Inheriting the City

Inheriting the City

The Children of Immigrants
Come of Age

Philip Kasinitz
John H. Mollenkopf
Mary C. Waters
Jennifer Holdaway

Russell Sage Foundation
New York

Harvard University Press
Cambridge, Massachusetts, and London, England | 2008

Library of Congress Cataloging-in-Publication Data

Inheriting the city : the children of immigrants come of age / Philip
  Kasinitz . . . [et al.].
      p.   cm.
    Includes bibliographical references and index.
    ISBN-13: 978-0-674-02803-6 (alk. paper)
    1. Children of immigrants—United States—Social conditions—20th
century.   2. Children of immigrants—United States—Social conditions—
21st century.   I. Kasinitz, Philip, 1957–
JV6600.I64   2008
305.23—dc22   2007036136

Contents

Acknowledgments

The idea of doing a study of the second generation of immigrants in New York originally emerged from the discussions of the Russell Sage Foundation's committee on immigration. As is the way of such things, the project that produced this book, as well as its companion volume, *Becoming New Yorkers: Ethnographies of the New Second Generation* (Russell Sage Press 2004), turned out to be much bigger and more complicated, and to take much longer, than we or anyone in that initial meeting could have foreseen. But throughout it all, Russell Sage was a partner in our efforts, and its president, Eric Wanner, was our biggest supporter. A worthy, occasionally stern, and always astute advisor and task master, Eric made this study possible. In addition to providing the funding for the project, Russell Sage also hosted Philip Kasinitz and John H. Mollenkopf for a wonderful year as visiting scholars in 2000–2001. We should particularly thank former Russell Sage Foundation vice president Reynolds Farley and program officers Stephanie Platz and Aixa Cintron for their invaluable help.

We began the project as novices in the field of survey research. We could never have pulled off a survey of this size without our friends. Garth Taylor was a huge help in the early stages of the first proposal. The telephone survey that is the basis of most of the quantitative analysis was conducted by the firm of Schulman, Ronca and Bucuvales Incorporated (SRBI), and we worked closely with the staff of SRBI, particularly Al Ronca and Michael Bucuvales, throughout the early stages of the project.

One of the first things we learned is that surveys are expensive. We spent much of the early years of our collaboration raising money. Fortunately, as the project grew, generous support was provided by a variety of sources. We owe thanks to the National Institute for Child Health and Development (for NIH Grants 5R03HD044598–02 and 990–0173), particularly our program officer, Rebecca Clark; the Ford Foundation, particularly Taryn Higashi; the Rockefeller Foundation, particularly Katherine McFate; the Mellon Foundation, particularly Harriet Zuckerman; and the UJA-Federation of Greater New York, particularly Caroline Katz and the late Gary Rubin. The final data-gathering phase of the project, re-interviewing our in-depth respondents in 2002 and 2003, was supported by the MacArthur Foundation and its research network on transitions to adulthood, led by Frank Furstenberg and wonderfully administered by Patricia Miller. Thanks to them both. In addition, Mary Waters was supported by a year at the Radcliffe Institute for Advanced Study, which provided valuable time to write as we brought the project to completion during the academic year 2005–2006.

The study was based at the Center for Urban Research at the Graduate Center of the City University of New York (CUNY). Thanks are due the Graduate Center business office and the CUNY Research Foundation for helping us to manage many aspects of a complex enterprise. Over the years, many people worked on this project at both CUNY and Harvard University. They often made substantial contributions, not only to getting the project done but also to the ideas that emerged from it. We had two crack, multilingual teams of in-depth interviewers, one at work from 1998 to 2001 and another who did the re-interviews in 2002–2003. We also had an outstanding team of ethnographers, whose work is presented in *Becoming New Yorkers* but who also contributed to the analysis in the present volume. We also relied on our data analysts, administrators, and research and editorial assistants—and some people filled multiple roles over the years. Our heartfelt thanks go to Robert Lee Adams, Linda Allegro, Merih Anil, Katsch Belash, Claudio Benzecry, Emily Bolton, Sherri-Ann Butterfield, Alice Cepeda, Karen Chai, Tracy Chu, Randol Contreras, Lauren Dye, Arianna Farinelli, Amy Foerster, Dorothy Friendly, Emily Gan, Alwyn Gilkes, Corina Graif, Christian Grov, Martine Hackett, Luisa Heredia, Diana Hernandez, Joshua Howard, Yvonne Hung, Miriam Jimenez, Yvanne Joseph, Rose Kakoza, Alison Khaskelis, Hosu Kim, Niels Kohlrausch, Sara Lee, Jacob Chong Li Lin, Laura Liu, Vivian Shuh-Ming Louie, Victoria Malkin, Nicole Marwell, Noriko Matsumoto, Monica McDermott, Tracy McFarlane, Tamara Mose Brown, Richard Ocejo, Carolyn Pinedo-Turnovsky, Jackie Piracini, Giorgio Pirre, Binh Pok, Andrew Reynolds, Michelle Ronda, Wendy Roth, Zoya Simakhodskaya, Ingrid Skadberg, Sarah Song, Audrey Thomas, Rafael Perez Torruela, Alex Trillo, James Trimarco, Debora Upequi, Susannah Vance, Linta Varghese, Natasha Warikoo, Suzanne Washington, and Henry A. Welcome, Jr.

A particularly important role was played by Dae Young Kim and Nancy López, who managed the project in its early, pretest years. They were succeeded by Jennifer Holdaway, who managed the project through the most crucial period of data gathering and who eventually became a full partner in the endeavor, at which point Ervin Kosta came to fill the project manager's role. We should also make special mention of Aviva Zeltzer-Zubida, who was an interviewer, an ethnographer, and a quantitative data analyst, and who made particular contributions to the education and labor market chapters. Cheri Minton at Harvard was invaluable in helping with computer matters. The interviews were transcribed by Lynn Karow and Elinor Bernal. Steve Romalewski of the CUNY Mapping Service created the map on page xii.

Helen Marrow, Van Tran, Rubén Rumbaut, Roger Waldinger, and Eric Wanner all read and provided extremely useful comments on an earlier version of the manuscript. Richard Alba deserves our special thanks for having read both an early and a later version and making wonderfully incisive comments on each. Significant portions of early drafts of the work were read or listened to by Nancy Foner, Kathleen Gerson, Charles Hirschman, Jennifer Hochschild, Peggy Levitt, Tomas Jiménez, Stanley Lieberson, Douglas Massey, Joel Perlmann, Alejandro Portes, Aristide Zolberg, Jeffrey Reitz, Carola Suárez-Orozco, and Marta Tienda. In addition we all gave many talks based on this research, both throughout the United States and in Europe. We cannot list all the different audiences and individuals who gave us valuable feedback, but we deeply appreciate the responses we received and believe they helped us to clarify our argument.

In addition to this volume and *Becoming New Yorkers*, several other works draw, at least in part, on data from this study and contributed to our overall intellectual arguments. These include López (2004), Kim (2001), Zeltzer-Zubida (2004), Louie (2004), and Roth (2006). (These works have also been the basis for numerous journal articles.) Data from the second round of in-depth interviews will also appear as part of two edited volumes commisioned by the MacArthur Network on the Transition to Adulthood.

Because this is a co-published volume, we have two sets of publishers to thank, Michael Aronson at Harvard University Press and Suzanne Nichols of the Russell Sage Press. Suzanne especially had a great and lasting impact on us, most notably when she proved that New York really is not as big a city as some people might think.

We owe a great debt of gratitude to our thousands of respondents. Busy young people, they took the time to share their stories with us, often for many hours and in some cases as many as three times. Usually they did so because they believed, as we do, that their story is an important one to tell. What we can offer, by way of recompense, is that we tried, to the best of our limited abilities, to get the story right.

Finally, we would like to dedicate this book to our families. They lived with this project for more years than any of them would have liked, usually cheerfully, though occasionally reminding us of the need for balance between work and family. We are deeply grateful for their patience and support and advice. We dedicate this book to Lisa Gibbs, Basya Kasinitz, Mira Kasinitz, Kathleen Gerson, Emily Mollenkopf, Ric Bayly, Katie Bayly, Harry Bayly, Maggie Bayly, and Guy Padula.

Inheriting the City

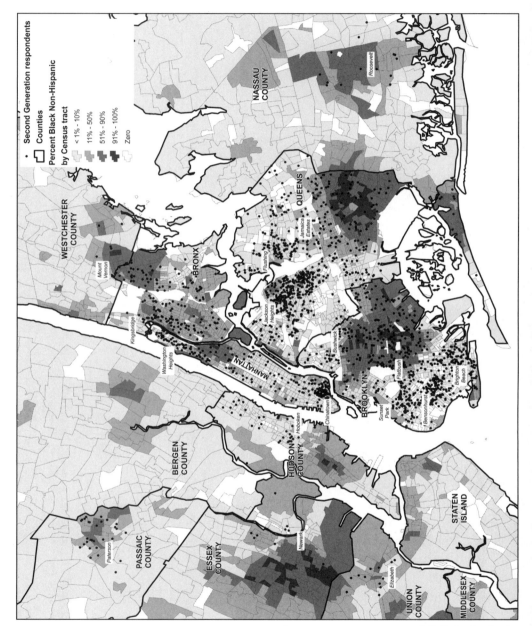

CUNY Mapping Service

1

Introduction: Inheriting the City

Immigration is squarely on the American political agenda. With the influx of migrants continuing at high levels, it is destined to remain there. Although its salience as an issue may rise and fall, immigration poses fundamental questions about what it means to be an American and whether the nation can deliver on its historic promise to provide upward mobility to newcomers and their children.

Scholars usually frame the debate in terms of the economic and demographic impacts of high levels of immigration. Yet the broad passions excited by the issue point to deeper concerns about the ways in which mass migration is reshaping American society and culture (Zolberg 2006). Many wonder what sort of Americans the latest immigrants will become and what sort of America will be their legacy—and ours. Even those who think that immigration has a generally benevolent economic impact often worry that the huge numbers of largely nonwhite immigrants who have come to the United States since the mid-1960s will not "assimilate" or will put native born minorities at a further disadvantage.

The answer to the question of what large scale migration will mean for American society, however. lies less with the immigrants themselves than with their ambivalently American children. The March 2005 Current Population Survey (CPS) reported that this new "second generation"—the children of at least one immigrant parent born in the United States or who arrived by the age of 12—accounted for one out of six 18- to 32-year-olds in the nation and one out of four of all Americans under 18. In many ways, they will define how today's immigrant groups become tomorrow's American ethnic groups. In the process, they will not only reshape American racial and ethnic relations but define the character of American social, cultural, and political life.

This book is about their lives. It is the culmination of a decade-long

1

research project by a large team of researchers who interviewed members of the second and 1.5 generations in and around New York City. (We define the second generation as those born in the United States to at least one immigrant parent and the 1.5 generation as those born abroad but who arrived by age 12 and then grew up in the United States.) By looking at what life is like for them and those who will follow them, the project sought to understand the longer term consequences of immigration for American society. Over time, however, it also became a study of what it is like to be a young adult in New York today. We learned about the struggles and joys experienced by young adults coming of age in a tough town, a place of ever-present dangers, of backbreaking competition, but also of extraordinary possibilities.

As such, it is also a book about New York City. This city of "eight million stories" houses more adult immigrants and more children of immigrants than any other city in the United States and its metropolitan area more than anywhere else but Greater Los Angeles. Yet while large scale international migration to Los Angeles did not take place until well into the twentieth century, it has a much longer history in New York. Indeed, the children of immigrants, past and present, have often been seen as the quintessential New Yorkers. Today's second generation grows up among local institutions and attitudes that were shaped by the region's long, deep, and diverse immigrant traditions.

Writing this book has made us more aware of how difficult it can be to grow up in New York, yet how the city can still welcome newcomers. These qualities will no doubt lead some readers to think our research and conclusions apply only to New York. The city's enthusiasts and detractors alike tend to exaggerate its difference from the rest of the United States—an "island off the coast of America," in the words of Spalding Grey. Yet the problems faced by the second generation in New York are pretty much the same as those anywhere else. If New Yorkers have forged distinctive answers to those problems, they may offer positive or negative lessons to the rest of the nation.

Why is it important to assess how New York and the nation are incorporating this new second generation? One reason is sheer numbers. Immigrants and their children now form a majority of the population in New York, Miami, and Los Angeles. According to the March 2005 CPS, 35 percent of all New Yorkers were foreign born, and their native born children constituted another 17 percent. Their presence is even greater among the city's 18- to 32-year-old residents, more than a fifth of whom were born here to immigrant parents; another fifth arrived by age 12 and grew up here, and a final fifth arrived as young adult immigrants. In short, most young adult New Yorkers are of immigrant origin. These trends are even more pronounced among those who are under 18. Thus, even if immigration were to end magically tomorrow, the question of how the children of immigrants will fit into U.S. society would be with us for decades. Simply put, the children of immigrants are the future of New York and many other parts of the nation.

A second reason to study the children of immigrants involves the future of American ethnic and racial relations. Before 1965, immigrants to the Unted States were overwhelmingly European. Since then, most have come from other parts of the globe. Given how the United States has historically constructed racial categories, they are not generally regarded as "white." Yet they are not African Americans either. Since the cleavage between the "white" descendants of immigrants and the "black" descendants of American slaves has so strongly marked big cities, the emergence of a large and rapidly growing group that does not fit easily into either of these categories has enormous potential consequences. To a degree, the arrival of this group was presaged by New York's large Puerto Rican population, which is also neither unambiguously white nor unambiguously black. Glazer and Moynihan (1963) suggested that this large "intermediate" group would temper the city's race relations. Since that largely turned out not to be the case, we must be careful about any conclusions we draw from the experience of the new immigrants.

New York City is a rich site for studying how immigration is affecting race relations. Its immigrants are staggeringly diverse, and newcomers have altered the makeup of every racial category. No one group dominates the flow of immigrants to New York as Cubans have in Miami or Mexicans in Los Angeles. About 45 percent of the city's black population are immigrants or the children of immigrants, as are 40 percent of the white population. The same is true of 59 percent of the Hispanic population and 95 percent of the Asian population. Most native Hispanics with native parents are Puerto Ricans who were born on the mainland but whose parents or grandparents migrated from the island, so even they have a strong migrant heritage, though they are all American citizens.

Immigrants are having a huge impact on the city's labor market. Like other American cities, New York incorporated the nineteenth- and early twentieth-century immigrants in part because their arrival coincided with, and fed, the growth of its manufacturing sector, which provided jobs and a living to people with limited education or who did not speak English. Today, many wonder whether a service sector economy that places a premium on education and communication can accommodate new immigrant workers. As the top of the city's household income distribution pulls away from the bottom, others worry that while immigrants may find low wage jobs, their children will lack opportunities for upward mobility in an "hourglass"-shaped economy.

Unlike their predecessors, the children of the current immigrants are becoming American in the midst of continuing immigration. Our understanding of assimilation has been largely shaped by the experience of the descendants of the southern and eastern European immigrants who came to the United States between roughly 1882 and 1924 (Foner 2000, 2005). Their incorporation took place after legislative changes in the 1920s, the Depression, and World War II sharply reduced new immigration. Their children came of age in a context of low immigration with few new arrivals to reinvigorate ties to the old country or to reinforce old country ways. Americanization was further reinforced for many by the experience of serving in the American armed forces in World War II. Today, by contrast, members of the new second generation rub shoulders with recently arrived immigrants their own age in the streets, classrooms, and workplaces of New York. There is therefore a good deal less distinction between the first and second generations than in the past (Rumbaut 2004; Waters and Jiménez 2005; Foner and Kasinitz 2007).

Today's second generation also grows up in communities where the parents have more transnational connections than in the past. Modern communications and cheap transportation enable immigrants to remain socially connected to their home communities. Today's transnational immigrants (or "trans/migrants") and their children remain active in social networks that make it possible for them to live in more than one society at a time, perhaps never fully committing to either (Glick Schiller, Basch, and Blanc-Stanton 1992; Portes 1999; Levitt 2001, 2007; Levitt and Waters 2002). New York's immigrant neighborhoods are jammed with businesses selling low cost phone calls and instant money transfers to remote parts of the globe. In every group, some second generation people remain strongly tied to their parents' homelands. They visit often, send money back, and even contemplate settling there. A surprising number of first generation West Indian and Latin American parents "send back" children to live with relatives when the dangers of the New York streets terrify them or they suddenly lose their child-care arrangements. These transnational connections may be quite important to the American lives of the new second generation.

Finally, it is important to study the second generation because so many first generation parents worry about what will happen to their American children. While social scientists cannot automatically accept their view of their community's problems, we should nevertheless take their concerns seriously. Anyone spending time in America's growing immigrant communities will hear parental concern over the second generation. "We are afraid for our kids," we have been told. With a mixture of awe, fear, and disdain, immigrant parents say their children are "becoming American." This is the stuff of sermons in Korean churches, of discussion in Ecuadoran hometown associations, of debate in Chinese newspapers.

Sometimes this is only a vague but nagging fear about cultural loss among people who are otherwise quite happy in America. Jhumpa Lahiri's fictional couple, for example, find themselves inexplicably afraid for their U.S.-born son at Harvard: "So we drive to Cambridge to visit him or bring him home for the weekend so that he can eat rice with us with his hands and speak Bengali, things we sometimes worry he will no longer do after we die" (Lahiri 1999:197). Other times the fear is more pointed. West Indian Brooklynites told Mary Waters that "we are losing our kids to the streets," a shorthand both for the manifold dangers of the American ghetto and for the less well understood but nonetheless frightening impact that being considered a black person in racist America was having on their children (Waters 1999).

This fear is part of the paradox of the immigrant experience. Immigrants come to America to improve their lives and those of their children. Most manage to do just that. They overcome hardships and obstacles to give their children the chance to become Americans. At the same time, parents are often uncomfortable with and anxious about the future of the new Americans they have created. Whether the experience of the immigrant second and 1.5 generations in New York justifies these fears or not is the most important question that we hope this book can answer.

The State of the Debate

The discussion of how America will incorporate today's immigrants always involves an implicit or explicit comparison with the experience of those descended from the last great wave of immigration. This is unfair. It is also inevitable. Americans, and particularly New Yorkers, justifiably celebrate the incorporation of that group of immigrants and their descendants. We have made the Statue of Liberty and Ellis Island into shrines for what makes America unique. At the same time, America's (and especially New

York's) proud history of incorporating immigrants stands in sharp contrast to the troubled history of America's native racial minorities.

Social scientific observers of the last great wave of European immigrants tended to assume that assimilation was both probable and desirable. Writing at the height of American self-confidence, they saw assimilation as closely tied to upward mobility and often wrote as if assimilation, acculturation, and upward mobility were virtually the same thing. While they disagreed on whether immigrants would drop immigrant values in favor of Anglo-Saxon norms or develop some hybrid instead, they assumed, as the popular discourse continues to assume, that immigrants would achieve upward mobility by embracing the main elements of the culture of the dominant society. Whatever the psychic toll the shedding of old cultural identities might cause, substantial upward mobility would be the reward (Hansen 1938; Park 1950; Gordon 1964; Shibutani and Kwan 1965).

William Lloyd Warner and Leo Srole's (1945) study of ethnic groups in "Yankee City" remains the most complete discussion of the identity and experience of the second generation of this historical period. Warner and Srole describe a generational march of the ethnic groups from initial poverty amidst residential and occupational segregation to residential, occupational, and identity integration and Americanization. This orderly pattern of mobility has come to be called the "straight line" model of assimilation (Warner and Srole 1945:72): "Each consecutive ethnic generation pushes progressively farther out of the bottom level and into each of the successive layers above. That the class index of an ethnic group is related to the length of its settlement in the city is a manifestation of the continuous advance achieved in the hierarchy of each new generation."

In a chapter on the children of the immigrants, Warner and Srole explore the forces affecting the children's relations with their parents' generation and the wider society. They argue that the parents orient the child's early socialization to the values and beliefs of the old country. As soon as the child enters into social relations outside the home, however, he begins to reorient himself toward the wider American society. The child quickly absorbs values and skills specific to American society and experiences tension when these clash or disagree with those of his parents. Schools, peer groups, and the mass media all teach American ways. As the child absorbs these values, he or she often leads the rest of the family in adapting to the new world. This process, Warner and Srole argue, can turn the traditional parent-child relationship on its head. With knowledge about U.S. society, the child teaches the parent. This role reversal often leads to conflict within the personality of the child as well as between children and parents.

Looking back with the advantage of more than a half century of historical knowledge, we can see the weaknesses of this approach. Warner and Srole assumed that immigrant children would be absorbed into a single, unified, middle class "American culture." They ignored the diversity among natives and the ways in which immigrants were being assimilated into distinct segments of U.S. society (Portes and Zhou 1993). They also ignored the possibility that immigrants might improve their prospects for upward mobility by *retaining* their immigrant culture. The model also discounted the ways in which immigrants, in the words of Alba and Nee (2003), "remade the American mainstream" and gradually brought the immigrant world and American world closer together. Their model takes for granted that "American" culture has a higher status than immigrant culture (Warner and Srole 1945:145): "In any judgments of rank, the American social system, being the most vigorous and having also the dominance of host status, is affirmed the higher. Since the child identifies himself with it, his position in the present reciprocal is higher."

Straight line theory also proposes a one-dimensional model of assimilation. In fact, however, groups often assimilated in one sphere of life while remaining distinct in others. Eastern European Jews, for example, are often considered the archetype of immigrant success. Starting out low status and highly stigmatized, they achieved substantial educational and economic mobility in one generation. As the straight line theory predicts, they evinced clear signs of acculturation in their rapid adoption of English, their almost complete loss of Yiddish, their residential assimilation, and so on. At least through the 1960s, however, Jews remained the least assimilated of European immigrants in many other respects. They maintained highly developed ethnic organizations and exhibited high degrees of occupational concentration and distinctive voting patterns. Despite the fretting of Jewish leaders over the rise of out-marriage, Jews are not likely to "disappear" into mainstream America even today, upward mobility notwithstanding.

The straight line model came under increasing attack after the 1960s. As intellectuals lost confidence in America's ability to overcome its racial problems and the civil right movement waned, some critics reminded us that "assimilation" had historically been for "whites only." Others (Novak 1974) celebrated the "unmeltable" white ethnics. Yet while the line may

have been more "bumpy" (Gans 1979) and the ethnic cultures more re-
silient than predicted, the large majority of the second, third, and fourth
generation descendants of European immigrants did join the American
mainstream in most respects, albeit remaking that mainstream in the process (Alba and Nee 2003). Those "white ethnics" who asserted a "symbolic ethnicity" during the 1960s and 1970s usually did so in the form of
individualistic and "optional" celebrations of culture, often mediated
through mass consumption. Although important to many people's self-
concept, such cultural celebrations had little direct bearing on their daily
life or life chances (Gans 1979; Alba 1990; Waters 1990).

Will the contemporary second generation follow this path? Many social
scientists have been skeptical. In 1992 sociologist Herbert Gans (1992)
inverted the straight line model of assimilation by proposing what he
termed the "second generation decline." Gans outlined ways in which
members of the post-1965 second generation could do worse than their
parents. Children who refused to accept the low level, poorly paid jobs of
their parents could face a difficult bind (Gans 1992: 173–174): "In adulthood, some members of the second generation, especially those whose
parents did not themselves escape poverty, will end up in persistent
poverty, because they will be reluctant to work at immigrant wages and
hours like their parents, but lack the job opportunities and skills and connections to do better."

By having the same reactions toward these low level jobs as poor young
native whites, blacks, and Hispanics, members of the second generation
might risk sliding into persistent poverty. Indeed, some may "become
American" by adopting negative attitudes toward school, opportunity,
hard work, and the "American dream." By contrast, those who retain
their ties to their parents' ethnic community may, Gans suggests, do
better while assimilating less: "The people who have secured an economically viable ethnic niche acculturating less than did the European 2nd and
3rd generation and those without such a niche escaping condemnation to
dead end immigrant and other jobs mainly by becoming very poor and
persistently jobless Americans."

Alejandro Portes and Min Zhou (1992, 1993) greatly expanded on
these notions by proposing the idea of "segmented assimilation." Perhaps
the single most influential concept in the contemporary study of the
second generation, this notion was further developed in Portes and
Rubén Rumbaut's 2001 book, *Legacies* (see also Rumbaut 1997, 2004,
and 2005b; Zhou 1997a, 1997b; Feliciano and Rumbaut 2005; Portes

and Rumbaut 2005). The segmented assimilation model argues that the varying modes of incorporation of the first generation endow the second generation with differing amounts of cultural and social capital in the form of ethnic jobs, networks, and values and expose it to differing opportunities. This in turn exerts differential pulls and pushes on the allegiances of the second generation.

Second generation youth with strong ties to American minorities, whose parents lack the ability to provide them with jobs or to protect them from the influence of the native poor, tend to develop an "adversarial stance" toward the dominant white society similar to that of American minorities. According to this view, those facing high levels of discrimination or who live close to American minorities are particularly likely to adopt such a "reactive" ethnicity. They may become skeptical about the possibility of upward mobility and the value of education. Like Gans, Portes and his colleagues concluded that second generation young people who cast their lot with America's minority groups will experience downward social mobility, in part because high levels of discrimination will preclude the option of joining the white mainstream, even if they are highly acculturated. Joining the native circles to which they have access may be a ticket to permanent subordination and disadvantage (Portes and Zhou 1993).

While Gans stresses that deindustrialization has sharply reduced the kinds of jobs that eased generational mobility a century ago, Portes and Zhou focus on how cultural organization interacts with economic opportunity. Gans believes that the second generation must attain skills in one generation to succeed, that took European immigrants several generations to gain. Portes and Zhou instead highlight how strong kinship ties among the Chinese, or the religious affiliations of the Koreans, constitute "social capital" that increases the ability of the first generation to instill loyalty and obedience in their children. Simultaneously, they involve few ties to U.S. minorities. When these groups resist acculturation into the broader American culture—or allow their children to acculturate only selectively while retaining strong ties to the ethnic community—they paradoxically provide their children with better means to get ahead.

The idea that assimilation has costs and "paradoxes" is not new, as Rumbaut carefully notes (1999). Observers of early twentieth century immigrants often commented on the heartache produced by intergenerational conflict (Thomas and Znaniecki 1927). Leonard Covello, a leading educator in New York's Italian American community in the mid-twentieth century, famously recalled of his own second generation childhood: "We were becoming Americans by learning how to be ashamed of our parents" (quoted in Iorizzo and Mondello 1980:118). Years later, as principal of an East Harlem high school, Covello introduced the teaching of Italian as a means of preserving ethnic heritage and keeping assimilation partially at bay.

Complaints that the children of immigrants were becoming the "wrong kind" of Americans are also not new. As early as 1906, *The Outlook* magazine warned "against rushing Italian children into the 'streetiness' and 'cheap Americanism' which 'so overwhelms Italian youngsters in the cities" (Kahn 1987:244). Even the notion that a dense "ethnic enclave" can provide a bulwark against the worst effects of the American street, a case made forcefully by Zhou and Bankston (1998), is foreshadowed by studies of New York's Jewish community in the early twentieth century in which juvenile delinquency among boys and sexual promiscuity among girls are seen as the result of overly rapid Americanization (Landesman 1969; Prell 1999).

Yet if the literature on the last great wave of migration contained most of the arguments made in the segmented assimilation model, such skeptical voices were very much in the minority. Against a background of falling real wages, rising income inequality, and continuing racial conflict, doubts about the possibility and value of assimilation are more common today. Some have nevertheless taken up the tattered banner of assimilation. In their major book on the subject, Richard Alba and Victor Nee (2003) argue that assimilation not only accurately describes the experiences of white immigrants from Europe and their descendants in the twentieth century; it is also happening among new nonwhite immigrants and their descendants in the twenty-first century. They argue that the segmented assimilation model exaggerates the factors working against assimilation among contemporary nonwhite immigrants, and the scholarship on the revival of ethnicity among whites misses the forest for the trees. Ethnic occupational niches have diminished for the latter over time, while a declining portion of ethnic populations live in ethnic neighborhoods. Intermarriage is eroding ethnic boundaries among Asians and some Latino groups as well as whites.

Few immigrants in any period, Alba and Nee remind us, ever made a conscious decision to "assimilate." Assimilation is the sum of a million small decisions and tiny changes in daily life that often occur despite the immigrant's efforts to ward off assimilation. Many immigrant parents, past and present, make heroic efforts to inculcate "old country ways" in their U.S.-born children. They lecture their offspring on the virtues of traditional values and of speaking the parental language. Yet they also tend to support their children's use of English, move them to "better"—that is, less ethnic—neighborhoods, and send them to "better"—that is, less ethnic—schools.

The debate over the new second and 1.5 generations has been lively, but largely speculative. Until recently, this group has been too young to permit a robust assessment of their educational attainment, labor force participation, marriage and fertility patterns, and political participation. Data have also been lacking. The U.S. Census stopped asking about parents' place of birth in 1970. While the Current Population Survey did begin to ask this question in 1994, this sample survey permits fine-grained analysis only of the largest first and second generation groups, like Mexicans, mainly at the national level (J. Smith 2003; Perlmann 2005). Most other surveys use categories like "black" and "Hispanic" that do not distinguish the children of immigrants from native stock populations, so the second generation statistically disappears into increasingly problematic racial categories. Valiant efforts have been made to draw conclusions about adult life chances from surveys documenting the expectations and attitudes of adolescents (Suárez-Orozco and Suárez-Orozco 1995; Portes and Rumbaut 2001); but as any parent can attest, this is a questionable enterprise. Excellent case studies of particular communities provide some indications about the adult second generation (Min 2002; Smith 2006), but not broad evidence.

Until recently, then, we have not been able to *assess* how the second and 1.5 generations are actually doing *as adults*. This provided the impetus for our effort to gather data. Our way was paved by Portes and Rumbaut's path-breaking Children of Immigrants Longitudinal Study (CILS), which initially studied eighth graders in Miami and San Diego and has now followed respondents into their mid-twenties (Portes and Rumbaut 2005). Data-gathering efforts shaped partly by our study have also recently been completed in Greater Los Angeles and the big cities of eight European countries. These studies have begun to permit meaningful comparisons of second generation young adults from different backgrounds and in different settings.

Our Study

This book is based on a three-part study of five immigrant-origin groups and three native born comparison groups. Between 1998 and 2000, we conducted a telephone survey of 3,415 young adults (aged 18 to 32) living in the ten counties within metropolitan New York where the 1990 Census indicated our target populations were present in sufficient numbers to be sampled economically—in at least 1.5 percent of the households. (This sample frame included New York City except for Staten Island; the inner suburban counties of Nassau and Westchester in New York; and Essex, Hudson, Passaic, and Union counties in northeastern New Jersey.) This area contained about 12 million of the region's 21 million people in 2000, and our study groups made up 81 percent of that total population. Eighteen was our lower age boundary because it did not make sense to collect data on education and work data on younger people. Thirty-two was the upper boundary because that was the oldest a child born in the United States to a post-1965 immigrant parent could be when we went into the field.

We located respondents in two waves of screening. The first round of "random-digit dialing" within the study area produced the necessary quota (about 400) of native white, black, and Puerto Rican respondents, along with varying numbers for the other second generation groups. A second round of random-digit dialing took place only in telephone exchanges that yielded at least one eligible respondent in the first wave. The response rate among those who were identified as eligible for an interview was 53.3 percent. Response rates were higher among the second generation groups and lower among all three native groups–whites, blacks, and Puerto Ricans, ranging from 67 percent among the Chinese to 41 percent among the native born blacks. The telephone interviews were thirty to forty minutes long and provided many of the statistics presented in the following chapters. (See the Methodological Appendix for more information on the technical aspects of this survey and for response rates by group.) The map on page xii provides an overview of where our respondents lived.

In the second stage of our study we conducted detailed, open-ended, face-to-face interviews with 333 of our telephone respondents. The interviews began a month after the respondents answered the telephone survey and continued into 2001. Our interviewers were advanced graduate students in the social sciences. They used an interview protocol but were encouraged to follow the conversation where it led when that seemed appropriate. These interviews lasted from two to four hours. Most took place in the respondents' homes, although some were conducted at university facilities or in public places. These respondents are broadly representative of the wider sample, although they have slightly more educational attainment. (The characteristics of the in-depth interview sample and the total telephone sample are further discussed in the Methodological Appendix.) Then, in an effort to learn more about how the 9/11 attacks and the subsequent sharp economic downturn affected the respondents, we re-interviewed 172 of these respondents in 2002 and 2003. All the interviews were taped, transcribed, and coded. The quotations presented in the book come from these in-depth interviews.

Finally, since surveys and interviews can reify ethnic groups and miss the importance of institutional context, we also fielded six ethnographers to investigate domains where second generation and native groups were interacting between 2000 and 2002: high schools, community colleges, university campuses, workplaces, unions, community organizations, and church congregations. These projects, along with other qualitative research by the in-depth interviewers, are presented in a companion volume, *Becoming New Yorkers* (Kasinitz, Mollenkopf, and Waters 2004). Many insights drawn from the ethnographic work inform this volume as well.

Our selection of groups reflects several strategic choices. We considered gathering data from a representative cross section of all second generation young people, rather than by specific ethnic groups. Yet if we had done so, the fact that New York's immigrants come from so many different national origins would have prevented us from being able to make meaningful group comparisons. We also felt that many previous studies of the second generation had suffered from the lack of native born "control groups." We wanted to be able to compare the second generation groups with black, white, and Latino natives of native parentage.

Dominicans were an obvious choice. They are the largest national-origin immigrant group and play an important role in the city's economy and politics. Because most Dominicans appear racially "mixed" by North American standards, having African, European, and Amerindian ancestry, the group is also theoretically interesting. It does not fit easily into North American racial categories. Our study often compares the Dominican second generation with New York's longstanding Puerto Rican and "Nuyorican" population. We surveyed only Puerto Rican young people who had been born on the U.S. mainland, most of whom were lifelong New Yorkers, as were many of their parents.

We also wanted to compare both Dominicans and Puerto Ricans with New York's growing population of non-Caribbean Hispanics. Because no other single Hispanic national group was large enough to be sampled on its own, we combined the three largest South American groups, Colombians, Ecuadorans, and Peruvians. First generation South American immigrants tend to have more education, slightly higher incomes, and less African ancestry than first generation Dominicans. Although there are differences among these three groups, they tend to live near each other, work in similar occupations, and often intermarry. (We discuss their similarities and differences in Chapter 2.) They generally have more in common with each other than with Dominicans and Puerto Ricans. We did not study New York's rapidly growing Mexican population because it is still new and has a small adult second generation (Smith 2006).

We also wanted to compare the children of Caribbean Hispanic immigrants with those of English-speaking West Indian parents. By "West Indian," we mean the thirteen Caricom nations making up the "British West Indies" prior to their independence starting in 1962. These former colonies have different cultures and histories, but their premigration commonalities far outweigh these differences and, in any event, they constitute a single ethnic group in New York City (Kasinitz 1992; Waters 1999). Taken together, West Indians are the largest immigrant community in New York City. Although Indo-Caribbeans play a fascinating role in the racial stratification of West Indian New Yorkers (Warikoo 2004), we interviewed only those West Indians of African descent.

The Chinese are the largest Asian population in metropolitan New York. We oversampled Chinese respondents in order to distinguish those with parents from People's Republic from those whose parents hail from Taiwan, Hong Kong, and the Chinese diaspora. Finally, we selected the largest "white" second generation group, the children of Jewish immigrants from the former Soviet Union, whom we compare with native white New Yorkers of native parentage. We selected only those with a Jewish background in part to control for religion and in part to approximate the boundaries of ethnic solidarity as it is lived in daily life in New York today. Such boundaries are often imprecise and shifting (Zeltzer-Zubida 2004a), but this group does clearly have a subjective sense of identity.

Our book investigates many aspects of the lives of members of the new second generation. Chapter 2 begins with how the second generation's immigrant parents came to New York, where they settled, what kinds of jobs they do, and what kinds of families they formed. Chapter 3 introduces the reader to our second generation respondents and examines how they sort themselves into the ethnic groups. Chapter 4 describes the dynamics of the families in which they grew up and how they experienced the neighborhoods where their parents had settled. These neighborhoods varied greatly in terms of the quality of their schools, the mixture of groups and classes, and even their physical safety. Chapter 5 follows the second generation young people as they enter their crucial high school years and the many who go on to some college experience. Chapter 6 examines their entry into the labor force, the jobs they do, and the ethnic composition of the places where they work. Chapter 7 asks when and how they have children of their own and form marriages. It also examines the surprisingly different ways in which groups time and combine parenting and marriage. Chapter 8 explores the extent to which immigrant cultures continue to shape the patterns of adaptation of these young people. Chapter 9 examines questions of civic engagement and politics, a topic that contemporary immigration scholars too often ignore. Chapter 10 takes up the thorny issue of the continuing salience that racism has in shaping people's life chances.

Second Generation Advantage

This book does not tell a simple story. The data we gathered are rich but complicated. They provide exceptions for every generalization and require caveats for every assertion Although there is considerable variation across ethnic groups, there is also much variation within each group. Both dimensions must be taken into account in order to understand the relationship between cultural adaption and economic, social, and political status. Incorporation is also not a single story. Young people are being incorporated into different spheres in different ways.

Attempting to measure the progress or the "assimilation" of the second generation immediately poses questions: Assimilation into what? And progress compared to whom? Second generation young people may see themselves as very "American" compared to their immigrant parents and yet still feel—and seem—very much like foreigners compared to the children of natives. Further, the United States remains very much an ethnically and racially stratified society. It is probably unrealistic to expect black and Hispanic immigrants to come to resemble white natives in one generation. The fact that often they have not achieved parity with native whites is, we feel, too easily seized upon by those who would minimize the progress these second generation young people are making. (Indeed, in the past it often took *white* immigrants more than one generation to reach parity with white natives.) Of course, it *is* important to note those areas in which the children of immigrants do not do as well as the children of white natives. At the same time, it is equally if not more important to see how the black and Hispanic second generation compares with the black and Hispanic children of natives. In the pages that follow we make all these comparisons. We feel, however, that the clearest reference groups for the second generation are other young people who share their "racial" backgrounds. Thus we compare second and 1.5 generation Dominicans and South Americans with mainland born Puerto Ricans, West Indians with the children of native born African Americans, and Russians with the children of native born whites. There is, of course, no obvious large racial comparison group for the second generation Chinese. Here, comparison with native whites probably gives the clearest benchmark.

Given these comparisons, we are guardedly optimistic about the second generation. On measures of educational attainment and labor force status, two-fifths of the second generation have already gone beyond their immigrant parents. Except among Dominican men, there is little evidence of second generation decline. In every case, the second generation young people we have studied are doing at least somewhat better than natives of the same race, even after adjusting for various advantages in family background. Indeed, we find the greatest evidence of persistent disadvantage, not among the second generation groups, but among African Americans and Puerto Ricans—particularly among young men.

The children of immigrants have not achieved these successes by clinging to the networks and enclaves of their immigrant communities. Instead, they have joined the mainstream, at least in the sense that their educational and occupational profiles look more like those of each other and native young people their age than they do those of their immigrant parents. Chinese youngsters have achieved the greatest educational and economic success relative to their parents' often humble origins. Members of the Chinese first generation often live and work within a well-developed ethnic enclave (Wilson and Portes 1980; Zhou 1992). Yet their children have moved farther than any other group in terms of their distance from their parents' occupations, educational levels, and even attitudes. Whatever advantages the enclave provided their parents, the second generation young people did not embrace them. As a result, the Chinese enclave appears largely to be a first generation phenomenon. (Portes recently reached a similar conclusion about the Cuban enclave in South Florida [Portes and Shafer 2007].)

Nor are Chinese second generation young people unique in distancing themselves from their parents. Most members of the other second generation groups are forsaking ethnic niches and joining the mainstream. This does not mean they always experience rapid upward mobility. Many members of this generation are in fact joining New York's working class. Yet their problems and opportunities are generally common among young people working in entry level positions. Rarely do they stem from the status of being the children of immigrants.

In addition, many black and Hispanic second generation young people have benefitted from civil rights era policies and institutions initially designed to help African Americans and Puerto Ricans. While originally intended to address the age-old racial cleavages in American society, such policies may actually be more effective in aiding the incorporation of recent immigrants "of color" and their children. As a result, we conclude that being racialized as a member of a "minority" group can have positive impacts in contemporary America along with the negative effects stressed by segmented assimilation theory.

The second generation is also remaking the mainstream with a truly remarkable speed and creative energy. By and large, black and Hispanic members of the second generation have not closed their gap with native whites (although Chinese and Russian Jews have done so on many measures). Given the continued salience of race in American society and the low human capital of many minority parents, it would be highly unrealistic to expect minority members of the second generation to close the gap with whites within a single generation. Yet second generation minority youth rarely worry about how they stack up to native white young people, perhaps because they rarely meet native whites in their schools, work sites, and neighborhoods. They do meet and compare themselves to members of native minority groups and are often doing quite well by that metric. They also meet each other. As they interact with each other and native minorities, the children of immigrants are creating a new cultural and economic landscape.

Of course, there is no one measure of "doing well." Different groups achieve varying levels in different spheres of incorporation. The dynamics of the spheres themselves are distinct. Economic mobility, for example, does not guarantee cultural inclusion, and neither economic mobility nor cultural inclusion correlates perfectly with political inclusion or political efficacy. Relatively well-off West Indians, for example, are just as likely to think that the police single them out for abuse and disrespect as do African Americans. This may lead them to feel less at ease and less comfortable as "Americans" than members of other groups, despite their comparative success in the labor market. Upwardly mobile Russians and Chinese are not the most likely to participate in American civic or political life. Nor does upward mobility guarantee happiness and harmonious family lives. The Chinese second generation has had a steeply rising career trajectory, but many second generation youth express profound personal dissatisfactions and difficulties communicating with their parents—with whom they nevertheless live longer than most other groups. In short, progress in one sphere of incorporation does not guarantee forward movement in all the others.

Finally, we have concluded that culture counts. Despite their overall assimilation, the different groups organize their lives in markedly different ways in terms of timing and sequencing major decisions in the transition to adulthood. They vary in when they leave home, finish their education, begin full time employment, find spouses or partners, and have children. We have some trepidation in saying that culture counts. Social scientists often shy away from culture when discussing ethnic and racial differences for fear that mentioning culture will lead to invidious distinctions, stereotypes, "victim blaming," or racism. Yet even when distinct groups face common problems of survival in New York, they bring different ideas, values, repertoires of action, and strategies to bear on these problems. At the same time, we understand that culture is highly contingent on social structure. What aspect of a cultural repertoire an individual brings to bear on any particular problem depends on a host of considerations. Social context facilitates some approaches and discourages others. Further, different cultural strategies also have different practical results in people's lives.

How do we explain why we reach more optimistic conclusions that do some other researchers, or indeed than do worried immigrant parents? One reason is that we undertook our research in more prosperous times. Gans (1992) developed his "second generation decline" scenario and Portes and Zhou (1993) originally formulated the segmented assimilation model at a time when the crack epidemic, crime, and the growing concentration of poverty were having a devastating impact on inner city neighborhoods. By the time our research began, many urban areas, particularly New York, had begun to reinvent themselves amidst a long national economic expansion. In particular, New York City's declining crime rate yielded a dramatically improved quality of life.

Lack of legal status may also have been less detrimental for the parents of our respondents than for more recent immigrants, or indeed for the first and second generation in other parts of the country. Our second generation respondents are all citizens, and only a few of our 1.5 generation respondents reported not being legally documented. Although many of their parents had been undocumented at some point in the past, the vast majority of them had found ways to become legal residents or U.S. citizens. The earliest members of one group, the Russian Jews, were cold war refugees who obtained legal status quite easily. Among the other groups, most of the parents came to the United States between the late 1960s and late 1980s, when becoming "legal" was easier than it is today.

New York's immigrants are also less likely to be undocumented than those in many other parts of the country. The undocumented are estimated to comprise between 15 and 20 percent of New York's foreign born as opposed to around 40 percent in California and over 50 percent in Greater Los Angeles. (We also did not study Mexicans, a group with comparatively high levels of undocumented people.) As a result, even respondents whose parents were originally undocumented did not grow up in communities where most adults lacked legal status. Indeed, their families tended to be of mixed status, containing U.S. citizens and legal permanent residents along with temporary visa holders and undocumented persons.

New York's undocumented are not clustered together or especially stigmatized. Most entered on a temporary visa that they subsequently overstayed. It was unusual to have the traumatic experience of being smuggled across the border. It is reasonable to assume that as visa abusers rather than illegal border crossers, having once obtained a tourist or student visa, they were better positioned to become legal permanently. The immigrants most likely to enter the country without documents, Mexicans, have only recently become a growing presence in the city. While Mexicans constitute more than 40 percent of the immigrants in Chicago, Los Angeles, and Houston, they are less than 5 percent of the foreign born population in New York (Foner 2005).

New York also has an extensive public sector, a well-developed social welfare system, and a large and open public university system developed in large part in response to earlier waves of immigrants and their children. Immigration is a messy business. False starts and disrupted trajectories are common. New York's institutional structure allows for many "second chances." New York sees itself as a place where people can remake themselves, and the local culture celebrates those who do. That one is allowed second, third, and fourth chances is a particularly good fit for the children of immigrants.

Finally, many previous observers have worried that the children of immigrants will be caught between two worlds, rejecting their parents' "old country" ways, yet not fully Americanized. While this may sometimes be a problem for them, we feel that social scientists have not sufficiently appreciated how "in between-ness" can provide the second generation with real advantages.

Park and Warner and Srole assumed that members of the second generation could share the *native advantages* of the majority by distancing themselves from their immigrant parents. Through assimilation, they would become familiar with American culture and access a relatively open opportunity structure. Perhaps they understood that these were white native advantages. In assimilating, European immigrants were, in effect, becoming fully and unambiguously white. On the other side, Gans, Portes, and Zhou posit that the children of nonwhite immigrants would come to share the *native disadvantages* of racial minorities. Discrimination and racial segregation would block their access to educational opportunities and decent jobs. To avoid this tendency, some members of the second generation would retain the *immigrant advantages* stemming from their parents' positive selection, their embeddedness in ethnic networks and economies, and their cultural orientations (Rumbaut 2004). Of course, their parents' *immigrant disadvantages,* such as lack of English, low human capital, and discordant cultural orientations, might also hold them back.

While our research yields examples of all these scenarios, it suggests an additional possibility: members of the second generation can sometimes negotiate among the different combinations of immigrant and native advantage and disadvantage to choose the best combination for themselves. In other words, we believe that the ability to select the best traits from their immigrant parents and their native born peers yields distinct *second generation advantages*. Members of the second generation neither simply continue their parents' ways of doing things nor simply adopt native ways. Growing up in a different society from that of their parents, they know they must choose between immigrant and native ways of doing things. Sometimes they choose one, sometimes the other, and sometimes they try to combine the best of both worlds. They also sometimes create something wholly new. They do not always choose wisely or well. But they are more aware than most people that they have a choice. Being "in between" allows many members of this generation to engage in forms of cultural innovation that New Yorkers have received well.

Just as we have learned about how young people come of age, we have also learned about New York. Our respondents constantly reminded us just how hard it can be to grow up in the city. Even middle class youngsters and their parents had to compete ferociously for things that middle class Americans elsewhere can take for granted, from a seat in a good elementary school to a spot on the little league team. The situation is many times worse for the poor. The crack epidemic of the late 1980s ravaged many of the neighborhoods in which our informants grew up. Housing remains extremely expensive for young people starting out, even in the poorest neighborhoods. Competition for jobs is fierce, not only from the constant supply of new immigrants, but from young educated people moving from other parts of the United States to try to make it in the city that never sleeps.

As tough as New York is, it is has also historically been good to immigrants. It offers extraordinary opportunities and rewards the improvisation that comes easily to the second generation. Immigrants and their children, past and present, have helped New York emerge as the dominant city in American (and perhaps world) culture and commerce in the mid-twentieth century. New York's brusque local culture is not exactly welcoming, but it offers a rough-and-tumble tolerance to newcomers who can use second generation advantages to best effect. Its native white population celebrates its immigrant origins. If their cousins turned into "unhyphenated" whites after crossing the Hudson, the remaining native whites continue to have social networks and life chances shaped by ethnic histories.

Ethnicity thus has legitimacy. To borrow Elijah Anderson's (2004) phrase for physical and social spaces that celebrate difference, the city's "cosmopolitan canopy" is large and vibrant. When Republicans in Congress proposed criminalizing illegal immigrants and building a fence at the border, New York's Republican mayor dismissively called on them to "get real." Only the chair of the City Council Immigration Committee, a 1973 migrant from Guyana, disagreed: he chided the mayor for not coming out strongly for an unconditional amnesty (Chan 2006:B6). That the city has no clear ethnic majority means that it was "no big deal" for our second generation respondents to have immigrant parents. They rarely felt like outsiders or exotics. Most of their friends were in a similar situation, and anyway, everyone is from somewhere. "Immigrants" are the people who arrived last week, while the only native white "Americans" without accents they know are the ones they see on television. They are New Yorkers, comfortable with the city they have inherited. Without thinking too much about it, they live multicultural lives in the streets, workplaces, and nightclubs of a city that put the tortuously self-conscious "diversity" of elite educational institutions to shame.

Our young respondents appreciated this cosmopolitanism. Cultural diversity was one of the things they liked most about their city. Of course, their explanation of why diversity is good often began and ended with the variety of restaurants. Still, even if practice falls short of theory, they take it for granted that one *should* have friends of many races and backgrounds and think contact with people different from oneself enriches one's life. That belief is important. It is one of the best things about this generation and about New York.

Thinking about Groups

A few caveats are in order before proceeding. Most of the analysis presented in this book is structured around the comparison of ethnic groups. We hope that our evidence will convince the reader that these groups are in some sense real, not just our own nominal creation. Indeed, we think the data make clear how group membership shapes people's lives. Time after time in the pages that follow we will present evidence that even after controlling for all the other relevant variables we have measured in our study, there is still a group effect that we cannot explain away. Nevertheless, we are aware that intergroup comparisons—"the Chinese do this, the Dominicans do that"—sometimes reify groupness more than reality warrants. The variation within the ethnic groups is often as great as the differences between them. When we focus on the differences between ethnic groups, we do not mean to imply that this is the most important factor in their lives, or that other factors like gender or age or race are not sometimes more important. We also recognize that the importance of ethnic identity, as well as the degree to which ethnic groups actually function as groups, varies from group to group and rises and falls over time (Cohen 1974; Brubaker 2004).

We further recognize it is possible to read group comparisons as stereotypes or even racist generalizations. Let us be clear: any reference to group differences makes groups appear more homogenous than they actually are. Our young respondents belonged not only to ethnic groups but also to social classes, genders, social groups, and neighborhoods. Like all modern people, they had a multiplicity of interacting social roles and identities. Although a quick reading of a table comparing groups will not always make this apparent, we have tried to remain sensitive to individual variation without losing sight of the real difference that ethnicity makes. When we highlight ethnic group differences, we are referring to differences in central tendencies with larger, overlapping distributions.

Further, when we or our informants refer to the norms, values, or cultures of any particular group, we are talking about the particular, historically selected group now present in New York. When we refer to the "Chinese" or the "Ecuadorans," we are talking about the specific people who migrated to New York and raised children there between the late 1960s and early 1990s. They represent specific regional, class, linguistic, political, and occupational segments of their countries of origin. They have sometimes created communities in New York that are bizarre parallels to their homelands. "Russian" New York is made up of urban mostly Jewish Russian speakers. "Chinese" New York is disproportionately comprised of Cantonese speakers from particular villages in southern China, with struggling newcomers from Fujian and middle class migrants from Taiwan. Needless to say, the "Russian" or "Chinese" cultural practices of these communities may seem odd to many people in Russia or China.

With all these caveats in mind, we nonetheless believe that membership in and differences among ethnic and racial groups have real and important impacts on the lives of children. As Glazer and Moynihan (1963) argued, later members of ethnic groups inherit a social position derived from the ways in which earlier members entered and became situated in the city, and they function as interest groups that transcend waves of arrival. When members of the Russian Jewish second generation get help from social service agencies created by an earlier generation of Russian Jewish New Yorkers, or when a West Indian avails him- or herself of programs originally created to help African Americans, past group identities, networks, and social positions are shaping their lives, even if they are not fully aware of it. Even when children do not think that their parents' national origin is particularly important, they inherit structures of advantage and disadvantage. Native born white Americans, for example, need not be aware of their "white privilege" to enjoy what Roediger (1999) terms the "wages of whiteness."

Ethnic groups have different modal levels of education, employment, and social capital. Although, as we recognize, all groups vary along these dimensions in ways that overlap with one another, their central tendencies differ significantly, reflecting the group position within the larger society. Moreover, the ways in which traits vary around those central tendencies also differ systematically across groups. Put in plain English, it is better to be part of a poor group that has some well-off members than to be part of a uniformly poor group. These patterns of difference reflect not only conditions in the home countries but also the "selection" of the immigrant first generation from these national populations. While immigrants from poor countries have fewer advantages than those from rich countries, even immigrants from poor countries usually have advantages over those whom they left behind. Groups also have different connections with their home country, proximity to native born ethnic groups, and legal status on entry. Finally, groups vary in how tightly and how densely members are bound to each other and how much they function *as* groups. Given the larger society's tendency to hold ethnic stereotypes, these patterns clearly have real consequences for group members.

Ethnic differences as experienced in the United States are constantly being shaped and reshaped as the groups interact with the larger society and as its patterns of race, social class, education, and a host of other factors evolve. Men and women experience ethnic differences in divergent ways as well. By itself, ethnicity explains nothing. Yet ethnic differences are not a myth obscuring some more fundamental underlying reality. As E. P. Thompson (1966) remarked about class, ethnicity is a historically contingent event, constantly changing, but real nonetheless, and of vital importance to the young people whose lives we are striving to understand.

2

The Worlds of the Fathers and Mothers

Everybody, back then, came to New York because they wanted to pursue a better life. For the Chinese it's very 'whatever you suffer is for the benefit of the children.' Everything, in terms of working and saving money, is to leave behind to your children. Buying a house is to leave behind to your children. It's all for the potential of what they can bestow to their kids.

CHINESE 27-YEAR-OLD WOMAN

The story of the second generation begins with the parents' journey to New York. These first generation immigrants faced struggles, found jobs, formed families, settled in neighborhoods, and were received by native New Yorkers in ways that all set the stage for their children's lives. Here, we draw on the literature on migration to Greater New York, reports from our respondents, and the 2000 Census to paint the portrait of the first generation. We begin by outlining the paths by which the various immigrant and native born racial and ethnic groups came to Greater New York. We discuss how the smaller, more recently arrived immigrant groups fit into the social, economic, and political matrix of the region alongside the larger, older native born groups. We then turn to the 2000 Census for the ten county area in which the telephone survey took place to compare people belonging to the likely age cohort of the parents—foreign born people aged 40 through 60 who immigrated between 1965 and 1990—with their native born counterparts along a series of key dimensions. Taken together, our eight groups comprised 74 percent of the 12 million people in the sampling area for the study.

Immigrant Groups

Dominicans

The United States has a long history of involvement in the Dominican Republic, having occupied it between 1916 and 1924. After the decades-old repressive regime of dictator Rafael Trujillo ended in 1961 and the U.S. Marines invaded in 1965, an initial wave of middle class flight from political unrest began. The first wave included critics of the regime, labor union organizers, and dissident students (Pessar and Graham 2001:252). The dismal state of the Dominican economy, plagued by massive foreign debt and soaring oil prices, led a broader group to migrate for economic reasons starting in the 1970s. Pessar and Graham report that real per capita income on the island in 1992 had fallen below the level of the early 1970s. New York City became the primary destination for Dominican immigrants, with smaller numbers going to New Jersey, Florida, Massachusetts, Rhode Island, and Connecticut (Hernández and Torres-Saillant 1996; Hernández and Rivera-Batiz 1997). As a result, Dominicans are now the area's largest national origin group, with 640,000 people living in households headed by Dominican immigrants in the ten county study area in 2000.

The Dominican Republic shares the island of Hispaniola with the Republic of Haiti. The troubled relationship between the two nations has shaped Dominican national-identity. The first black nation-state, Haiti repeatedly laid claim to the Dominican Republic in the nineteenth century. Dominican nationalist identity was thus constructed in opposition to Haiti—"antihaitianismo" (Paulino 2006). Dominicans often associate blackness with Haiti and non-blackness and Hispanic roots with being Dominican, even though most Dominicans have mixed African and Spanish heritage. (About 12 percent of adult Dominican immigrants in the study area reported to the Census that they were black.) That many are considered phenotypically black on arrival in the United States further complicates their ideas about national and racial identity (Itzigsohn and Dore-Cabral 2000; Itzigsohn, Giorguli, and Vazquez 2005).

As we will see, the Dominican first generation is the most disadvantaged immigrant group in our study. Although a few came from wealthy or middle class families, the parental generation is the most likely (along with the Chinese) to lack formal education and the least likely to have a college education. Dominican families are also the largest, on average, and most likely of the immigrant groups to be headed by a single parent without a partner present. Although Dominican respondents spoke of having extended family in New York, they rarely received financial assistance from them. The Census indicates that the parental generation was also most likely to use public assistance, had the lowest labor force participation rates, received the lowest median earnings, and had the lowest household incomes.

Despite their relative poverty, one-fifth of our Dominican respondents reported that their parents regularly send money to relatives in the Dominican Republic. This high level of remittances helps families back home and yields continuing involvement with the home country, but it also drains family resources. Many parents build homes in the Dominican Republic for retirement. Given that one parent often migrates first, many children are separated from a parent while growing up (Levitt 2001). A parent's return, usually the father's, can also lead to separation. These factors also help explain why Dominicans have the lowest home ownership rates of the groups in our study.

The Dominican second generation thus grows up with more disadvantages than do the children of the other immigrant groups. Many of this generation's members are dark skinned and thus subject to racial discrimination. Their parents are poorly educated, have less fluency in English than do Puerto Rican and South American parents, and speak Spanish at home. Many second generation Dominican respondents did not speak English until they went to school. While Dominican New Yorkers have somewhat more self-employment than blacks or Puerto Ricans and have developed an entrepreneurial class of bodega and supermarket owners, their rates of self-employment and incomes are still lower than those of the other first generation groups.

The Dominican first generation is also more concentrated in dense, poor neighborhoods than are the other immigrant groups. The biggest Dominican settlement is in Washington Heights, north of Harlem in Manhattan (Pessar 1995). but Dominicans have also crossed the Harlem River into the western Bronx, while better-off Dominicans have sought out the Latin American neighborhoods of Queens. Geographic concentration has enabled Dominicans to produce a thriving political class. Dominicans have served in the city council and state legislature since 1991, and they also play a role in Dominican politics. (One recent Dominican president, Lionel Fernández, spent much of his life in New York's Dominican community.) A dense transnational network of personal and ideological connections links neighborhood political and social service groups, Democratic Party political clubs, and the Dominican political parties (Marwell 2004; Morawska 2007).

South Americans: Colombians, Ecuadorans, and Peruvians

First generation immigrants from the three largest South American national origin groups have similar socioeconomic profiles, migrated to New York for similar reasons, live near each other, and often intermarry. Though these sending countries have significant differences with each other, their emigrants are far more like each other than like Puerto Ricans, Dominicans, or Mexicans in New York. Ecuadorans and Colombians are the larger groups, at 213,000 and 168,000 living in households headed by immigrants from these countries in the ten county study area in 2000, along with 89,000 in Peruvian households. Taken together, the group thus rivals Dominicans in population size.

New York's Ecuadoran population grew dramatically in the 1980s and 1990s. A modest flow began from the coastal towns soon after the new U.S. immigration law was passed in 1965. As Ecuadorans filled the quota for legal immigration and the Ecuadoran economy declined in the 1980s, the flow of undocumented workers, many from inland Andean parts of the country, increased sharply (Kyle 2000:29; Marrow 2007:597). In the mid-1990s Ecuador had the highest inflation rate in Latin America, which led the country to freeze dollar bank accounts, causing further emigration. By 1993 Ecuadorans had become the largest undocumented group in the city (New York Department of City Planning, quoted in the *New York Times*, September 2, 1993: B1).

This made New York the "third city of Ecuador" behind Guayaquil and Quito. As sociologist David Kyle noted, "During a visit [to Quito] in 1990 . . . professionals and cabdrivers alike [were saying] what sounded to my ears like 'la YANY.' I asked a taxista what it meant and was told 'Tú sabes, yo amo Nueva York—Y ♥ NY.' *(You know, I love New York—I ♥ NY.)* Everyone I met talked about who was in New York or about to go there, what they were doing, and when and if they were coming back" (Kyle 2000:2). The Ecuadoran immigrants to New York reflect Ecuador's diversity of regions and ethnic groups, with more than 100 sports clubs and civic associations forming to reflect these origins, as in the case of the Chinese-Ecuadorans of New York City Social Club (Kyle 2000:37).

Colombians are the second most numerous South American group in the metropolitan area. Decades of political violence and economic upheaval, beginning with "La Violencia" (1948–1962), led to a steady stream of migrants. The first Colombians in New York were mostly lower middle class people from Bogotá, Cali, and Medellín fleeing instability and seeking economic opportunity (Collier and Gamarra 2001; Guarnizo and Espitia 2007). After the late 1970s, drug-related violence drove a second wave of middle and upper class migrants to leave despite Colombia's improving economy. Although the best-off Colombians tended to settle in South Florida (Collier and Gamarra 2001), New York's Colombian community is generally more middle class than are the communities of Hispanic immigrants from the Caribbean or Mexico.

Peruvian immigrants have been coming to the United States since the late nineteenth century, but their numbers increased dramatically after the 1960s, with the emigration of professionals, technicians, and manual workers (Marrow 2007). As in Colombia, political crises and armed conflict promoted migration from Peru during the 1980s. The Sendero Luminoso (Shining Path) campaign from 1979 to 1992 caused great bloodshed in the Andean highlands and Lima. The political and economic instability of the 1980s became known as the "lost decade" or the "decade of chaos," leading to the rapid growth of the Peruvian population not only in metropolitan New York but also in Florida and California (Sabogal 2005; Marrow 2007).

Immigrants from these three South American countries tended to be lighter skinned than the other two Hispanic groups we studied. Although all three countries have large indigenous Indian populations and small African ancestry populations, these groups were not predominant among those who migrated to New York. (According to the 2000 Census, 2.1 percent of the Colombians in the metropolitan area report being black, and less than 1 percent report indigenous ancestry.) Our South American respondents reported lower levels of racial discrimination than did the Dominicans and Puerto Ricans. When other New Yorkers tried to guess their ethnicity, many of our South American respondents told us that they were most often mistaken for Italian Americans.

First generation South Americans in metropolitan New York have higher levels of education than do Dominicans. South American first generation adults are comparatively likely to live in married couples and have high levels of labor force participation. Although many South American parents send remittances home, their transnational ties are not as strong as those of Dominicans parents. Continuing violence discourages Colombians from frequent or long term visits home. Few Ecuadoran and Peruvian respondents said their parents planned to return to the home country on retirement, and even fewer thought about living there themselves.

South American immigrants have largely settled in the middle class neighborhoods of northern Queens, particularly Jackson Heights and East Elmhurst, as well as in the older, working class sections of New Jersey towns along the Hudson and in Westchester County, often in formerly Italian American neighborhoods. Although these neighborhoods are run down by suburban standards, they usually afford access to decent schools and have less crime than poor inner city neighborhoods. The neighborhoods where these immigrants have settled in New York became among the most ethnically diverse anywhere in the world (Winnick 1990; Jones-Correa 1998; Sanjek 1998; Maly 2005). No Colombian, Ecuadoran, or Peruvian has yet held political office in the city, although there is a rich supply of civic and business organizations that serve these communities.

West Indians

English-speaking West Indians have a long history in New York City. In 1920, 41,000 Caribbean born blacks lived in New York City, making up a quarter of its black population (Kasinitz 1992). For many years these immigrants and their descendants remained "invisible" because society saw them only as blacks (Bryce-Laporte 1972). Yet they played prominent roles in the political, cultural, and intellectual life of New York, producing such luminaries as nationalist leader Marcus Garvey, poet Claude McKay, psychologist Kenneth Clarke, Congresswoman Shirley Chisholm, and former Secretary of State Colin Powell. These figures were clearly part of *black* New York, however. While rigid segregation and discrimination circumscribed some of the achievements of West Indian politicians, professionals, and intellectuals, the growth of New York's black population provided many of them with a base of constituents.

The West Indian share of New York's black population fell during and after World War II as black migration from the South burgeoned, but the perennial economic stagnation and unemployment of the Caribbean, the region's historical links with New York, and British refusal to accept further West Indian migration after 1962 set the scene for renewed large scale migration to the United States. Though centered on New York, the post-1965 immigration also spread to the suburbs and other parts of the United States. Over time this group has developed an identity that is partly, though by no means entirely, distinct from that of native African Americans (Vickerman 1999; Waters 1999).

The former slave plantation societies of the English-speaking Caribbean are not as desperately poor as Haiti or the Dominican Republic, but they suffer from high unemployment, uneven development, and scant opportunities for advancement. Their educational systems are better than those of many other poor countries, yet opportunities for high school graduates are scarce, leading many to seek employment or higher education in the United States. Jamaica and Guyana also experienced sharp rises in crime and political violence during the 1970s, prompting a middle class emigration. The Jamaican dollar, which traded at parity with the U.S. dollar in the late 1960s, was worth less than two U.S. pennies in the 1990s. Since Jamaica imports most of its daily necessities, its families have grown heavily dependent on remittances. Migration thus became an expected part of the adult life course throughout the region (Kasinitz 1992; Richardson 1992). By 2000 the ten county study area contained 660,000 members of West Indian households, making this group about as large as the Dominicans. (Haitians, who are not included in our West Indian category, would add several hundred thousand more.)

Though they come from poor islands, many West Indians do arrive with real resources. Most members of the parental generation have a high school degree, and about one in five has a college degree. The parental generation of West Indians also has a high rate of labor force participation, particularly the women. The number of married couples is low: a quarter of the West Indian parental generation are divorced, separated, or widowed; another 16 percent never married. More than half of our respondents grew up without both biological parents in the home. Yet this did not seem to have as negative an impact on them as it did among native blacks and Puerto Ricans, perhaps because of the presence of extended family members. West Indian families are more likely than black or Puerto Rican families to contain an elder, and many West Indian respondents spoke of grandmothers playing the role of "second mother" in their lives.

West Indians also have strong transnational connections, and many respondents had visited their parents' homelands several times. However, this was mostly for short stays to visit relatives and take a vacation. While high, remittance rates were lower than among Dominicans and placed less of a strain on the higher West Indian family incomes. Although many West Indian parents talked of returning home on retirement, this did not prevent them from acquiring property in New York. Their rate of home ownership was significantly higher than that of the other immigrant groups or native minorities.

Many West Indian respondents told us that they had experienced prejudice or discrimination from the police. At the same time, they had some advantages over other immigrant groups. They spoke English on arrival, and members of the parental generation were almost as likely to have graduated from high school as native blacks and considerably more likely to do so than the Hispanic groups. Some New York employers may prefer West Indians to native blacks or Hispanics (Waters 1999). As New York City's labor market has become feminized, the long West Indian tradition of female labor force participation, sharply different from the Latin American tradition, has served West Indians well. West Indian women developed ethnic niches in nursing and health care, clerical and administrative work, teaching, and child care, while West Indian men found blue collar jobs, particularly in construction (Kasinitz and Vickerman 2001).

The relative prosperity of West Indian parents came at a price. Despite colonialism, blacks have long held positions of wealth and power on the sending islands. Being black in America thus often came as a deep shock to them (Vickerman 1999). Less affluent West Indian parents living in racially segregated neighborhoods with inferior schools were deeply worried that they would lose their children to "the streets" (Waters 1999). This sometimes prompted parents to send their children "back home" for a time, even though doing so might trigger feelings of abandonment in their children and lead to difficulties in their readjusting to life in the United States upon return. Although the first generation parents see themselves as distinct from native blacks, the distinction has a "now you see it, now you don't" quality within the second generation, as young Caribbean Americans insist that they are both African American and West Indian (Butterfield 2004).

The West Indian first generation had established distinctively West Indian neighborhoods near those of African Americans. Its members avoided older African American neighborhoods like Harlem and also did not live in public housing. They concentrated in working and middle class areas like Crown Heights, Flatbush, East Flatbush, and more recently Canarsie in Brooklyn, the Northeast Bronx and Laurelton, Queens Village, and Cambria Heights in Southeast Queens. Their relatively high levels of household income and home ownership, together with their facility in English and long family histories in New York City, enabled community members to produce a strong political leadership cadre. Shirley Chisholm, in 1968 the first black woman elected to the U.S. Congress, was a second generation West Indian, partially raised in Barbados. In 2006 Brooklyn sent Yvette Clarke, a second generation Jamaican American, to Capitol Hill.

The Chinese

New York has long had a small community founded by southern Chinese migrants who had initially come to the West Coast as laborers in the mid-nineteenth century but later moved east seeking work and fleeing anti-Chinese violence. Since the United States heavily restricted Chinese immigration until 1965 and the People's Republic of China and Taiwan governments both restricted Chinese emigration even after that, this community grew slowly with small numbers of migrants from Hong Kong or Taiwan, many of whom came as graduate students. In the early 1970s, however, China liberalized its emigration policy. Most of this wave of migrants had family ties with earlier migrants from Guangdong Province, but soon more and more Chinese came from other regions as well. After 1979 the Taiwan government followed suit and allowed more Taiwanese to enter the United States through family reunification visas (Skeldon 1994; Wong 1999). People of Chinese descent from Malaysia, Singapore, Thailand, Vietnam, and Indonesia as well as the Caribbean and South America also migrated to New York during this period. These populations have widely varied backgrounds (Ong, Bonacich, and Cheng 1994; Holdaway 2007; Yin 2007), yet they all seem to consider themselves more or less "Chinese" and share institutions and neighborhoods with people coming directly from China. By 2000 the ten county study area included 368,000 living in households headed by foreign born Chinese.

These population flows have been matched by capital flows. The migrants brought personal funds from Taiwan and Hong Kong, while Taiwan's economic boom, capital flight from pre-1997 Hong Kong, and China's recent rapid growth fueled investment in New York (Zhou 1992; Kwong 1996; Lin 1998). In 1958 the city had two Chinese-owned banks; by 1988 there were thirty-nine. Chinese language media and professional services have mushroomed, as have restaurants and garment factories, creating a diversified and substantial economic enclave (Zhou 1992:95). Rising prices and density in Manhattan's Chinatown have spurred the growth of satellite Chinatowns in Flushing and Elmhurst in Queens and Sunset Park in Brooklyn (Chen 1992; Zhou 1992).

These migration streams have diversified the Chinese population in and around New York. Although their median level of education was similar to that of many other groups, they were more likely to be found at the two extremes: a third of the Chinese in the parental age group had a college degree, but even more than a third lacked a high school degree.

While many Chinese parents were poor and had little or no education, their family and social networks usually connected them with others who had high levels of education and strong professional aspirations for their children. These "weak ties" (Granovetter 1973) helped even poor Chinese children with uneducated parents.

The parents' generation entered a city with a strong Chinese ethnic economy that provided them with jobs and access to credit to buy homes or start businesses. High levels of education allowed some parents, especially those from Taiwan, to get well-paid professional jobs, although many of our respondents told us that their parents encountered "glass ceilings" in predominantly white settings.

Chinese families have the highest average number of workers of all our study groups and very high levels of labor force participation. They also have high levels of self-employment and are the most likely to receive income from assets and to own homes. Thus, even though many individuals work at low-paying jobs, members of the Chinese first generation have pooled resources to achieve an extraordinary level of asset accumulation. The first generation Chinese are also the most likely to live in married couple families with other adults who contribute to caring for the children.

Transnationalism seems to have facilitated the flow of financial capital *into* the Chinese community in New York. Because most working class families came as family units, it is rare for children to be separated from their parents. Until recently, conditions in China were such that few parents intended to return to their homeland, so they concentrated their energy on succeeding in New York. Their remittance levels were, and continue to be, relatively low and infrequent, suggesting symbolic gifts rather than maintaining extended families back home. On the other hand, capital has flowed from Taiwan and Hong Kong into North American Chinese communities (Lin 1998).

Future migrants from China may not share these advantages. Economic reform in China and the attendant loosening of controls on emigration have stimulated new waves of migration from the poorest regions of that country, including undocumented migrants from around the city of Fuzhou and skilled workers laid off from China's rust belt. Few of the newer immigrants have family here, and many start out as undocumented workers on the lowest rungs of the garment and restaurant industries, often burdened with debts of up to $50,000 to criminal immigrant smugglers.

The initial zone of settlement for the Chinese first generation was the historic Chinatown of Lower Manhattan. This densely packed residential, commercial, and industrial neighborhood is characterized by crowded streets and small apartments. Because it is close to many gentrifying neighborhoods in Lower Manhattan as well as the municipal government buildings, Chinatown rents have risen rapidly in recent years. Consequently, Chinese families searching for better housing at more affordable prices have followed the subway lines that run through Manhattan's Chinatown into the white ethnic neighborhoods of southern Brooklyn and northern Queens, such as Sunset Park and Flushing. In these areas, working class Chinese parents found neighborhoods with decent if not outstanding schools and relatively little crime. They often came into contact with other Asians, better-off Hispanic immigrants, and Russian Jews as well as native whites. Better-off Chinese immigrants have bought homes in middle class neighborhoods east of Flushing, such as Bayside and Whitestone. Our Chinese respondents rarely mentioned parents facing discrimination when looking for housing. Although the Chinese are slower to naturalize and less likely to join American political parties or to vote when they do, their community's growing size, affluence, and organization led to the election of the first Chinese member of the city council from Flushing in 2002.

Russian Jews

After Jews were allowed to leave the Soviet Union in the early 1970s, more than half a million came to the United States, and most settled in metropolitan New York (Kasinitz, Zeltzer-Zubida, and Simakhodskaya 2001). The first settlers were "Refuseniks," who had actively opposed the Soviet regime. Later, many left Russia and the other republics of the former Soviet Union for economic reasons or because of political upheaval. As a result, their backgrounds ranged from professionals, artists, and scholars to working class people. A few were religious Jews, others were staunchly secular, and most were somewhere in between. In the ten county study area, about 50 percent came from Russia, 28 percent from Ukraine, and 3.9 percent from Belarus, with the rest from Azerbaijan, Kazakhstan, Uzbekistan, Tajikistan, and the Caucasus. Thus it is probably more accurate to call this group the "Russian-speaking Jewish community." Because members of this community arrived recently, most of our respondents are 1.5 generation. Their parents tend to be older than those of the other first generation groups. In 2000, 220,000 people in the study area lived in households headed by people born in the former Soviet Union.

The members of the parental cohort of those from the former Soviet Union are highly educated. More than half have college degrees, and more than a quarter have graduate degrees. All but a handful graduated from high school. Most of the parents' cohort, including the majority of the mothers, had professional positions in the former Soviet Union as doctors, engineers, and professors, although discrimination against Jews there meant that some individuals held more modest occupations than their education would suggest.

In the United States the parents' generation benefitted from its refugee status, which came with welfare benefits and early naturalization. More than any other group, the Russian Jews also benefitted from a close connection with earlier immigrants, the huge wave of Jewish migration that arrived between 1882 and 1924. Over time the descendants of that group become one of New York's largest and most powerful ethnic communities and established an extensive network of social and religious institutions. By the 1980s these institutions were running out of traditional clients and warmly embraced the new arrivals. The "new" Russian Jews rarely had direct family connections to the "old" Russian Jews. The Holocaust and the cold war had largely severed those. Yet community institutions helped to forge a strong ethnic bond (Zeltzer-Zubida 2004a; Zeltzer-Zubida and Kasinitz 2005). Organizations like the United Jewish Appeal-Federation (UJA) and the New York Association for New Americans (NYANA) provided an array of social services and supports. Our respondents reported that half their parents received help from Jewish organizations (the organizations believe they helped even more), and many Jewish schools offered special scholarships to enable the children of these immigrants to attend when their parents could not afford the full fee (Zeltzer-Zubida and Kasinitz, 2005). Although many Russian Jewish respondents also received public assistance growing up, they were the *least* likely to be receiving public assistance as young adults.

Many well-educated Russian Jewish parents were able to reestablish their credentials and practice their professions in the United States, but others took relatively modest jobs. Still, the Russian parents' cohort had the highest household incomes, the most self-employment, and among the highest rates of return on assets of all the groups except for native whites. Although members of this cohort were less likely than the Chinese or native whites to own homes, those they did own had high values.

Russian families generally make a "clean break" with the former Soviet Union. Few send remittances and very few plan to return. To the extent that transnational ties are important to the Russians, such ties are with Israel. Russian Jewish families are small, and Russian Jewish parents tend to stay married. Most of our respondents report that they grew up with two working parents, often with grandparents helping to care for them.

Religion complicates the question of Russian identity. The Soviet Union stigmatized Russian Jews for being Jewish. In New York, Jewish host organizations, schools, and sometimes parents have pressured the second generation to become more religious, which many individuals resist. Whereas their families did not feel entirely "Russian" in Russia, members of this group have the option in New York of participating in a growing and vibrant Russian-speaking community that includes non-Jews as well. As one young man put it, "It's like a joke. Back in Russia, I was considered to be a Jew. Here I'm considered to be a Russian!" Of course, the United States also considers him "white." While relatively poor at the outset, the first generation settled in neighborhoods with good public schools and city services. With access to Section 8 housing vouchers, they were preferred over minority renters by landlords in white neighborhoods thought to be at risk of "going black."

Many Russian Jews moved to Brighton Beach in southern Brooklyn. At the terminus of several subway lines near Coney Island, this neighborhood was a northern urban version of a declining South Florida Jewish retirement community, with dense apartment buildings bordering the boardwalk and beach. Beginning around 1980, Soviet Jewish families established a residential enclave and thriving commercial district known as "Little Odessa" under the elevated train along Brighton Beach Avenue. As Russian Jews became more established, they spread to neighboring Manhattan Beach, Midwood, and Bensonhurst, as well as suburban communities on Long Island. Other "Russian" Jews, particularly those from Central Asia or the Caucasus, have concentrated in the Briarwood, Forest Hills, and Rego Park sections of Queens. They share these neighborhoods with non-Jewish Russian speakers, American Jews, and Chinese, South Asian, Pakistani, and Middle Eastern immigrants. It is relatively rare for them to encounter blacks and Puerto Ricans. Because they settled in areas represented by an entrenched group of white ethnic politicians, this community has been slow to gain political representation, but the first Russian member of the state legislature was elected from Brighton Beach in November 2006.

The Native Born Comparison Groups

Native Whites

Unlike the other groups in our study, many young whites in metropolitan New York grew up in other parts of the country and came there to get an education or launch their careers. While this skews the educational profile of our native white respondents upward, even those individuals who grew up in New York started with more advantages than the other groups we studied. Some had professional and managerial parents who lived in upper middle class suburbs; others grew up in the city's middle class Irish, Italian, or Eastern European Jewish neighborhoods. Few in the native white parents' age group lacked a high school diploma, and two-fifths had college degrees. They had the highest household incomes, the most self-employment income, the largest assets, and by far the highest levels of home ownership. Even respondents growing up in working class neighborhoods had parents with jobs that afforded a modicum of financial stability. Their neighborhoods had decent public schools, and many of our respondents attended Catholic or Jewish schools for at least part of their education. They also comprised the single largest group in the ten county region, accounting for 3.9 million of its 12 million residents.

Despite this, native whites in our study lacked some "immigrant advantages." Although the rate of marital breakup was lower than that of Latinos and blacks, it was far higher in the parental generation than among the Chinese and Russian Jews. Unlike in immigrant households, it was also a rare native white household that included adults who could help compensate for the absence of parents. Young native white New Yorkers are also the likeliest to leave the area for college or to pursue career opportunities. They are thus more distant from family connections. This exodus of young native whites is often overlooked, since they are replaced by well-educated native whites about the same age from other parts of the country. These native white in-migrants tend to be secular, highly educated young people. Most live in Manhattan or brownstone Brooklyn. The native whites who grew up in New York, by contrast, often identified with an "ethnic" background. A third described themselves as Italian and a quarter as Irish, and one-sixth said they were Jewish. In the parents' generation, native whites were the largest single racial-ethnic group, but they comprised only just over a third of the total population. Though the population living in native white households within the city and region is steadily declining, people from this group continue to hold most positions of authority in politics, government, and private institutions.

Native Blacks

African Americans have been in New York City longer than any white group other than the Dutch. Colonial North America's largest concentration of African slaves outside the South was in New York. At the time of the Revolution, blacks constituted 17 percent of New York City and Kings County residents (Rosenwaike 1972:8). Slavery was legal in New York until 1826, and blacks, slave and free, unloaded ships, staffed kitchens, and served as laborers and artisans in early nineteenth-century New York (Binder and Reimers 1995; Burrows and Wallace 1999; Foote 2004).

After 1840 the huge European migration overwhelmed the city's relatively stable black population, leading to patterns of racial conflict and exclusion that continued to shape intergroup relations for the next century. By 1920 blacks had dropped to 2 percent of the city's population (Rosenwaike 1972). Pervasive and persistent discrimination and exclusion from white ethnic networks drove African Americans out of trades where they previously had a foothold, save for the most menial and least lucrative (Model 1993; Waldinger 1996; Foner 2000). Native blacks came to be concentrated in the poorest, most crime ridden areas of the city, where they lived with the poorest white immigrants (Anbinder 2001).

Most African Americans in and around New York today are descended from people who came north in the great migration during and after World Wars I and II. The closure of the United States to international migration after the 1920s created a demand in the North for low-skilled labor from new sources, while agricultural modernization and Jim Crow racial restrictions pushed blacks out of the South. The city's black population grew sevenfold between 1920 and 1950, creating new black neighborhoods in Harlem and Brooklyn's Bedford Stuyvesant (Osofsky 1966). These neighborhoods soon became among the city's most overcrowded, with rents far higher than in comparable white neighborhoods (Kasinitz 1992).

Between 1950 and 1980 natural increase and continued migration from the South increased the black population and enlarged the boundaries of black neighborhoods. By 1980 three-fifths of the city's native black population had been born in New York, but one-fourth still hailed from South

Carolina, North Carolina, Virginia, and Georgia. (Even in the 2000 Census more than a third of the region's native blacks in the parents' generation had been born in the South.) The civil rights movement and growing political empowerment opened up new employment opportunities for blacks in the government and social services that expanded in the wake of the racial turmoil of the 1960s. Black women, who always had high rates of labor force participation, moved into clerical and administrative positions in these sectors. This substantial new black middle class diversified the class composition of the black community. At the same time, much of the black population remained stuck in poverty. By 2000, people living in households headed by native blacks were the second largest ethno-racial group in the ten county region, accounting for 14 percent of the total.

The educational attainment of the African American parental generation is highly diverse. While almost a quarter of the parents' generation lacks a high school degree, 17 percent had a BA or more, and another 29 percent had some college. While the median household income of the native black parental generation in 1999 exceeded that of the Dominicans and Puerto Ricans, it was lower than that of the South Americans and West Indians and far below that of the Chinese, Russians, and whites.

Native black households had the lowest average number of workers in the family. Members of the native black parental generation were least likely to live in married couple families and most likely to live in single parent families without a partner. They were also most likely to report that they had never been married. Apart from native whites, their households had the smallest average size and a relatively low presence of older members. Less than half our native black respondents reported that they had grown up with both parents, and only 21 percent reported that their parents were still together at the time we interviewed them. They also came from the families with the most siblings.

Native blacks remain the second most heavily segregated group in New York, after native whites. For the most part, the parents' generation lives in overwhelmingly black neighborhoods. If the parents have white neighbors, it is usually so only during the short period between when the first black families move in and the last white families move out. Although highly racially segregated, New York's native African American neighborhoods are economically diverse. Not only do native African Americans live in the city's largest, poorest, and most crime-ridden public housing projects, they also live in modest working class row houses, the beautiful brownstones of Bedford Stuyvesant, and semi-suburban enclaves in Queens.

Politics and public sector employment have been central to upward mobility in New York's black communities. Black political representation increased dramatically after the adoption of the Voting Rights Act in 1965, and native blacks now wield a substantial amount of political influence in the city. The city comptroller and the borough president of Queens are both African Americans, as are many members of the city council and the city's delegations in the state legislature and the U.S. Congress. New York's African American neighborhoods feature many political organizations, community organizations, and churches. (All three are rolled into one at the Greater Allen AME Cathedral in Queens, led by former congressman Floyd Flake.)

Puerto Ricans

Puerto Ricans occupy an ambiguous position in our study. On the one hand, Puerto Ricans are not "foreign born." They have been U.S. citizens since the adoption of the Jones Act in 1917. On the other, the parents and grandparents of our Puerto Rican respondents uprooted themselves from a Spanish-speaking island home and relocated to the New York region, much like the Hispanic immigrant groups. Arriving mainly in the 1950s, most have been in New York more than a half century. Our study includes only those young people who were born on the U.S. mainland to a Puerto Rican parent. By 2000, people living in Puerto Rican households made up 8.2 percent of the study area's population, or almost 1 million people. About two-thirds of the Puerto Ricans in the parental generation were born on the island and about one-third in New York. Of the island born, the median year of arrival is 1965 and the median arrival age is 17, indicating that the bulk of the Puerto Rican parents' generation arrived as children. Our Puerto Rican respondents are thus "2.5" to third generation.

Puerto Rico became a U.S. possession in 1898 after the Spanish-American War. The Jones Act removed all restrictions on Puerto Ricans' entry into the mainland. In 1952 Puerto Rico was designated a commonwealth, a "free state associated with the United States." The residents of Puerto Rico do not have voting representation in Congress, do not vote for president, and pay no federal taxes. Currently 3.5 million people live on the island, while another 3.4 million Puerto Ricans live on the mainland, where they make up 1.2 percent of the U.S. population.

After World War II Puerto Rico adopted a program of rapid industrialization. From 1948 to 1965 the number of agricultural jobs fell radically while mainland companies recruited Puerto Rican laborers to work in agriculture and factory jobs, mostly in and around New York. In essence, Puerto Rico exported its surplus poor people (Rivera-Batiz and Santiago 1996; Baker 2002). By 1970 approximately 835,000 Puerto Ricans had left the island for the mainland (Rivera-Batiz and Santiago 1996). As the Puerto Rican economy grew during the 1970s, this flow slowed, only to rise again as crime and unemployment spiked on the island in the 1980s and 1990s (Rivera-Batiz and Santiago 1996:3). Many Puerto Ricans who originally settled in New York have moved to the declining small cities of New England, such as Hartford, Connecticut, and Springfield, Massachusetts, where they faced less competition from new immigrants for low wage jobs and much lower housing costs. Better-off Puerto Ricans also suburbanized. New York City's share of the mainland Puerto Rican population has thus fallen from 98 percent in 1950 to 64 percent in 2000.

The 2000 Census indicates that of those Puerto Ricans moving into and out of New York between 1995 and 2000, higher-income households are moving to the suburbs, but movement out of the metropolitan area or back to the island takes place disproportionately among the poor. In short, the Puerto Ricans who remain in the ten county study area are, if anything, better off, not worse off, as a result of selective migration in the five years prior to the Census. That said, New York City still had almost 800,000 Puerto Rican residents and the ten county study area more than a million in 2000, nearly twice as many as San Juan. Puerto Ricans remain the country's second largest Hispanic group after the 21 million people of Mexican ancestry.

The island's population reflects a heritage of European settlers, African slaves brought to work on the plantations, and the indigenous Taino and Arawak Indians. Although Puerto Ricans distinguish among themselves on the basis of race and phenotype, their history of racial mixing and lack of hard racial boundaries created a relatively flexible system of racial stratification and many racially mixed families on the island. On the mainland, Puerto Ricans' notions about race thus often conflicted with North American racial norms (Rodríguez 1989; Duany 2002).

Puerto Ricans are quite poor. The 1999 median household income of $40,000 among the parents' generation in the ten county study area was lower than among any other group except Dominicans. Initially concentrated in low wage manufacturing jobs, New York's Puerto Ricans bore the brunt of the city's deindustrialization (Tienda 1989). Scholars paid a great deal of attention to Puerto Rican poverty in the 1960s. Oscar Lewis's study

La Vida (1966) explained the Puerto Rican plight as an example of the "culture of poverty," a self-defeating culture that led to intergenerational transmission of poverty and lack of mobility. Many felt that this "blamed the victim" for structural problems like discrimination and colonialism. The advent of large scale immigration from other parts of Latin America, especially Mexico, diverted scholarly attention from the continued poverty among Puerto Ricans, but they continue to have significant problems.

Among the parents' generation within the ten county study area, 42 percent of individuals lacked a high school degree, and only 10 percent had a college degree or more. Only native blacks had fewer average workers in the family, and Puerto Ricans in the parental generation were least likely to be self-employed or receive income from assets. Only Dominicans were less likely to own their homes or had lower rates of labor force participation. After native blacks, Puerto Ricans were least likely to live in married couple families. Yet unlike the immigrant groups, they lived in relatively small households unlikely to contain elders to help with child care.

The parents' generation overwhelmingly continues to speak Spanish at home. Of those individuals who do, 48 percent told the 2000 Census that they did not speak English well. Like Dominicans, the Puerto Rican parents have experienced many disadvantages—low levels of education, racial discrimination, low rates of labor force participation, work in low wage occupations when employed, and high rates of single parent families (Massey and Bitterman 1985; Bean and Tienda 1987; Massey and Denton 1989). As with Dominicans, a continuing high rate of transnational connection with Puerto Rico involves frequent visits and some remittances but rarely yields capital transfers from the island to New York.

Finally, after Dominicans, Puerto Ricans were most likely to live in low income neighborhoods in New York City and most likely to live among African Americans, often in public housing. These neighborhoods usually have low-performing public schools and high crime rates. Originally concentrated in Manhattan's Lower East Side and East Harlem, Puerto Ricans gravitated toward the South Bronx. Many of our Puerto Rican respondents lived in the Castle Hill, Classon Point, and Soundview neighborhoods of the Southeast Bronx and the Tremont, East Tremont, Mount Hope, and Bathgate neighborhoods of the Central Bronx. Castle Hill is dominated by large public housing projects with such a serious problem with drug dealing and associated crimes that they drew a targeted intervention from the U.S. Attorney's Office (Glazer 1999). Tremont epitomized neighborhood decline in the Bronx during the 1970s and 1980s, experiencing widespread housing abandonment and arson (Jacobson and Kasinitz 1986), but extensive city investment in rehabilitating the abandoned buildings has enabled the neighborhood to rebound.

Although Puerto Ricans are now a minority of the city's Hispanic population, they remain the majority of its Hispanic voters and elected officials. Puerto Ricans have represented New York in Congress since the 1960s, and Fernando Ferrer, a Puerto Rican former borough president of the Bronx, was the Democratic mayoral candidate in 2001 and 2005. After African Americans, Puerto Ricans are also the group most likely to work in the public sector, and their paths of incorporation are parallel in many respects. Puerto Rican youth played a prominent role in the development of hip hop and other cultural forms usually associated with inner city African Americans (Flores 2000; Rivera 2003).

Comparing the Groups

We can compare the conditions of the different parental groups within the 40 to 60 age cohort using the Public Use Microdata Sample (PUMS) of the 2000 Census for the ten counties included in our study area. To construct a profile of the second generation's parents, we look at foreign born people who migrated to the United States from 1966 through 1990 defined in the same way we chose respondents to the telephone survey. The native counterparts are Puerto Ricans born either on the mainland or the island, native blacks who did not give West Indian or other specific foreign ancestries, and native born whites. (The actual parents of our respondents may be a little older and have spent more time in the United States than this Census cohort because they raised children to adulthood in America.) These data provide a portrait of the parental generation on dimensions such as earnings, assets, education, and family form that were not reliably available through our telephone survey.

Human Capital

The single most important factor in explaining intergenerational mobility is family background, particularly the education, work experience, and earnings of the parents. Of these, parental education and familiarity with English are paramount. Beginning with English abilities, Figure 2.1 shows that virtually all members of the immigrant groups, except for the West Indians, speak their language of origin at home, not English.

(On this and all following figures, the native whites are on the right end and the two native minority groups on the left end, with the Puerto Ricans, generally the most disadvantaged, on the far left. The immigrant origin groups are arrayed in between in terms of their general level of advantage, with Dominicans being most disadvantaged, West Indians and South Americans having moderate advantage, and the Chinese and Russians being most advantaged.)

The ability of members of the parents' generation who speak other languages at home to speak English varies widely, however, with only 16 percent of Russians not speaking English well, but more than half of the Chinese and Dominicans not doing so. (Although many Puerto Ricans speak Spanish at home, fewer than one in five of them report not speaking English well.) Although a few West Indians, native blacks, and native whites speak another language at home, almost all report speaking English well.

Similar patterns may be seen in Figure 2.2, which shows educational attainment among these adults. As one might expect, few of the native whites and Russians of the parents' cohort lack a high school degree, but

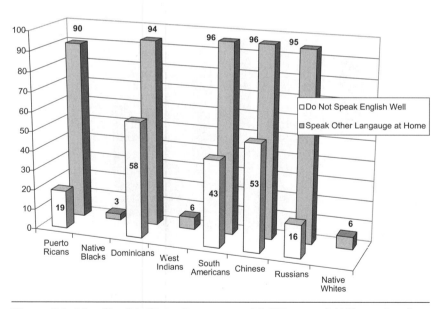

Figure 2.1. Non-English Home Language and Self-Reported Ability to Speak English (%), Parents' Generation. *Source:* U.S. Census, 2000, 5% Public Use Microdata Sample, ten county study area.

this is true of a quarter of the native blacks and West Indians. The Puerto Ricans, South Americans, and Chinese are also comparatively likely to lack a high school degree. The Dominican parents fall the farthest behind, with only two-fifths having as much as a high school degree. College graduation rates follow a similar pattern: highest among the native whites and Russians, comparatively high among the Chinese, lower among native blacks and West Indians, and lowest among Puerto Ricans and Dominicans. The Chinese pattern is distinctive in having both a relatively high share of college graduates and a high share of those who never earned even a high school degree.

Work, Earnings, Household Income, and Home Ownership

The different parental groups also had widely varying levels of labor force participation, earnings, workers in the family, household income, self-employment, and assets such as home ownership or stocks. Figure 2.3 shows

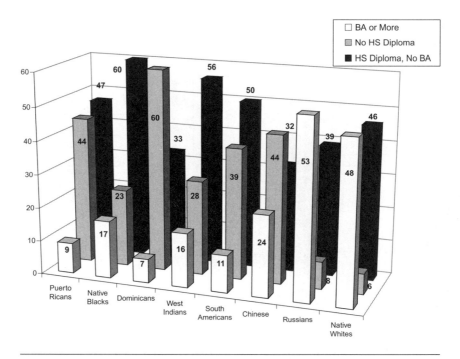

Figure 2.2. Educational Attainment (%), Parents' Generation. *Source:* U.S. Census, 2000, 5% Public Use Microdata Sample, ten county study area.

labor force participation by gender and median annual earnings for those working regular hours for most of the year. Every group displays a gender gap in labor force participation and earnings, with men working and earning more than women, but the gendering of work varies considerably across the groups. The gaps in share of population working are small among West Indians and native blacks, rise to ten points among Russians and twelve points among the native whites, and are thirteen to sixteen points among the other groups. Considerable differences may be seen across groups in terms of the levels of work as well: highest overall among native whites and Russians, lowest among the Dominicans and Puerto Ricans, a bit higher among native blacks and South Americans, and significantly higher among the West Indians and Chinese. Clearly, both the generally low level of work and fairly strong gender differences in work contribute to putting the Hispanic groups toward the low end of the group distribution of work.

Similar patterns between men and women and across groups may also be seen in earnings: men earn more than women, though the gaps are

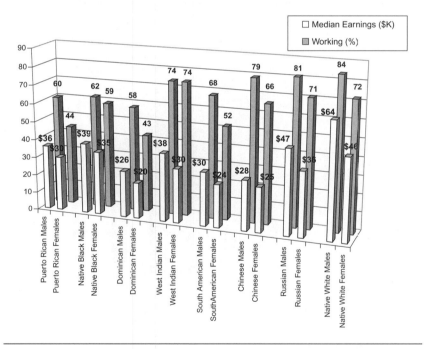

Figure 2.3. Employment (%) and Earnings ($K) of Full Time Employed, Parents' Generation. *Source:* U.S. Census, 2000, 5% Public Use Microdata Sample, ten county study area.

smallest among native blacks and greatest among the relatively high earning native whites. Among them, the female median annual earnings are 71 percent of the male median. Women do best relative to the men among the native blacks (89 percent), Chinese (89 percent), and Puerto Ricans (84 percent).

When combined with the share of families that have two or more workers, Figure 2.4 shows how these employment rates by gender and earnings by gender add up into median household incomes. Native whites in the parents' age bracket have the highest median household income ($88,000) even though they are less likely to have multiple workers in the family because they have by far the highest earnings. Russians ($63,000) were in a similar position. Perhaps counter to stereotype, native blacks ($44,000) did not have the lowest household incomes, which fell, rather, to Puerto Ricans ($36,000) and Dominicans ($35,000). These groups had the lowest incomes because they had the lowest employment rate, lowest individual earnings, relatively big gender gaps in these rates, and low shares of families with two or more workers. Native blacks and

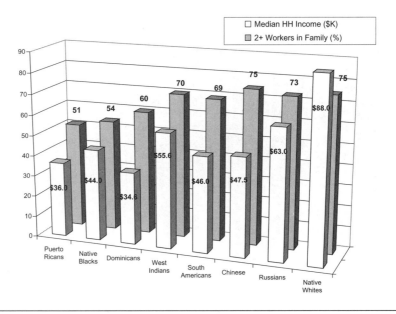

Figure 2.4. 2+ Workers in Family (%) and Median Household Income ($K), Parents' Generation. *Source:* U.S. Census, 2000, 5% Public Use Microdata Sample, ten county study area.

South Americans ($46,000) did somewhat better on these factors, but the West Indians ($56,000) and Chinese ($48,000) did better. They showed how gender parity in work and earnings, high group engagement with work, and multiple earners in the family could offset relatively low individual earnings to generate higher household incomes.

The variation in earnings within the group can also be an important factor. The Chinese, for example, include a larger upper middle class (as well as more poor people). Despite regional and class differences within this group, better-off co-ethnics evidently felt a connection with the poor "downtown" Chinese (Louie 2004). The intensity of connections within the community helped poor members to access cross-class networks that provided information, financial resources, role models, and practical assistance.

Finally, the groups also differ in how much capital they have, how it is distributed within the group, and how group members accumulate it. Ethnic banks and informal lending associations play an important role for many immigrant families. Groups with access to credit are more likely to generate small business ownership. Though only a small portion of any group is self-employed, *all* the immigrant groups have higher rates of self-employment and get more income from their businesses than the two native minority groups. In this respect, the immigrants are more like the native whites, who get the most income from self-employment. They are all twice as likely to be self-employed as native blacks and Puerto Ricans. (African Americans are much more likely to be employed in the public sector, where they benefit from good health insurance and pensions, but this may also deter them from building business equity.) Immigrant and native white families also have significantly higher average numbers of workers in their families than do blacks and Puerto Ricans. Finally, the native white, Russian, and Chinese households also have substantial income from dividends, interest, and rents.

Owning a home provides the single largest asset for most families. Racial discrimination, segregation, and income differences have produced a large gap in home ownership and home equity between black and white Americans—a wealth gap that has remained wide even as the income gap has narrowed (Oliver and Shapiro 1995; Conley 1999). Similar home ownership and home value gaps exist across the groups within the metropolitan region.

Figure 2.5 shows patterns of self-employment; receipt of income from assets that generate interest, dividends, or rent; and home ownership.

Only a relatively few members of the parents' age cohort are self-employed, but small differences seem to count: the shares are lowest among Puerto Ricans and native blacks and more than twice as high among South Americans, Chinese, and Russians, with a high rate among native whites as well. Even more important, the mean earnings among self-employed Russians and native whites are $40,000 and $50,000 per year, compared with $20,000 for Chinese and less for the other groups. Patterns of asset holding are similar, with native whites, Russians, and Chinese being distinctly more likely to have income from this source, followed by West Indians.

A home is generally a family's biggest and most important asset, and the rate of home ownership shown in Figure 2.5 ranges from a high of 72 percent among native whites in the parental cohort to 63 percent for Chinese, 54 percent among West Indians, 48 percent for Russians, 37 percent for native blacks in the parents' age group, down to 32 percent for South Americans, 26 percent for Puerto Ricans, and a mere 17 percent for the Dominicans. Median values of the homes owned are also much higher for the native whites, Chinese, and Russians than for the other

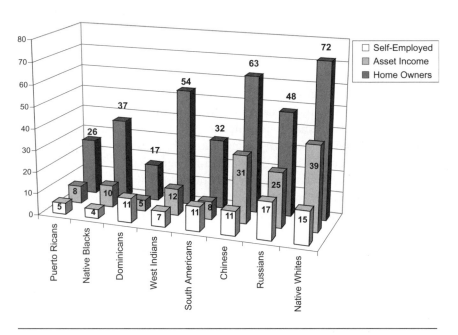

Figure 2.5. Household Assets (%), Parents' Generation. *Source:* U.S. Census, 2000, 5% Public Use Microdata Sample, ten county study area.

groups, with the Puerto Ricans and Dominicans owning the least valuable homes. Clearly, home ownership gives some groups a substantial asset advantage over the others.

Because housing is so expensive in New York and because neighborhoods with high rates of home ownership tend to have good schools, inheriting or being able to buy a home in such areas has a strong influence on children's early education. Native whites are far more likely to be in this position. Discriminatory real estate and lending practices and lack of enough money to make a down payment consign many immigrant minority families to renting in neighborhoods with fewer good schools. Even when immigrant minority families buy, their houses are worth less and appreciate more slowly. Native blacks and Puerto Ricans are also far more likely to live in public housing. Although this gives them respite from New York housing prices, it also ties them to low-performing school districts and prevents them from accumulating home equity.

Family Form

Finally, Figure 2.6 shows that the groups have also formed different types of households and families. It shows three patterns. First, native whites, Russians, and Chinese are much more likely than the other groups in the parents' generation to be living in married couple families, followed by the South Americans. Rates of married couple families are lowest among native blacks and West Indians. Second, the native born groups—native whites, native blacks, and Puerto Ricans—are all more likely to be living in nonfamily households, the most common of which is an individual living alone. Finally, the black and Hispanic groups are all much more likely to be living in single parent families than are the Chinese, Russians, or native whites.

Except for the Russians, the immigrant groups—the Chinese, South Americans, West Indians, and Dominicans—are more likely to live in households containing both people over 65 *and* children under 18. (These households are also more likely to contain subfamilies, which is to say a child with his or her own child.) As a result, they are more likely to include grandparents or other elders who might be able to stay at home to watch over small children as their parent or parents go out to work—as well as more adults who could contribute to the household income. Contrary to the popular but evidently dated image of kin networks among native blacks (Stack 1974), native blacks and Puerto Ricans are *less* likely to live in multigenerational households than are immigrant groups. (In Stack's study, the eldest and usually central members of the extensive "kin networks" were almost all first generation migrants from the South. After more than four decades in the urban North, this "immigrant" pattern seems to have eroded among African Americans.) Since the Russian immigrants arrived more recently, were older to begin with, and brought their children with them, the Russian parents' generation lives in households with the fewest children. Its members are also most like the native whites, who live in the smallest households with the least prevalence of either elders or children.

These differences in family form reinforce the previously described patterns of work across the groups. More Chinese adults live as married couples with both partners working than is true of any other group, followed by Russians, native whites, West Indians, and South Americans. Native blacks, Puerto Ricans, and Dominicans are only half as likely to live in such households. Conversely, Dominicans, Puerto Ricans, and native blacks are twice as likely as the other groups to live in female-headed households where the parent does not work outside the home. Among female-headed families, West Indian and South American mothers are

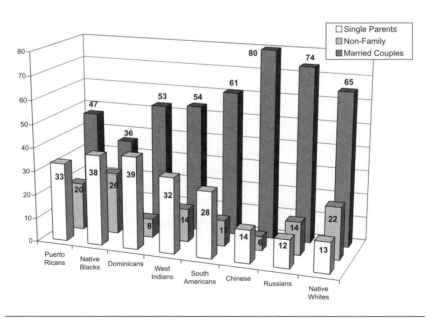

Figure 2.6. Family Form (%), Parents' Generation. *Source:* U.S. Census, 2000, 5% Public Use Microdata Sample, ten county study area.

most likely to be in the paid labor force, whereas the Puerto Rican mothers are the least likely.

Social Networks

Social networks—including the extended family, parents' co-workers and friends, and also teachers, guidance counselors, and peers—are a crucial source of information and even practical or financial help. Parents may hope that their children will go to college, but they must know the system in order to get them there. Our in-depth interviews show that parents from different backgrounds have highly uneven levels of information about local schools and how to compare them. Groups also vary in terms of how important they think early education is for future opportunities. Some parents assume that any local school should give their children an adequate start; others realize that their children can get into college only if they get a good grounding in high school.

In some cases social networks provide practical support. Co-workers and extended family members may allow youngsters living elsewhere to use their addresses so that the children can attend better schools, or may contribute to their college fund. Jewish groups in New York often provided scholarships or financial assistance for the Russian youngsters to attend yeshivas. Networks also shape expectations and provide role models not available in the immediate family. The peers surrounding a young person can affect the youth's behavior for better or worse. (The literature generally focuses on worse, but Margaret Gibson [1988] points out that peers can play a positive role.) Relationships with teachers, counselors, employers, and other nonparental adults can be crucial in providing information, encouragement, and opportunities. We do not have direct measures of social networks for the parents either from the Census or from our survey, but our in-depth interviews underscore their importance.

Transnational Ties

Some immigrant groups are more likely than others to maintain ties to their countries of origin. On the whole, the literature on transnationalism focuses on the fact that many immigrant groups *do* send significant remittances back to their home countries and that these financial flows have an important economic impact there. The literature also shows how transnational ties can promote immigrant entrepreneurship in the receiving societies and by and large argues that such transnational connections enhance integration in the United States rather than detract from it (see Basch, Schiller, and Blanc 1994; Portes 1999; Levitt 2001; Smith 2006). Finally, students of international migration also acknowledge that a shift of resources from the sending country to the United States transpires when, for example, they send bright and well-schooled young people to the United States for graduate study or work as professionals. Much less attention has been paid, however, to the circumstances under which sending substantial remittances to the home country may constitute a burden on immigrant communities and reduce their resources for investing in their host country.

Our interviews confirm that some families do come to the United States at least partly in order to give their children better educational opportunities. Some arrived knowing quite a lot about the local school system from relatives who migrated earlier. The maintenance of transnational ties probably facilitates the flow of such information back to peers in the home country, as well as helping immigrants to compare their progress with that of their cousins back home. If members of the second generation rarely or never return to the home country, their reference point will be their peers in New York. These different reference points could serve to raise or lower expectations depending on the prevailing levels of education, but generally those in New York are higher.

It is important to measure not only the degree of transnational resource flows but also their direction and their positive and negative impacts at both ends. Given that geographic proximity, sending-country support for dual nationality, and the level of commerce between the United States and the sending countries all promote transnationalism, it is clear that some of our groups can be expected to have higher levels than others. Transnationalism can be expected to be relatively high for the Dominicans and West Indians, somewhat lower for the South Americans, and lowest for the Chinese and Russians. The direction of resource flows is mostly outward for the former groups and perhaps inward for the latter.

Transnational flows can take many forms. Where movement across borders is easy, for example, families may send their children "back home" for part of their education. This may get children out of a negative environment in New York and perhaps expose them to a more rigorous education, but it can be personally disruptive, a reentry into the U.S. system may be difficult, and it may retard English-language ability. Politics in the sending countries can also be influential. Concern about Hong Kong's return to

China in 1997 and uncertainty about Taiwan's future caused large capital flows into the Chinese communities of the United States. This drove up real estate prices, but it also provided a new source of capital.

Norms, Repertoires, and Expectations

Material resources clearly matter a great deal, but so do the ways in which families put them to use. Group-specific ideas about how much education a child should get, what occupations their children should or may pursue, and how critical education is for success shape how parents from different ethnic and class backgrounds seek to guide their children's education. The groups vary considerably about when they feel young people should leave their parents' home and what age is appropriate for them to settle down and have children. These norms and expectations also vary by class and are strongly gendered.

Such norms are not simply a matter of choice but are shaped by a complex interaction of factors operating within the family, the community, and even transnational relations. For immigrant groups, they reflect not just the culture of the home country but also the subset of people who migrated to New York. These norms also evolve as immigrants interact with the broader co-ethnic community in New York. The high expectations that working class Chinese have for their children result partly from the presence of so many well-educated professionals in the community. They can also be learned by interacting with native born ethnic groups, as when Dominican parents settle close to Puerto Ricans and native blacks. Strong transnational ties can also affect expectations, norms, and repertoires as young people compare themselves with peers in the home country (Louie 2004).

Our respondents all said that their parents wanted them to "finish school," but they meant different things. Even working class Chinese parents pushed their children to pursue careers requiring a college degree and saw getting one as a necessary part of success. South American youth and their parents, by contrast, often aspired to getting a stable job with good benefits and did not necessarily think that going to college was essential for reaching that goal. The impact of such different expectations can be seen well before the children reach college-going age; parents who saw college as optional were much less concerned about whether their children attended a high quality high school than those who saw high school as a stepping-stone to college and beyond.

All parents were concerned about their children's safety. Some would allow their children to travel across the city to better schools, however, while others kept their children, especially the girls, close to home because they feared what might happen if their children traveled long distances to school. Dominicans and South Americans were particularly reluctant to let their children travel far from home, but this was also true of Puerto Rican and Russian families. Chinese and West Indians, by contrast, were far more willing to let children travel if it meant going to a better high school, though they generally did not want their kids to leave the city for college—something native whites, blacks, and Puerto Ricans often took for granted.

These expectations are expressed at the family level, but they also reflect and are experienced as community and ethnic group norms. Our Chinese respondents, for example, talk about feeling strong pressure to excel in school from extended family and the larger community. Young people who dropped out of high school in communities where that was fairly common were far less disappointed than those where graduation was expected. While gaining admission to a public City University of New York college was an achievement for young people from many groups, other groups saw attending a local public college as an embarrassing shortfall.

As young people reach adolescence, expectations and norms relating to other aspects of their lives also begin to have an impact. If having a family is an important goal, for example, young people are more likely to end their education sooner or to try to combine school with parenting and perhaps also with work. There are marked differences across the study groups in terms of the timing and sequencing of marriage and child-bearing, which feeds into respondents' attitudes toward education. Russian Jews, for example, feel strong pressure to get married in their mid-twenties—much earlier than others with similarly high educational attainment. This puts them in sharp contrast to the Jews (usually of Russian descent) among the "native whites."

Residential Concentration

Although scholars have studied how residential segregation affects the quality of schooling received by black and Hispanic children, we know less about the impact of residential concentration on children of immigrants (initial evidence is provided by Ellen et al. 2002; Capps et al. 2005). Where immigrants settle is shaped by their financial resources, ethnic networks, and ability to speak English, but also by discrimination in housing and credit markets. Our respondents grew up in settings that put them at an immediate advantage or disadvantage in terms not only of the local schools but also of poverty, crime, access to employment, and amenities such as parks, libraries, and cultural institutions. Since our respondents grew up in the latter 1980s and early 1990s, when violent crime reached a peak in and around New York, physical safety was no small matter.

As expected, native whites are clustered in the most well-off suburbs and New York City neighborhoods, while the native blacks and Puerto Ricans are concentrated in the poorer areas of New York City and the New Jersey cities and are among the least likely to be present in the suburbs. Of the first generation groups, the Colombians, Ecuadorans, and Peruvians are the least concentrated in New York City, though half do live there, and also have a significant presence in the cities on the west side of the Hudson. By contrast, the regional settlement patterns of the Dominican first generation resemble those of the native blacks and Puerto Ricans more than the other immigrant groups. West Indians are more likely to be found in the suburbs, especially on Long Island, than native blacks. Yet West Indians, the Chinese, and Russian immigrants are all still highly concentrated in the city.

The Racial and Ethnic Division of Labor in New York City

Racial and ethnic groups thus occupy widely different positions in the social, geographic, and political hierarchy of Greater New York. When Americans think about immigration, their first concern may be what effect immigrant workers may have on their own jobs and wages. Immigrants are accused both of not working enough—that is, "coming to collect welfare"—and of working too much—"taking jobs" from Americans. The vast academic research on the economic role of immigrants does not add up into a single, clear picture on this score (Smith and Edmondson 1997; Borjas 1999; Carter and Sutch 1999; Friedberg and Hunt 1999; Hirschman 2005).

Regardless of their overall economic impact, we know that first generation immigrants are concentrated in certain occupations and industries. Lacking English, not being familiar with the larger society, and suffering discrimination, immigrants may have little choice but to accept lower wages or more difficult working conditions than natives. At the same time, "ethnic niches" (Waldinger 1996) provide job opportunities to immigrants that the larger economy does not, and "ethnic economies" (Light and Gold 2000) may create employment and wealth that otherwise would not exist.

Ethnic niches are most visible in the form of self-employment in small businesses, a well-known feature of the urban landscape. New Yorkers often call a particular kind of small fruit-and-vegetable shop a "Korean store," and everyone knows that a "Greek diner" describes the origins of the owner, not the cuisine (or even of the kitchen workers, who are today likely to be Mexican). Ethnic concentrations may, however, be equally important in less entrepreneurial arenas and even the public sector. For example, a third of the West Indian women in the parents' generation in the New York region work as nurses, nurse's aides, or home health-care attendants. This is not because West Indians own the hospitals and nursing homes.

As striking as these ethnic niches is the high overall level of commitment to work among the first generation immigrants. Apart from the Dominicans, the immigrant parental generation has higher labor force participation, more working women, and more workers in the family than do the native born minority groups. Multiple-wage-earner households are particularly common among the Chinese, the South Americans, and the West Indians. Sheer labor force participation, even at low wages, can create household incomes that lead to home ownership, better neighborhood schools, and the resources to start businesses.

Our second generation respondents often grow up in families where jobs come through ethnic ties. Their first generation immigrant parents are almost stereotypically concentrated in immigrant occupations and industries. (Only the West Indian fathers and the Russian Jewish mothers do not have a clear ethnic niche.) In fact, the parents are more concentrated than first generation immigrants in the region as a whole. For example, 20 percent of the working mothers of our Dominican and South American respondents and a staggering 47 percent of the working mothers of Chinese respondents had jobs in garment and other factories. Nurse's aides, nurses, and health technicians were the jobs most commonly held by the mothers of our West Indian respondents, accounting for 35 percent of those working. Some 40 percent of Chinese fathers worked in restaurants, mainly as cooks.

That the immigrant parents are even more highly concentrated in ethnic niches than first generation immigrants in general, not to mention the native born minority groups, should not be surprising. The parents are older than other immigrants, have been here longer, and were among the first to enter and build these niches. Their place in the labor market partially reflects the composition of New York's economy two or three decades ago. The heavy concentrations of Chinese, Dominican, and South American mothers in garment manufacturing must be understood in light of the fact that they entered the labor force when New York had many more manufacturing jobs than it does now.

This racial and ethnic division of labor certainly has a strong impact on where members of the parents' generation end up working. We usually think of ethnic niches as a form of "positive" discrimination, but other groups can be negatively affected when one group monopolizes jobs in an area. In New York, extensive ethnic niching in the parents' generation may exclude members of native minority groups from a significant portion of the unskilled and low wage labor market.

Of course, native blacks have their own ethnic niches and may strive for ethnic closure in the workplace. As one second generation Dominican retail worker noted:

The owners of the store, they're white. They have stores all around the country, but my manager was black. And she's racist. When I started working, there was a lot of Dominicans. And she started hiring blacks. She prohibited us from talking in Spanish. She was like, "This is America, and you only talk Spanish if a customer doesn't understand or needs help, but besides that, I don't want to hear you talking Spanish, or you're gonna have to find yourself another job." And she fired every Spanish person in the place.

Native blacks have also built an important niche in public service employment and nonprofit social services closely tied to the public sector.

Many earlier ethnic niches were a transitory feature of life for first generation immigrants, with the second and succeeding generations moving on to better jobs. Other ethnic niches, however, were created and sustained over generations and served as paths to group-level upward mobility. The Irish involvement with politics and government led from the Irish cop in one generation to the Irish mayor in the next and the Irish investment banker in the following generation. More than a century and a half after the potato famine, many more New York City fire fighters are of Irish ancestry than is true of the metropolitan population as a whole. Generations past Ellis Island, New Yorkers still expect their teachers and psychotherapists to be Jewish and their most skilled construction tradespeople to be Italian.

Although protected "white ethnic" niches have been in decline for decades, they continue to enhance the life chances of working class white young people, particularly those without a college education. A 32-year-old Italian American man from Carroll Gardens in Brooklyn, for example, grew up in a family of carpenters. He told us that only after a great deal of reflection and conflict with his family did he decide to defy his father, uncle, and brothers—by becoming an electrician. He never seriously considered attending a four year college or following a white collar career. Given his family and neighborhood connection with the highest-skilled and highest-paid segment of blue collar employment, there was little reason why he should.

Waldinger (1996) shows that while recent immigrants working in ethnically concentrated industries earn less than those who do not work in ethnic niches, the reverse is often true among longtime New Yorkers. After all, assimilated groups cling to the best niches and seek to pass them to their children. Some longtime New Yorkers are as ethnically "niched" as new immigrants, although in well paying occupations it is easy to mistake group upward mobility for assimilation. On the other hand, as Alba and Nee (2003) point out, the proportion of native born people working in ethnic niches has declined, perhaps less among New Yorkers than among their cousins who crossed the Hudson. The man from Carroll Gardens was probably well aware that most people like him do not get jobs through ethnic and neighborhood links. Even though his neighborhood has been dramatically gentrified, his parents' decision to buy a home decades ago has given him and his siblings a valuable resource. As his friends from the neighborhood have moved to distant suburbs, his once dense ethnic networks are fraying. At 32, he already feels nostalgic for a lost social world.

The Relative Position of Native Born and Immigrant Groups

The sequencing and circumstances under which groups have entered the New York metropolitan region, the varied resources they brought with them, and the highly unequal opportunities they found upon arrival have put them into quite different positions in the social and economic structure of the metropolitan area. Though highly schematic, Table 2.1 provides a provisional summary of how the factors reviewed here have affected the parents' generation in each of our groups. The Dominicans and Puerto Ricans face the greatest array of disadvantages in terms both of group characteristics and the context of reception. The parental generation does not speak English as a matter of course; its members are often

Table 2.1. Factors Affecting Position of First Generation Parents

Domain	Puerto Rican	Native Black	Dominican	West Indian	South American	Chinese	Russian	Native White
Language	–	+	–	+	–	–	–	+
Family Structure	–	–	–	–	m	+	+	m
Parental Employment	–	+	–	+	m	+	+	+
Parental Education	–	m	–	+	m	–	+	+
Racial Discrimination	–	–	–	–	+	m	+	+
Transnational Flows	m	na	–	–	m	+	na	na
Residential Location	–	–	–	–	+	+	+	+
Class Heterogeneity	–	+	–	+	+	+	+	+

– overall disadvantage on this measure
+ overall advantage on this measure
na neutral or not applicable on this measure
m mixed

single parent families; they have low levels of education and labor force participation, particularly among women; they often have African ancestry that leads to discrimination against them; and they live in the poorest neighborhoods. Particularly with the Dominicans, remittances tax an already struggling community. Though the other Hispanic immigrant group, South Americans, have some of the same issues, such as lack of familiarity with English, they have a different profile—more two parent families, more workers in the family, and more education—and they often live in better neighborhoods. Similarly, although the South Americans arguably face some discrimination, their lighter skin color, better residential locations, and class diversity set them apart from Dominicans and Puerto Ricans.

Though beset by centuries of racial inequality and discrimination, native blacks are in a more ambiguous position. They are also highly disadvantaged, facing high levels of segregation and discrimination, relatively low levels of parental education, and a high likelihood of having been raised in single parent households. Nevertheless, they are English-speaking citizens and have developed a greater degree of class heterogeneity, with a significant well-educated, middle class minority, a strong ethnic niche in public and social service jobs, and well established political positions.

West Indian first generation immigrants present an even starker mix of circumstances. Like African Americans, they face high degrees of discrimination and residential segregation. They also frequently live in single parent families. On the other hand, their families are often multigenerational, involving several working adults. Their parental employment rates are high, and the community has achieved a high level of home ownership. It has also become more diverse in terms of education and occupations. While West Indians do send capital abroad, doing so does not seem to have a negative impact on their ability to invest at home. Speaking English on arrival, with a strong tradition of female labor force participation outside the home, West Indians are well positioned in New York's service economy.

At the other end of the spectrum, the native whites and Russian Jews occupy the most systematically advantaged positions. Both groups have well-educated parents, access to jobs, and no serious problem with discrimination. Russian Jews have a family structure conducive to upward mobility with low levels of single-headed households and high intergenerational living. Whites have a higher divorce rate than some of the second generation groups and much less intergenerational living; thus they are mixed on the measure of family structure. Transnational commitments do not drain resources from the community. Even disadvantaged members often have connections with better-off co-ethnics. Although the Russian Jews are the most recently arrived group in our study, their extensive connections with the well established native Jewish community and its social service infrastructure have clearly been an advantage.

Like the West Indians, the Chinese present a mixed picture. On the one hand, a great many of the Chinese parents arrived in the United States with little education and no capacity to speak English. Despite these modest circumstances, the group comes with many assets—high levels of labor force participation, a tendency to sustain two parent and extended families, and a great deal of class diversity within the group that seems to help even those at the bottom find opportunities. If anything, transnational flows are positive for this group. While the Chinese do face racial discrimination, it has much less impact on residential location or access to jobs than it does for other minority groups.

Stepping back, two groups face the highest barriers—Dominicans and Puerto Ricans—and two have the most advantages—native whites and Russian Jews. In between are three groups, the South Americans, West Indians, and Chinese, who present a mixed picture.

The children of the first generation immigrant and native born parents have thus grown up within a set of opportunities and barriers that are strongly shaped by the position of their parents within the larger social structure of New York, as measured here by parental income, education, neighborhood location, family form, English-language ability, and many other factors not measurable in a census or survey. The parents have also developed cultural understandings and strategic repertoires for responding to this set of opportunities and constraints—scripts for how to live in the world, how to decide what is important, and how to reach one's goals.

What would we predict if their children's lives were only a straight line extrapolation from the trajectories of their parents' groups? Naturally, we would expect the children of the native whites to have the easiest time and the most success in schools and the job market. It would be reasonable to expect the children of the Russian Jewish families to do almost as well. After all, their parents were even more highly educated than those of the native whites and they received a warm and supportive welcome from a highly successful white ethnic group as well as the U.S. government. Such handicaps as not initially being as familiar with English ought to be a small challenge for this group.

The prospects for other groups are less clear, especially when compared with the native born minority groups, the African Americans and Puerto Ricans. We should expect native blacks to do better than Puerto Ricans, given their parents' advantage in English-language ability, education, and employment. We should also expect the two native minority groups–African Americans and Puerto Ricans—to have a significant advantage over their closest second generation counterparts, the West Indians and Dominicans. After all, the former have been in New York City for several generations. They have waged a long struggle for group advancement and have built an infrastructure of community institutions. They have achieved a significant level of community organization and political representation. West Indians and Dominicans have started down this path only in the last decade. Although the two immigrant groups have some advantages in labor force participation levels, the two native minority groups are better educated and work at higher-paying jobs. We should thus expect the West Indian and Dominican second generation to be doing better than their parents, but perhaps less well than their native born African American and Puerto Rican counterparts. The South Americans, as the next most "white" immigrant group after the Russians, can be expected to do better than the other Hispanic groups.

The Chinese present an ambiguous case. On the one hand, the low levels of education and occupation of many first generation parents, combined with a lack of English facility and a concentration in poor neighborhoods, might argue for a relatively low trajectory for the second generation. On the other hand, the high levels of parental labor force participation, the high ratio of care-giving adults to children in the families, the occupational, educational, and class diversity within the community, and the relative lack of racial discrimination might suggest a higher trajectory. Perhaps the safest prediction would be a bifurcated pattern, with many succeeding while others do not.

The following chapters show what the young people who have shared their lives with us did with these inheritances. The next chapter takes up the question of ethnic identity—how much our respondents see themselves as members of a racial or ethnic group, under what circumstances, and what it means to them to be an American from an immigrant background. The succeeding chapters take up neighborhood, family, and early schooling growing up; the transition to high school and, for some, college;

entry into the labor market; and patterns of civic and political participation. A final substantive chapter examines the impact of race and continuing racial discrimination. The conclusion returns to the question presented here: did things turn out as might have been predicted from family background and the trajectories of the parental generation? If not, why not? And what lessons do these stories have to tell us about the ways in which large scale immigration has transformed the nature of life in America's largest metropolitan area?

As we shall see, differences in cultural norms and expectations as well as group circumstances result in the next generation taking different approaches to some key issues. These norms and expectations shape ideas about success, choices regarding education and employment, and the timing of partnering and childbearing, leading respondents with similar levels of resources to pursue quite different trajectories in life. Growing up, the children in our study have used the resources of their parents to forge their own new realities that are quite apart from both the world of their parents and white "middle American" society.

3

Ethnic Identities

> I have been asked if I am Egyptian, Cuban, Greek, Pakistani. I say no, I am Peruvian, Spanish. I like my culture and I am proud to be Peruvian, the Incas and all that.
>
> 18-YEAR-OLD PERUVIAN AMERICAN FEMALE

One need not dig far in New York City to find ethnicity in all its dramatic complexity. The city has always served as an immigrant gateway to America, and three-fifths of its population are now immigrants or their children. Ethnicity is woven into the fabric of everyday life. Encounters between strangers often begin with questions about origins, identities, language, race, looks, and ethnic practices and beliefs. People naturally ask each other where they are "from," what they "are," and whom they identify with. Our second generation young adults were happy to talk about their ethnic and racial identities, experiences, beliefs, and behaviors. As social scientists, we asked questions about their experiences in ways that resembled how they talk every day—how Puerto Ricans and Dominicans are different from or similar to one another, or how different American-born Chinese (ABCs) are from Chinese immigrants (Fresh off the Boats—FOBs), or whether the children of immigrants are more like their parents or like people born in America, or why some groups are doing better than others.

People often attribute the success or failure of a group in schools or the labor market to different "cultures," such as Chinese "Confucianism" or Caribbean "island laid-back culture." Such facile answers presuppose two things we seek to take apart here—how individuals sort themselves into different ethnic groups and what aspects of premigration "culture" persist into the second generation. We explore how our respondents categorize themselves into ethnic groups, and we begin to look at how those attachments relate to other kinds of outcomes.

Ethnic groups encapsulate three differences among people—subjective identity, social networks, and a historical accumulation of specific traits. When we say that individuals are members of Group A rather than Group B, we mean that they see themselves as belonging to A and not B, that people in Group A have social networks that look different from those in Group B, and that they inherit a bundle of human and social capital and outlooks on life that comes from being A and not B. These traits include a position in society—living in certain neighborhoods, having certain jobs, being treated by the larger society in a certain way—and participating in a shared culture—holding certain norms and having specific repertoires about how to be in the world. None of these are uniform across all the individuals in a group—individuals differ in how much they identify with ethnicity, with how varied their social networks are, and in how much they internalize and act on the norms and values they inherit from their parents and extended family. But these three aspects of ethnicity do tend to add up in consequential ways. The pattern of advantages and disadvantages outlined in the previous chapter shapes outcomes in the second generation even when they do not identify strongly with their parents' ethnicity or even when they have parents from different ethnic groups.

So what kinds of racial and ethnic boundaries do our second generation respondents draw around themselves and each other? What do these boundaries enclose in terms of the behaviors, beliefs, and norms that characterize these ethnic groups? First we focus on how people identify themselves and others in ethnic and racial terms. We look at what our survey questions and in-depth interviews tell us about how second generation individuals take on identities and think about ethnic and racial boundaries. We argue that surveys and censuses, including our own, do a poor job of capturing the complex reality of these matters. Identity is situational, variable, and often hybrid. Survey questions do not capture the subtle differences between identifying as Puerto Rican versus Hispanic, or African American versus black, or Chinese versus Asian. This does not mean that such ethnic labels do not hold strong political, ideological, or emotional meanings for people. But it is often impossible to discern these emotional meanings from a survey response. It is in the in-depth interviews that we are able to capture much more of the complexity and ambiguity that characterize ethnic identity.

We then explore how culture can help us to understand some of the outcomes explored subsequently in the book, such as schooling, jobs, and civic engagement. Despite the complexity and flux in how our respondents think about ethnic categories, ethnicity shapes many aspects of life. Indeed, ethnic differences inflected the ways in which our respondents think about what it means to be successful. When we asked our respondents an open-ended question about how they would define success for themselves, people from different ethnic groups had systematically different answers.

The Complexity of Identities

It is fashionable in academic circles to talk of multiple identities, hybridity, multiraciality, and the fluidly situational nature of ethnicity and identity. At the same time, our national Census and survey researchers are busy dividing the population into separate categories, measuring the type and intensity of their ethnic identity, and relating those measurements to such outcomes as education, family formation, and employment. The Census and these surveys tell us that immigrants and their children are transforming the demographic profile of the United States and allow us to measure how well we do in incorporating them. To the extent that immigrants and their children do not fit neatly into boxed categories, they are complicating the task of measuring ethnicity, race, and ancestry.

It was simple to arrive at an abstract rule for defining the groups we examine in this study. It was more complicated in practice. We included any respondent who had at least one parent who fit the designated native born or foreign born group. If a person had parents from different origins—say, an Ecuadoran mother and a Dominican father—we asked which group the respondent identified with most and then assigned the respondent to that group. Many respondents ended up identifying primarily with one parent while losing contact with the other parent because of divorce, death, a parent's never coming to the United States, or other forms of family change. In all, 23 of our 3,415 respondents qualified for two of our study groups. (Many more, however, had multiple ancestries involving one study group and an ancestry or race not included in our study.)

We began the telephone interview by asking about Hispanic origin, race, and ancestry with the same questions used in the 2000 Census so that we could compare them to official data in the Census and the Current Population Survey (CPS). We coded up to two responses for the Hispanic origin and race questions as well as up to three responses for the ancestry question. The results made it abundantly clear that our respondents do not come in neat ethnic packages. Though we ultimately placed our respondents in eight categories, they gave us 27 different responses to the Census race question and over 100 different responses to an open-ended question about ancestry.

All but a handful of our West Indian respondents' parents came from the Caribbean countries we designated, but a few West Indian parents had spouses from Africa or the United Kingdom. Seven percent of our West Indian respondents also had a U.S.-born father and 2 percent a U.S.-born mother. Among our South American respondents, 39 percent reported having two parents born in Ecuador, 30 percent both parents from Colombia, and 10 percent both parents from Peru. When their parentage was mixed, it was usually with members of one of the other two groups, but a few respondents reported an Asian, European immigrant, or native white parent.

While we expected the "constructed" groups to have parents with different national origins, we were impressed by how much the respondents from other groups were also the product of ethnic intermarriage. Even though the Dominican Republic, Russia, China, and Puerto Rico are (or were) nations with clear boundaries, the parentage of our respondents often transcended them. For example, while 85 percent of our Dominican respondents reported that their mother and father were both born in the Dominican Republic, the other 15 percent included parents from China, Dominica, Haiti, Hungary, Jamaica, Japan, and Spain as well as from other Latin American origins. About half our Puerto Rican respondents reported that both their parents were born in Puerto Rico, and another third reported that both their parents were born in the mainland United States but were of Puerto Rican origin. Of the remaining sixth, non–Puerto Rican parents were mostly from Latin America, although they included native whites and blacks, West Indians, Filipinos, and Lebanese.

We oversampled the Chinese to attain an accurate cross section of the countries from which Chinese immigrants came to metropolitan New York. About 62 percent of the Chinese respondents had two parents from mainland China, 11 percent had both parents born in Taiwan, and 6 percent reported two parents from Hong Kong. The rest reported parents who hailed from Chinese communities throughout the world as well as a few non-Chinese parents. Our Russian sample was restricted to respondents who had at least one Jewish parent from the former Soviet Union. Only 28 percent of our respondents reported that both parents were born in Russia proper. Another 28 percent reported that both parents were born in Ukraine, 6 percent had both parents from Belarus, and 10 percent had both parents from Uzbekistan. Most of the rest reported having Jewish parents from other former Soviet territories, the United States, or

Israel. A few of those from Russia or Ukraine reported a non-Jewish parent, and others reported having one non-Jewish parent from China, Germany, Luxembourg, and, in one case, Pakistan. However distinct as selection criteria, the national origins of the parents of the second generation are sometimes fuzzy in practice.

We asked all respondents to answer the Census race question, and Table 3.1 summarizes the results. Overall, Russians, native blacks, and native whites gave the most consistent responses about their race. The Hispanic groups gave the least consistent responses. Russian Jews are the only completely homogeneous group, with 100 percent reporting that they are white. Just one native black respondent reported being a Native American as well, and another reported being "mixed." Native whites, at 96.3 percent, are almost as homogeneous. (Despite having been identified in a screening interview as having two native born white parents, a few whites reported their race as American, Latino, or Hispanic on the main survey.) Nine out of ten Chinese respondents said their race was Chinese, while 3 percent chose the pan-ethnic American racial term "Asian American." A few chose other Asian national origins, such as Burmese and Vietnamese. West Indians also overwhelmingly reported their race as black, with 4 percent reporting West Indian and a few reporting mixed race or a Hispanic race.

In contrast with these groups that were nearly unanimous about their race, our three Spanish-speaking groups reported diverse racial origins. This is not surprising given the high degree of racial mixing among whites, blacks, and indigenous peoples throughout the history of Latin America. Indeed, given that history, the amount of racial mixture reported on our survey and in other surveys in the United States is likely on the low side. The South Americans had the highest percentage reporting that they are Hispanic (37 percent); about 11 percent gave a Colombian, Ecuadoran, or Peruvian national origin as their race; and another 5 percent each reported being Spanish or Latino. In addition, 8 percent reported that they do not know their race. The South Americans are our "whitest" Hispanic group, with 19 percent who reported being white, while only 4 percent reported being black, as compared to 12 percent of Dominicans and 11 percent of Puerto Ricans. Puerto Ricans were least likely to say they are Hispanic, at 26 percent, and 30 percent reported their race as Puerto Rican. Another 17 percent said they are white, and 11 percent said they are black. They were less likely than the other two groups to say they do not know their race (3 percent). Dominicans were almost as likely as South Americans to say they are Hispanic (34 percent),

Table 3.1. Racial Identification by Group

	Study Group of Respondents							
Race Given	Puerto Rican	Native Black	Dominican	West Indian	South American	Chinese	Russian Jewish	Native White
White	16.6		12.1	0.2	19.5	0.5	100.0	95.9
Black	10.8	99.5	11.7	92.9	3.7			0.2
Native American Indian		0.2	0.2		0.2			
Chinese				0.2		95.0		
Japanese								
Vietnamese					0.2	0.2		
Hawaiian					0.2			
American	3.2		2.1		3.2	0.2		1.0
Asian					0.2	3.3		
Burmese						0.2		
Colombian					5.2			
Dominican			15.2					
Ecuadoran					4.7			
Hispanic	26.0		34.3	0.5	36.9	0.2		0.2
Human	0.5		0.2	0.2	0.5			
Indigenous Indian	0.5		1.9		1.0			
Latin American	0.5		1.9		1.7			
Latino	2.8		4.9	0.2	4.7			0.2
Mixed	0.7	0.2	1.4	0.5				
Peruvian					2.0			
Puerto Rican	30.4				0.7			
South American					0.5			
Spanish	3.0		4.7		5.0			
West Indian			0.2	3.9				
Malay						0.2		
Other Race	3.5		0.2	0.2	0.5			0.2
Don't Know			7.2	0.7	8.5	0.3		0.5
Refused	1.6		1.6	0.2	0.5			1.7

Source: Study of the immigrant Second Generation in Metropolitan New York (ISGMNY).

with another 5 percent each saying they are Spanish or Latino. The same number claimed to be white and black (12 percent each), with 15 percent claiming the Dominican national origin as their race.

The 2000 U.S. Census did not allow respondents to give "Hispanic" as their race but asked a separate (and prior) question about Hispanic origin. This decision was based not on social science or survey research but on politics. When the Census included "Mexican" as a racial category in 1930, the Mexican government immediately objected, insisting that Mexicans were white. After the civil rights movement and the adoption of the Voting Rights Act, both African American and Latino or Hispanic organizations have argued against a Hispanic category on the race question because it might reduce the counted size of their groups. Even though ordinary citizens find the Census race question confusing and even irritating, especially immigrants who want to claim their Hispanic identity when asked about race, the Census does not give them that option; so many chose, or were reclassified as, "some other race."

That scholars and statisticians have noted that people of Spanish origin have the most difficulty with the race question has not prevented researchers from asking important research questions about whether Hispanics who identify as black on the race question are more likely to live in or near neighborhoods with African Americans and West Indians, and whether those who answer white are more likely to have higher incomes, either because white skin conveys advantage or, as in Latin America, "money whitens." Some have argued that people who embrace a pan-ethnic identity such as Hispanic or Latino as opposed to a national origin identity such as Mexican or Cuban are making the political statement that they are a "racialized minority."

Our in-depth interviews suggest that such thinking may be misguided. Our Dominican, Puerto Rican, and South American respondents made clear to us that they found our race question problematic because it did not permit a category that reflected who they were. They sorted out these categories in many and varied ways. When followed up in person, some denied what they had told the telephone interviewer or explained that they had chosen a category under the duress of an insistent telephone interviewer with a very misguided question. One 25-year-old Puerto Rican man described his reaction thus:

I: What is your race?
R: I guess I'm a Puerto Rican, well, I guess I'm a New YorRican.

I: But when you "bubble" in the circle, what race do you put down?

R: Oh God I don't feel like I'm any race; I just feel like I'm me. It sounds so cliché but I do. I usually bubble in Hispanic if it's there and I always cringe when I do so.

The choice of "white" on the race question does not necessarily reflect a racial identity, and as the Census has documented, many people believe that they are answering a question about their ethnicity when they answer the race question. This is how an 18-year-old South American reacted:

I: You told us that you consider your race to be white and didn't give a category for ethnicity.

R: They asked me, "What do you consider yourself?" I was "Hispanic." Then they asked me, "A black Hispanic or a white Hispanic?" I said, "White Hispanic." And I guess that's how they classified me in the computer or something. They wanted to know my skin color and what ethnicity so I guess they heard white and just put white.

Some Puerto Rican, South American, and Dominican respondents chose "white"—or were pressed into it by the telephone interviewer when they were stymied by the race question. Others chose "black," but most were no more committed to the "black" category. This 32-year-old Dominican man had answered black on the race question on the survey:

I: You said in the survey that you consider your race to be black and your ethnicity to be Dominican, is that correct?

R: Yeah, that's because they didn't give me Hispanic. Black is the closest one to Hispanic of the choices the guy gave me.

This is not to say the South American, Dominican, and Puerto Rican respondents did not think with American racial terms. Many were just trying to say that Hispanic or Latino was a particular mix of these racial categories.

The Census question frustrates respondents like this 22-year-old Puerto Rican man who does not see a category that captures his own racial mixture:

I: What is your ethnicity?

R: Hispanic, Latino.

I: And what is your race?

R: [Pause] I guess I would probably be white or mixed race. Actually I

would probably classify myself as mixed race . . . Black, white, Indian. You know.

I: If someone asks you where you're from?

R: Someone asked me that question the other day. I'll say I'm from
Brooklyn! And if they want more, I'll say, "Ok, my parents are from
Puerto Rico," or "I'm from Puerto Rico."

While American racial terms assign individuals to mutually exclusive categories based on skin color, physical appearance, and what is known about
ancestry, many respondents gave a Latin American interpretation of race,
focusing on variations in skin color. Spanish has a long list of terms for skin
colors between white and black, and these are then used differently in
different countries. Itzigsohn, Giorguli, and Vazquez (2005) note that
Dominicans on the island most frequently identify as "Indio," literally
meaning Indian, but connoting mixed race. People call themselves "indio
claro" (light Indian), "indio oscuro" (dark Indian), or "indio quemado"
(burnt Indian). The categories on the Census do not allow these distinctions, so the question forced our respondents to respond categorically with
"white," even though it is not what they meant. As one 23-year-old Dominican female put it, she has white skin, but she is not a "white person."

While many people chose a race haphazardly, a few chose deliberately
because the race question captured something meaningful for them. One
20-year-old Dominican put it this way:

In Dominican history we have a strong African influence. A very
strong influence that most Dominicans don't see. As an ethnicity
we're in denial about our African heritage and that's why I identify
with African Americans because they have embraced that part of
themselves and they advertise it and that's what attracts me to them.
They celebrate their Africanity, Africanness, whatever.

In the 2000 Census most Dominicans (58 percent) reported themselves as "some other race," 20 percent said white, and 8 percent reported
that their race was black. A far greater percentage of the Dominican population would most likely "look" black to the average American. Yet the
history of the Dominican Republic teaches a strong resistance to identifying one's African heritage, and most people identify with intermediate
racial categories, distancing themselves from Haitians, who are identified
as "black" (Itzigsohn, Giorguli, and Vasquez 2005).

Some respondents side-stepped the entire process by insisting that their national origin was their ethnic identity and also their racial identity, even though ethnicity was not one of the provided categories. Still others, especially the Puerto Ricans, wanted to assert a New York–based identity, sometimes using the word "New Yorican," and sometimes just stressing their New York roots.

I: You didn't tell us what you consider your race to be.

R: New Yorican. Because I'm a Puerto Rican descendant and I was born in New York.

I: Can you tell me more about why you feel like a New Yorican?

R: Well, I'm an American who speaks Spanish. Who is a descendant of Spanish. Of Puerto Ricans. That's why I can't say I'm Puerto Rican because I'm an American but I do have Puerto Rican blood. I mean if you want to get technical, I would be an American. But if you were to ask me what is my race, I would say Puerto Rican.

Complexity can go beyond the difficulty of combining birthplace, race, ancestry, Hispanic origin, and parental birthplace. One young woman reported that she was half Dominican and half Chinese and identified more with the Chinese side. In an in-depth interview, she told us her Chinese father had migrated from Taiwan to the Dominican Republic in the 1970s, when it was easy to get residence. He met and married a Dominican woman and they moved to New York. Her Dominican mother died when she was young, and her father, unable to cope with a young child, sent her to the Dominican Republic to live with her mother's relatives. She became fluent in Spanish and called her uncle "Dad."

By the time she was 13, her father had established a business in New York and bought a house. He brought his mother over from China so she could look after his daughter, whom he brought back from the Dominican Republic. She said she hated moving back to New York. She could not understand her Chinese grandmother, whose cooking she could not abide. (The respondent reports that she only liked "the kind of Chinese food that all white people like.") Her father was oddly quiet and reserved compared to her Dominican uncles. But she stayed with him, attended a private prep school, and went to an elite college. Seeing a Hong Kong action movie in college exposed her to a heroic macho Asian male image and provoked her to re-evaluate her Chineseness. She became a fan of Asian films and even went to work for a while in Hong Kong, reconnecting with her father's Taiwanese family during a visit there. Her father remarried a woman from Taiwan, and they had several children. Our respondent is now working in an investment bank, living at home with her father and his wife and her half sisters, and identifies strongly as Chinese American.

While this is an unusual story, it demonstrates the sometimes wildly contingent nature of ethnic identity. Depending on what stage in her life course we interviewed her, we would have gotten a very different response about her primary identification. Although one might describe the Dominican and Chinese communities as being quite different in any number of ways, one can see that this respondent could be deeply at home in either place at this point. One also wonders whether the presence of a large number of Chinese students at her college disproportionately affected her ethnicity. If the Dominican presence had been strong, might she have made a different choice about her own identity?

The contingent nature of her outcome is clear in the contrast with another mixed-ancestry respondent's story. He has a Salvadoran mother and a Chinese father. His father left China at the age of 10 and with his family went to Cuba, where they ran a bodega. The father developed an interest in architecture and took technical drawing. When the father was 18, Castro came to power and the family left for Spain; but the father could not make a living there. Moving to New York, he got a job in a Cuban Chinese restaurant, where he met some architects who hired him as a draftsman. Frustrated with the mysteries of Catholicism, he became a Jehovah's Witness and married a Salvadoran woman of the same faith whom he met on a bus. Though he taught her to cook Chinese food, they speak Spanish at home because it was both his and his wife's first language. Growing up in this household, our second generation respondent does not have a strong Chinese identity. Beyond the food, being Chinese has little meaning for him. His primary identity is religious, and he spends long hours trying to evangelize his neighbors in Washington Heights.

Proximal Hosts

While our Hispanic respondents had the most trouble with the race question, other respondents also expressed dissatisfaction with it. This is not just an exercise in showing the futility of using a survey question to tap into complex identities. The in-depth interviews showed that our respondents were grappling with how to relate to their "proximal hosts" (Mittelberg and Waters 1992). Proximal hosts are the American racial and ethnic grouping in which native born Americans would tend to place the new immigrant ethnic group. The general public and statisticians would be most likely to assign Russian Jews, for instance, to American Jews. African Americans are the proximal host for West Indians because white Americans tend not to notice differences among people with black skin (Kasinitz 1992; Waters 1999). As the largest and most established Hispanic group in New York City, Puerto Ricans are the group to which native New Yorkers are most likely to assign any Hispanic or Latino person they encounter.

When we asked our respondents about how they balance a pan-ethnic category like Latino or Hispanic against their specific national origin—Puerto Rican, Dominican, or Colombian; Ecuadoran or Peruvian—people most often described Puerto Ricans to be the default group. In the 1960s more than 80 percent of all Hispanics in New York were Puerto Rican, though the figure is well under half now. The historical demographic predominance of the Puerto Ricans means that our Hispanic respondents were often aware that people they encountered in New York were very likely to assume they were Puerto Rican unless they signaled a different identity. Some people thought Latino referred only to people from South America; others thought Hispanic was a better term because it made reference to speaking Spanish. Some Dominicans and Puerto Ricans thought Latino referred more to people from Central or South America and that Hispanic was a better term for them. For those with complex identities, choosing a specific national origin seemed like the simplest way to convey a Hispanic identity. One 24-year-old Colombian man told us that

R: I never use that [Latino].

I: Why?

R: Latino is like Puerto Rican and Dominican. That's what people think. Most people tend to think of Spanish people as dark, like Caribbean. I don't know why. I may be wrong. And that is not the way it is. People in South America are as white as any European. My skin is olive. When people ask me I say I am Spanish. I speak Spanish with my parents.

The South Americans and Dominicans find themselves needing to decide whether or not to choose an identity that distances them from or identifies them with Puerto Ricans. One 29-year-old Dominican woman told us that until fifth grade she didn't even know she was Dominican. "I thought everyone who spoke Spanish was Puerto Rican. I thought *I* was Puerto Rican." The varied meanings that individuals attach to the terms "Hispanic," "Latino," and "Spanish" and the frequency with which they switch back and forth among them and with specific national origin labels would suggest that there is no right or wrong label to use with this population and that academic debates about whether Hispanic or Latino is more correct are truly academic in nature.

The Chinese lack a native born proximal host in New York. Indeed, the Chinese play the role of proximal host to other East Asian immigrants such as Koreans in New York City. Yet they also face the question of whether to identify with the pan-ethnic racial classification of Asian American or to specifically identify as Chinese American. A question about race or ancestry brings up all these issues but ignores the situational nature of ethnicity and how people go back and forth in dealing with the choices available to them.

While most respondents did grapple with how they related to their proximal hosts, a survey question may not capture the ultimate choice respondents make and definitely does not capture the issues raised by the topic. For instance, those West Indians who chose "black" on the race question are not necessarily telling us about how they relate to African Americans. Many in fact actually distanced themselves from African Americans (Waters 1999; Vickerman 1999; Kasinitz, Battle, and Miyares 2001). As a 29-year-old West Indian notes:

> R: In a general sense, yes, I consider myself African American 'cause I'm black. People don't really say "Negro" or "black" anymore. The politically correct term is "African American." Whether you consider yourself African American or not, is another talk show!
> I: However, what is more common for you to say, to describe yourself to other people?
> R: I really don't use African American. I'm black. People ask you where you come from I say I was born here but my parents are Jamaican. I don't say I'm Jamaican because I wasn't born there.

The Census race question includes a number of specific Asian national origin groups, including Chinese (Perlmann and Waters 2002). Our Chinese respondents thus overwhelmingly chose Chinese with fewer of the difficulties facing the other groups. Most saw Chinese as interchangeable with Asian American, as one 30-year-old Chinese woman demonstrated:

> I: Which is more common for you to identify with, Chinese or Asian?
> R: It depends. When you fill out the ethnic group it has Caucasian, Hispanic, Asian, so if they have Asian I check Asian, if they have Chinese I check Chinese.

Some respondents saw the term "Asian American" as implying a more assimilated, less culturally bound identity than being Chinese American.

> I was pretty much raised near Chinatown and I was raised like a Chinese person and I'm more of a traditional Chinese American than I would say Asian American 'cause Asian Americans don't celebrate Chinese New Year, but Chinese New Year means a lot to me.

Others preferred the term "Chinese" to "American," not to signal that they are less assimilated but because they did not want to be classified together with other Asian groups. A 20-year-old Chinese man put it this way:

> I: Which is more common for you to say, Chinese or Asian?
> R: Chinese, definitely. Because there are a whole mess of other Asians. There's Korean, there's Japanese, there's all the Indians. When you just say Asian, people might not know what kind of Asian you are. I don't want anybody to think I'm Japanese. Or Filipino. I'm Chinese. So I say Chinese.

Because the former Soviet Union discouraged the practice of Judaism as a religion but defined Jewish as an official nationality, Jews from the former Soviet Union often come from secular families, yet nevertheless strongly identify as being Jewish. In the United States "Jewish" is more often thought of as a religious identity and less of a national or racial one. Thus many of our respondents did not feel particularly Jewish in this context. Now being away from Russia, they find that speaking Russian, liking Russian foods, and being different from Americans make them identify as Russian, sometimes for the first time in their lives. As one 23-year-old man put it:

> I don't understand here. When I was in Russia, I wasn't Russian. Right? So for me to consider myself Russian would not necessarily be correct. Because I never consider myself to be Ukrainian or Russian, maybe Soviet, which is not ethnicity obviously. So, I guess Russian Jew, Ukrainian Jew.

This is further complicated by the fact that many "Russian" Jews in New York are actually from non-Russian republics of the former Soviet Union that are now separate countries. Georgia is a particularly amusing source of confusion.

> R: My ethnicity is Georgian. The only thing is that when people ask me where I'm from, and I tell them Georgia it never fails. "Really?

Where's your southern twang?" I'm like it's not that Georgia! It's the Georgia in the Soviet Union. They're always like "What? Where?" So just for the sake of not having to go through the same explanation over and over again I just say I'm Russian.

I: What does it mean to you to be Georgian?

R: That's deep. I think it's a great culture. I think there are very beautiful things about it and I love it. I love the music and I love the food. I love the closeness that Georgian people have among one another.

The demise of the former Soviet Union stimulated new identities as borders shifted and new nation-states were created. With all the shifting political borders the one sure identity the young people have is that they are Jews. One 26-year-old Russian Jewish man who grew up with one identity suddenly found that the political terrain has shifted and he needed a new label.

I: What would you consider your ethnicity to be?

R: I have no idea. White. Jewish? What's ethnicity? We all came from the same thing in the long run so I guess at first I thought it was Russian, now I'm not Russian. Now I'm Moldavan. Now I don't even know if I'm Moldavan, I'm Ukrainian. If I'm not Ukrainian, I'm someone else. Whatever. But at least I can say I'm Jewish.

While the Census does not allow people to identify with a religion and would not record any reference to being Jewish, most of our Russian Jewish respondents did not want to separate the two terms. For many of these young people, forging a new identity in New York is a self-conscious process of combining their Russian-ness and their Jewishness. They are not "just Russian" and not "just Jewish." Only the intersection makes sense to this 23-year-old young man:

I: You said that you consider your ethnicity to be Russian.

A: Yes. Russian Jewish to be more precise. I wouldn't want to be Russian. Russian Jew.

I: What does that mean?

A: It's that I'm not Russian but I come from Russia. To me, it's nothing else but having Jewish blood in me and living in Russia. That's what it means, a Russian Jew to me. The fact is that I'm Jewish and I've been Jewish all my life and I have lived with Jewish people.

Yet when most respondents say they are Jewish, they are often not re-ferring to a religion.

> For me it is primarily ethnic and cultural. A level of history that I completely accept and adopt. It doesn't extend to religion for me. I think that you can be just as Jewish without being religious at all.

No wonder some of our Russian respondents so quickly see themselves as New Yorkers. Being a minority yet absorbing aspects of the culture around them has been a hallmark of their own cultural heritage.

Brubaker (2004:13) asks social scientists to explore "the ways in which the categorized appropriate, internalize, subvert, evade or transform the categories that are imposed on them." Our in-depth interviews suggest that it is difficult, indeed, we would argue impossible, to use survey re-sponses to make the subtle contextual distinctions necessary for under-standing the subjective meanings of identity. Yet because surveys and the Census classify people and because society places significance on this clas-sification, people are strongly tempted to make conscious choices about them. For instance, Rumbaut (1996a) distinguishes four types of ethnic identity choices among young second generation respondents in the Chil-dren of Immigrants Longitudinal Study (CILS): (1) national origin iden-tities, (2) hyphenated identities, (3) assimilative unhyphenated identities, and (4) dissimilative racial and pan-ethnic identities. A respondent whose parents were born in China could be Chinese, Chinese American, Amer-ican, or Asian American. Rumbaut argues that these identity labels capture feelings about the nature of American society and how integrated into and accepting of it the young person is.

Our interviews show that some young people do indeed consciously choose to be Asian American, often after taking Asian American studies classes in college or joining Asian American organizations or churches. Our respondents also sometimes self-consciously label themselves "Amer-ican," particularly when contrasting themselves with immigrant family members. But when asked about such identities, they are almost always implicitly answering the question with another question: "Who's asking?" They may be "American" compared to newly arrived immigrants, "Chi-nese" if they were among other Asians, or "Asian American" if they were around whites or blacks.

> I say Asian when I'm talking to somebody who isn't Asian and when I'm talking to somebody Asian, I would say that I'm Chinese. A lot

of times I would say I'm Asian because I say I'm Asian before I say I'm Chinese.

A rigid Census or survey question about race clashes with the multiple and complex origins and layers of meaning available to these young people when they think about racial and ethnic identity. Our evidence suggests that the Census's refusal to recognize Hispanic origin and religious identification is producing the sharpest clashes between self-definition and official classification. The Russian Jews also have a hard time stating their identification because they do not feel only Russian or only Jewish. Because they are officially classified as white, this disjunction will not have many political or social repercussions. The clash between Hispanic origins and the Census race categories is more consequential. Our respondents made it abundantly clear to us that they were neither black nor white, but Hispanic or Spanish. If the government continues to insist on a distinction that the first and the second generation do not accept as legitimate, it will continue to misinterpret the answers of a large number of people.

Using Culture as an Explanatory Variable

One might ask why we bother categorizing people by race and ethnicity when any such classification obscures so much interesting complexity. Average New Yorkers inquire about ethnicity because they have a folk theory that different groups have different cultures that explain their attitudes and behaviors. They often invoke "Chinese culture" to explain why Chinese succeed at schools and rarely get divorced. Social scientists are strongly oriented in the opposite direction. They turn to culture, if at all, as the last possible explanation for different outcomes, trying to exhaust all other explanations. The preferred approach to explaining differences in Dominican and Chinese educational attainment would examine family background, sources of migration, differential treatment by schools and teachers, and the social class mix of the communities the working class immigrants join, and would discount the premigration cultures and beliefs of the immigrant generation.

The reluctance to use cultural variation to explain the patterns of success and failure among different ethnic and racial groups stems from two developments in scholarly research. In the field of race relations, cultural explanations for group differences in the United States fell out of favor in the 1960s and 1970s after the rejection of the "culture of poverty" explanation for Puerto Rican and black poverty and the controversy generated by the Moynihan report on the Negro family. The cultural argument of that report was criticized for blaming the American victims of centuries of racism for failing to succeed. As Patterson (2000:203) points out, folk theories using culture to explain African American problems were too often circular, reductionist, and static. They relied on a "simplistic or untenable conception of culture that was used in a crudely deterministic way to explain Afro American social problems." In response to this critique, many scholars argued that poor native minorities had the same values as middle class whites, but they faced structural obstacles that prevented them from reaching the same goals (Liebow 1967).

As cultural explanations fell out of favor among academics studying race, they also receded in the study of ethnicity. Most theorizing about ethnicity has followed Fredrick Barth's insight that the best way to study ethnicity is to understand how boundaries are erected, maintained, or reduced between groups, not by cataloging the content of the ethnicity delimited by those boundaries. Many scholars of ethnicity in the United States have been concerned with how people distinguish themselves from each other and not how different ethnic groups are from each other or from the American mainstream. This concern with ethnic options made sense in the middle and end of the twentieth century as scholarship concentrated on assimilated white ethnics and racial minority groups who had become over time quite similar (Gans 1979; Alba 1990; Waters 1990).

Perhaps as an inevitable result of immigration and the production of new ethnic groups filled with first and second generation immigrants, scholars have become more interested in the cultural content of ethnicity and race. Some reject the idea that culture plays any role in ethnic difference (Steinberg 2007). Others, such as Cornel West (1994) and William Julius Wilson (1987), have pioneered a reexamination of the role of culture and values in understanding differences in racial behaviors. Social scientists have developed a new and more sophisticated understanding of culture in recent decades that moves beyond the culture-versus-structure debate that pitted conservative scholars stressing cultural explanations for group success and failure against liberals who refused to recognize any consequential cultural differences between ethnic groups (Lamont 1999; Waters 1999).

A new model of ethnicity for the twenty-first century obviously has to take into account the very different structural constraints and opportunities facing different racial and ethnic groups. But it must also give full credence to the different cultural repertoires and beliefs emerging from the different backgrounds from which the group comes, which are reinforced, undermined, or modified in the new environments in which people find themselves. The culture of any ethnic or racial group is continually formed and reformed in the United States. It is not essential or unchanging. But it is also real and consequential. Different cultures interact with American social structure in different ways that can lead some groups to have better outcomes than others and enable some subcultures to be more or less persistent within the wider American culture.

How might we measure cultural differences among groups? We can begin by thinking about the formal cultural practices that differentiate groups. Language, religion, dress, food, holidays, music, and political, economic, and social ties to the sending country are all examples of formal cultural expressions. We can also assess culture in terms of values, attitudes, and beliefs—motivating scripts that guide how people see and behave in the world. The idea that the patterns by which people understand and act in the world vary by ethnic group lies beneath both the layperson's view of these issues and the social scientist's often reluctant assumption that "culture" explains important differences in outcomes after social structural factors have been taken into account. For instance, even after accounting for parental education, occupation, neighborhood and school characteristics, and the presence of racial discrimination, there remain significant differences in educational outcomes and labor force participation between African Americans and West Indians. Waters (1999) posits that two groups have cultural differences in their approaches to education and work that help to explain these differences in outcomes. The point of this approach is not simply to say that all unexplained variance in outcomes is simply attributable to "culture" but to specify what it is about cultural practices that produces the differences.

Social scientists have tended to look at culture as a result or a *dependent* variable. Sociologists have used these more or less easily measured aspects of culture (such as language preferences) to assess acculturation (Gordon 1964; Alba and Nee 2003). They have been examined as a function of generation or time in the United States. The main question is how immigrants become more like Americans, in terms of language use, food eaten, music listened to, visits home, and holidays celebrated, as time passes. But culture can also be an *independent* variable, as we ask how a system of values and meanings influences individual choices. The different ways in which groups see the world influence their trajectory into the American mainstream.

Once we factor in demographic and structural context, we have to turn to ethnically grounded norms, values, expectations, and repertoires of action to understand how ethnic groups make different choices on such matters as the importance and timing of marriage, when to have children, whether to live in multigenerational families, what constitutes success, how important an education is, what should be expected of men and women, and so on. Many analysts have fallen into the trap of essentializing differences on these questions—of seeing them as unchanging, uniform, and uncontested aspects of any particular group. A more dynamic view of culture recognizes that cultural differences are socially constructed and evolve in response to changing circumstances. Indeed, the cultures of countries that are sending migrants to the United States are changing so rapidly that immigrants are now coming with cultural orientations that are very different from those brought by their predecessors thirty years ago.

Orlando Patterson (2000:208) argues that culture can be defined as a "repertoire of socially transmitted and intra-generationally generated ideas about how to live and make judgements, both in general terms and in regard to specific domains of life." Groups inherit these cultural dispositions from previous generations through socialization and intragenerational learning from peers and the media. Culture constantly interacts with social structure as conditions change and humans innovate in the face of new situations. Patterson rightly cautions that cultural and noncultural factors can be both independent and dependent variables in one's causal model.

Take the example of gender relations among Dominicans, a subject often brought up by our second generation respondents and examined in more detail in Chapter 7. Dominican immigrant parents transmit a model of "proper" gender relations. Women should not go out alone and teens should not date in the American fashion. Women should do all the housework, while men are expected to live in "the streets," where they may be tempted and sometimes succumb to extramarital affairs. Yet, as Patterson suggests, such models are not static. They are "the outcome of changes in the inherited models due to transmission errors in teaching and imitation, as well as adjustments to new strategies of coping with the environment learned by trial and error." Dominican parents in New York are the traditional models for their children. Yet they are already changing their behaviors and beliefs in response to migration. These immigrant parents even send these modified models back to the Dominican Republic. Levitt (2001) has argued that new gender relations patterns learned in the United States are an important "social remittance" sent back to the Dominican Republic, changing ideas and beliefs there. And peers in the United States whom the second generation encounter also give them new messages about what women and men are capable of and how gender equality might work. The structural environment in the United States leads people to change their cultural models. For example, as Dominican women work outside the home in order for the family to make ends meet, they gain greater autonomy, which changes cultural models about proper female behavior.

Individual behaviors of second generation respondents are thus a direct response to their parents' transmitted cultural models, to the modified cultural models of their Dominican peers and siblings, and to the media and American peers. Their behaviors are also direct responses to a different structural environment—the economic opportunities for women, enforcement of laws against domestic violence, and so on. The different behavioral outcomes contribute to modified cultural models. Patterson even leaves out a feedback loop—modified cultural models exported back to the source country identified by Levitt as changing the cultural models transmitted to future generations of Dominicans, migrant and nonmigrant alike. Perhaps more important, the interaction of structure and culture opens up choices, particularly for the second generation. The fact that they have choices, and that they are often conscious of the fact that they have choices, is perhaps more than anything the distinct advantage of the second generation.

The idea of looking at how different ethnic groups vary culturally and how groups change across generations once they migrate to the United States also begs the question that inspired the segmented assimilation approach—exactly what is it that groups are assimilating into? What does it mean to come of age of immigrant parents in a city like New York, where the majority of the city are minority group members, either immigrants or their children or native racial minorities? How does one define the mainstream in a truly multicultural city? What are the boundaries or markers that people cross over to become truly included into the category "American"? Are these groups reacting to some mainstream American set of values and expectations? By including native whites and blacks in our study, we are able to identify some "American" as opposed to "second generation" cultural beliefs and practices. White and black Americans have remarkably similar expectations about gender equality, children becoming independent at 18, and relations between adult parents and children. These beliefs and values are invisible to the American respondents we interviewed, but our second generation respondents often describe them as the "American way." Yet some "American values" can be counterproductive in terms of socioeconomic mobility, such as the expectation of moving out of your parents' home when you are 18, whereas some immigrant values fit better, such as multigenerational living in an expensive housing market.

The following chapters show some of the ways in which our respondents are combining American and parental cultural beliefs and practices and creating new norms and beliefs about how to live in the world that vary across groups. This is very evident in the systematic differences across groups in the timing and sequencing of the major milestones of becoming an adult—leaving home, completing an education, finding work, partnering and marrying, and having children. Many of these differences are shaped by structural realities—parental human capital, the quality of schools available to the second generation, and racial discrimination or affirmative action in different industries or workplaces. But these outcomes also reflect values and decisions on the part of the young people we interviewed about what is important to them, what they want to achieve in their lives, and how best to go about reaching their goals.

Ideas about Success

These ideas about what is important in life are best captured in some of the open-ended questions we asked in the qualitative portion of our study, such as "How would you define success for someone your age?" as well as "Did your parents ever give you advice about how to be successful in life?" and finally, "What would you like to be doing in ten years?" We also asked what the respondent thought about education: "Some people say education will help you find a good job. Others say that whether you have a high school diploma or college degree it does not matter much these days. What do you think?"

The pattern of responses yielded some fascinating differences across groups. We took all the open-ended responses to this question and coded the most common themes by group. Our respondents use very different frameworks to judge their own situations, they have different goals for themselves, and they have different priorities for reaching those goals.

Their answers reflect their different class origins as well as the collective experiences of their group in New York and of their parents in the sending countries. The Chinese respondents, for example, mentioned gaining a professional occupation, money, education, discrimination, and knowing your future goals. Not one Chinese respondent mentioned having friends, just meeting basic needs, or having money at the end of your pay period as examples of success, answers that were common among African Americans. Nor did any Chinese person express the opinion sometimes heard from other groups that education might not lead to success. Indeed, the Chinese and the Russian respondents could not even understand the question. Yet the Chinese respondents were the most likely to spontaneously mention discrimination as something they would face in trying to be successful. They said their parents made a point of telling them that they should expect to encounter discrimination, but they should not let it keep them from being successful. They did, however, think that they would have to try harder than a white person would to be successful in the United States.

African Americans, on the other hand, mentioned education, money, fun, material goods, stability, discrimination (meaning the possibility that they would have to deal with discrimination in achieving success), and being their own boss as signs of success. A few defined success as just being alive or avoiding trouble. Many said their parents pushed education and considered themselves successful because they had gotten educated, but many others doubted whether education led to success. Several reported knowing of highly successful people with poor educations and highly educated people who were having hard times (homeless people with PhDs and CEOs who were high school dropouts). A number of African Americans mentioned "having their own business." This theme appears to cut across class and is pronounced in this group, despite the fact that their parents have the lowest rates of self-employment among the groups in our study. For this group autonomy, rather than economic benefits, seems to make self-employment attractive. Consider, for instance, the response of this 27-year-old African American man:

I: How would you define success for someone your age?
R: Now? Their own business. That's the only thing I can see. Open a barber shop or something. That's the only thing I can see. I mean, I'm for real. I'm being honest. If I had money, I would be in the laundromat. Put my money into it. That's the only thing I can see, some kind of your own business. Not the drug business.

I: Some people say education will help you find a good job. Others say that whether you have a high school diploma or college degree it doesn't matter much these days. What do you think?

R: I say 50/50, man. 'Cause I have a lot of friends that have a college education now and they got shit. They try. They got a nice little degree and some of them ain't got nothing, some of them do. That's why I can't say yes to that question. I would say yes and no. Some do, some don't.

Neither the Chinese nor the African Americans ever mentioned having children, and only one mentioned being married (because her mother was concerned about it) as milestones of success. Yet respondents whose parents came from Colombia, Ecuador, and Peru frequently mentioned this topic and often linked it to stability. The other common themes for this group were stability, education, and material goods. South Americans reported mixed attitudes toward education; many said their parents wanted them to finish high school, but fewer talked about college. A 28-year-old South American woman talked about having a trade, getting a "good job," and, most of all, stability.

I: How would you define success for someone your age?

R: Probably somebody who has a nice stable job, that's not hopping around from job to job. Who, at this point, is either close to being settled down as far as marriage and family. Probably, by now, at almost twenty nine, I'd say to probably have children by this point.

I: Do you think school has to be part of that?

R: No. I don't think so. I think that the opportunities are out there in a lot of different companies, but it depends on what you do . . . You just got to know the right people and do the right things while you're there. Be confident and do your best and you can get ahead very far.

Dominicans frequently reported concerns with discrimination; they mentioned education, but often in the context of wondering whether it would matter in the long run. The third most common theme was avoiding trouble, followed by being the boss, knowing your goals, and occupation. Avoiding trouble was a large part of how they talk about success, as was getting out of New York. (They were the only group that had some people define being successful as moving *out* of New York.) One Dominican young man showed even more ambivalence about education than African Americans:

I: How would you define success for someone your age?

R: Being able to say that you're alive.

I: Why do you say that?

R: Look at the news, you know. Look at the newspaper. You don't hear about too many twenty-five, twenty-six-year-old males Hispanic African American you know, doing anything with their lives other than dying or going to jail, so you know.

I: Some people say that education helps you find a job. Other people say that whether you have a high school diploma or a college degree doesn't matter much. What do you think?

R: It doesn't. It doesn't at all. I don't think education has a thing to do with success . . . I think education, being educated is a condition, you know. I think that your own success comes through your own determination and your own will to be successful. You know, I know college graduates that are drug dealers.

I: Why do you think they're doing that?

R: Because they can't get jobs!

Puerto Ricans also questioned whether education matters to success and focused on being the boss and not being dependent. They were not sure education was the right route to success, telling many stories about highly educated people who were not successful. They used the idea of family to refer to an extended family, not just a spouse. As one 26-year-old put it:

How would I define success? I don't know, I don't know if I'm there yet. For me it's like being able to own your own home, having responsibilities that you know you can handle, having a good family support, maybe a girlfriend or wife who I can always have somebody stand by me. Where I'm happy.

Among Russian Jews, the most common themes were money, occupation, discrimination, education, and being aggressive. They were distinct in thinking that "being aggressive" was a good way to become successful. While the Chinese said that their parents told them all the time that education was the key to success, the Russian Jews took completely for granted that they would proceed through school to an advanced degree. Interestingly, Russian Jews included the only respondents who felt that success might be attributable to good luck. When asked about discrimination, they said their parents told them how much they experienced in

Russia, but that they were not subject to it here in the United States. Starting a family was also important to our Russian respondents.

> I: Did your mother or father give you advice about how to be successful?
> R: Sure. They wanted me to go to college, finish college, and get a nice job.
> I: Did they encourage you to pursue a particular major or career?
> R: Of course every Jewish person wants you to be a doctor, if you're very smart. If you're not so smart, maybe a lawyer. If you're real stupid, then an accountant. That is what I would teach my son. Go to college, get your degree and if you want to sweep the streets, that's fine, but you got to get a degree. Even when you get a degree, 90 percent of the time, you're going to pursue a better life. Nobody spends four or five years in college and then does nothing.

A 27-year-old Russian woman put it a similar way:

> I: How do you define success for someone your age?
> R: Should be already at least a college graduate, living independent from their parents, either married or [in a] relationship, starting a family and stuff, with their own career already at this point. I would think they would be successful.

The most common themes for West Indians were discrimination, education, getting into a good occupation, being happy, being alive, avoiding or getting out of trouble, and being the boss. This group was the most likely to spontaneously mention conflict with parents over what it meant to be successful, with people talking about how their parents were pushing them to succeed. Showing ambivalence about her chances, a 23-year-old West Indian female responded,

> R: Success would be if I had a father that worked in a big corporation that would pull strings for me to get a good job.
> I: That's how you would define success for someone your age?
> R: Opportunities for success. That's how to define it. I mean what the hell is success anyway? When you get to whatever you think you're successful, it's probably not going to be fulfilling to you emotionally. I don't even know if I know the answer to that question.

Another West Indian man expressed skepticism about the value of education.

I think [education] matters but you have to have more than a college degree to get a good job now. You have to be super smart. There's no guarantee that if you have a college degree that you're going to get a good job. Because I know people with a college degree and [no job]. I saw this girl a couple of days ago and she just graduated from Brooklyn College and she was working at Macy's as a cashier. So I know. And my sister graduated from school and she still hasn't gotten a good job yet. I know you have to know where the opportunities are. Like for a long time I looked for a job in the newspaper. You have to go to an employment agency. That's the only way. And they're so racist there too.

Native whites showed great concern for having money, education, and occupation; knowing future goals; and getting married and having a family. Native whites were also the only ones to mentioned concern for inner goals, such as being happy, being a good person, and making the world a better place. Native whites appeared to be the only group with the luxury of being worried that success should *not* be defined through material goods, which a number of respondents saw as being shallow.

> *I:* Ok. How would you define success for somebody your age?
> *R:* My age, I would say you have a solid foundation as far as education goes. You have a good job that you're well into, that you're comfortable with, you're settled in. That your have good personal life, you have good home social life and all that. I would not necessarily say that we're all in my age, I mean, married and have family and all that, but a good personal and professional life.

It would be a mistake to conclude from these ideas about success that our respondents are free to choose the overall outcome of their lives in an unfettered way. There are class divisions that make some young people see education as a route to success and do not make their view evident to other young people. But it would also be a mistake to deny that these ideas about what is important in life and how to achieve them reflect cultural differences across groups.

These values are important in their own right in explaining the choices young people do make. For Dominicans and Puerto Ricans early childbearing and parenting is a value they inherit from their parents and share with their peers, just as for black Americans autonomy on the job is something important to their sense of who they are. Although these notions of success and the routes to it vary across groups, they are also in flux as wants and desires meet constraints and opportunities.

It would not be surprising at all if the children of our respondents—the third generation—reflect very different priorities when they reach young adulthood. The children of our Chinese respondents might define success in terms of friendships, romantic relationships, and childbearing in order to counterbalance their parents' accounts of delayed partnering and loneliness. The children of the South American second generation might have achieved the stability their parents strived for and they might choose educational advancement as their definition of success. In sum, culture and values matter, and they evolve. Thus an accurate understanding of individual and group outcomes must take cultural matters into account.

Whether they are aware of it or not, the immigrant parents' origins shape the lives of the second generation. This is so because of the conscious decisions they make about being "ethnic" or "American" as well as the structural barriers they encounter to full inclusion in American society such as racial discrimination. In the chapters that follow, we examine the patterns of outcomes among the second generation and the native groups and we try to unbundle the advantages and disadvantages that their ethnic origins and identities bring with them.

4

Family and Neighborhood Origins

Most people would agree that one's family has an enormous impact on one's formative years and often provides important resources later in life. Debate arises, however, about exactly which aspects of family background have what effects on a family's children under what circumstances. Contemporary families certainly face vastly different circumstances than those experienced by "traditional families" in the 1950s. Nevertheless, when families work well, children feel solidarity with their parents, develop self-esteem and high aspirations, and use parental support to gain high levels of achievement. According to one recent study, families remain a significant influence:

> Our results demonstrate the continuing influence and enduring importance of families across recent generations, despite the effects of divorce, alternative family forms, and changing gender roles on family commitments and functions . . . Despite this, family influences across generations are strong, and families still matter—much more than advocates of the family decline hypothesis would admit. (Bengtson, Biblarz, and Roberts 2002:156–157)

People often organize their social networks around their families and other kin, especially when they live close by (Logan and Spitze 1996). Support from parents and other relatives can help the next generation connect with job opportunities, learn how to deal with various challenges, and provide financial assistance in times of need (Hauser et al. 1992).

One important aspect of family life has to do with how parents make investments in their children. Our quantitative and qualitative evidence suggests that the ratio of working adults within a family to the children they have to support has an impact on family outcomes. Different groups appear to have evolved different practices or approaches to what might be called "family strategies for the intergenerational transfer of human and social capital." (See also Nee and Sanders 2001.) When more working parents and other relatives care for and support fewer children, each of these children has more resources and often develops higher aspirations than when fewer working parents or, indeed, one nonworking mother supports a larger number of children.

The conditions in a youngster's neighborhood may also have a lasting impact on youthful trajectories, particularly in a dense city like New York. Neighborhood networks and peer groups offer a variety of positive and sometimes negative influences on young people in the city (Williams and Kornblum 1985). Neighborhoods with high levels of civic organization give some of our respondents a leg up in life. Such places usually have less crime, better-maintained housing, and better-quality schools. Local communities with vibrant public spaces can promote connections between area residents. Such places foster "social capital" and a sense of political efficacy among their residents (Nyden et al. 1998; Saegert, Thompson, and Warren 2005; Putnam 2000). Conversely, growing up amidst high levels of crime and disorder can have long-lasting negative effects (Sampson, Morenoff, and Gannon-Rowley 2002).

Although many of these "neighborhood effects" may simply represent the combined traits of the people living in the communities, many scholars think that neighborhood-level processes have important impacts of their own—in other words, the neighborhood can be more than the sum of its individual residents' parts. Life is more difficult for a poor person living in a poor neighborhood, for example, than for a poor person living in a more affluent setting (Wilson 1987; Jargowsky 1997; Anderson 1999; Small and Newman 2001; Small and McDermott 2006). Communities can also differ in how their social and political organization and institutional resources affect children who grow up under their influence (Small 2007).

Here, we review the varied family circumstances and neighborhood settings in which our young respondents grew up, and we discuss how the settings and circumstances affected their subsequent lives. Many respondents still live with or near their parents and other relatives in neighborhoods where the family has lived for many years. Other respondents have recently moved—sometimes over long distances—to resettle in New York, particularly many of the young native whites and some blacks who came to New York to make their careers. Most of these in-movers have had few local family members to help them but have relied on formal labor market mechanisms (such as recruitment by a firm) or the "weak ties" of college friendships to find jobs and establish themselves. Yet others may have grown up in and around New York but have moved many times and are less tied to any one neighborhood.

Families of Origin

The form and dynamics of the families in which our respondents grew up tended to vary considerably by group. The most fundamental question is whether our respondents grew up with both parents—something that has been decreasingly true for Americans in general. The final row of bars in Figure 4.1 shows that only two-fifths of the native blacks and just half of the Puerto Ricans and West Indians grew up with both parents, compared with three-fifths of the Dominicans, about 70 percent of the South Americans and native whites, and more than four-fifths of the Chinese and Russian Jews. Moreover, as indicated by the bars immediately in front, a large share of the families that had been intact in the childhood of the native

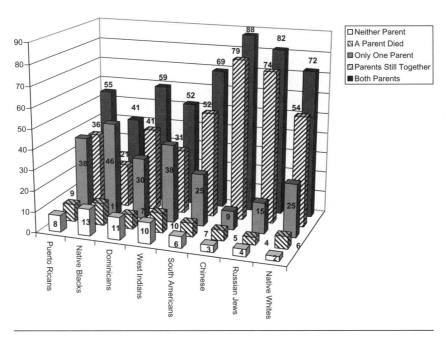

Figure 4.1. Family Form Growing Up (%). *Source:* ISGMNY.

black, West Indian, Puerto Rican, and Dominican respondents were not together at the time of the interview, compared to the vast majority who were still together among the Chinese and the Russian Jews. Native blacks, West Indians, and Puerto Ricans were also more likely to have reported to our survey that one of their parents had died by the time of our interview. Starkly, one out of eight native blacks and one out of ten West Indians and Dominicans reported not growing up with *either* their biological mother or biological father. Although the reasons for an absent parent varied, and an absent parent could mean different things in different settings, most often such absence meant that a principal wage earner was missing.

Absent Fathers

Since the vast majority of respondents in every group grew up with their biological mothers—including seven out of eight native black respondents—the missing parent was almost always the father. We asked those respondents who had not grown up with their fathers if anyone had served as a father figure. The nonwhite groups were most likely to answer "none," followed by "older brother," whereas the native whites and Russians gave "stepfather" as their second most likely answer. In short, many of our respondents with absent fathers also lacked any adult male to serve as a father figure, acting as a breadwinner and role model. The distribution of this experience was a mirror image of the likelihood of having two parents: a quarter of native blacks and West Indians had no father figure, compared to one-sixth of Puerto Ricans and Dominicans, about one-eighth of South Americans and native whites, and fewer than one in ten Russian Jews and Chinese.

Even when both parents were present during our respondents' childhoods, many parents were no longer together when we conducted our interview. Still together were roughly three-quarters of the parents of our Russian and Chinese respondents, and 40 percent of the Dominican parents, but less than one-third of the West Indian parents, and only a fifth of those of native blacks. The groups least likely to have two parents in the first place were also the most likely to have those parents separate after the respondents' childhoods. Among second generation respondents, especially West Indians and Dominicans, growing up in a single parent family sometimes resulted from one parent, usually the father, never having migrated to the United States.

That our black and Hispanic respondents were more likely to have parents who were apart when we interviewed them as young adults was not because of minority status or poverty alone. Only half our wealthiest group, native whites, had parents who were still together, a rate closer to those of the South Americans and Dominicans than to the Chinese and Russian Jews. Indeed, if growing up with two parents rather than one or none is an advantage, and the research literature suggests it is a distinct one, then this is a prime example of the second generation advantage. Every second generation group was more likely to report parents being still together than was true of their native born counterparts: West Indian parents, though frequently separated, were less so than African Americans; South American and Dominican parents were more likely to be together than Puerto Ricans; and Russian Jews more likely than native whites. Indeed, even when their marriages were not close or warm—as our respondents often reported—the Russian Jewish and Chinese parents were significantly more likely than other groups to stay together.

Extended Families

Parents, of course, are not the only family members who can help raise children. Other adults, such as grandparents, uncles, or aunts, helped to raise many of our respondents. We asked our respondents whether any other adults lived with them and helped to raise them while they were growing up. This scenario was fairly common among the children of immigrants but unusual for the children of all three native groups, including whites. More than a quarter of the Chinese and Russian respondents reported that their families contained "extra" adults beyond two parents, as did a fifth of the West Indian and South American respondents. (This reflects, in part, the circumstances of their migration to the United States, which in the case of the Chinese and Russians promoted family members coming together.) Many respondents from these groups, particularly the Russian Jews, reported that their grandparents took primary care of them during their childhood. The West Indians and South Americans often report the presence of a parent's siblings and other relatives. In both cases, these relatives provided a considerable immigrant advantage. Additional working adults contributed to household finances, while nonworking adults (typically grandparents) provided free child care and allowed both parents to be in the labor force with minimal child-care costs. Sometimes this continued even after the additional relative had moved out of the family home. One Ecuadoran 1.5 generation respondent rarely lacked for adults in her life, despite an absent father and a working mother:

> I was raised by my mother, my grandmother, and my aunt. The three of us—we always were together when we lived in Ecuador. Later we all came here. My aunt took care of me in the morning and I was just fine here, and at about four o'clock my uncles came and they were at home with me. We all lived here.

A Russian Jewish respondent, whose mother started out as a manicurist and ended up owning a beauty salon, remembers how relatives aided her mother's upward mobility.

> *I:* Who took care of you?
> *R:* Either my grandmother or my sister.
> *I:* How did you feel about that?
> *R:* Fine. [My mother] would be working across the street from where we lived. So I would always stop in. As a young kid I would hang out in the salon, help out.

There may be less tangible benefits as well. Richard Sennett's (1974) study of earlier newcomers to the city illustrated how extended families brought "adult talk" into the home and thereby increased and broadened the family's knowledge of and contacts in the labor force as well as diversified knowledge of educational opportunities. Finally, the presence of additional adults appears to "soften the blow" materially and psychologically in groups with high levels of family breakup and parental mortality.

This pattern was far less likely to prevail in our native families. The presence of adults other than parents in the family of origin was *least* common among native African Americans, despite popular images of multigenerational black families. This may reflect the fading heritage of the original postwar black migration from the U.S. South. Indeed, as Chapter 7 will elaborate, our native black respondents are more likely than any other group except native whites to report living on their own as young adults. Native blacks (and to a lesser extent Puerto Ricans) share the native white reluctance to have "extra adults" present in the household.

Number of Siblings

Differences in the number of parents and other adults in households are compounded by differences in the number of children these adults are raising. The final row in Figure 4.2 shows the mean number of children growing up in our respondents' families of origin. The Russian youngsters grew up with the fewest siblings, averaging just under one; the native blacks the most, averaging 2.6. The Puerto Ricans, West Indians, and Dominicans were all on the higher end, with averages of 2.2–2.3 siblings; whereas the South Americans and native whites averaged well under two siblings, and the Chinese were closest to the Russians (1.5). Indeed, almost one-third of the Russian Jewish respondents grew up as only children. (A third or more of the native blacks, Dominicans, West Indians, and Puerto Ricans grew up with three or more siblings.) The median Russians, Chinese, and native whites grew up with one sibling, whereas the median in all the other groups was two siblings.

Growing up in a family with a high ratio of parent figures to children is a considerable advantage for both material and nonmaterial reasons. The incidence of two parent families, the presence of "extra" adults, and the typical number of children come together in different ways to shape the ratio of adults to children in the groups we studied. This ratio is shown in the first row of bars in Figure 4.2, which indicates the ratio of the number of

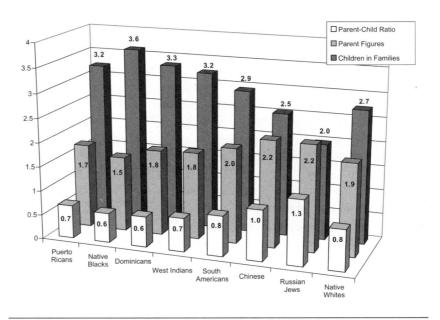

Figure 4.2. Family Composition. *Source:* ISGMNY.

parent figures (biological parents, stepparents, and additional parent figures) to the number of children (respondent plus siblings) in each group. The Chinese and Russian families had the highest ratios, with an adult to care for each child. The native whites and South Americans were also high (.83–.84). Native blacks, Dominicans, Puerto Rican, and West Indians were all at the low end of the distribution, with only an average of .60 to .67 of an adult per child.

Of course, the number of adults living in a household only approximates the number of adults who can play an active role in a child's life. Kin or even close friends living down the block or down the hall may fill these roles as well. Many African American respondents recall having been cared for by grandparents or other kin while their parents worked. It is possible that the disinclination of native families to have "extra adults" living with them is more a matter of housing patterns than caring practices. Native blacks and Puerto Ricans are the most likely groups to live in public housing, where small apartments and long term tenancies may allow kin and neighborly "fictive kin" to help with child-rearing even when such caregivers do not live with the family. Yet while such patterns may temper the underlying differences between the immigrant and native minority groups, they do not seem to be large enough to overcome them.

Parents, Extended Families, and Children

Our respondents' families during the years respondents were growing up thus show both broad variation and systematic differences across groups in terms of how they were organized. At one end of the spectrum are those who grew up with two parents and perhaps even "extra" adults who helped raise relatively few children. Although this pattern occurred in all groups, it was markedly more prevalent among the Russians and Chinese and far less prevalent among the native born and second generation minority groups, with the South Americans and the native whites in between. At the other end of the spectrum are respondents whose parents never lived together, whose families contained no other adults who could step in to help the primary caregiver, usually the mother, and who had two or more siblings, including half-siblings. This pattern, too, could be found in every group, but it was most prevalent among native African Americans and Puerto Ricans and fairly common among West Indians and Dominicans.

The Impact of Absent Fathers

What are relationships within families like? Because the presence or absence of fathers is fundamental to the variation in family forms, it is important to examine the effects of fatherhood. The literature on this question suggests that absent fathers are strongly associated with negative outcomes for the children (McLanahan 1999, 2001), whereas present and engaged fathers have a modest but clearly positive impact on their children's development, with the benefits to the children likely outweighing the fathers' costs of involvement (Pleck and Masciadrelli 2004). McLanahan (2001:1) concludes as much in her review of the key studies:

> Children raised apart from a biological parent are disadvantaged in numerous ways. They are more likely to drop out of high schools, less likely to attend college, and less likely to graduate from college than children raised by both biological parents. Girls from father-absent families are more likely to become sexually active at a younger age and to have a child outside of marriage. Boys who grow up without their fathers are more likely to have trouble finding (and keeping) a job in young adulthood.

McLanahan is careful to note that growing up without a father does not guarantee bad outcomes and that the absence of fathers may not be the direct cause of these outcomes, but simply a marker for deeper difficulties that cause both absent fathers and worse outcomes for their children. She notes, however, that studies attempting to control for these deeper factors, such as conflict between parents, show that the departure of a father by itself seems to worsen the situation for the children. In her view, this happens through loss of economic support for the children, reduction of the number of adults who are available to provide support for children, and the disruption of social networks that frequently occurs when, for example, divorce means moving. Children of never-married parents suffer even more than children of divorced parents, and getting a stepfather does not improve matters (McLanahan 2001).

On the positive side, American fathers are becoming substantially more involved with raising their children (Gerson 1993; Pleck and Masciadrelli 2004), and this seems to be clearly associated with positive outcomes for children. This pattern of greater paternal positive involvement spans racial, ethnic, and income categories. Reviewing studies that controlled for maternal involvement and had independent measures of child outcomes,

Pleck and Masciadrelli conclude that the evidence suggests that positive paternal involvement is associated with better outcomes for their children. Among these outcomes are less psychological distress when the children are growing up, higher self-confidence and self-esteem, higher achievements in education and employment, and lower delinquency (Harris, Furstenberg, and Marmer 1998; Pleck and Masciadrelli 2004:253).

Many of our respondents never had a father or a father figure while growing up, stopped living with their fathers at some point during their childhood, or lost their father to an early death. Indeed, the loss of a father was a common theme in our respondents' lives. As is already clear, our native black respondents were most likely to experience an absent father: three-fifths did not grow up with both biological parents, and a quarter report no father figure at all. Many never knew much about their fathers, either because they had never lived with their mothers or because their fathers had died long ago.

Respondents were often sensitive about the subject. When asked what he knew about his father, who "cut out" when he was 5 years old, one 27-year-old black man said at first "that's a question we can avoid. Because I don't know and I don't really care. Honestly, I understand you want to get to the answers but I can't tell you something I don't know." But he had tried to make contact with his father, a senior postal worker, who lived not far away:

One day his [other] son and I almost got into a big thing. I knocked on his door and the son say, "Who are you?" I said, "I'm Darrell. I want to speak to Sonny." That's my father's name. So, "He not here." So I said, "I'm his son." "He ain't here." This, that, and the other thing. Mouthing off. "Man," I said, "Yo, I just asked you one question. All the other remarks you're making, man, I ain't the one that trying to hear that right now." He mouthed off. But I left 'cause it would have been dumb for me to sit there and fight this guy. I don't know him even though he's my brother.

Like other respondents with absent fathers, many Puerto Rican respondents did not know much about their fathers. Some expressed anger toward their absent father for not being present or for having other women besides their mothers. One 26-year-old Puerto Rican woman expressed dismay at her father:

My father denied me when I was little, but now, I speak to him on the phone. I met him when I was twenty years old, then stopped seeing him, but now we got back in contact. Every time I call, he's never home. It's only his wife. Why am I gonna waste my time calling him, when he's always in the street.

The experience of absent fathers also shaped relationships between African American mothers and their children, particularly the daughters. Many respondents emphasize how their mothers tried to teach self-reliance and sometimes passed on a distrust of their fathers and other men in general.

[My mother] told me to be independent. Don't depend on a man. Don't get caught up in one friend or just have a lot of friends. Don't trust too many people.

Mothers in single parent families also introduced their children to the world of work, something that fathers more commonly did in more traditional families. Of course, being single, most often poor, the mothers often had limited knowledge of and contacts in the labor force. Nonetheless, mothers' careers were frequently mentioned as a source of pride by our respondents. Respondents who have grown up in single parent households often become extremely close to their mothers. Putting the story in starkly racial terms, a 25-year-old African American woman recalls how her single mother sacrificed for her and her sister:

My mother's friends would be like, "You bring those kids up like they was white kids." It bothered my mother a lot because my mother was like, "I'm not giving my kids anything that they don't deserve. It wasn't that I'm trying to make them white or anything like that," it was just that she wanted me and my sister to have a future. My mother didn't have a lot of things that she gave me and my sister. When she grew up, she always said, "My babies is going to have something different and going to be treated different. They aren't going to grow up in what I grew up in!" And to a certain extent, we had a better lifestyle. The love between me and my mother and my sister is extremely close. And nobody can break that, even though we had family and friends, boyfriends who tried to. They can't stop that. That's something that is just there and is strong and that's something that's not going to be able to break. A lot of people think it's weird because the love is so close. But it's not weird. That's how we are. It's the three of us. This is our family.

Many West Indian respondents also grew up without their fathers, but they tended to recall their fathers more favorably than did the African

Americans. One 20-year-old woman said of her church deacon father, "My dad, if he had his last couple of dollars in his pocket and we had to do something for school, he would rather give it to us than him have it. He would give it to us." The West Indian respondents recalled that their fathers had helped with homework, used to take them to their job sites, and played with them. As one 24-year-old man whose father was from Grenada said:

> When I was little, we was always going to the beach. He taught me to swim, dive, drive, everything. He taught me everything pretty much that I know as a guy. I can honestly say he never hit my mom, and he and my mother been together since they were fifteen years old and are still together, so at least I picked that quality up too.

West Indian fathers and mothers did seem more strict with their children than other groups and fairly commonly applied mild corporal punishment. Indeed, tales of "good parents" getting in trouble with the authorities for suspected child abuse and of children threatening to report parents to child welfare authorities circulate frequently in New York's West Indian community (Waters 1999). One young West Indian man, whose father was a union organizer, had this to say:

> When I was young he was actually very key in my education. He taught me how to read so I knew how to read before I ever started school. He was also very strict about my learning so that when I was young we used to study stuff. We'd get up on Saturday morning, before any cartoons, before going out to play, and it would be "we're going to read. We're going to learn." He is responsible for my current love of reading. As I got older, he became more the disciplinarian, the one I had to watch out for if I was doing something I wasn't supposed to be doing.

Many West Indian fathers had other women in their lives, and this was an ongoing source of tension. One 29-year-old West Indian male described the men in his family thus:

> My dad, my uncle, they used to have a lot of women. Their friends used to have a lot of women friends and I used to hang out with them. As a matter of fact, I used to have older women just like them too 'cause I was always hanging out with older women. When I was fifteen, my first girlfriend was twenty-nine-years-old. And she was a friend of my mom's. Twenty-nine-years-old. These women taught

me a lot. And also I think the reason also was why I ended up with a lot of women was because in the household my dad was very abusive . . . I think that rubs off. It trickles down. So that's why I say [parents need to provide] good support, good role models.

These sentiments were echoed by a 31-year-old West Indian male who remembered his father as a disappointing presence in his life, and yet he notes:

Basically I'm like him . . . This is the problem with children. They grow up in a home with a low socioeconomic class background and they achieve very low standards of education, particularly for boys, when there is not a man in the house. The way the economy is today, it's too much for either parent, male or female, to do it by themself. I feel my education was put on hold because I did not have the guidance of my father . . . The fact that he wasn't there, and our lives were affected by people that did not have our best interest in their minds, meant that by the time I was ready to go to college, I was underachieving in school. I didn't know what I wanted to do. Looking back I realize I am intelligent. If somebody had cared, I would have done a lot better.

Women were particularly angry with fathers they felt had treated their mothers badly, had cheated on them, and put their own interests first. A 24-year-old West Indian woman who often visited her father, who had returned to Barbados, said:

He thinks because he grew up hard that he doesn't owe anyone anything. And thus, whatever he does, he does and that's just that. Whether it hurts someone or not. And he has little or no remorse for what he does. You get older, you start hitting adolescence, you start noticing things you didn't notice before. Daddy's not this king that I thought he was and daddy was abusive to women. And daddy is sneaky and daddy is a liar. And I didn't want to be a part of that.

As one 29-year-old West Indian woman summed up, "Can you tell it's not one of my favorite subjects?

Some West Indian fathers never migrated to the United States, whereas others returned to their home countries fairly early in our respondents' childhoods. While these situations seemed most common among West Indians, they occurred among Dominicans and South Americans as well. (Given the long distances and circumstances of departure, spreading families across home and host countries was far less common for our Russian and Chinese respondents.) Although rare for our working class Chinese parents, when divorce did occur, it was often attributed to the disruptions and long separations caused by immigration. Yet growing up in a single parent family has a somewhat less negative effect on educational attainment and adult labor market participation for West Indians than for native blacks. (See Chapter 5.) This may result from the larger number of adults, particularly working adults, in West Indian immigrant families and the higher rates of labor force participation among West Indian mothers.

Fathers and Work

Puerto Ricans and Dominicans were more likely to grow up in two parent families than native African American and West Indian respondents but less likely than our other groups. In this regard the South Americans were closer to the native whites than to the other Hispanic groups. About 55 percent of our Puerto Rican respondents reported growing up with their father and mother, and another quarter had a father figure who was not their biological parent. They generally reported that their fathers provided financial support, taught them skills, and served as a positive role model.

Most Puerto Rican fathers worked in blue collar jobs, and so their children did not expect many material benefits from them but appreciated spending time with them and having some security about their basic needs. One 24-year-old Puerto Rican young man whose father drove a tow truck said, "He did good. You can't complain. As long as we got food in the refrigerator, clothes on our back, it's a different story. We had all that. We had clothes. Any time we wanted something we got it, so it was good." Another young man noted, "He was always there and he always did make sure that we went to Little League, but he didn't really participate much. I guess that was the support, knowing that he was there." A third young man said, "We used to go to the baseball games, football games, to the park, hang out. We used to go to his relatives' house, hang out together. Take trips to Manhattan and go sight-seeing. If I had to go to the doctor's, he would go with me. So we were always tight."

But many other respondents described fathers who had bad experiences in the New York City labor market. Many Puerto Rican fathers worked in manufacturing during a period of rapid deindustrialization. They often lost jobs and had a hard time finding new ones, sometimes having to commute long distances. One father who was a store manager in a family-owned supermarket was demoted to assistant manager when the store was bought out by a corporate chain. Another was murdered in the night club he owned.

Dominicans reported that their fathers had similar experiences. Many of them worked as building superintendents, taxi drivers, and mechanics and often asked their sons to help them out. One young man reported:

> R: When I was growing up, he was taking care of me. He had a business in the Dominican Republic which, you know, he would always go and come back. It was like a pizza shop. So yeah, I was always with him. I was his right-hand man.
> I: How did you feel about that?
> R: It's like, forget it. I mean, everything, anything that I wanted to do, anything he wanted to do, we'd just do it.

A young man whose father worked in a hospital using a computer system to keep inventories also spoke warmly of his father:

> R: Oh, he used to babysit us sometimes. For my mother, he would actually take days off, whatever, like when I was sick. We played basketball, baseball, football. He would take me to his job, like in the hospital. That's where I first saw handicapped people. I was like ten or eleven. I was like—I want to work with handicapped people.

At the same time, many also told stories of having distant fathers. Traditionally, Dominican, South American, and Puerto Rican men and women tend to live in separate spheres and the male sphere, is largely in public, out of the house. The "togetherness" of the idealized American family is not always valued, a fact their second generation children feel acutely:

> R: Me and my dad weren't really close. Like most Dominican fathers, they're pretty much in the streets. I would have to say my mother took a lot of the father role when I was growing up, more than he did. He was always out.

Not all Dominican respondents were as accepting of this behavior and of their father's ideas about gender roles. One 21-year-old Dominican woman describes the men in her family thus:

> Cheap, big egos, want to the be strong one, "can't do this, can't do that. You do what I say!" Very opinionated . . . "You're a girl, you shouldn't have to work, you serve me!"

Women rarely worked outside the home in the Dominican Republic, Ecuador, Colombia, or Peru until recent decades, particularly among rural families. For many of the mothers of the Hispanic second generation respondents, moving to New York brought their mothers increased independence and led them to question the gender roles they had grown up with. Even very low-paying jobs or the opportunity to go on public assistance made the women less dependent on men and, as a result, often less willing to put up with abuse, extramarital affairs, or men who live "in the streets," as respondents frequently put it (Grasmuck and Pessar 1991; Levitt 2001).

Changes in women's expectations also brought tensions, and in some cases considerable conflict, into the family, leaving one Dominican woman to wonder whether it was such a good thing for her family to have stayed together:

> When I was growing up, all [my mother] did was cook, clean . . . as she got educated, you know, she became, if you want to call it, rebellious. He never hit her or anything like that, but his ego was so big it took up all the extra room in the house. He was the man of the house. He's like, "You respect me, I'm your father." [My mother] kept saying she was going to divorce my father, but didn't, for us. We probably would have been the only kids to benefit from those two getting away from each other! I call him the sperm donor. He provided the sperm, and we gave him a roof in exchange for it.

Finally, the wounds of a difficult life are easily passed on to the children even when parents don't intend to do so. As this Dominican woman observes:

> It's like never enough with the both of them; you can't do enough because they feel like we owe them or something, like they deserve. It's not our fault. We didn't make him work in the fields, we didn't make her work in people's houses at the age of nine, you know? It's like a pattern; she's trying not to do it, but she's doing it, and so is he. All I can do is not do it to my kids. I hope I don't. I have a lot of pent-up anger and feelings, and all that, but I'm going to try to forget about it.

Our native white, Russian Jewish, Chinese, and South American respondents generally grew up with fathers who held jobs that brought significant incomes into the household. These respondents also told us many stories of things they did with their parents and lessons or skills that they learned from them. These fathers sometimes even helped their young adult children start businesses, lent them substantial amounts of money, or made it possible for them to attend a college. The other side of this coin, however, is that upwardly mobile parents could demand more of their children, which was not always appreciated. As one 26-year-old Russian respondent said of his father:

> He wanted me to be a perfect chess player. He had a lot of wonderful qualities that were not of interest to me too much. His lack of information on how to approach children, I think, always made it a little bit of a rift. I felt like I had to do this activity rather than it being something that we could both enjoy.

Another Russian young woman noted of her father, "He became much too involved, like when I would come to him for help with school projects he threw himself into that and wouldn't let go." Similarly, another Russian father made a point of taking his daughter to music lessons:

> Every Sunday I went to music school. My father took me to Manhattan and spent the whole day there with me while I took piano lessons, ballet lessons, theory of music. And he waited. He took turns with one of my friends' fathers. But every Sunday he knew that he had to do this.

Among all immigrant groups, many respondents recalled that their fathers worked very long hours and consequently could not spend as much time with their children as respondents might have liked. An 18-year-old Russian woman commented: "When I was younger he spent a lot of time with me because he worked 9 to 5 or 9 to 4. As I got older, less and less. Like really less. Now he'll come home like 10 o'clock or something."

It is also significant that many Russian Jewish parents lost professional status when they immigrated, at least initially. For many of the Russian Jewish respondents, the story of their parents' professional background, occupational downward mobility (often accompanied by periods on public assistance), and eventual but often successful attempt to regain middle class status has left a deep impression. The experience of witnessing the parental drive to recapture lost status—and parental bitterness and depression when that proved impossible—may account for much of the young people's own drive to succeed. In some cases, the experience may have led respondents to distance themselves from their parents' experience.

I: What work did your father do back in Georgia?
R: Chief engineer.

I: Did your father's work situation improve or get worse over time in the U.S.?

R: Improved. He started out as a taxi driver. He worked his way up to owning medallions. He bought real estate, for investment. He's a diamond dealer right now.

I: Would you ever work at his job?

R: Would I ever? No!

I: Why not?

R: Because it's still more or less, it's like a blue collar job. It's great. It will make you money but I am lucky that I have grown up here and I have an education I don't have to do that.

Like the South American and Dominican respondents, Russian Jewish respondents often commented on how their mothers enjoyed greater freedom in the United States than "back home" and explained that this had required some renegotiation of household roles after immigration (for a discussion of a similar situation among Korean New Yorkers, see Min 2002). Unlike the Latin mothers, the mothers of the Russian Jews almost all worked outside the home prior to immigration, many in professional jobs. Yet most respondents report that their mothers were able to recapture professional status in New York faster than their fathers were, and even when they did not, mothers were more able to find satisfactory work and adjust to their new status. Fathers, by contrast, sometimes became depressed. This situation is rife with possibilities for tension within the family. A respondent from Brooklyn notes:

R: [My mother] is working as an accountant right now. But [when she arrived] she worked as a sewer. She sewed clothes in Borough Park for Jewish women. That's what she was doing on and off. That was temporary. She cleaned apartments for Jewish people and she even sewed at a factory, at a Chinese factory. She volunteered at the hospital trying to get some work there. She was doing the bookkeeping job. And accounting jobs . . . She was an accountant in Russia. Here she went to college, to get a degree to become an accountant again.

I: Generally, would you say your mother's work situation improved or got worse over time, here in the U.S.?

R: Comparing it to the past I think it's a lot better . . . We have a house now. We have several cars and stuff like that. Financially, it's a lot better. And of course, in other ways too. Her English is getting better and stuff like that. Emotionally, she feels better being in this country. So it improved a great deal. [My father] had several jobs. First, he started working at a car wash. And then he got a job at this mortgage company, where he works as a messenger. He delivers money to banks and he delivers important mail and he has been working there all along. He was a technician at a factory back in Russia.

I: Would you say your father's work situation improved or got worse?

R: I think it got worse . . . Working in that place all these years, it wears him out. He gets tired more. He just comes home all beat up. He's sick of it.

Despite tensions and depression over loss of status, and the usual family conflicts, marital dissolution was less frequent among the parents of the Russian Jews than other groups (with the exception of the Chinese). This finding is striking, since both Jewish tradition and Soviet law made divorce relatively easy. Indeed, divorce appears to be less frequent among the Russian Jews in New York than it was back in Russia.

Among the Chinese respondents, working extremely long hours was also common for fathers and for some mothers as well. One Chinese respondent recalled that after his father had opened a laundromat: "I only saw my dad a little bit. I didn't even see him in the morning because he would get up later than I did because I had to go to school so I would see him when he came home around 10:30 or 11:30. I'm supposed to be in bed so I would only see him for an hour." Another Chinese woman also experienced a father who was distant because he was working so many hours:

I didn't really see him that much. My dad didn't really raise us. He kind of fed us. And there was a point in our lives where he realized that we were growing up and he stayed home on Tuesday nights because that's when it was slowest at the restaurant and he would make us dinner. But the three of us felt guilty too that we weren't closer to our father, but our father was kind of trying. So he didn't really impart any . . . like my mother was very good at giving us all this motherly advice and teaching us things and driving us to wherever, and my father was kind of . . . he didn't even know how old I was sometimes.

This lack of communication with parents, particularly fathers, is compounded by language difficulties. Compared with other groups, fewer

Chinese respondents are fluent in their parents' native language, and fewer Chinese parents are really fluent in English. As one Chinese respondent notes, "In my thirty-some years of life, I've never really had a deep conversation with my dad." (See also Qin 2006.)

If emotional distance and a lack of communication characterized relations between parents, particularly fathers, and children in many of the Chinese respondents' families, relations between the parents themselves were often not much better, at least so far as their second generation children remember. While some Chinese respondents recall their parents' marriages as deeply loving, and others remember them as an at least amiable domestic partnership, often the respondents described their parents as inhabiting very separate social spheres. At least one working class Chinese respondent says that his parents literally did not speak for decades, despite sharing a tiny Chinatown apartment. For Chinese fathers to have extramarital relationships was also not uncommon. Yet this behavior does not seem to have inspired in their children the bitterness that we see in other groups, nor was infidelity usually grounds for divorce.

One reason the Chinese families, and perhaps the Russian Jewish families, were more able to stay together may be their expectations of marriage. Loving, companionate relationships, while desirable, may have been less important than establishing a workable partnership for economic stability and raising children. (It is interesting to note that among the generally better-off Taiwanese parents the divorce rate was higher, approaching that of the native whites. In this case, divorce may be a luxury that only the better-off can afford.) For the Chinese second generation, being raised in an American culture that continually tells young people to "follow their dreams," that places paramount importance on individual happiness, and in which "love conquers all," the distance between the model of love and marriage they learned from their parents and the one they learn from the U.S. media and their American peers is vast. How they try to bridge that gap, particularly when members of the second generation begin their own families, is a subject we take up in Chapter 7.

The South American families, particularly those with more resources, had perhaps the most traditional division of labor. Having a mother at home, sometimes with other relatives to help out, was often remembered fondly by respondents. These traditional gender roles, however, take a clear toll on women's aspirations, a fact that their second generation children, who often have greater expectations of gender equity, are well aware of. This 30-year-old new mother reflects on her parents':

R: I guess my father did sacrifice. I mean he was working two jobs! But I don't know. He's the one who was working! I don't know what his sacrifices were. I know his life is better now than it was in Ecuador. I think it was my mother who sacrificed a lot because she raised four kids and she was always home. Now that I'm home with one, I see what I sacrifice! And I'm just assuming here, pretending I could read her head, but as soon as my brother was in school, my mother started taking a class here and there and she went to work. My mother never worked while we were little. So we're talking about I was fifteen, sixteen before she finally started doing anything for herself. She's sixty-two and she's just graduating now with a four-year degree.

I: That's great.

R: Yeah, but at sixty-two, what are you going to be working for? Definitely she sacrificed a lot, my mom.

South American families also tend to be relatively small in New York, far smaller than in South America. The Ecuadoran mother with four children described earlier had a large brood by New York standards, and certainly her daughter sees the situation that way. Yet many Ecuadoran, Colombian, and Peruvian respondents recall with awe how their grandparents raised eight, ten, or more children. This intergenerational drop in family size may account for the high ratio of aunts and uncles to children among the South Americans and the significant role that parents' siblings often played in the respondents' lives.

The families in which our native white respondents grew up often had a traditional division of labor, particularly the families who were not upper middle class. One young woman had a father who did a considerable amount of travel for a telephone company while her mother took care of the family:

He was there. He definitely had a say in what went on but he did have to work a lot. It was difficult because we couldn't go all together on family vacations because he'd have to work and that was one thing that me and my brother kind of missed out on. Otherwise, you know, we don't have any grudges against him or anything like that.

Another young man related a similar story:

He was always working. *Always* working. We had arguments about this. I mean he's there if I really, really, really needed him, but he was never there when I was growing up.

As with working parents from other groups, both fathers' and mothers' work experience could hold lessons for the children, if only by showing them by example careers to be avoided. One young man from a blue-collar background told this story:

> He always brought me to work. Dealing with the sheet rock and the insulation was a nightmare. It turned me off to it completely . . . It's a rough life. It's hard. He showed me because he wanted me to experience that plus he was bringing me along to keep me out of trouble. And when I did it, I just knew that this is not for me. I don't take nothing away from carpenters. There are very skilled tradesmen out there, but it's not for me.

In every group, having fathers who could provide financial support to the family and be involved in family life provided many advantages to the children. Nowhere is this clearer than among the native whites, the group with the highest incomes. White respondents often learned about the world of work from their fathers and benefitted from their contacts when it came time to go to work themselves. Their fathers often stressed the importance of goals and pressured their children to succeed. One young white respondent said:

> I was trying to satisfy him, you know. Kind of sounds weird, but, um, that was important to him. And maybe it was, not like an obsession, but maybe a little bit too important to him at one time. Especially in high school. That was the only thing he talked about, homework, homework, homework. You got home, you go to work studying. Don't have a personal life, don't have any free time to yourself, you have to study, study, study. And if you do anything less, then, you know, you're inferior. That was hard.

The kinds of families in which our respondents grew up varied tremendously in many ways that had an immediate impact on the opportunities or barriers they faced. Foremost was the impact of working adults on family income. Even when parents held relatively modest jobs, having two or even more adults contributing to the household gave that family a leg up compared to others with fewer sources of income. As Figure 4.2 shows, a clear majority of the Russian Jewish, Chinese, and West Indian respondents grew up in households with two or more working adults. This was true of only two-fifths of the South American, Dominican, and native black respondents, and only one-third of the Puerto Ricans. One source of second generation advantage, then, was that parents in many immigrant groups were able to pool income from several working adults, even when our respondents were often growing up apart from their fathers. Immigrant families, not the native born minority families, seemed most able to compensate for absent fathers with fictive or other kin.

A second source of immigrant advantage was that the larger number of working adults generally had fewer children to support, at least compared to their native born counterpart groups. (Dominican families were the only exception to this pattern.) The Russian Jewish and Chinese families had the smallest number of children, while the native black families were the largest on average. The groups with the highest levels of parental labor force participation also had the lowest number of children to support. The result was more resources per child.

Neighborhood Context

Family dynamics are interwoven with the fabric of their local neighborhoods. Most of those who grew up in single parent households, for example, also grew up in neighborhoods where such families were half again more common compared to the neighborhoods of our respondents growing up in two parent families. Such neighborhoods also had fewer working adults, lower median incomes, and higher school dropout rates. These conditions compounded the difficulties and challenges of growing up in a single parent household. A high concentration of resource-poor families can overwhelm local institutions and social networks, even undermining those individuals and families with more resources (Anderson 1999; Kasinitz 2001).

Conversely, those respondents growing up in households containing two parents plus other working adults also tended to live in neighborhoods where this type of family is common. In such communities, even those families with fewer resources may be able to draw on neighbors and local kin, and local institutions can concentrate their efforts on the relatively smaller numbers in need. At the same time, worse-off members of better-off groups living in such communities may experience relative deprivation. They may feel their problem more acutely than those in neighborhoods or ethnic groups in which their situation is the norm (Lee 2004).

The degree to which individuals and families are embedded in local communities varies greatly across metropolitan New York. Other factors being equal, we would expect families with a longer history in New York to have deeper and thicker kinship networks that would provide our respondents with more resources and connections. Other factors are rarely equal, however. It turns out that the second generation groups were more likely to have been born in and grown up in New York City to parents who still live there, compared with the children of natives. In some ways this reflects and may account for some of New York's storied combination of cosmopolitanism and parochialism. The young people with foreign born parents and the strongest connections to other countries are also the ones least likely to have experienced life in any other part of the United States. More than 37 percent of the native whites—the most advantaged group in the sample—grew up in other parts of the United States and came to New York as young adults either to attend college or, more frequently, to pursue careers after finishing their educations. This tends to skew the native white education rates and income levels upward. In addition, just under 9 percent of the native African Americans are also newcomers to the city. Largely postcollege migrants, they resemble their native white counterparts. Some Chinese respondents (6 percent of the group), mostly the children of well-educated Taiwanese parents, also came to New York as adults after finishing their educations. This accounts for some of, but by no means all, the high Chinese educational performance.

By contrast, the children of immigrants are city kids. Of the native whites who did grow up in the New York metropolitan area, more than a third spent most of their childhoods in the suburbs. A smaller but still significant minority of native African Americans also hails from suburban parts of the region. Among the second generation groups, only among the South Americans, many of whom have settled in the declining downtowns of older suburban towns in Westchester and New Jersey, did a large minority hail from the suburbs. Among the children of other immigrants, 90 percent or more spent most of their childhoods and teenage years in New York City.

Neighborhoods and Ethnic Groups

A place of residence is not just a roof and four walls but a package of surrounding hazards (for example, violent crime or public health risks) and strengths (good local schools, availability of cultural and religious institutions, and community organizations). The parents in a neighborhood generally develop expectations about what activities their children should participate in, what schools they should attend, and what sorts of youthful behavior are appropriate. Neighborhoods with strong "social capital" (Putnam 2000) typically have parentally sanctioned activities for young people, such as sports leagues, cultural enrichment programs, and church programs. (Of course, youngsters may self-organize into cliques and gangs even in these areas.) Like family networks, then, neighborhoods also influence how young people develop strategies for growing up and getting ahead in life (Sampson, Morenoff, and Gannon-Rowley 2002).

The consolidation of Greater New York into a single city in 1898 created a 322-square-mile metropolis with a vast range of neighborhoods. Although much denser than other American cities, New York City nonetheless has many suburban areas. The 2000 Census showed that New York continues to be one of the most highly racially segregated cities in America (Logan, Stults, and Farley 2004)—meaning that blacks and whites are physically separated at the Census tract level. Yet whereas black-white segregation persists, segregation between other groups has dropped, with Hispanics and Asians increasingly likely to live among whites and blacks as well as with each other. New York also has a large number of areas where people with quite different racial and economic characteristics border each other. Since a half million overwhelmingly native black and Puerto Rican poor people live in public housing, the location of such housing has a considerable effect on the statistical measurement of segregation. Unlike many other American cities, public housing in New York has a stable population with long housing tenures and long waiting lists for apartments. As a result, today the demography of the projects looks more like the demography of New York's poor of several decades ago. About one in seven of our native black and Puerto Rican respondents lives in public housing, three times as many as any of our other groups.

Street Life

Except for the very wealthy, New Yorkers generally live in homes that are smaller, older, and more crowded than is typical of most American communities. New York compensates for the poor quality of its private spaces with a wealth of public spaces and facilities. Like other Americans, New Yorkers tend to speak of "the streets" as a place to be feared and avoided. Parents talk about "losing" children "to the streets." Yet traditionally

New Yorkers, young and old, have spent a great deal of time on the city's bustling sidewalks, on its subways, and in its parks. Since at least the work of Jane Jacobs (1961), this form of public life has been recognized as a source of the city's cultural and economic vitality (Whyte 1988). When the dangers of "the streets," real and perceived, lead some New Yorkers to withdraw themselves and their children from public spaces, group members suffer because their private spaces are often so poor and crowded. This is one reason that high levels of street crime took such a toll on the city in the late 1980s and early 1990s, when our respondents were growing up. It is also why the reduction of street crime since 1990 has been so important, particularly in poor and working class neighborhoods.

Many neighborhoods had a street life characterized by dangerous, sometimes illegal, activities. The exposure to violent crime followed the general pattern of race and income, though street crimes were far higher in areas with commercial traffic than in purely residential areas (Goldsmith et al. 2000). As crack use reached epidemic proportions in the late 1980s, the city experienced a spike in violent crime. During these years it became increasingly common for young males, especially, to carry weapons, including handguns, as a matter of course (DASH 1993; Fagan and Davies 2004). These problems were heavily concentrated in neighborhoods where our Puerto Rican, Dominican, African American, and West Indian respondents grew up but less prominent, though by no means absent, from those in which our native white, Russian Jewish, Chinese, and South American respondents grew up.

Analysis of the 1990 Census data for the zip codes in which our New York City respondents reported growing up indicates that the median native black, Puerto Rican, and Dominican respondents lived in areas with the highest values of female-headed households, 16- to 19-year-olds who had dropped out of school and did not work, poverty, and adults without high school diplomas (Figure 4.3). The West Indians lived in markedly less disadvantaged areas than these three groups. The South American, Chinese, and Russians lived in areas with even better median values on these dimensions, particularly in terms of the share of female-headed households with children. Still, these areas had higher levels of young high school dropouts and poverty than those of the native whites, who lived in the areas with the lowest median values of disadvantage. They grew up in areas consistently marked by higher levels of education, private school enrollment, labor force participation, and median household income.

That native born blacks and Puerto Ricans are likely to live in neighborhoods characterized by concentrated poverty and its associated social problems, and that only Dominicans live in equally troubled areas, is another structural factor that helps to explain why individual members of the second generation groups had better socioeconomic outcomes. The white concentration in better neighborhoods also demonstrates whites' continuing advantage in the American racial hierarchy.

We asked our respondents what they thought about the conditions of the neighborhoods in which they grew up. Figure 4.4 shows how our respondents felt about neighborhood problems. The most acute neighborhood issue facing our respondents was the open dealing and use of drugs. This was not an exclusively inner city problem. A considerable minority of every group, usually the men, reported engaging in criminal activity in their late teens and early twenties, with drug dealing being the most common, often accompanied by robbery and other gang activity. Most respondents had "aged out" of this activity by their early twenties, though a handful moved into more serious criminal activity and even criminal

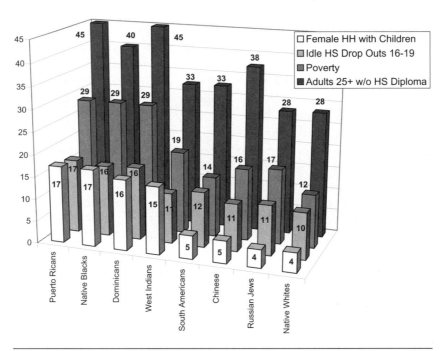

Figure 4.3. Neighborhoods Growing Up (Median %). *Source:* U.S. Census 1990, Standard File 3, Zip Code Level.

careers. Yet, even at the height of the crack epidemic, drugs and crime had much less effect on the overall environment in which most of our native white, Russian Jewish, and Chinese respondents grew up. Some individuals got involved in these activities, but drug-related street crime did not permeate their communities.

One respondent in four described "drug dealing" as a big problem in his or her community, but this situation was clearly most pronounced in the Dominican and Puerto Rican neighborhoods, particularly among respondents growing up in Washington Heights and the South Bronx during the 1980s. Indeed, more than two-fifths of Dominicans and Puerto Ricans reported that drugs were a big problem in their neighborhoods when they were growing up. (Williams [1992] and Jackall [1977] give accounts of Washington Heights during this period.) Respondents who still live in these neighborhoods frequently remarked on how much life has improved with the decline in crime since the mid-1990s. Even in the worst years, of course, most young people were not involved with drug dealing and drug-related violence. Yet such activity was prevalent at times, and virtually all the young people we surveyed knew someone involved in it. In such places crime shaped the friendships people would

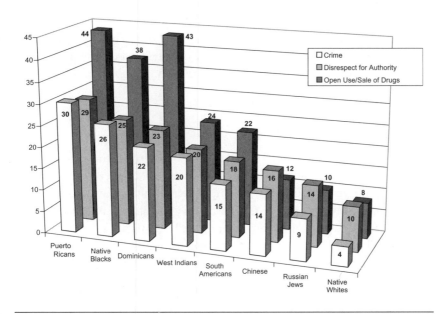

Figure 4.4. Neighborhood Problems Reported (%). *Source:* ISGMNY.

make, constrained the public facilities people would use, restricted whether residents could safely go out at night, and even determined what route young people would take to and from school. In many cases parents moved out of these areas because of their fears about crime; others sent their children to Catholic schools or to distant relatives to get them away from the "wrong crowd." Fear of crime also limited some parents' willingness to let their children take advantage of educational opportunities if doing so meant long commutes on public transportation.

The high levels of violence and insecurity surrounding the open air drug markets of the 1980s posed a real and direct threat to many of our respondents. One black respondent casually related to us that on the way to the store she was shot in the leg by a drug dealer's stray bullet. A native black young man related the following depressing story of how being a crime victim might have saved him from worse:

> *R:* When I was growing up it was drugs crazy. Crack on this corner, dope on this corner, weed on this corner. That's about the worst things I did. A lot of my friends were involved in this activity. A lot of them. Including myself. Just about all my friends now are locked up twenty-five to life and God forbid, if this didn't happen to me I'd be locked up too.
>
> *I:* What happened?
>
> *R:* I got car jacked. Got shot in my head. But I'm here to talk about it. I was in a coma for six months. But I'm here. So I do my physical therapy. It's getting better. I can't complain. I can't complain. I can't.

Another African American young man noted:

> It's like a cycle. For what I did, for what the kids did around my way, these [kids] around here are doing now. The drugs, the shootings, they doing it right now. So it's a cycle. From what I seen when I was growing up, these young boys doing the same things now. And when I see that, I say, "I used to do that." I try to talk them, "Don't do that man. Go get a job, do something." "Naw, I can't make no money like that." It's just another generation doing what I used to do when I was a kid. That's the only thing I seen now.

Of course, not every African American respondent grew up in a threatening environment. One young black woman observed of Jamaica, Queens:

It was pretty cool 'cause it's a quiet neighborhood. Nice neighbors. Lots of kids to play with. No fussing, no fighting, none of that kind of stuff. No gang wars and that kind of stuff. Working class neighborhood.

Another 32-year-old African American woman described how her current neighborhood in Queens, where she is raising her own children, differed from the area of Brooklyn in which she grew up:

This community is great. They have a lot to offer for the children. Like I said I have a lot of development, recreation centers and parks and it's just . . . the environment is so much different. It's better. I mean I cannot be afraid to let them run outside ahead of me, whereas in Brooklyn, you don't know where a bullet is coming from. So it's a big step up around here. That's the only thing I see.

Despite the popular imagery of the brutality of "Colombian cartels" and "Jamaican posses," our South Americans and West Indian respondents were less likely than Dominicans, Puerto Ricans, or blacks to talk about drugs as a neighborhood problem, though they were more likely to do so than Russian Jews, Chinese, or native whites.

A closely related pattern involved overall crime, which was slightly less likely to be named a big problem than drugs, but was still widespread, with more than one in six saying crime was a big problem overall. As with drugs, the variation in exposure to high-crime environments was wide, with relatively few native whites finding crime a major problem, but more than one in five Puerto Ricans, native blacks, Dominicans, and West Indians finding crime a big problem. Also seen as a "big problem," though with less variation across the groups, was youthful disrespect for authority. While this may be endemic to adolescent life, one in five respondents saw such disrespect as a big problem, with the highest rates in Puerto Rican, native black, and Dominican neighborhoods. Finally, young people growing up in the native born minority neighborhoods were three times more likely to say that the lack of after-school activities was a big problem for them.

A clear picture emerges from these responses: discounting the specific characteristics of their families or even the median family incomes of people in their neighborhoods, many of our respondents were growing up in areas that were physically dangerous, sometimes menacing, and often unresponsive to their needs as youngsters. These conditions were worst in the Puerto Rican and native African American neighborhoods, almost as bad in the Dominican neighborhoods, not as bad in the West Indian and South American neighborhoods, and noticeably better in the Russian, Chinese, and especially native white neighborhoods.

Indeed, the native whites and the Russian Jews often looked back on the communities in which they grew up as parochial and unexciting. Yet they also often remembered them as good places to grow up. As one Russian Jewish respondent put it:

> If I look back, I would say it was good that the neighborhood was decently safe. Everything is around the corner. You don't have to go far to the grocery store. The park. It's nice. I like it. I like it here. I will probably move to Manhattan when I have the money to buy an apartment, just because there's more life there than there is here but I'm grateful to the neighborhood.

A Russian Jewish young woman raised largely among native whites in the suburbs but now living in Brooklyn details the good and bad sides of the suburban American dream as lived by young people.

> R: It was great. Suburban. Very nice community. Safe, quiet. Good resources, nice stores. It was just a nice suburb . . . quiet, schools were good. People were very nice. Pretty much middle class. We have some African American families, not too many . . . You know, it was mostly white Americans, but there were some Jewish kids like myself and some minorities. Sometimes there was nothing to do for kids. You couldn't really [do much], if you couldn't drive. There was no transportation actually. There are some bad parts about it. I went to a public high school which is a very good high school but it was a very big public high school and sometimes that creates problems, and people get left out . . . They don't feel good about themselves and they want to shoot everybody else up.

Most of the Russian Jews still lived with or near their parents in New York City. For those raised in the heart of the immigrant communities, particularly Brighton Beach, a comforting haven for newcomers like their immigrant parents, such a community can seem more like a stifling ghetto for the second generation children. One young woman who came to Brighton Beach from Russia as a toddler explains, "It was okay, because not knowing English it was easier [for her parents] just getting around." Yet as she became a teenager, she found it annoying "to live in an community where everybody knows you, minds your business, and had an opinion on how you dress, whom you date and how much money you have."

Other Russian Jewish immigrant parents originally settled among Orthodox or Hasidic Jews in communities where most of the secular Jewish population had left for the suburbs. This created other problems, as this young man reports:

It was a little bit uncomfortable because [of] having to deal with all those customs that the Hasidic Jews have and that was hard for me 'cause I simply didn't want to [laughter] deal with those rules and stuff. We always used to clean our house on Saturdays. So that means that we would have to turn on the vacuum cleaner and everything and now that there's Shabbos and everything, my mom didn't want to do the cleaning and I'm used to that. So it was uncomfortable for me.

Some of those who have moved into non-Jewish communities report conflict with neighbors. This seemed to be a particular issue in Bensonhurst, where many respondents report conflicts between Russian Jewish and Chinese newcomers and the "Americans" of Italian descent. For the most part, however, respondents seemed happy with their neighborhoods and thought that the Russian influx had been good for the communities:

R: This is Forest Hills. It's mostly Jewish. High Russian population, growing rapidly. It [is] becoming much safer and cleaner.
I: So, you think this neighborhood is getting better?
R: It's hard to say. There are a lot of Russian immigrants moving in and because they're immigrants their social culture might be a little different and you might look down on them. But they do keep within themselves. They keep bad stuff out of the neighborhood. So it's a little change but I don't think it's getting worse. It's just different.

Native white and Russian Jewish respondents frequently mentioned lack of crime as one of the virtues of their neighborhoods. When they did talk about crime at all, it was usually in reference to organized crime, and often with a wink and a smirk implying that crime happened but did not endanger them or affect their quality of life. In general, while the respondents' neighborhoods were by no means free of criminal activities, and many respondents also used drugs at some point in their teen years, this environment seems not to have generally affected their life chances. The respondents also tended to recall good local facilities, good schools, decent neighbors, and a lively and friendly street life as among things they liked about their neighborhoods.

The Chinese American second generation presents something of a paradox when it comes to its members' memories of their neighborhoods, and particularly to gangs and violence. Many Chinese respondents recalled Chinatown as crowded and dirty; and even more than the Russians, they often found growing up there embarrassingly parochial and confining. Many respondents were glad when their parents moved out. At the same time, many members of the second generation continued to base much of their social life in Chinatown, even after moving to more commodious districts. Its commercial facilities, restaurants, and recreational life not only were important for their non-English-speaking parents but also continued to play a role in the lives of many of the non-Chinese-speaking members of the second generations.

Few Chinese respondents reported that drugs and crime were major problems for their communities, and the Chinese were the least likely to report having been arrested. On the other hand, Chinese gangs were clearly present in New York during the 1980s. Like gangs in Latino and black neighborhoods, the Chinese gangs were often involved in drug dealing. They also worked as enforcers for adult criminals involved in loan sharking, gambling, extortion, and prostitution; and they frequently recruited very young people. A few of our Chinese respondents, mostly 1.5 generation immigrants, belonged to these gangs. Other Chinese respondents report having friends in them. They found in the gangs a feeling of belonging and a sanctuary when things were going badly at home, as well as opportunities to make adult money and have adult thrills while still in their mid-teens. For most respondents, involvement with gangs was a short and passing phase with few serious consequences, although at least one respondent noted that his terrified parents moved out of Chinatown specifically to get him away from the local gang. Other respondents, however, admitted committing serious crimes. Some respondents were arrested—in one case for attempted murder—and a few spent time in prison.

Yet growing up around gangs and even having periods of serious criminal activity themselves seemed to have less debilitating long term consequences for the Chinese respondents than it did for the black and Hispanic second generation groups. Some respondents report a double life—keeping their gang activities secret from schoolfriends while hiding from their gang friends the fact that they were still struggling to get good grades in prestigious magnet schools. Others went through a period of serious delinquency but managed to recover with the help of many people in the community. One young man, a former member of the Ghost Shadows, quit high school and left home after a fight with his parents. He lived for two years under an assumed name as a full time gangster. During this time he committed numerous serious crimes. Yet after a brush with the law he quit the gang, got his GED, entered college, and eventually attended a prestigious law school.

A young woman began hanging out with gang members in her early teens to get away from an unhappy family life. She ran away from home in Queens and was arrested riding in a stolen car, but she was released when the gang members she was with told police she had not been involved in the theft. She was arrested again and taken out of school in handcuffs for beating a fellow student. Yet she too was able to turn her life around. Her dismayed parents turned to an uncle, a leader in a Chinese association who in turn appealed to gang leaders not to involve her in further criminal activity. At the same time, she was herself seeing no future in the gang life: "I saw a lot of people get killed. Others, with no schooling, ended up working in fish markets." Returning to school, she managed to graduate with a B average. She went on to graduate from a City University of New York college. When we last spoke to her, she was in her early twenties, and had recently been promoted to an executive position in a major financial firm. She was considering going back to school for an MBA.

Although the preceding respondents are both extraordinary individuals, their stories illustrate a broader pattern. In high-crime African American, Puerto Rican, Dominican, and West Indian communities, youthful involvement in criminal activities often had long term consequences. While many of these young people usually "drifted out" (Matza 1964) of this sort of activity as the got older, they often felt there was nowhere for them to "drift" into. Schools rarely wanted students back after they dropped out. Communities, and even families, overwhelmed by the large number of young people in trouble, were often quick to "write them off." With criminal records and no high school degree, these young people had difficulty finding jobs. This problem was compounded for native blacks in our study because they were most likely to rely on formal mechanisms and the least likely to use family connections to find jobs. Friends and other social ties were of little use: "social capital" does little good when it "connects" us to people facing the same problems. Indeed, in high-crime neighborhoods the most successful young people we spoke to often describe themselves as having been "loners," "nerds," or "mama's boys," who had kept their distance from the street life of the neighborhood and had few friends while growing up.

By contrast, in Chinese communities, even though gang activity was fairly widespread in the 1980s and early 1990s, the total number of young people in trouble was far smaller relative to the number of adults in a position to help them. This situation, plus the overall high ratio of adults to youth, meant that Chinese families and the broader Chinese community could invest more in a relatively small number of troubled young people. Families had more options to move if that meant giving young people a chance at a new start. Educational institutions were often willing to give young people a second or third chance. Local small business owners, could, if they wished, make exceptions to normal rules and provide jobs for young people without degrees or with criminal records. Dense social connections tied struggling families to those individuals in a position to help. Even the criminal gangs themselves could at times be called on to act in the community's best interest. Thus, locally based "social capital" proved effective in helping the community's least advantaged members in a way not evident among other groups.

Public Facilities

Of course, New York's "public life" is about more than just the streets. The city features a system of large and small parks, swimming pools, playgrounds and recreational facilities, a huge network of highly utilized public libraries, and the nation's largest concentration of museums and cultural facilities, to say nothing of a seventeen-campus public university. Even "high culture" venues, such as museums and performance spaces, frequently reach out to new immigrant communities as part of their mission. The city also has the nation's largest public transportation system, which makes its facilities accessible to those without cars or too young to drive. Indeed, the freedom from dependence on automobiles—and parental chauffeurs (Lareau 2003)—is a distinct feature of a New York childhood.

Nevertheless, New York neighborhoods vary in the type of facilities and amenities that are available and in how people make use of them. Not surprisingly, the qualities of public and private services in these neighborhoods are strongly linked with the ethnic group and social class of the residents. In this sense, public facilities sometimes reinforced the supports offered by family and could even compensate to a degree for supports lacking in those families. Other times, the lack of or low quality of public institutions and facilities compounded inequalities among families.

The first local institutions a child encounters are the "quotidian neighborhood organizations" that provide child care (Small 2007). Neighborhoods vary greatly in the availability and quality of child care. Private child care is extremely expensive in the city, and although publicly subsidized child care exists, demand often outstrips supply. The child-care system is also highly fragmented and is often run through religious groups and community-based organizations, which means that some communities and ethnic groups are better served than others. There are also substantial barriers to access to affordable child care, not the least of which is knowledge of what is available, which varies greatly from community to community (Carlson and Scharf 2004; Kelly 2005). City government has been notoriously bad about informing parents on Public Assistance about the child-care options available to them (Powell 2000), for example. Here again, different groups bring different material and cultural resources to the problem of child care. For groups with low rates of fertility, the problem is obviously less pressing; groups in which multigenerational households are the norm clearly have access to strategies that others do not.

The close link between elementary schools and neighborhoods is discussed at greater length in Chapter 5. Suffice it to say that while junior high and high schools draw from broad areas of the city, most pupils attending the city's more than 600 public elementary schools and the dozens of Catholic schools arrive on foot. These schools thus tend to reflect the demography of the local population. Further, although the "savage inequalities" (Kozol 1991) between the elementary schools are at least as large as those between the high schools, a high school student can use the mass transit system to attend better high schools, an option rarely practical for elementary school students with working parents.

Of course, not all schools that serve poor communities do a bad job. But their job is clearly harder. They almost always have a higher concentration of difficult-to-teach students and fewer resources to draw on from the parents. When located in out-of-the-way or dangerous neighborhoods, these schools also have a harder time attracting and retaining quality teachers. Their staffs thus tend to be less experienced and less well trained.

Groups also vary in the degree to which they make use of New York's other public facilities, and neighborhoods differ in how well they are served by them. To some degree this is also a matter of class composition, but not entirely. Many of the city's older neighborhoods are well served, while some of the more affluent, recently built areas on the city's outer edge and the suburbs are not. One West Indian woman recalls her childhood as "boring." Her strict parents were fearful of the crime-ridden streets:

> We weren't allowed to play outside so we couldn't go outside. I think it's that typical kind of West Indian immigrant thing. You don't mix with the Americans and all that foolishness.

Luckily, her neighborhood, Crown Heights, while relatively poor, had an illustrious past and good public facilities, including the Brooklyn Museum and the main branch of the Brooklyn Public Library:

> There were some resources. I guess it would be a lot worse if I grew up in a lot of communities. Because we had the museum there. We had the library, which I made full use of because coming up we didn't watch TV and that sort of thing. So the library was a big thing.

Indeed, many of New York's Libraries, YMCAs, boys' and girls' clubs, settlement houses, and Police Athletic Leagues were facilities created by nineteenth- and early twentieth-century movements to "Americanize" earlier immigrants and improve the conditions of the working class. Others, particularly swimming pools and recreation centers, were built in the 1930s by the Works Progress Administration. Thus, many public facilities are located in poor and working class neighborhoods. By the time today's second generation immigrants were growing up, such facilities were often looking much the worse for wear. Yet they remain a potential resource.

Who is able to take advantage of these public events and facilities? Almost every group uses the parks, and group members remember them as being important in their lives when they were growing up, often mentioning the parks as one of the good points of their neighborhoods. Parks seen as dangerous because of crime and gang activity, almost always constituted a major complaint among respondents. There was more local variation in the use of other youth-oriented facilities, such as athletic venues. This variation, however, did not map predictably onto divisions of ethnicity and class. African Americans often lived in areas well served by recreation centers and swimming pools, as did public housing residents. Public libraries were also widely used by poorer respondents as a place to do homework and as a safe place to socialize. Once again, residents of some of the more crowded inner city neighborhoods were most likely to have a library within walking distance.

Group and class differences in the use of public facilities grow, however, when one looks at "high culture" institutions like museums. Not surprisingly, these were most often used by the relatively well-educated native whites and Russian Jews, although some African American and West Indians used them as well. Despite the Chinese respondents' high levels of educational attainment, their use of museums and libraries was surprisingly low, probably because Chinese parents faced language barriers and worked long hours. Social class and parental education partially explain these differences, but not entirely. Use of museums and libraries while growing up is positively associated with high educational outcomes and probably high parental expectations. Of course, children rarely trot off to a museum on their own, so this positive effect is in part a proxy for parental education. Yet even controlling for parental education, the relationship remains significant, leading us to suspect it is also a proxy for something harder to measure but perhaps more important—high educational *expectations* on the part of parents.

Conclusion

The early family and neighborhood experiences of our respondents set a pattern of advantages and disadvantages that accumulated into young adulthood and beyond. Native born African Americans and Puerto Ricans were much more likely than members of other groups to grow up without a father or father figure. Despite the fact that many of the parents of our respondents immigrated from countries with high fertility rates, our native black respondents also reported growing up with the most siblings, further lowering the ratio of adults to children in those households.

All the second generation groups were more likely than native groups to grow up with two parents, with the Chinese and Russians exceptionally so. Beyond the nuclear family, the second generation also has an advantage in households that contained "extra adults"—most often extended family members. Once again, more than other groups, the Chinese and Russians benefitted from the presence of other adults in the household. These extra adults could provide help to the family through assistance with child care or through extra income if they were wage earners. South Americans and West Indians were also advantaged on this measure, whereas Puerto Ricans, Dominicans, and native born whites and blacks were less likely to have these supports. These patterns are in part the result of cultural differences between Americans, both black and white, and Puerto Ricans, on the one hand, and the second generation, on the other. Americans do not generally live in extended family households, whereas doing so is an acceptable and even preferable option for the second generation groups.

Native born blacks, Puerto Ricans, and Dominicans, who had less extended family support and higher levels of single-headed households, also were concentrated in poorer neighborhoods, with greater social problems. Dominicans were definitely the worst off of the second generation groups, with poverty levels in their neighborhoods very close to that of native born blacks and Puerto Ricans. Interestingly, the Dominicans report equally high levels of problems with drugs as do Puerto Ricans, but they complain less about crime and youth who disrespect authority than do native born blacks and Puerto Ricans, suggesting that the immigrant community helps to buffer at least some of the effects of crime and concentrated poverty (see Sampson, Morenoff, and Raudenbush 2005).

Family and neighborhood combine to stack the deck against native born blacks and Puerto Ricans, and to a lesser extent against Dominicans. Russians, Chinese, and South Americans have an advantage in terms of family structure and neighborhood. West Indians are better off than African Americans, Dominicans, and Puerto Ricans in terms of their family structure and the quality of the neighborhoods they live in. These early advantages and disadvantages broadly coordinate with the respondents' later socioeconomic trajectories. This correlation becomes evident as the second generation goes to high school and college, a topic taken up in the next chapter.

5

The School System as Sorting Mechanism

I: What does it take to be successful?
R: School. College. Because with a high school diploma, you can
get a job, but you can't get what you want and it's a battle out
there. In order to compete you have to have the material.

WEST INDIAN WOMAN, AGE 25

Educational attainment increasingly determines the opportunities open to young people. Although a few young people in metropolitan New York manage to find skilled blue collar jobs, often through family connections, most need a college degree to qualify for a position that offers a decent wage, benefits, and the possibility of advancement. One recent survey found that more than half the region's businesses required more than a high school diploma for entry level positions. Higher levels of education also lead to greater earnings. According to the 2000 Census, regional workers with only a high school education had median annual earnings of only $14,000 in 1999, the year we began interviewing. Those with some college earned $10,700 more, but those with a BA earned $45,000. In short, getting a college degree is the most direct route to achieving a middle class standard of living.

Our second generation and native born respondents faced a complex and differentiated system of primary and secondary schools and colleges. The 2000 Census indicates that just over a million students aged 6 through 18 enrolled in New York City public schools at the time of our study. They attended 1,350 schools staffed by 90,000 teachers. (The number of schools has grown since 2000, when the New York City Department of Education created charter schools and broke up many large, old high schools into smaller programs housed within the same buildings.) Another 245,000 New York City students enrolled in private primary and secondary schools. The Archdiocese of New York, which covers Manhattan and the Bronx as well as Westchester, operates 182 schools, 116 in low-income areas; the Brooklyn Archdiocese, which covers Brooklyn, Queens, and Staten Island, has a similar number. Many families are attracted to these parochial schools because of the schools' better educational quality and discipline, not because of their own religious affiliation. Many parochial school teachers do not belong to a religious order, and about a quarter of the attending students are not Catholic. In the ten county region outside the city that served as our sampling area, 590,000 more young people are enrolled in public schools and 101,000 in private schools.

Inevitably, these schools vary greatly in how well they prepare their students for the next level in the educational system. Since most of our second generation respondents grew up in New York City, we must consider its 872 elementary and middle schools. Unless parents can pay for private education—and even Catholic schools, generally less expensive than other private schools, cost about $5,000 a year—or "game the system" to get their children into better schools, their children attend neighborhood elementary and middle schools. Like the city's high schools, the neighborhood schools have highly varied track records. In some, many pupils do not learn enough to perform at grade level when they reach high school. Primary school performance is closely associated with the socioeconomic characteristics of the neighborhoods the primary schools serve. In 2001, the share of elementary and middle school students performing at grade level in New York City ranged from only 26 percent in the South Bronx to 76 percent in the Bayside–Little Neck area of Queens (Mei, Bell-Ellwanger, and Miller 2002).

After attending elementary and middle school, students in New York City or the inner city areas of Newark or Paterson must find a high school. Students in New York City may take the specialized high school test to enter one of nine selective high schools, some of which are harder to get into than Ivy League universities. (Some 26,000 students take this test, most seeking one of the 2,300 freshman class seats at Bronx Science, Brooklyn Tech, and Stuyvesant high schools.) The programs at these schools attract high achievers with well-informed parents, and virtually all graduates of these high schools go to college, many to the nation's best institutions. Few students who attend weak primary schools or whose parents are not attuned to getting them into these schools receive the preparation that helps many test-takers to score high enough to gain entry.

Instead, most middle school pupils go to local zoned high schools. In the majority of such high schools, less than half the freshman class graduates in four years and few of the schools offer Advanced Placement classes. In 2000 two-thirds of New York City's 650 high schools retained less than half the freshman class in their senior years, compared to only 8 percent of all high schools across the nation (Balfanz and Letgers 2004). Many students are behind or "age over grade" even before they enter high school. Only 20 percent of the entering classes in these weak high schools met grade standards in English and math. Although these students need high quality instruction, their schools often have the least qualified and least experienced teachers, since teachers gravitate toward better schools as they gain seniority.

Compounding the poor performance of many of the schools attended by numerous respondents are the low levels of parental education. Almost half the Dominican parents had not completed high school, as was true of more than a third of Chinese and Puerto Rican parents. (At CUNY, for example, the overwhelming majority of students are the first in their families ever to have gone to college.) These parents could not give their children much guidance about negotiating the school system. As Joel Perlmann (2005) has pointed out, children in this situation are trying to climb a ladder of intergenerational educational mobility that is missing its middle rungs.

One way out of this quandary is to resort to private schools, usually religious schools. A great many parents choose this option for at least some portion of their children's education. At any given time, about one-fifth of the city's school-aged population is enrolled in private institutions. Overall, about 11 percent of our respondents graduated from a parochial high school, and about 3 percent from a nonsectarian private high school, while 27 percent spent at least one year at a parochial high school. Almost half of native white respondents spent some part of their educational careers in private or parochial schools. So did a third of the South Americans and Dominicans, a quarter of the West Indians and native blacks, and even one in five of the Chinese respondents. (The Russian Jews often attended yeshivas for part or all of their educations.) Even when they were able to send their children to parochial schools in the early grades, however, many parents often could not afford the more expensive parochial high schools, especially when they had several children to educate.

Once through this maze of elementary schools, our respondents and their parents faced an equally wide and bewildering range of college options. In fall 2001, 126,000 young adults (mostly from New York City) attended one of the seventeen community colleges, BA-granting "senior colleges," and graduate programs of the City University of New York (CUNY). Many of the region's high school graduates also attend the State University of New York, which has university campuses at Albany, Binghamton, Buffalo, and Stony Brook and college campuses at Purchase, Old Westbury, and other locations in the metropolitan area, or they attend the Rutgers campuses across the river in New Brunswick and Newark. In the 2000 Census, about 60 percent of the region's college-goers attended a public institution. The region also has a huge range of private colleges and universities, from Ivy League institutions like Columbia, Yale, Princeton, and the University of Pennsylvania and first-rank universities like New York University (NYU) and Fordham, to nonselective institutions like Pace, Adelphi, and Long Island University. Finally, the 2000 Census suggests that several hundred thousand young people born in New York or New Jersey attend college or graduate school in other parts of the country.

Like the grade schools and high schools to which our respondents had access, these colleges vary hugely in terms of their cost, selectivity, competitiveness, course offerings, other resources, and value of their degrees in the labor market. In 2000, their tuition and fees ranged from $4,000 at CUNY to more than $25,000 at Columbia. Most Columbia and NYU undergraduates attend full time over four years, while many CUNY students attend part time over a much longer period (Attewell and Lavin 2007). Individuals who attend elite institutions clearly reap greater benefits in terms of income, occupation, and social status than those attending less selective schools.

Overall Patterns

To get a fair picture of how our respondents have navigated the educational system, we look first at those who grew up in the metropolitan area and are at least 24 years old. (The high levels of education among whites, and to a lesser extent blacks, who migrated from other parts of the country would set an artificially high target for comparison if we included them; by age 24, everyone has completed a high school experience and often college.) Four-fifths of these respondents grew up and received their high school education within New York City; the other one-fifth grew up in the surrounding metropolitan area, mostly central cities like Newark or Paterson. Figure 5.1 gives the rates at which each group, graduated from high school and college.

This figure reveals several key patterns. First, *all* the second generation groups fared better than native born minority young people in high school and college graduation rates. In each case, the second generation group did at least somewhat better than the comparable native born group—Dominicans slightly better than Puerto Ricans, South Americans substantially better than Puerto Ricans, West Indians better than African Americans, and so on. More members of every second generation group earned high school diplomas and college degrees than their Puerto Rican and African American counterparts. Even more strikingly, two second generation groups—Chinese and Russians—substantially outpaced native born whites in college graduation rates. In other words, these second generation groups did not only far better than native minorities but also noticeably better than native whites who grew up in and around New York. Finally, except for high school and college graduation among native whites and high school graduation among Puerto Ricans, the young women of each group are getting more education than their young male

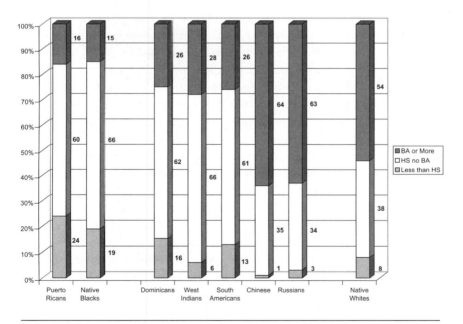

Figure 5.1. Educational Attainment (%) (age 24–32 grew up in New York metro area). *Source:* ISGMNY.

counterparts, despite the challenges in some instances of becoming a parent.

Dominicans were experiencing the most difficulty of the second generation groups, especially Dominican men. Their parents had the least education of any group, and the rate at which they failed to complete high school—16 percent overall, more than 20 percent for the men—was higher than for any other second generation group. At the same time, these outcomes were better than those of the two native minority groups. Despite having parents with somewhat more education than the parents of Dominican respondents, Puerto Ricans were having the hardest time making progress through the educational system. Ten percent more Dominicans got a college degree than did Puerto Ricans.

Native blacks were also well behind the other groups. Though their high school graduation rates were a bit higher than those of the Puerto Ricans, their college graduation rates were the lowest of any group. Only 15 percent of native blacks had completed a BA by age 24, compared to two-thirds of the Russians and Chinese, half the native whites, and a quarter of the West Indians, South Americans, and Dominicans. The noticeably lower college completion rates among Puerto Ricans and African Americans compared to all the other groups, including Dominicans, the most challenged of the second generation groups, represents a major dividing line in terms of access to future opportunities.

Gender also plays an important role. Except for Puerto Ricans and native whites, where men had a slight advantage, and Chinese, where the rates were almost the same, the women were more likely to have earned a high school diploma. Once again with the exception of native whites, where men held a slight edge, and native blacks, where both sexes performed about the same, women respondents were more likely to have earned a college degree. The biggest gaps were among the Chinese and Russians; three-quarters of the women held college degrees compared to just over half the men. The differentials among the other groups were far more modest. Still, it is clear that the opportunities to and barriers against educational attainment differ for the two sexes.

The ethnic segmentation into different educational trajectories first becomes deeply apparent in the high school years. Figure 5.2 shows that three-quarters of the Puerto Ricans and native blacks growing up in the region went to nonmagnet public high schools in New York City, as did most Dominicans and West Indians. That share begins to drop for the South Americans (many of whom went to public high schools in the surrounding area) and falls even lower for the Chinese and Russian respondents. Offering a sharp contrast, fewer than one-third of the native whites growing up in the region went to zoned New York City high schools, mainly because the native whites were schooled in the suburbs but also because they had the most other options.

Some of our respondents found routes out of the zoned high schools. The Chinese were most likely to find the best options within the public system—in an amazing feat, one in five attended a magnet high school in New York City. (About 8 percent of the Russians also attended these schools.) Of the other groups, West Indians were most likely to go to such schools, but only 4.4 percent did so. Roughly one in ten South Americans and Dominicans went to Catholic schools and almost one in six Russians went to a yeshiva. Many native whites also attended Catholic high schools, as did one in ten Puerto Rican respondents. Native whites were the only group to make more than negligible use of private nonsectarian schools.

Finally, we also looked at the performance rankings of the public high schools attended by our respondents in New York City. (This ranking was based on analysis of the "report cards" on New York City high schools from 1994 through 1996 concerning a wide range of indicators on test

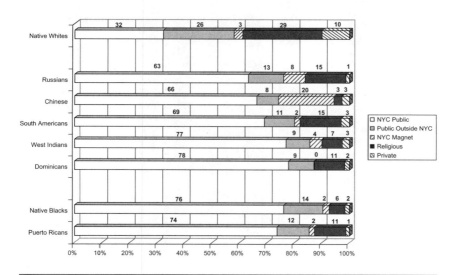

Figure 5.2. Type of High School Attended (%) (grew up in New York metro area). *Source:* ISGMNY.

scores, graduation rates, and so forth. These indicators were factor analyzed and then scaled into an overall performance measure, which was broken down into quintiles. See the Methodological Appendix for details.) Echoing the larger pattern, Figure 5.3 shows that more than a third of the Puerto Rican, native black, Dominican, and West Indian students attended high schools in the lowest quintile, compared to less than one-tenth of the Chinese, Russian Jews, or native whites; but a quarter or more of the latter groups went to high schools in the top quintile, compared to roughly one-tenth or fewer of the Puerto Ricans, native blacks, Dominicans, or West Indians. (The South Americans were more evenly distributed across the spectrum.)

This ethnic stratification continued into college. Among those respondents aged 24 and older who grew up in the metropolitan area and ever attended college, the groups attended starkly different institutions. As Figure 5.4 shows, few native whites, Russians, or Chinese went to a community college (roughly one in six), but a third or more of the Puerto Ricans, native blacks, Dominicans, West Indians, and South Americans did so. Scholars have debated whether community colleges create greater access to higher education or merely divert students onto dead end voca-

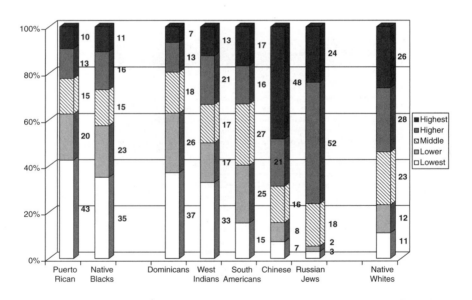

Figure 5.3. Performance Quintile of New York City Public High Schools Attended (%) (attended New York City high school). *Source:* ISGMNY.

tional tracks (Brint and Karabel 1989; Dougherty 1992: Rouse 1995). Among our respondents, few who went to community colleges went on to get a BA degree; and many of those who left college without a degree had attended a community college, mainly at CUNY. On the other hand, our data confirm Attewell and Lavin's (2007) conclusion that there are substantial benefits to attending community college even for those who do not graduate.

At the baccalaureate level, only a few black or Hispanic respondents (roughly 5 percent) attended a top-ranked public or private college or university (ranked Tier I by *U.S. News & World Report*), but three to four times that many Russians, Chinese, and native whites did so. Many in these groups also went to middle-rank colleges and universities (ranked Tier II), especially the public ones, while the black and Hispanic respondents (native and second generation alike) were concentrated in the lower-ranked BA-granting institutions, including many in private institutions (ranked Tier III and IV). Whereas a top-performing Chinese or Russian respondent went to Columbia, Massachusetts Institute of Technology (MIT), or NYU, the top performers among the West Indians or Dominicans went to one of the better CUNY or SUNY colleges like Hunter College or SUNY Stony Brook.

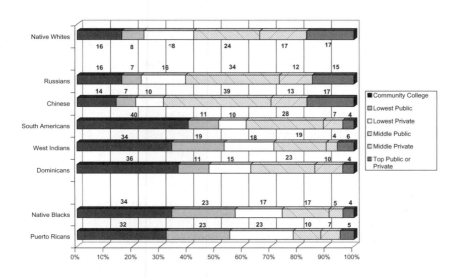

Figure 5.4. Type and Ranking of College Attended (%) (attended any college). *Source:* ISGMNY.

Explaining Second Generation Educational Attainment

That many second generation respondents are achieving more and better educations than their native minority counterparts—and, indeed, sometimes relative to native whites—is consistent with findings from many other studies on this issue (Kao and Tienda 1995; Fuligni 1997; Hao and Bonstead-Bruns 1998; Feliciano 2001; Hirschman 2001; Portes and Rumbaut 2001; Suárez-Orozco and Suárez-Orozco 2001; Kao 2004; Portes and Hao 2004; Feliciano and Rumbaut 2005; Pong, Hao, and Gardner 2005). A variety of theories have been offered about this pattern.

The segmented assimilation hypothesis suggests a basic attitudinal and behavioral choice toward education for second generation children and their parents. Portes and his associates argue that those who maintain ties to their immigrant parents' ethnic communities (selective acculturation) will have better outcomes than those who assimilate more quickly than their parents into American ways (dissonant acculturation). This is especially true for those who attend school with native born American minorities, who, Portes argues, have an "adversarial stance" toward education. In this view, maintaining strong ethnic contacts helps second generation young people to keep a positive attitude toward education. Maintaining parents' language is a key to this end. Min Zhou has stressed how the dense social networks of the Chinese ethnic enclave foster educational attainment through language and cram schools (Zhou 1997a; Zhou and Xiong 2005), while the Chinese media inform parents about navigating the local education system (Zhou and Guoxuan 2002). This view predicts that West Indians, Dominicans, and perhaps even South Americans would be at greatest risk, but that those who maintained their ethnic distinctiveness and distanced themselves most from their native born counterparts would do the best. By remaining inside ethnic networks, Chinese and Russians would avoid dissonant acculturation.

Kao and Tienda (1995) and Kao (2004) argue alternatively that "immigrant optimism" helps to explain the better performance of the second generation. They argue that immigrant parents have higher expectations for their children than do native born parents. Kao (2004) finds that immigrant parents are more likely than comparable native born parents to talk about college with their children. Fuligni (1997) adds that positive attitudes among the students themselves, reinforced by peer support, were also important. He stresses that the children of immigrants are motivated by obligations toward parents who have made sacrifices to help them succeed in school (Fuligni 2006).

Peer relations and school based programs are also important. They can support or impede attainment, and they can provide immigrant students with the practical and emotional supports that middle class native born students get from their families (Gibson et al. 2004). Positive relationships with teachers and other school personnel can have a positive influence on the academic orientation of the children of immigrants Suárez-Orozco, Suárez-Orozco, and Todorova (2007). Higher levels of parent-child interaction increase parents' and children's educational expectations and achievement (Hao and Bonstead-Bruns 1998).

We examined many of these factors to see how they have shaped the educational pathways of our native and second generation respondents. We drew on the in-depth interviews and survey data to explore how parents and children had different expectations about education and how the available bundles of resources helped them achieve their goals. Unlike many other studies, which focus mainly on immigrant group characteristics, we also examined the effect of institutions, particularly how different types of schools sort children of various backgrounds into different educational tracks.

Researchers have highlighted how residential segregation clusters native born minorities into underresourced and poorly performing schools (Neckerman 2007). Few researchers have asked where the children of immigrants may fit into the educational sorting system and how their families react to the options facing them (Ellen et al. 2002; Louie 2004). This is partly because national surveys rarely capture the local institutional opportunity structure, which is best understood through a combination of survey and in-depth interviews. We believe that the literature on educational attainment among the children of immigrants and native born minorities has not placed enough emphasis on the differences in group resources that immigrant families can deploy as they negotiate the educational sorting system.

Explaining Group Differences

Why do some groups among our respondents have better overall educational outcomes than others, and why do the outcomes differ systematically across groups? If we simply measure the statistical association between belonging to each group of respondents and an individual's educational attainment measured along a five-point scale—no high school diploma and not attending high school, high school diploma or attending high school, AA degree or attending community college, BA degree or attending college, and graduate degree or attending graduate school—the Chinese and Russians have statistically significantly better educational outcomes than native whites, the excluded reference group; the other groups are doing worse; and Puerto Ricans and native blacks lag furthest behind (first column in Table 5.1). What might lie behind these statistical patterns?

Table 5.1. Correlates of Educational Attainment
(Age 24–32, grew up in metropolitan New York)

Variable	Beta	Beta	Beta
(Constant)	3.49**	1.77**	1.16**
Puerto Rican	−.300**	−.141**	−.095**
Black	−.333**	−.190**	−.106**
Dominican	−.110**	−.003	.011
West Indian	−.096**	−.013	.011
CEP	−.093**	−.028	−.032
Chinese	.042	.092**	.066**
Russian	.040	.017	.032
Parents' Education		.307**	.269**
Age		.073*	.107**
Female		.072**	.088**
Grew Up with Both Parents		.061**	.019
Siblings Grew Up With		−.097**	−.054**
Times Moved 6–18		−.125**	−.094**
Has Had a Child			−.307**
Ever Arrested			−.077**
High School Average Hours of Homework			.039
Went to Parochial HS 1+ year			.051*
Used Museums & Libraries Growing Up			.070**
Adjusted R²	.105	.240	.335

*sig < .05. **sig < .01

Dependent variable is educational status: 1 = no HS diploma, 2 = HS diploma or in high school, 3 = associate's degree or enrolled in community college, 4 = BA degree or enrolled in college, 5 = postgraduate degree or enrolled in graduate school. Respondents are weighted to represent their group's share of the sample universe. Parents' education measured by highest level attained by either parent on a five-point scale.

We used multivariate analysis to explore two additional sets of explanatory variables that may be relevant. The first set includes basic demographic characteristics of the respondent and his or her family: parents' education, the respondent's age and sex, family background growing up, and the number of times the family moved. The second set involves choices made by respondents, such as having a child, being arrested, how hard they studied, and some educational choices they may have made under parental influence, such as how often they used libraries and museums growing up and whether they went to high school outside the public system. We consider these factors in three steps: first, just group membership; then, adding family background; and finally, adding life choices.

The coefficients for the additional factors shown in the middle column of Table 5.1 clearly indicate that parental education is indeed the single strongest factor explaining educational attainment among our respondents, as many other social scientists have previously found. This factor is four times stronger than any other family background characteristic. It is hardly surprising that native whites and Russians, whose parents have the most education and who experience the least racial discrimination, also have the highest rates of college graduation. Similarly, since more West Indian and South American parents than native born blacks, Puerto Ricans, and Dominican parents have college educations, the position of their children relative to the excluded group, native whites, also stands to reason.

It is noteworthy that after controlling for basic individual and family background characteristics, the second generation groups are all statistically indistinct from native whites except for Chinese, who are performing significantly *better* than native whites. In other words, accounting for these background factors substantially closes the statistical gap of each group with whites. Moreover, controlling for these factors significantly improves the strength of Chinese educational attainment relative to that of whites. Overall, taking basic family characteristics into account also doubles the explanatory power of the model.

Even though many Chinese parents did not complete high school, hardly any Chinese respondents dropped out of high school, and most had completed a BA by age 24. Similarly, though almost a quarter of the Puerto Rican respondents nonetheless had at least one college-educated parent, by age 24 or older only 16 percent of the Puerto Rican respondents had managed to complete college. Indeed, almost one in five

Puerto Ricans that age with at least one college-educated parent had become a high school dropout. Native born blacks followed a similar, if less pronounced, pattern. Two-fifths of the African American respondents had at least one college-educated parent, but only 14.5 percent of the respondents aged 24 and older had gotten a BA.

Taken together, all the other background factors added in this set have a larger impact on educational outcomes than does parental education. The most negative of these additional factors is the number of times that respondents moved during their school-going years. While many reasons may contribute to frequent moves—low family incomes, difficulty paying rent, family instability, or negative neighborhood conditions—the impact is clear. Shifting from school to school disrupts the continuity of the educational experience. The next most important factor is the number of one's siblings growing up. More siblings mean that parents had to spread scarce resources farther and perhaps give each individual child less attention. Our respondents growing up in a one-child family were better off than those respondents with many brothers and sisters. On the positive side, growing up with both parents, being female, and, obviously, being older enabled respondents to get more education.

Our finding that women tend to get more education than men agrees with the findings of other researchers (Jacobs 1996; Portes and Rumbaut 2001; Feliciano and Rumbaut 2005). When we analyze men and women separately, however, the factors have different relative weights. For example, parents' educational attainment is more important for men than women, and so is growing up with two parents, probably because an absent father has a more negative effect on sons than daughters. Having more siblings has a more negative effect on women, perhaps because women play a greater role in helping to raise their brothers and sisters.

This "standard model" does a better job of explaining native born white outcomes than for other groups. When the model is run separately for that group (not shown), parents' education accounts for more than a third of the variance for whites, but less than 10 percent for native blacks and Puerto Ricans; the second generation immigrants are in between. Among the factors that might account for this is that black and Puerto Rican parents tend to have gone to college later in life, probably attended less prestigious institutions, and thus experienced fewer returns to their education than native white parents enjoyed. The second generation parents varied considerably in the timing and quality of their educations.

Many Taiwanese parents had graduated from elite schools in Taiwan, whereas West Indian parents often earned degrees as mature students after arriving in the United States.

Interestingly, in these separate models (not shown), growing up in a single parent household also seems to have had a less negative impact on the children of immigrants than on native born minorities. In fact, growing up in a single parent household is a significantly negative factor for native born blacks and Puerto Ricans, and to a lesser extent for Chinese, but not for Dominicans or West Indians, many of whom also grew up with only one parent. Quite likely, the presence of other relatives in extended immigrant families who could provide emotional and financial support for the children made a difference. Our West Indian respondents also told us that grandparents and other relatives played an important role in their lives.

As yet unobserved factors may be accounting for the persistence of significant differences for the native minorities and Chinese. The final column in Table 5.1 takes a further set of factors into consideration: decisions undertaken by the respondents, sometimes under the influence of their parents. On the negative side, these decisions include having had a child or getting arrested. On the positive side, doing homework, utilizing public libraries and museums, and going to a parochial school all foster educational attainment. Predictably, having a child has a strongly negative impact on educational attainment. Indeed, among all the factors taken into account, having a child has the strongest and most negative impact. This, too, comports with a wide range of previous studies. These factors greatly strengthen the overall explanatory power of the model and reduce the size of the coefficients for native blacks, Puerto Ricans, and Chinese, though the coefficients remain significant.

Parental Expectations

All parents urge their children to do well in school, but they have different ideas about how much schooling their children should get, what occupations they find acceptable or desirable for their children, and how important education is for entering these occupations. These expectations are rooted not only in the parents' own educational and work experiences but also in examples drawn from the extended family or other community members. In particular, working class families were better able to take advantage of opportunities when their community included middle class and professional role models, as is the case for our Chinese respondents. For highly transnational groups like the Dominicans, education levels in the home country can also be significant, as young people compare themselves to peers there (Louie 2004).

Parental expectations operate from an early age. Parents who saw college as an optional extra were less inclined to push their children to study and less concerned that they go to a high quality high school than were parents who saw high school as a critical stepping stone to college. In a context where educational stratification starts in the early grades and is hard to reverse after students enter high school, this difference had significant consequences. The highly educated Russian and Taiwanese parents pushed their children firmly toward college educations. All the acceptable occupations for their children required college, and the children knew they would be seen to have let down the family if they did not go to college.

Whites from well-educated families sometimes saw education as a means of personal fulfillment. One white respondent, who grew up in an upper middle class Maryland suburb, said that her father encouraged her "pure intention" to learn and never tried to steer her toward practical courses. Now a schoolteacher, she finds her students' instrumental attitude about education upsetting:

> In my opinion, it takes . . . knowing yourself and knowing what you're interested in. Spending time with something that you love, more than just thinking in terms of money. So many of the kids I teach here are under such pressure to follow a particular field that's lucrative, at the risk of something that they really like."

Most white families were financially secure enough that their children did not feel they would end up in a dead end job if they did not get a good education. Indeed, some Irish and Italian American male respondents had family connections to jobs that would give them a decent living without a college degree. One said his working class parents did not insist that he go to college:

> Growing up as a teenager, being interested in girls and money, you tend to veer away. Not that it's any of their fault, but my parents didn't ride me. I'm not saying they should have, but it was a different household as opposed to maybe two lawyers or two doctors who keep riding their children.

The more frequent response among the native whites, however, was to note that getting a good education at a prestigious institution was the best way to make a good life for themselves.

Those respondents who grew up with immigrant and native born minority parents had less option to think about education in terms of personal fulfillment. Almost all these respondents thought that education was the only route out of poverty. As one college-educated Dominican woman who had gone to public schools said:

> Basically, they said that's the only way out for us. We don't have any money to inherit. We don't have a guaranteed job when we graduate.

A Russian woman said, "It was just assumed. It wasn't told. That was the presumption." Indeed, Russian respondents found it amusing to be asked whether they were expected to go to college.

At the same time, many working class parents could not offer their children much advice about what educational path to follow in order to become a professional. According to a 29-year-old South American woman:

> R: See they're not those type of parents that they sit down with you.
> I: Did they tell you how far they wanted you to go in school?
> R: They wanted me to graduate from high school. And then from there I don't know.

Many working class Chinese parents had little education, but they were nonetheless confident that their children could realize the high educational expectations they had for them. Chinese respondents talked about feeling strong pressure to excel in school from their extended families as well as their parents. They often mentioned how their parents would compare them—usually unfavorably—with the children of relatives and friends who were doing well. One respondent recalled how his father urged him to avoid his fate as a restaurant worker:

> R: And he came in and I was in bed and I was about to go to sleep and he goes, "Look, my life is hard." I said, "Yeah, I kind of realized that." He said, "I don't want you to grow up like me." So it was his story of shape up in school, do well and be like your uncle . . . "Be like your uncle who is an engineer. He's a professional. He makes good money. He's well respected in society." And that's when it hit me. I was, "Wow, okay." And that's why I majored in engineering in college.

Although we have no direct survey evidence of parental expectations about education, our respondents from the immigrant and minority groups frequently reported that their parents stressed that they would have to work harder than other groups to get ahead. The importance of using museums and libraries in the multivariate analysis is another indirect indicator of how parental expectations could shape children's educational trajectories.

Finding Neighborhoods with Good Elementary and Secondary Schools

Expectations aside, families still positioned their children at the educational starting gate by choosing a neighborhood in which to live. Their ability to choose a neighborhood with good schools reflected family resources, the class differentiation of the group, and the degree of residential segregation. Even families with high expectations, adequate information, and the resources needed to live in a neighborhood with well-performing elementary schools still face hard choices in navigating the New York City school system. Middle class, native born parents agonize over whether to buy a more expensive house in a better public school district or pay for private education. Immigrant families typically have less information about the school system and fewer options about where to live.

Residential segregation not only channels some groups into lower-quality schools but also hinders families from moving to neighborhoods with better schools. The families are less likely to purchase homes; and when they do, these homes are less likely to provide the real estate asset growth that might help them pay for private education for their children. As Dalton Conley (2001) has shown, parents draw on this asset to finance their children's undergraduate educations, which affects what kinds of colleges they can attend. The availability of formal and informal credit mechanisms enables some immigrant communities to get a foothold in the housing market; continuing discrimination from formal lenders can hamper native born minorities from following the same path.

As Chapter 4 showed, most white parents lived in decent neighborhoods that provided their children with access to good primary schools. Although not always highly educated, most native white parents had well-paid jobs that enabled them to buy homes at the lower prices that prevailed in and around New York before the early 1980s. Some native white families sold their homes in the city and left for the suburbs during the severe recession of the mid-1970s, but those who stayed predominantly raised their children in Queens and Brooklyn neighborhoods with adequate if not always stellar public schools. As property values appreciated in these neighborhoods, home ownership provided options for moving to areas with better schools, paying for private or Catholic school, or going to college.

Native black families were often stuck in segregated neighborhoods (Massey and Denton 1993). A combination of low incomes and mortgage lending discrimination meant that fewer blacks than whites could buy homes and their property values did not appreciate as fast (Yinger 1997). Arriving in the 1950s and 1960s, Puerto Ricans mostly settled close to black neighborhoods with high poverty rates as well as in rapidly dwindling working class Italian neighborhoods. They often remained in poor neighborhoods even when their socioeconomic status improved (Massey and Bitterman 1985; Rosenbaum 1994). Many of our native black and Puerto Rican respondents grew up in public housing, which the native white or immigrant families rarely did. Although this provided cheap accommodation in an expensive city, it also trapped people in areas with poor schools and prevented them from building home equity.

Of the second generation groups, Dominicans, who settled closest to Puerto Ricans and native blacks, lived in the worst school districts and had the most limited mobility. This reflects not only their comparatively low incomes but also the fact that many Dominican families chose to buy homes in the Dominican Republic rather than in New York City. Even higher-income Dominicans showed lower rates of home ownership. As these families paid larger shares of their income as remittances, the quality of public schools in the neighborhoods they could afford declined.

South Americans and West Indians settled in neighborhoods with more varied local schools. Some South American respondents grew up in predominantly Puerto Rican neighborhoods like Williamsburg in Brooklyn, or in black neighborhoods in northern Manhattan, but most lived in neighborhoods like Sunset Park in Brooklyn or the Elmhurst–Jackson Heights area of Queens—declining white ethnic or Jewish areas with middle-range public schools. West Indian families settled close to but not within native black neighborhoods in Brooklyn and Queens, or they moved out into white neighborhoods like Canarsie, where they subsequently became the majority. Some areas had quite good public schools or magnet schools offering special programs. Since many West Indians in our study owned homes, they also gained a financial asset. Perhaps because they were more likely to be subject to discrimination in the housing market, West Indian families did not talk about choosing a neighborhood primarily to get better schools.

The Chinese and Russians were able to seek out neighborhoods with comparatively good public schools. Taiwanese families moved directly to affluent semi-suburban neighborhoods like Bayside and Whitestone in Queens, while working class Chinese families mostly settled in white or mixed ethnic neighborhoods with decent public schools. Respondents whose families remained in Manhattan's Chinatown were the most likely to attend weak schools, but many individuals talked about how their families moved to the emerging Chinese neighborhoods in Brooklyn and Queens to get more affordable housing and better schools. Chinese families appeared to face little or no discrimination when they chose to move, and even low income families seem to have been pooling funds to buy houses and get mortgages from Chinese banks on more flexible terms than mainstream lenders would offer.

Finding Good Schools outside the Neighborhood

Families faced with bad neighborhood schools employed a range of tactics to avoid them: transferring their children or testing them into better schools outside the neighborhood, paying for Catholic school, or even sending their children back to the home country to study. Working class Chinese actively negotiated their options within the public system. One Chinese American respondent who attended a top magnet high school and a selective college explained that her parents had sent her to a Catholic school while they lived in Elmhurst, a dense zone of new immigrants. After they had saved enough money to move to the middle class Whitestone neighborhood, she shifted to a public school:

> It was excellent. It was a really good school. We got the best reading scores and it was one of those schools where you had small classes. The teachers would have a cow if there were more than twenty-five students. So it prepared me pretty well to go to a specialized high school. If I had stayed in Elmhurst I don't think I would have done as well.

Family, co-workers, and the Chinese media provide information about the magnet schools. Nearly all Chinese respondents said their parents encouraged them to take the entrance test for these schools, even if they spoke little English and had a limited education.

The Dominicans and South Americans had more limited information. Parents were often not aware of the specialized high schools or did not realize that the quality of early schooling might make a big difference for their children's future. Fewer than half of Dominicans told us they knew about the selective high schools, few took the entrance test, and only one respondent attended such a school. Dominicans did not always encourage their children to attend even when they did pass the test. One young woman said she did not want to travel to a distant school every day and liked the legal studies program at a local school. She later found that this high school had not prepared her well for college.

> R: My parents left it totally up to me . . . I filled out the applications, I went to sign up for the test, I took classes studying for the test, I took the test.
> I: Did they know that Stuyvesant is a top school?
> R: Not really. They just know it is a specialized school.
> I: Do you think they would want you to go there?
> R: Oh yeah, now, with my little brother, they are pushing him to go to Stuyvesant.
> R: They know about it.
> J: Exactly 'cause I'm the oldest and the first. This is the first time they are dealing with the public school system.

As noted, many parents send their children to Catholic schools to avoid the bad elementary and high schools. Over half the native born whites attended private or Catholic schools at some point, and more than a third graduated from these schools. Yeshivas served a similar role for Russians. The other groups were much less likely to go outside the public system— about a third of South Americans and Dominicans attended Catholic school at some point, as did slightly smaller percentages of Puerto Ricans, native blacks, and West Indians. Far fewer graduated from those schools, however, with native blacks being the most likely to have attended but not graduated.

This is an expensive option for high school. Although not a single white respondent talked about having to leave Catholic school for financial reasons, many native minority and immigrant respondents said their families could not afford to put them all the way through high school. Dominican respondents talked about how their parents made sacrifices so they could attend Catholic school, often working long hours or multiple jobs. But many had to leave before the end of high school. This may explain why attending Catholic school had a less beneficial effect on Dominicans' educational attainment than it did for other groups. Catholic high schools also vary considerably: some have entrance tests and expel students who do not maintain good grades; others are less academically oriented (Louie and Holdaway 2008).

Russian Jews also turned to religious schools as an alternative to the public system. Money was sometimes a consideration, but yeshivas charged different amounts, ranging from a few hundred dollars to over $9,000 a year. Some offered scholarships to children of Russian Jewish immigrants in an effort to foster their religiosity. This had mixed results. Some parents who hoped that sending their children to a yeshiva would make them more religious found that they rebelled and wore jeans on Jewish holidays instead. In other cases, nonreligious parents who sent their sons or daughters to Jewish schools were unpleasantly surprised when their children wanted to start keeping kosher at home (Zeltzer-Zubida and Kasinitz 2005).

The negative consequences of the concentration of some groups in worse neighborhoods with lower-quality schools are exacerbated by the fact that these groups—native blacks, Puerto Ricans, West Indians, and Dominicans—are also less likely to strategize about the schools and to send their children to schools outside the neighborhoods.

Weighing Alternatives

Gender concerns also came into play. All parents worried about their children's safety, but some parents would not allow their children to travel across the city even for better schools. Many families especially wanted to keep girls close to home. Chinese and West Indian parents were more willing to let their children travel some distance for a better high school but wanted them to remain in or near the city for college. Dominicans and South Americans were particularly wary of allowing their children to travel far, but so were Puerto Rican and Russian families. One young South American woman told us that

> I wanted to go to Junior High School 56 because that was the top school . . . My mother said that I couldn't go there because it was too far . . . I actually got accepted and the teachers told my mother that I belonged [there], [but] my mother said I couldn't go over there.

Some respondents did not think they would fit in socially at the specialized high schools. They did not want to be one of the few minority students in a predominantly white and Asian school. One Puerto Rican man, who gained entry to Bronx Science, explained:

> I didn't want to go . . . I went over there for sightseeing and for some reason it didn't catch my eye over there. Something about it I didn't like.

He went to a general high school, where he cut class a lot and did not do that well. His first job was in the factory where his father worked, and he later joined the military.

Transnational Solutions

If children were doing particularly badly in school, parents who felt they had exhausted local options sent their children back to the home country for a time. Dominican parents, for example, had relatives back home who could keep an eye on the children. Sometimes this helped turn the children around. One 24-year-old Dominican man told us that he left the United States when he was 11 and lived with his grandmother in the Dominican Republic. Although he had a difficult adjustment, he graduated with honors, went to college in the Dominican Republic, and later returned to the United States. He explained:

> I went with my little brother. They decided that things were getting very bad. People were missing out of school, especially the Dominicans. They decided that I had a better chance of graduating and being somebody in the Dominican Republic than staying in the United States. Not that, you know, it's any better in the Dominican Republic. But in the Dominican Republic you actually find people that enjoy studying. You actually find people that want to go that extra mile. Here they'll just stop. You have a lot of peer pressure; you have a lot of drugs.

But going back to the country of origin could also create problems. Hispanic children often had trouble studying in Spanish when sent back, and then their English-language skills deteriorated, making it hard to return to the United States. This young man described returning from Ecuador:

Actually, yeah, I had an accent. I had an accent since then. I was in Ecuador for two years and that's where I learned to master how to speak Spanish. So then I was constantly speaking Spanish and my English started to deplete. I was forgetting my English. When I came over here I had to relearn English . . . I didn't recall much of the words, the grammar part in English.

Other groups found fewer educational opportunities "back home." West Indians returned frequently to the Caribbean for vacations but rarely went to school there. Working class Chinese rarely considered sending their children back to China. Coming from a wealthier country with more family resources, Taiwanese families had stronger transnational ties, and Taiwanese children who got into trouble would occasionally be sent back for a spell. One young woman became involved with a Chinatown gang and was sent back to Taiwan to live with her father to straighten out. The plan backfired, however, when she proceeded to get involved with the same kind of crowd back home. When she finally decided to turn things around, her father got her a fake school record that enabled her to go back into high school on her return to the United States.

High School Quality

Residential segregation and constraints on the family's ability to navigate the school system meant that many children attended poor neighborhood primary and middle schools that gave them a poor level of preparation for high school. In turn, they often attended the least well-functioning high schools in New York City. The Russians and native whites were entrenched in the top three tiers of public high schools (although 20 percent of whites did attend high schools in the bottom two tiers [see Figure 5.3]). The Chinese also managed a striking degree of access to the better public high schools, even when they came from working class families. The ability to negotiate this system effectively compensated for the parents' lack of human capital. While 75 percent of Chinese respondents with a parent from Taiwan graduated from a top-tier high school compared with only 37 percent of those with mainland-born parents, nearly half of all Chinese respondents graduated from schools in the top quintile, and 65 percent attended schools in the top 40 percent of the range.

This contrasts sharply with the Puerto Ricans and Dominicans, more than half of whom attended schools in the two lowest quintiles. The children who were most in need of strong schools thus got their education in the poorest-performing schools. West Indians attended better schools than native born blacks, as might be expected, given their somewhat better-educated parents and better neighborhoods. South Americans largely avoided the bottom rung of the public school system, but half attended schools in the third and fourth lowest quintiles. Black and Hispanic respondents—of immigrant origins as well as native born—were also far more likely to attend vocational high schools.

The High School Experience

School environments profoundly affected our respondents. Those in schools performing at the bottom end of the public system described large, anonymous schools with indifferent teachers who expected little of their black and Hispanic students. Despite the security guards and the metal detectors, the teachers made little effort to maintain discipline. Students cut classes freely, and fights, open drug dealing, and sex in the bathrooms were not uncommon. This picture came through most clearly in the accounts given by students who switched schools. One West Indian mother bussed her son to a white suburban school but withdrew him after he started to get into fights. But the local high school was no better:

> At first I was still soft—sheltered with my parents, I didn't know much about anything and I was scared to go there. And after I got up in there and got into fights and got a rep, I loved it. Had respect just for going there. I took on that thug mentality and there was no other place I would have been. That's when I started chillin'. I started drinkin' 40s. Hanging around with the guys who were around my way. I started putting on size. I started getting into a few fights. Put a few heads out. And everything was lovely after that. Had girls up in the school. Southside. Hollis, it was beautiful.

Even where violence was not a problem, respondents in these large public high schools often told us that their teachers had low expectations of them and were indifferent to them. The respondents had responded by disengaging. Many respondents talked about having high grades in elementary and middle school but becoming bored and disaffected in high school. A 24-year-old West Indian woman was a gifted student until she attended a large public high school, where her grades fell to Cs:

I think I was a very receptive child and I saw that the teachers didn't care whether you came or not. I had teachers who sat and read their paper when we were doing tests and were not really watching us . . . You could see people clearly having fun and playing around and the teacher is just sitting there and not doing anything and not being stern and I just lost respect . . . I had teachers that I was fond of who were interested in what I was learning and how I was learning. And I did better in their classes, but once I lost the respect for the teachers, it was, "I don't even know why I come here." And a lot of my teachers, which I think is wrong, give that message. "Y'all ain't gonna do nothing anyway so do what you want."

In addition to finding differences among the schools our respondents attended, we also found evidence of systematic differences within schools with differential achievement and differential enrollment in special education by race. Black and Latino respondents were most likely to have been held back in high school. This happened to a quarter of South Americans, West Indians, Dominicans, and native blacks and a third of Puerto Ricans. In all groups except the Puerto Ricans, men were much more likely to have been held back than women. (Men of all groups, including whites, were also more likely than women to have been in special education programs.)

Coping with Discrimination in High School

Although most black students did not think their schools treated them any differently than they treated other children in school, often this was so because the other students were black too, not because the respondents felt well treated. A few respondents gave accounts of overtly racist comments from teachers, as when one girl was told to "sit down, you nigger bitch." These incidents seem to have been more common for native blacks. West Indian respondents talked about native black students laughing at their Island accents and sometimes making racist comments about them, but they did not feel mistreated by teachers. In fact, several said they thought teachers favored them because they were good students.

Native blacks were more likely to say that they or their parents had responded directly to discrimination from teachers. This African American man recounted his mother's response to a racially charged incident:

They had an altercation with a teacher one time . . . She said something that offended me, something like "that's why you people something . . ." At the time, I was young and I went home and she [my mother] explained it to me . . . She went to the teacher and she was seething with rage, telling her not to put things like that on her child. She came home and explained it to me. That those are the people that you just ignore.

Less affected by structural discrimination, Chinese respondents still had bad experiences at school. A quarter said they experienced prejudice. Chinese men often spoke of feeling socially excluded or being bullied by other students at school. At the same time, teachers and guidance counselors often treated Chinese as "model minorities." Counselors advised them to apply to selective high schools, providing information and encouragement not available at home; teachers assumed they were good at math and science even when they weren't. These expectations caused some anxiety among students who were not academically inclined, but they also reinforced their academic performance. One Chinese man explained his ambivalent feelings about these expectations:

Well I guess it could be a good and a bad. Being Chinese and being among all the different racial groups. I was always pointed out as "He's Chinese: he must be the smart one. If he's not, oh man is he in trouble. He must be retarded or something." And it is bad. We carry that as Chinese. "Hard working, comes from a very good family background and really, really smart." And in a way, that has helped me, because that has always pushed me. I have a standard to uphold. And also from my parents, you got to do better. You got to do better.

This respondent told us the clichéd story about his cousin coming home with 98 out of 100 on a test and having his grandma ask him what happened to the other 2 percent. After he was sent to the principal's office for talking back to teachers, his parents sent him to Catholic school for the discipline. But "the teachers didn't know how bad I was. They were 'He's from a Chinese family, he must be pretty good.'" On this assumption, they asked him to tutor other students. In retrospect, he felt that "growing up I guess I had a free pass" and credited his school experience with enabling him to go on to college and encouraging him to get involved in community work.

In spite of bad schools and discrimination, few of our second generation or native minority respondents developed an "oppositional identity" or saw doing well as "acting white." Although some successful students faced this accusation from their peers, our respondents uniformly rejected this idea even when they had not done well in school. Native blacks and West Indians both said that the real issue was whether or not you denied your background and distanced yourself from your old friends. One native black young man put it this way:

> *I:* Some people say if African Americans do well in school people say they're selling out or acting white. What do you think?
> *R:* Not really, it depends on how they act. If you get successful and then don't want to recognize where you came from or where you was raised, then you selling out. Or if you stay in the same neighborhood, do the same things, but you just do good in school, you ain't no sell-out, you're just doing your thing.

In the words of a West Indian man:

> *R:* Mostly I say somebody's acting white 'cause of the way they act and talk. The grades ain't got nothin' to do with being white but it's your whole ideology and your mentality. Thinking like you want to be white, they're the only people you can relate to—that's acting white [and] you can be dumped for that. You don't have to have good grades for that. But just getting good grades in itself and studying, I don't see anything wrong with that.

Chinese students did not model themselves on white students either. They saw the idea of becoming like native whites as slightly ridiculous because they thought their white classmates were less driven to succeed, if not actually lazy and irresponsible. If hours spent doing homework are any indication, they are right: only 17 percent of native whites reported that they spent more than two hours of homework a night while in high school, compared to 36 percent of Chinese and 34 percent of West Indians. Some Chinese parents intimated that their belief that Chinese are smarter than other ethnic groups gave their children confidence in their ability to succeed despite obstacles. As one 25-year-old man with Taiwanese parents explained:

> Asian parents for the most part think they are better than white people. You can do better, so you have to do really well. That's what they tell their children.

The Transition to College

Overall, seven out of eight of our respondents who grew up in the New York metropolitan area and received a high school degree went on to college. As Figure 5.3 indicated, this experience ranged from taking classes but never graduating from a community college to getting an advanced degree from a prestigious research university. Studies of ethnic stratification in education usually examine the number of years of schooling and the kinds of degrees individuals attain—Associate, BA, MA, PhD, and professional degrees. Now that growing numbers of young people are entering and graduating from college, scholars are paying greater attention to stratification within the post-secondary sector.

The information we collected on the specific colleges attended by our respondents enables us to examine how young people are sorted across more or less selective institutions. We coded their institutions of higher learning using the eight-category ranking system developed by *U.S. News and World Report*. This system ranks four-year institutions based on whether they draw on a national student body (national) or recruit from the nearby region (regional). Within these broad categories, *U.S. News* ranks the institutions on how selective they are (with Tier I as most selective and Tier IV the least). Over half the native blacks and Puerto Ricans attended regional Tier III or Tier IV schools, as did nearly as many West Indians and Dominicans. This contrasts with about 12 percent or less among the native whites, Russians, Chinese, and South Americans. This category of colleges includes weaker colleges within the CUNY system as well as a number of small private schools. Although graduates of these institutions will have a college diploma, it will not convey the same benefits or prestige as one from a national Tier I or II school or even the higher-ranking CUNY colleges. Native whites and Chinese who grew up in New York and went to college are well represented at elite schools. Two-fifths of all Chinese and half of all respondents with a parent from Taiwan attended a national Tier I or II college. Most other Chinese respondents attended national Tier III schools or the more prestigious regional Tier II colleges within the CUNY system, including Hunter, Queens, and Baruch. Baruch and NYU were the top colleges attended by the Chinese respondents. Despite their highly educated parents, fewer Russian respondents attended top schools (40 percent were at regional Tier I or II institutions), and they were clustered more in higher ranking state university campuses, Pace University (a private national Tier III college in Manhattan), and the Brooklyn and Baruch campuses of the

CUNY system (both ranked regional Tier II). Brooklyn, Pace, and NYU were the top colleges for the Russians. (Hunter, Fordham, and NYU were the top colleges for native whites growing up in New York.)

The South Americans fall between the whites and high-achieving second generation groups, on the one hand, and the native blacks, Puerto Ricans, West Indians, and Dominicans, on the other. Of those who attended college, less than 20 percent went to a national Tier I or II school. But they were more likely than native minorities to attend the regional Tier II CUNY colleges. West Indians and Dominicans were more likely as well to attend these schools than the native minority groups. Nevertheless, substantial shares of all these groups, including 30 percent of South American college-goers, attended regional Tier III or IV institutions.

Although women were about 15 percent more likely to attend college than men, men were more likely to attend the national Tier I and II institutions, whereas women were more likely to attend the regional Tier I and II institutions. Women leaving the region for school were also more likely to go to lower-ranked institutions. In other words, attending less prestigious institutions partly offset the higher rates of college attendance among women. It appears from these patterns that women with the credentials to attend top-tier institutions are more likely to stay near home, while the men go farther afield. Of all respondents, Puerto Rican women attended the weakest institutions, with almost 57 percent in regional Tier III and IV and unranked schools, but they were closely followed by 55 percent of Puerto Rican men and West Indian women and 54 percent of native black women. (Some 47 percent of native black and 42 percent of West Indian men fell into this category.)

The same background factors that influenced earlier schooling—a family's social, human, and financial capital, family expectations, and the constraints of discrimination and segregation—shaped the types of college attended by our respondents and how well they did. Although they did not always realize it at first, attending low-performing high schools ill prepared many respondents for college work. Even those who were ready to succeed often had their choices constrained by what their families could afford or whether they needed to stay close to family for personal or financial reasons. Young people who had started families, who just wanted to move out of their parents' homes, or who needed to contribute to their parents' households faced additional pressures.

Of our respondents who grew up in the New York area, got a high school degree, and were aged 24 through 32 (and thus likely to be beyond their college-going years), the number of individuals getting a BA degree falls along now-familiar patterns: lowest among Puerto Ricans and native blacks, high among native whites, but even higher among Chinese and Russians, with the other second generation groups falling between but substantially above the native minority level. As Figure 5.1 shows, in virtually every case except for native white and black women, women are more likely to have earned college degrees than their male counterparts. Indeed, the gap is large in some instances, reaching 26.5 percentage points among the Chinese. The Chinese men do no better than white men, and the Chinese women have very high levels of college attendance. (If we looked at any other measure of educational attainment, such as the quality of the college attended, the results would be similar.)

Moreover, multivariate analysis of the determinants of these college outcomes yields results similar to those reported in Table 5.1. The main differences are that some family circumstances, such as the presence of both biological parents or the number of siblings in the home when respondents were growing up, fade in significance, whereas factors like the quality of the high school attended and self-reported grade point average (GPA) increase in significance. Having a child continues to have the most negative impact on completing a college education. The respondent's parents' education continues to have the most positive impact, closely followed by high school GPA. As before, controlling for a host of factors, African Americans do significantly worse than native whites on this outcome, Russians and especially the Chinese do significantly better, and the other second generation groups are statistically indistinguishable from native whites.

Respondents told us that weak high school counseling services or sometimes deliberate steering influenced their choice of college. A West Indian law graduate said he felt that guidance counselors routinely discriminated against black students:

> I think the guidance office as a whole were not giving black students their due in helping people figure out what schools to apply to. I think that's a systemic problem. I think if you go to any school where guidance counselors [are] dealing with black children, they are not as good at identifying the right opportunities for those children as they would be with other types of kids . . . I've heard from a bunch of different friends who went to school at a bunch of different places that when you get to the guidance counselor's office, they don't want

to maybe deal with your trying to get into Harvard or Yale or wherever and so they try to steer people toward other places.

For some groups, ethnic peer networks favored certain schools, not
always for reasons that seemed sensible in retrospect. Russians often chose
relatively weak private schools over CUNY colleges, but some individuals
later transferred to Brooklyn College or Baruch. One Russian Jewish respondent chose a local private college because her friends were going:

> I had this big stigma against Brooklyn College because my parents
> really wanted me to go there. And everybody was saying it was the
> stupidest college, it has the worst reputation, it was really so not true.
> It was something that they implanted in my head. Not my parents,
> just people around.

She later decided this was "a stupid decision."

Family expectations and community norms also have a big impact.
Whereas some parents are satisfied to see their children just graduate from
high school, many families pressure their children to complete college or
pursue a particular career. Family expectations were particularly high
among Chinese families, especially Taiwanese. Community norms reinforced these family expectations. A Chinese woman who attended Wes-
leyan, an excellent college, felt acute disappointment when she did not get
into Harvard:

> Even though my father never spoke to me about schoolwork or any-
> thing like that, there is always the implicit thing in most Chinese
> households that you will either go to Harvard or Yale. When you're a
> little kid, Bronx Science and Stuyvesant and then Harvard or Yale, or
> Princeton maybe. And once you go to college, you're either going to
> be a lawyer or a doctor. In my household, it was never really stated,
> but I was so upset . . . that I didn't get into Harvard that I just sort
> of went with my guidance counselor's recommendation.

Working class respondents in general, including the Chinese, tended to
stay near home and go to a CUNY school. As Min Zhou and Vivian Louie
have pointed out, parental involvement in favoring a particular career can
present problems for second generation Chinese whose interests or talents
are at odds with parental choices (Louie 2004; Zhou and Xiong 2005).
Many working class Chinese reported that their parents wanted them to
pursue practical majors offering job security. The competitive atmosphere

also makes average Chinese students feel inadequate. One young man who was studying finance at Baruch, CUNY's business college, felt his aunts looked down on him:

> They would tell me, "You don't always have to live up to the standards of what Asian people do about going to Ivy League schools." But I think they're lying [laughter]. I think they're just trying to make me feel better because my aunts both went to Barnard, and they would always talk about people whose sons went from Stuyvesant to Columbia . . . [When] my older aunt says, "Whatever you make a living it's fine, at least it's honest work," I know she's saying, "I'm not so sure you can succeed to those standards that we have made for you."

Girls often felt pressure to choose a school close to home. One woman who did not attend Stuyvesant because her father did not want her leaving the neighborhood was accepted by several colleges outside New York, but once more she did not go "because I had to be a good girl and stay home and it wasn't an option." A West Indian woman observed that

> in the Jamaican family, the girls are lower than the guys. Boys being boys . . . it is okay for them to stay out late. But if you are a girl, you've got to be home by 8:00. My younger brother, next year he's going to college and he is allowed to go away to campus. When I was applying to colleges, you had no choice but to commute. My dad didn't want me to go anywhere.

The transition to college often challenged our respondents. Many students who graduated from weak high schools had a nasty shock their first semester. A Dominican woman who went to Fordham said:

> [It was] the biggest and most powerful experience to date in my life. Coming here, I found myself very unprepared. In high school I graduated with a B average. I think public school really cheated me out of an education . . . Here there were students who were a lot more well rounded, I would say, than I was. And were able to write long papers. A lot more was required from them when they were in high school, which prepared them for college. Whereas in my case, I had no preparation for college whatsoever, as far as academics go. I would get an A and have 20 million mistakes. Coming here, my first English class I got a C− on the first paper. I was so upset.

Students who had attended magnet schools had a much easier time. Asked whether going to Brooklyn Tech had prepared him for college, a Temple University student replied:

> My high school did. I don't know if *every* high school—I heard a lot of stories about that. Brooklyn Tech was set up like college. You had admittance to certain majors depending on your grade point average. College is a "whole 'nother world" but you know, [Brooklyn Tech is] a *really* good school as far as what they teach, and the depth of the stuff they teach. If you look at the stats—the time I was there, anyway—it was 95 percent of people going to college whereas other schools were 95 percent other things. Drop out rate or pregnancy, stuff like that.

Respondents who left New York to go to college often experienced a culture shock. Melanie, a Chinese American woman, looked forward to "going away" because growing up in Chinatown, she had had lots of conflicts with her parents After a short time at Vassar, however, she transferred to Columbia. She described meeting her roommate there:

> I'm so used to the city being diverse enough that people are not staring at you just because you look different. But at Vassar, only two hours away, it was a whole different scenario. Freshman year, my roommate is some white hick from Massachusetts. I had no preconception of her whatsoever, you know, yet she had [one] about me. After our parents left and it was our first meal to walk down to the cafeteria together, she actually said to me, "Do you need to bring chopsticks?" I'm like, okay, I always thought that education brings you to a higher level but only ignoramuses say things like that. I'm like, "I can use a fork." "Oh, I didn't know you could." Where do you think I came from?

Students who continued to live at home felt less pressure to earn money and tended to finish their degrees on time. This may help explain why so many Chinese and Russian respondents finished college within four or five years, whereas members of other groups often remained in college in their mid-twenties or later. Over half the Chinese and almost half the Russians enrolled in two- or four-year institutions did not work. Almost three-quarters of the Dominicans combined studying with working, followed by native whites, native blacks, South Americans, and Puerto Ricans.

Those respondents who had children of their own faced the greatest challenges. This group includes respondents who had children in high school but nonetheless continued on to college and others who had children in their early twenties. Over 20 percent of women who were working while attending school also had children. This situation was most common among native black women, 48 percent of whom had children; but it was also common among Puerto Ricans, Dominicans, and West Indians (about 30 percent). Few Chinese and Russian women bore this triple burden, and not many more native white women. Since many of these women were single mothers, they often balanced school, work, and parenting with little help from anyone else. Any additional problem could upset the delicate balance and force these single mothers out of school, at least for a while. (That few Chinese respondents had become parents, discussed at length in Chapter 7, and that some groups sequenced childbearing later than others, gave them a real advantage in educational attainment.) One 22-year-old Puerto Rican woman told us about her regrets at not finishing school:

> R: I wish I would have finished school. I really really really would have finished and then had my son. I never regret having my son, but I really, really, really wish I would have finished school first.
> I: Is it hard to go back when you have a kid?
> R: It is hard. It is a little bit harder. Also because there's the gap, the gap that I haven't been in school. It will take a little time to get back on track, but I think I'm doing it.

Although many of our respondents were young and still pursuing an education, we can already see that a college education pays off for them. Of those who were no longer enrolled in school, 48 percent of the high school dropouts and 33 percent of those with high school degrees were not working, compared to only 20 percent for those with some college and 9.2 percent of those with BAs. At all levels of education, native blacks were most likely to be unemployed, but their jobless rate fell from over 40 percent of those without a high school diploma to less than 10 percent among those with a BA. Despite this evident payoff, many young minority people, particularly men, told us they were skeptical about the value of education. Many talked of college-educated friends who were "still working at Macy's" or, worse, unable to find a job. That native blacks, Puerto Ricans, Dominicans, and even West Indians tended to be concentrated in the lowest-ranking schools may explain this attitude.

Conclusion

The high school and college experiences of these young New Yorkers give cause for optimism, as well as a few concerns. On the positive side, the children of immigrants showed no sign of "second generation decline." Most members of the second generation were attaining much more education than their parents and surpassing their native born minority counterparts, although the high dropout rate among Dominicans remains worrying. As we have seen, taking family background characteristics into account, the educational achievements of two second generation groups—Chinese and Russians—statistically exceed those of native whites who grew up in and around New York, whereas those of the other second generation groups are statistically more or less the same and those of native blacks and Puerto Ricans remain statistically worse.

That Puerto Ricans and native blacks lag behind not only whites but also the second generation groups is disturbing. Puerto Ricans have the highest high school dropout rates, are most likely to have been held back, and are most likely to have been in special education programs. As we have seen, they have been the least able to use parental human capital—college-educated parents—as a buffer against dropping out of high school. Only in this light is the performance of native born blacks somewhat better. The negative racialization of native born blacks and Puerto Ricans in New York appears to be exacting a continued toll that the black and Hispanic children of immigrants—despite being subject to racial prejudice—have not, so far, had to pay.

The expectations about getting an education that parents expressed to their children reflected their own levels of education as well as community norms. High parental expectations are not enough to explain why some groups had more academic achievement than others, however. To realize high expectations, families need good options available to them, good information about how to pursue those options, and the resources to realize them. Our respondents describe situations in which the settlement patterns of families from different class, race, and ethnic backgrounds yield unequal access to decent public education in the earliest years. Families from different backgrounds have widely varying amounts of information about how to navigate the educational system as well. Virtually all the Chinese respondents knew how to take the selective high school test, whereas less than half the Dominicans did. This reflected the levels of media information and co-ethnic connections with kin or community members who had personal experiences with these institutions. Being part of an ethnic community whose networks spanned class boundaries, rather than one that was homogeneously poor, clearly constituted a group advantage.

The school system also treated the different groups in markedly different ways. Reactions from teachers and guidance counselors affected students' levels of motivation. Not only does structural discrimination channel many native black and Puerto Rican children into low-performing schools, but many respondents reported that these schools treated them with indifference or even hostility. Of the second generation groups, Dominicans seemed most likely to have experienced such discrimination. West Indians and South Americans were less likely to report this. At the other end of the spectrum, Chinese children were given extra encouragement and advice.

These cumulative patterns of advantage and disadvantage help to explain why the second generation and native born groups show divergent outcomes during and after high school. Relative to native blacks and Puerto Ricans, many children of immigrants benefitted from living in families with more working members and more adults to care for them. With the exception of Dominicans, they also settled in neighborhoods with better schools and had more educational options open to them.

The contrast between Chinese and Dominicans highlights how these factors led to divergent educational outcomes. Both groups had many poorly educated parents, but even poor Chinese families have some advantages over the Dominicans. Most Chinese arrived through the family reunification policy, so households nearly always included both parents and often additional relatives. The Chinese settled in formerly white or mixed ethnic neighborhoods with relatively good grade schools. The Chinese community contains highly educated middle class parents who share their knowledge about public schools, and the Chinese language media provide extensive information on the best public schools. Chinese immigrants invest their savings in the education of their second generation children, of whom they have relatively few, rather than sending savings back to China as remittances. In addition Chinese second generation students benefit from the model minority stereotype through teachers' expectations that they will do well just by virtue of their being Chinese.

The Dominicans experienced cumulative disadvantage. The migration process often disrupted families, often separating parents and children for some time. Housing discrimination and segregation channeled them into neighborhoods with low-performing elementary schools. Poorly educated parents may have high hopes for their children, but they do not have much information about how to get their children into better schools, partly because they are a relatively homogeneously poor group. Although high levels of remittances certainly help sustain families in the Dominican Republic, they drain resources from the community in New York. Dominican parents with high expectations did send their children to Catholic schools, but this cost too much for most families to sustain. Respondents who were "sent back" often told us that switching schools was disruptive and they fell behind in both countries. This same pattern was found in a study of the effects of transnationalism on the educational performance of Italians and Turks in Germany (Alba, Handl, and Müller 1994).

While the presence of "ethnic capital" (Zhou and Lin 2005) clearly benefitted many second generation youth, we found little evidence that maintaining ethnicity per se—or "consonant assimilation" in Portes and Rumbaut's (2001) terms—helped them get more education. The most successful group, Chinese Americans, concentrated in the best segments of the public education system. While many Chinese Americans attended Chinese schools as a form of child care, these schools generally did not supplement the regular curriculum then in the ways that many now do. Few learned Chinese or knew much about Chinese culture beyond food and a few holidays. Lacking facility in their parents' language and rapidly surpassing their parents' educational level, even working class Chinese respondents engaged in highly "dissonant" acculturation. The lack of communication with parents often pained our Chinese second generation respondents.

Similarly, competence in speaking or writing Spanish did not seem to be a major factor promoting educational attainment among the Dominican or South American second generation. Dominicans were the most likely to live in ethnically concentrated neighborhoods but did not seem to have benefitted from that. To the contrary, living in ethnic enclaves confined them to the worst segments of the public school system. The transnational connections of this community led families with few resources to divide available funds across two locations. As Crul and Doomernik (2003) have pointed out for second generation Turks and Moroccans in the Netherlands, ethnic solidarity can work in positive or negative ways depending on the resources, information, and norms circulating within a given community.

Regardless of the group to which they belonged, the children of immigrants often followed their parents' wishes even when they did not want to. The children also tended to think about the family as an economic as well as a social unit. This reflected attitudes in many sending countries and young people's awareness that their parents had made large sacrifices in migrating. This motivated many of our respondents to work hard in school.

In a society where the income distribution has become more unequal over time and where education plays a growing role in determining income, getting a good college education has become the gateway to middle class status. Having some college education is important even for the better jobs within the region's growing service sector. While it is heartening to see that many children of immigrants are still able to use public schools in and around New York as a vehicle of upward mobility, it is depressing to see how stratification within the school system compounds the class, racial, ethnic, and gender inequalities evident among the families of our respondents. Children of the highly educated Russian parents have taken well to New York City. Children from working class Chinese families have also largely succeeded in using public schools to compensate for their parents' lack of education.

Children from the other immigrant and especially the native born minority groups have much less access to the factors that have enabled these groups to succeed. The parents of these children have less education, have higher rates of marital dissolution, live in poorer neighborhoods with low-performing schools and high rates of crime and other environmental risks, and constitute communities with fewer middle class and professional members. Even so, those who grow up with immigrant parents nonetheless appear to have some real advantages over poor native born blacks and Puerto Ricans, who have the least family resources and the most exposure to structural disadvantage and discriminatory treatment. Children from these backgrounds dearly need a good education, but they end up in schools that barely teach them in neighborhoods where they are often exposed to drugs and violence. Some native born black and Puerto Rican respondents described their schools in ways that make their decisions to turn their backs on education seem almost rational.

We thus conclude that the negative impact of race—or more broadly native minority status—on the educational outcomes within the second generation stems not so much from individuals developing an "adversarial" outlook on education as from the ways in which deep patterns of racial and class inequality channel some members of the second generation directly into poorly performing schools in which, not surprisingly, they do less well.

At the same time, our study provides examples of how the region's educational system also provided "first and second chances" to many who face barriers to quality education—GEDs and community colleges for those who went to poorly performing high schools; CUNY and SUNY campuses for upwardly striving children of working class families whose parents did not graduate from high school, much less college; and attendance at some of the nation's leading colleges and universities for those who went to public magnet schools, higher-tier zoned high schools, and Catholic high schools. This allowed not only some Chinese respondents to attend NYU and Cornell but also some West Indian students to go to Columbia and Penn and some Dominican students to go to City College and Fordham. Taking as a standard the young whites who moved to New York City after their college educations makes second generation immigrant educational trajectories look less successful. Taking the modal experience of an African American or Puerto Rican who grew up in and around New York City, however, makes the second generation immigrants' glass look more than half full.

6

The Second Generation Goes to Work

Is there any job you would never take? "I will *never* deliver Chinese food."

27-YEAR-OLD CHINESE AMERICAN MAN

Few aspects of contemporary migration to the United States have received as much attention as the role of immigrants in the economy and labor market. When asked about what motivated their parents' decision to leave their homeland, the young people we spoke to recounted many complicated stories, but most began or ended with some version of the cliché, "They came for a better life" for themselves and their children. While a "better life" means many different things, improving a family's economic fortunes was a central part of it. But do immigrants find this "better life"? We can gain important clues to the answer to this question by looking at how members of the second generation are entering the workforce. We can begin to see whether their parents' sacrifices have been worthwhile, whether their own educations will "pay off," and how parental human and social capital is being transferred to the next generation.

We know from research and everyday observation that today's immigrants are concentrated in certain occupations and industries. These ethnic concentrations result partly from a lack of options. Without being able to speak English, lacking familiarity with the larger society, and suffering discrimination, immigrants may have no choice but to accept lower wages or more difficult working conditions than would natives. Under these circumstances, "ethnic niches" may provide immigrants with advantages in the labor force, giving them access to jobs they might not otherwise get or even creating jobs and wealth that would not otherwise exist (Waldinger 1996; Light and Gold 2000).

Less clear is what these parental job concentrations mean for the working lives of the immigrants' children. The classical assimilation perspective implies that the children will move away from the parents and into the mainstream economy. As a result, across generations, ethnic concentrations in particular occupations and industries should diminish over time (Neidert and Farley 1985; Lieberson and Waters 1988; Farley and Alba 2002; Alba and Nee 2003). Indeed, Gans (1992) argues that in the face of racial discrimination, the children of immigrants who develop an American disdain for "immigrants' jobs" may suffer downward mobility. Other scholars stress the enduring role of ethnicity in economic life (Model 1993; Light and Gold 2000; Waldinger and Lichter 2003). According to this perspective, ethnic and racial concentrations will not disappear even among groups that are highly assimilated in other spheres.

The segmented assimilation approach argues that both outcomes are likely, but for different segments of the second generation population. Some groups will lose their distinctiveness over time and eventually come to have an occupational profile much like the mainstream population. Others will reject their parents' niches but also find themselves rejected by mainstream employers, and so they will experience downward assimilation into an increasingly multiethnic urban "underclass." Finally, those whose parents have developed successful economic niches will seize upon them as sources of second generation opportunity. They may thus achieve upward mobility through selective acculturation.

Until recently these arguments have been speculative. Now that many second and 1.5 generation young adults are entering the labor force, however, we can assess what is actually happening to them, though we must bear in mind that their careers have only just begun. We cannot know whether even the upwardly mobile may eventually hit "glass ceilings" or how future economic transformations will shape their work lives. Given that today's young people often change jobs (Appelbaum, Bernhard, and Murnane 2003), current job status may not accurately predict future earnings. Those workers in their twenties and thirties who remain in professional or graduate schools often report modest incomes that belie their long term prospects, whereas their peers with manual jobs may already be close to the peak of their earnings. These caveats aside, we can learn much from the experiences of the new second generation as it goes to work.

Working and Earning

On the whole, second and 1.5 generation young adults are less likely to be working full time than their older first generation immigrant parents (reported in Chapter 2), but about half of them do so. As Figure 6.1 shows, the women are less likely to be working full time than the men, and the full time employment rate ranges from a low of 37 percent among the Chinese and Russian women to a high of 66 percent among the native white men. But Figure 6.1 also shows that relatively few members of the second generation are neither in the labor force nor attending school (bottom category), though this is more common among the women than the men. Many of the second generation are still in school full time, particularly among the Chinese and Russians, but also among the West Indians and South Americans. Many members of the second generation mix education and part time work well into their twenties, so it is not surprising that they are all more likely to be working part time. Going to school full time kept few native blacks and Puerto Ricans out of the labor force. (Dominicans are the second generation group that most resembles the "native minority" pattern.)

Combining both sexes, native whites have moved most fully into the labor market, with 63 percent working full time. Among the second generation respondents, South Americans are most likely to work full

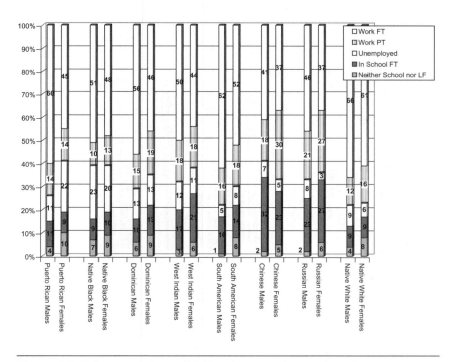

Figure 6.1. Labor Force Status (%) (Part Time Work Not Shown).
Source: ISGMNY.

time, at 57 percent. In every group, women are both less likely to be in the labor force and less likely to work full time than the men, though, as with the parents described in Chapter 2, the gender gaps are narrowest for native blacks and West Indians (and, for the children, the Chinese), and larger for other groups. The major factor behind this difference is that having children takes many more women than men out of the labor force.

Though relatively few respondents are neither working nor in school full time, the share ranges from a low of 6 percent among Chinese men and women and 8 percent of Russian Jews up to 23 percent among Puerto Ricans and 26 percent among native blacks, men and women combined. (Once more, Dominicans, at 18 percent, are the second generation group closest to the native minorities.) Early fertility is clearly a factor for native black, Puerto Rican, and Dominican women.

What do the different groups of workers earn? Average hourly wages, depicted in Figure 6.2, vary from a low of $12.32 among Puerto Rican women to a high of $17.71 among native white males but these figures

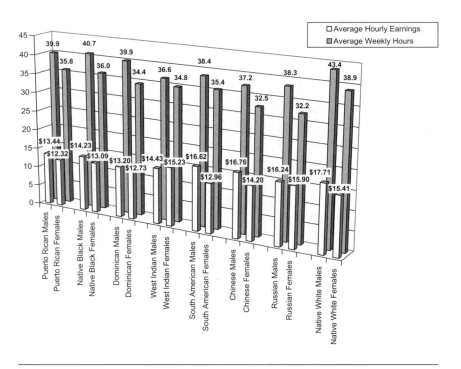

Figure 6.2. Hours Worked and Hourly Earnings. *Source:* ISGMNY.

show familiar patterns: the native whites, Russian Jews, and Chinese earn the most and the native minorities the least, with the West Indians and South Americans doing better and the Dominicans most resembling the native minority groups. Wages are relatively low, since many of our interviewees are working part time in entry-level positions. As our respondents age, they clearly earn more. Across the groups, women work an average of about four hours less per week than men, who average around thirty-eight hours per week. Despite the fact that women perform better at school, they earn less than men (except for West Indians).

Among those who are working twenty-five hours a week or more, native whites earn significantly more than the black and Hispanic groups, but not the Chinese and Russians Jews (Table 6.1, first column). Some of those differences reflect the age and gender distribution of our respondents. Once we control for those two factors, it turns out that white advantage over the other second generation groups becomes statistically insignificant (Table 6.1, second column), but the advantage over the two native minority groups remains. (Indeed, the Chinese and Russian Jewish respondents earn more than native whites, though the statistical significance is just above the .10 level). Finally, after controlling for education as well (Table 6.1, third column), the model explains much of the variation in hourly earnings, but all the groups continue to earn more than native blacks and Puerto Ricans. In other words, when the second generation groups—including the relatively low paid Dominicans—achieve levels of education comparable with those of whites, they are also earning comparable wages. This is not true for native African Americans and Puerto Ricans.

Of course, hourly earnings differences tell only part of the story about work experiences among young people. Jobs also vary in terms of their potential for advancement. Some groups are concentrated in retail sales or clerical work, while others are in more promising positions. This suggests that earnings gaps among the groups may widen over time. At least so far, however, adjusting for the obvious factors, most second generation young people seem to be earning close to what native whites earn, whereas native blacks and Puerto Ricans are not. The best-off second generation groups, the Chinese and the Russian Jews, may actually earn more than the native whites after these adjustments. This is clearly not evidence of second generation decline.

Getting the First Job

How does the second generation enter the labor force? Young New Yorkers from all backgrounds often do not have clear transitions demarcated between the stages of their lives. Many enter the labor force early, before finishing their educations. (In this regard, native white respondents growing up in New York stand in sharp contrast to those who arrived after college.) Even so, getting a job during high school did not seem to have a negative impact on progress in school or subsequent employment patterns. Indeed, having an after-school or weekend job seemed to have a positive overall influence on the educational progress of our respondents. Only among Dominicans was having had a high school job correlated with higher current earnings, and the effect was small.

Young people usually get their first jobs through kin and friends, often co-ethnics. Being a member of a group that is well embedded in the labor force thus has clear advantages. As one 20-year-old Russian Jewish man who worked three to four hours a day through high school recalls:

Table 6.1. Determinants of Logged Hourly Earnings (working twenty-five hours a week or more with reported wages)

Variable	Beta	Beta	Beta
(Constant)	2.69**	1.16**	1.00**
Puerto Rican	−.230**	−.186**	−.073*
Black	−.187**	−.194**	−.088**
Dominican	−.138**	−.089	−.033
West Indian	−.118**	−.085	−.031
South American	−.109**	−.063	−.016
Chinese	.001	.035	.029
Russian	.006	.035	.034
Age		.460**	.372**
Female		−.057**	−.078**
Educational Attainment			.319**
Adjusted R^2	.053	.260	.339

*sig < .05.**sig < .01.
Educational attainment: 1 = no HS diploma, 2 = HS diploma or in high school, 3 = associate's degree or enrolled in community college, 4 = BA degree, 5 = postgraduate degree. Respondents are weighted to represent their group's share of the sample universe.

[In high school] I worked in this salad bar place in the city, bringing lunches to all these rich people. Great tips! My mom's friend's son used to work there, so when he left there was an opening. Then I worked in a pharmacy for a while, also [because] my friend used to work there. He went to college—opening—so I got it.

Young people whose relatives owned businesses often reported that "helping out" in them as teenagers taught them about work, made them feel grown up, and inspired them to have their own businesses one day so they could avoid "dealing with bosses and managers." Yet such jobs rarely proved to be much of a stepping stone, largely because most had no interest in working in the immigrant enclave. As one Russian Jewish man said about working in his father's small store:

> *R:* It was okay. No big deal. You work for your father, it's no big deal. You see how we're sitting here? I'm getting paid for it. What I don't like about it is that it doesn't pay me well. That's why I'm going to school!
> *I:* Would you ever take over your father's business?
> *R:* No! I'm not into the store!

Respondents often mention that working in a family business was a burden and source of tension within the family. They saw even successful family businesses as robbing the young people of their independence and childhoods, sometimes involving them in family fights or disputes with co-workers long before they felt ready for such adult roles. One Chinese American woman was so put off by the long hours and constant tension of her father's small financial firm that medical school seemed less stressful to her. Another confessed to being relieved when her father sold his struggling restaurant and took a lower-status, but also less taxing, job as a factory worker.

The parents' stereotypically immigrant businesses also embarrassed some young people. Many respondents shared the sentiment of a Chinese restaurateur's son who said:

> *R:* I kind of get a little embarrassed. I feel like, "Why couldn't my dad be a doctor or something." I could at least say, "My dad's this." To say My dad's a take-out owner is almost like being ashamed of it.
> *I:* So would you ever own your own restaurant?
> *R:* No, never. I wouldn't want to go near that stuff I don't like working with food. It's not for me.

Some saw "helping out" in family businesses while in high school more as a family obligation than as a source of income. Many second generation young people recall deeply resenting having to do this kind of work. Others accepted it more or less willingly. Few of them thought it would translate directly into their own careers. A Chinese woman whose parents, a bus driver and a bus conductor back in Taiwan, had in New York run a typical ethnic enclave firm notes that she was expected to "help out"—but only in limited ways:

> R: Luckily for me, the type of business that we had, the wholesale restaurant supply business is like—it's like warehouse stuff. A lot of like deliveries, trucks and stuff, so as a girl, I didn't have to 'cause it was kind of rough-and-tumble kind of work. Primarily what I was expected to do was in the summertime to go work in the office part of the warehouse, take orders, answer the phone, and, you know, write up orders.
>
> I: So how did you feel about having to help out?
>
> R: I didn't mind that much. Growing up, I watched the *Brady Bunch* and it was always wonderful to hear about oh, you know, you have to save up your allowance money in order to buy this one toy you'd want. My family wasn't like that! My parents never gave me an allowance, but they never deprived me of anything. So working for my parents, it was just—I was glad to help out. I didn't mind that much. Plus, it made me feel like useful.
>
> I: Was it ever expected that you take over the business?
>
> R: No. I think because I was a girl, they never, never thought that that was the case. I think they *did* harbor some deeper fantasy that I would marry a Chinese guy who might have taken over the place and then the two of us can run the business! But, ultimately because I'm a girl, I don't think they expected that of me.
>
> I: Well, your husband's Korean. Why couldn't he take over the business?
>
> R: Our customers are mainly—actually, 99 percent—Chinese restaurants, so you've got language barrier. That's really pretty much why he couldn't take over.

If some Chinese, Russian Jewish, and South American respondents were ambivalent about working in their parents' businesses, the West Indian, Dominican, and Puerto Rican respondents were bitter about their parents' less successful businesses. In these communities, self-employment was often an immigrant's alternative to unemployment, and many children saw this work as appropriate only for immigrants. One 24-year-old Dominican recalls hating to work in her aunt's perennially struggling restaurant: "I speak English, I should do something better." A Puerto Rican teenager remembers difficult conditions ("no air conditioning!") and lack of pay when working in his parents' failing fruit store, but he also recalls the toll it took on his parents' marriage and health. A Puerto Rican 23-year-old whose father was murdered in his own night club made clear that he wanted nothing to do with that sort of work: "I want to sleep at night, at home, next to my wife."

While kinship ties can be a solid basis for business arrangements in relatively well-off communities, family businesses can lead to perceived exploitation in less well-off communities. A West Indian College graduate whose father once owned an auto repair shop but who sold the business to take a job with the Transit Authority spoke about how much better off his family was as a result. He noted that "relatives always tell you they will pay you later, and never do." Another West Indian college graduate resisted her father's offers to work at the family restaurant. "He's cheap. He won't pay me." Still, she sometimes considers going into the family business when she is having a hard time with her (white) bosses and managers. A 30-year-old-Colombian man whose successful father had several small businesses recalls that he left school at 19 to manage one of his father's video stores. Looking back, he recalls liking the independence. Now in college pursuing a professional degree, however, he regrets the five or six years he feels were "lost" to the business: "I could have graduated by now."

Few second generation youngsters ended up in family businesses. Family business employment is fairly high among the fathers of all groups, particularly the Russian Jewish, Chinese, and Dominican fathers, almost a third of whom had businesses. But family businesses account for over 10 percent of the second generation jobs only in one group, Russian Jews. Despite their well-developed ethnic enclave (Zhou 1992), fewer than 5 percent of the Chinese worked in such businesses. And only among the South Americans did working in a family business have a statistically significant positive impact on earnings.

Few members of the second generation aspire to own their own businesses, especially among those whose parents have the most entrepreneurial experience. The Russian Jews and the Chinese clearly see education and professional credentials as the preferred route to success. As a 23-year-old Chinese community college student whose parents own a small Chinese restaurant put it:

My father and mother would like me to go into a white collar job . . . a white collar environment with computers . . . just go into the air conditioning, come home at five. Not like my father.

Many parents share this view. A 30-year-old Dominican woman graduate student in clinical psychology helped out in her parents' small garment factory but recalls their discouraging her from taking too much interest in their business and pushing her instead toward higher education. A 27-year-old Chinese financial services worker, whose father owns a successful Chinatown jewelry store, sums up this way:

> *I:* Was it expected that you take over your father's business?
> *R:* No! My father wouldn't. He doesn't hate me enough to ever want me to take over his business. The reason he worked so hard is so that we wouldn't have to live that kind of life. You don't want your kids to . . . It's like indentured servants, that is what it feels like. Your life is not your own. I feel sorry for him.

Respondents without self-employed parents were more likely to see small business ownership as a measure of success. Despite native African Americans' lack of experience with family business ownership, our native black respondents commonly aspired to self-employment. This may have reflected their dissatisfaction with limited opportunities and "dead end jobs," but native blacks with college degrees and well-paying positions said the same thing. They had few illusions about small businesses and were well aware of the advantages of professional jobs. The key was their desire for autonomy, wanting to be free of workplace "politics" and to be in charge of their own destinies. Their view may also have reflected their wanting to be free of racism and constant second guessing to distinguish racism from the simply normal unpleasantness of the working world. These respondents saw "being my own boss" as providing a way not to have to deal with whites in positions of authority.

> *R:* I want to be able have my own business. That's *why* [at age twenty-six] I am going to college. I already have my future planned, but everybody's plans don't go the way they planned. So I just have to prepare myself for the bumps in the road, so I want to have my own business. I already have a title. It's called Black MOB, meaning, black men owned business. It would be several things: clothing, dealing with fashion, music, acting dealing with computers, a whole lot of things.

Relatively few second generation young people got their first job through formal summer youth employment programs or cooperative programs in high school. This route was most common among native blacks. Unclear, however, is how later employers or, indeed, the young people themselves evaluated this work experience. Despite the programs' attempts to serve as apprenticeship experiences, they were often perceived as "make work," a thinly disguised extension of the welfare state rather than a real introduction to the world of work.

The Informal Economy

Youth culture provides many early labor market experiences. As Robbin Kelly (1997) notes, the world of hip hop sometimes allows inner city youth to turn cultural production into economic production, or at least that is their hope. Surprising numbers of native black, Puerto Rican, West Indian, and Dominican respondents had earned money as DJs and entertainers while still in high school. This sometimes continued as a source of extra income for people in their twenties.

> *I:* Have there been specific times when you feel you benefitted from being Jamaican?
> *R:* Yeah, as far as being in the music industry, the reggae, being a DJ. This is happening now, a lot of the music or a lot of the artists and rappers are incorporating some form of reggae flavor or style or coming together with reggae artists to do their songs nowadays. So that was a good advantage. A good benefit. It brought Americans and other races together too. It's a fun thing and I like it and it's extra money, yeah, and it does make ends meet. I put it toward paying bills and saving to buy the house I want right now. My nice car and stuff like that. Clothes, etcetera. Take care of the kids, go to the movies, go to the park, all kind of stuff.

An 18-year-old West Indian retail worker also got work as a musician:

> *R:* [The store] is my first job on the books. Off the books, I'm in a steel band so we get paid. I've played drums for concerts and I did some sound engineering at a studio. My band played at a church and the lady said she didn't have a drummer and she asked me if I would like to and she would pay me to be a drummer for her church and that was it.

I: How much money would you say you made?

R: In a year off the books probably $1,000 probably. Depends on how many shows I did. At one church I get $20 every two weeks and the other one I get $65 every four weeks. And when I would lend if another church wants me, like this church down here, they use me sometimes for when guest choir is coming and they want a drummer they use me. Since I'm a musician I can charge them basically what I want so $20 an hour. So I would say $1,000 or $1,200 a year.

Taking advantage of these part time work opportunities shows considerable entrepreneurial drive and requires more initiative than simply being handed a job by one's relatives. It is also consistent with ideas common in the hip hop youth culture: the celebration of autonomy and "keeping it real" and the paradoxical combination of blatant materialism and disdain for "selling out." Yet skills acquired in such work rarely translate into the skills needed for mainstream employment. Indeed, it is the rare employer who will even see the weekend DJ or musician as having "work" experience at all.

Some young people did manage to create small, cash-based enterprises out of the needs of their fellow young people. One young Russian Jewish woman law student recalls her lucrative high school career as what she wryly describes as "a professional student":

R: I did a lot of writing for college kids while I was in high school. I wrote essays for cash.

I: Was it like, friends would ask you, or . . . ?

R: No, it was more, it was like a business type of thing. It was unbelievable. I had to get my own phone line and I would work a lot. I'd get paid pretty well for a high school kid. And the funniest thing is, they still call. My mom is like "She's in law school, she doesn't do that stuff." But I had a very large clientele, from like four colleges. I'd work probably like twelve hours on the weekend. And I'd make like, $300.

I: Was this editing, or you'd just write their papers for cash?

R: Right. Papers. On any subject. Um, a lot of times they'd bring me books, and I would read the book, and then you have to like, you know, write like an essay on the book or something.

I: How much did you charge?

R: Seven dollars a page. At one point I had three persons [working for me]. This went on for, probably, five years.

I: Five *years you* did this?

R: I started out by just typing essays for people. That was in eighth grade. And then, ninth grade, someone asked me, "Why don't you just write it for me?" And so, she would tell her friends, and they told their friends. People got like B pluses, A minuses. I wouldn't write A plus papers because I didn't have time for that. I would bang 'em out.

Her parents were well aware of the business. They could hardly have missed it, as it brought her clients to the house as late as one in the morning. Yet so long as her own grades did not suffer, they saw nothing wrong with it. She was proud of making adult money and outsmarting the educational system, which, like most teenagers, she saw as arbitrary and silly. She notes ruefully, however, that she is still not sure how to "put it on my resume."

Some young people got their first work experience in the more sinister—and dangerous—parts of the underground economy. Many grew up in neighborhoods where drug dealing was a significant industry that hired at a young age. Many respondents who grew up in New York at the height of the crack epidemic talk about the dangers of "getting into drugs," meaning *selling* drugs, not taking them. One African American from Brooklyn recalls:

R: When I left [school], I got a lot of jobs off the books. Bars, construction, repair banisters, interiors, housework, bricklaying. It was off the books, they was paying me cash . . . [But] I was caught up in hustling. I was always hustling. So I was really not caring if I had a job or not, because I had another job in the streets, which was the wrong route.
I: "Hustling?"
R: My definition of hustling, for me, was getting drugs and distributing them. And getting money for it! That's hustling. On the block. Every day, morning, noon and night!

While some people in all the groups dealt drugs, this activity evidently played a large role in the early work life of the Dominican men, particularly those from Washington Heights, the epicenter of the crack trade of the late 1980s and early 1990s. For some, drug dealing supplanted the legitimate work force. One young man, recently released after six years in prison, remembered drug dealing not only as his first paying job but also as a lifestyle. Now 30, only sporadically employed, he is nostalgic for those days, though he knows the toll that this lifestyle took on him and his family. With a prison record and little legitimate work experience, he seems at a loss as to what to do next.

I: At what age did you get involved in that [i.e., the drug] business?

R: Like sixteen. [I got into it] through friends. This was a big drug area back in the days so . . . When I was a freshman, I was looking out. I started working as a lookout for my man . . . when I was a freshman in high school . . . as like I didn't work for nobody and nobody worked for me. But we all just worked together. Like if I get something, it' difficult to explain. Okay, let' say us two and him we all grew up together. It' all good. We all grew up together, we all know each other, and he got a connection that will give him so-and-so amount of whatever. And I don' have nothing. And then I'll be like, "Yo, let me get so-and-so 'cause I got somebody coming right now." So he give it to me, I give it to them, I give him the money, I take my percentage and that's it. But then when he comes to me and tells me, "Yo, wazzup?" Then we do the same thing. Like that. That' how we used to work.

I: And eventually you left it because you were busted?

R: Yeah. But I didn't get busted for drugs. I got busted *with* drugs, but that wasn't what I did time for. We got into some beef with some kids and they was trying to shoot us and we shot at them and a couple of people got hit.

I: What was the best thing about your business? And the worst things?

R: You make a lot of money, you know. You get to do a lot of things that I guess normal people wouldn't do, like I used to go to a club, spend $1,500 drinking Moets and Doms and I didn't sweat it. Go back the next night, do the same thing. Meet a lot of women. Have fast cars. Had my own apartment in Riverdale. It was cool. When I first started, I was getting like $400 a week, for seven days, for like twelve hours a day. [Eventually, he worked his way up.] At one point, in the summer of '89, we was clocking in about $18,000, $19,000 per week. It wasn't bad but you got to understand the lifestyle is different. How you live is different. Like, I had to maintain two cars in a garage. My motorcycle. My apartment over there. A girl over here. A girl over there. Maintain appearances—you live a different lifestyle. Like I could get up and say, "Oh, let's go to DR [Dominican Republic] right now." Boom, and we could just get up from right here and *bam!*

I: Did you ever consider leaving that?

R: Not before I went to jail. Naw.

I: How do you feel about it now?

R: I don't want to make my mother go through it. That's the only thing that would prevent me from doing it right now. I wouldn't want to make my family go through what I made them go through again. It's not worth it. But besides that, it's all good. But you got to understand that if you get into that, you got to be ready to die. You got to be willing to go to jail.

Most of the former drug dealers who spoke with us had less dramatic lives of crime—a few years, a bit of "crazy money," quickly earned and quickly spent, followed by "drifting" out of crime and into legitimate employment when adult responsibilities took hold (Matza 1964; Sampson and Laub 2003). More than other underground economy jobs, drug dealing and criminal activity left few skills or experiences that could be translated into the mainstream economy. Having little legitimate work experience and few educational credentials, but adult obligations and having become accustomed to adult incomes, former drug dealers in their late twenties had a particularly difficult time entering the legitimate labor force (Contreras forthcoming).

Whether immigrants create crime is a question that drives the debate over immigration. Many Americans assume that crime goes up when the number of immigrants in a community increases. Research suggests otherwise. While the evidence is mixed, most studies show that immigrants are about as law abiding as natives; an influx of even poor immigrants is often accompanied by a *decline* in urban crime (Sampson, Morenoff, and Raudenbush 2005). Other research has found that crime increases in areas where immigration is leading to a rapid turnover in population, but crime is lower in residentially stable immigrant communities (Skogan 2006).

Many studies report that immigrant crime rates are closely connected to police practices and the relationship between immigrants and the police (Martinez and Valenzuela 2006; Peterson, Krivo, and Hagan 2006). In New York crime fell dramatically during the 1990s. Although this is usually attributed to changing police practices, the ebbing of the crack epidemic, and the decline of the teenage population (Karmen 2000), it is significant to note that the immigrant share of the city's population was rising rapidly during the same period. Finally, much of the journalistic and criminological writing on crime and recent immigrants has focused on organized crime (Friedman 2000; Horowitz 2001). While organized crime is indeed a serious problem, increases in organized crime activity or sophistication does not necessarily mean that street crime or violent crime is taking a greater toll on community life.

Even if immigrants do not commit more crime than natives, some critics worry that the immigrants' children might, with potentially severe consequences for the second generation's long term incorporation. The "downward assimilation" scenarios suggest that some members of the second generation will be caught up in gangs and criminal activity on the "mean streets" of urban America. This sometimes clearly does happen (R. Smith 2006). Even if the children of immigrants are more likely than their parents to commit crimes, however, the children's behavior needs to be compared to that of their American peers. Figure 6.3 shows the rates of having been arrested and jailed—admittedly imperfect measures of criminal activity—by group and gender. Being arrested is clearly a fairly common experience among all young men, especially African Americans, and much less common among young women. Men from two groups—the Chinese and the Russian Jews—have noticeably lower arrest rates, less than half those of native whites. While Dominicans, West Indians, and South Americans having arrest rates higher these two groups, are almost the same as those for native *whites,* despite the fact that all these groups perceive police as more likely to discriminate against minorities.

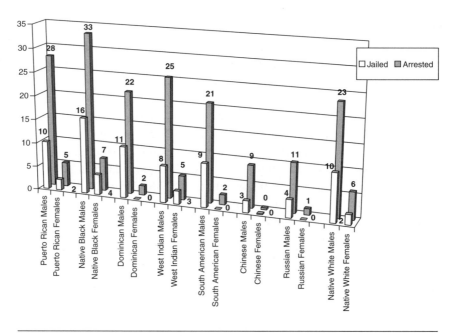

Figure 6.3. Contact with Criminal Justice System (%). *Source:* ISGMNY.

The arrest of nearly a quarter of the young men in some of these groups cannot be taken lightly. We suspect that being arrested will have more serious long term consequences for them than for native whites. While we have already seen that arrest has a negative impact on educational progress, it does not seem to have a uniformly negative impact on labor force participation. The most negative impacts are among native black, native white, and Russian men, where those arrested are ten points less likely to be working than those who were not. Working rates are actually *higher,* however, among West Indian, South American, and Chinese young men who were arrested. Certainly these patterns do not suggest that young second generation men are joining a native minority underclass.

From First Job to Current Job

The current jobs held by our respondents make a strong case for Granovetter's (1973) "strength of weak ties." While many second generation young people got their *first* jobs through family connections, they usually found their current job through friends their own age, many of whom worked at the places where our respondents found their current jobs. The Chinese and Russian Jews, whose parents had the strongest ethnic niches, were the least likely to get their current jobs through their families. They were significantly more likely than other groups to use college placement programs, reflecting the fact that they were also more likely to get college educations. Family played the biggest role for the least well-off groups: Puerto Ricans and Dominicans.

More formal channels, like answering an ad or using employment agencies, played a bigger role for African Americans and West Indians. These groups are also the most likely to seek jobs through governmental agencies and training programs, although this route was not common for anyone. African Americans were particularly likely to find jobs through formal mechanisms. Native blacks often seemed wary of informal job search procedures and using "connections" to look for work. They were also concerned about office "politics" and problems with bosses and the most comfortable with formal business relationships. They often saw the informal networking of other groups as unfair, exclusionary, and possibly racist (Kasinitz and Rosenberg 1996; Newman 1999; Mouw 2003; Fernandez and Su 2004; Smith 2005).

Relying on formal programs can sometimes be a distinct disadvantage.

Informal connections often proved the better route to employment opportunities, although the widespread reliance on friends underscores the importance of group characteristics in shaping individual access to opportunity. After all, if you get jobs through friends, where they work becomes very important. Formal training programs also have a poor record in providing the skills required in a dynamic labor market. One African American ex-convict, having recently completed a mandated training program and receiving his printer's licence, was frustrated by having been trained for jobs that no longer seemed to exist, compounding the problem of having a criminal record:

> *R:* For the first three to four months, I was not allowed to go for jobs, because I was basically training; learning a lot of the basics. Then, for the last two months . . . I would go job searching. So I have been putting my résumé out, Newsday, Times, companies like that. There's a lot of places on freeze right now. That's not hiring.
> *I:* Have you tried the local print shops?
> *R:* Yeah. I tried them. But the local ones always have . . . they already have their one person . . . they are really not so big and they don't need a lot of people.
> *I:* Do you think your problems with the law have made it difficult to find work? Do they ask about that?
> *R:* On the applications, yeah. And I put down "Will Explain" and I try to explain my situation. Do I find it difficult? In some cases yeah, because you can't lie on the application. You got to be straight up because lots of them do background checks. And they look at you different . . . They don't see a person. They see a crook.

African Americans and West Indians also relied on business and vocational schools. Whereas those institutions that trained nurses and medical technicians often did an adequate job of preparing people for real employment opportunities, many other schools had a poor reputation and did not. Although not accredited colleges these institutions can process college loans, and they encourage young people to incur debt for training that does not ultimately yield a good job.

Shifting Away from Parents' Industries and Occupations

Second generation and native born people work in industries and occupations that differ strongly from those of their parents. They also strongly resemble each other. Most young people work in retail, business services, and professional services, where few of their parents work. Manufacturing employment, particularly garment manufacturing, plays a huge role for the Chinese, Dominican, and South Americans mothers, as well some Russian Jewish fathers, but employs a negligible number of the second generation. While this may partly reflect the precipitous drop in manufacturing employment in the region, the dropoff is far too sharp to be explained this way.

A Colombian young man's sentiment that "I don't do that factory thing" seems widely held in the second generation, whose members saw such jobs as hard, dirty, and dangerous immigrant jobs that they would prefer to avoid. The Russian Jews had particularly strong feelings about the "ethnic imperative" of leaving the parental niches. As one young man explains:

> It's stressed within the family, so it's almost like 'God, I can't be a bum. I can't be like an Italian or anything. I'm Jewish!' We can't work with our hands. We have to work with our minds. So that's it. I would say that's how Jewish people are.

The authoritarian work relations of the factory floor often rankle the U.S. born. A 27-year-old Colombian from Queens recalls his ill-fated career as a machine operator:

> R: I got elected by all the employees as a shop steward, a union representative. If you really do your job good as a union representative, the enemies are going to be the bosses. They are not going to like you, because you are defending everybody else and you are making problems. So they started giving me a hard time. They started looking at how long I took in the bathroom, how long I took to do this. It wasn't that they were pushing me out the door but just that they were looking at me, timing me. I don't like that. And plus, I guess there was another thing they didn't like. I was born in this country. But if I can speak Spanish or English, I'd rather speak Spanish. And maybe that's weird because I can talk English, but I can express myself more in Spanish . . . and they [management] didn't like that because they'd say, "O, look at this guy, he could be talking behind my back."
>
> I: The management was English speaking?
>
> R: They were Americans. Like me. But the thing is, I'm Spanish too! I'd rather talk in Spanish. I'm proud of my heritage! I guess they

didn't like that . . . I'm not saying they hate me but . . . They thought maybe I was a smart guy.

About a year after he quit the factory, a friend told him about a position driving a delivery truck for a wholesaler. Although the money is not dramatically better, he greatly prefers the autonomy of his new position.

So where is the second generation going if not into the factories employing many of their parents? Many find the kind of entry level jobs open to any young New Yorker in white collar retail, clerical, and service work. Many have entered New York's all-important financial and professional services. Having grown rapidly in recent decades, these sectors were hiring vigorously when many respondents entered the labor force in the mid- to late 1990s, as the New York City economy reached an all-time high of employment in 2000. This does not mean that these young people all became brokers, analysts, and other "masters of the universe"— the most frequent job titles being things like "administrative assistant" or "customer service representative." A significant number also had job titles like "manager" or "office manager." Yet these positions usually pay better than similar jobs in manufacturing or the public sector.

Even during the late 1990s, the growth of financial and professional service employment did not lift all boats. The men and women from American, Chinese, and Russian Jewish backgrounds made significant advances over their parents in financial and professional service employment— even when their parents were already well represented there, as in the case of the Russians. The West Indian second generation, however, was slightly less likely to hold finance and professional service jobs than their English-speaking immigrant parents, who had, in fact, established a significant presence in these industries. Dominican young women were more likely to have entered these sectors than their mothers, but Dominican young men were not. Among the native groups, native African American young people advanced over their parents' share of employment in these areas. The picture was mixed among Puerto Ricans, where the young women were more likely than their mothers to work in these sectors, and the young men less so. Young native whites were also not as well represented as their parents, but their parents were the most heavily represented in these sectors.

Generally, the growing high skill sectors of New York City's economy have provided employment opportunities for many young New Yorkers, but the Chinese and Russian second generation have moved the furthest into them. The Russians have followed a pattern set by their parents. For the Chinese, however, this move into high skill areas represents a spectacular departure from their parents' industrial location.

High skill jobs and many other opportunities made available through the Internet, popular culture, and computer programming hardly existed for the respondents' parents. These jobs patterns offer strong counterevidence to the claim that the second generation might assimilate downwardly in the labor market. Even when the children of immigrants hold jobs that pay little more than their parents' jobs, or when career prospects remain limited, they see their work as thoroughly preferable to that of their parents. One 20-year-old Chinese college student explains:

> *R:* My father, he is always working (in a restaurant). Never home. My mom works like six days a week and my dad works six . . . [I] don't think he likes it. It is just to make money, pay my tuition, my brother's tuition, pay the bills.
> *I:* Would you ever work that job?
> *R:* No! Too much running around. My parents work long, long hours. I want to work nine to five! I guess it's all right for someone with his level of education. For them it's good, but not for me. I would not want to do it.

Parents with lower class or "ethnic" jobs can embarrass their upwardly mobile children. A 24-year-old man's Ukrainian Jewish father had continued his premigration profession as a waiter:

> I tell him, people go to computer jobs now, and they change careers and Pop, what are you doing? What are you doing working as a waiter? People work as waiters when they're like trying to get their acting career or something going but not like all your life. He's like, "Well, I've been doing that ever since I was in Russia and, you know, it's too late for me now." And I'm like, "Oh, please." Basically he thinks it's too late for him. He actually expresses the fact that he really enjoys it. He's like, "It's my job, and I have friends there and this is what I do and I've been doing this forever." I don't think he's too much of a thinker [little laugh] you know?

Even those respondents with limited job prospects share this sentiment. A currently unemployed 24-year-old Dominican woman with an arrest record recalls:

R: My mom, she didn't have papers. So she was working under the table, cleaning, ironing for people. That's like an Hispanic thing, you know? It was a way of getting through rough times.

I: Would you ever see yourself working that kind of job?

R: I never say "never" but . . . I wouldn't want to. Because I was raised here, you know? I speak very good English! So, I don't know . . .

We can appreciate just how far second generation young people have moved beyond their parents' labor market position by calculating an intergenerational index of dissimilarity across industries. This index, shown in Figure 6.4, compares the industry distribution of the respondents with those of their same-sex parent. It measures the share of each group that would have to move in order to produce the same distributions (Duncan and Duncan 1955). Three findings stand out. First, members of all the groups have moderately high differences (ranging from .2 to .5) with their parents. Second, these patterns show strong gender differences. For the most part, the women have moved further from their mothers' industry profile than the men have from their fathers. Change has been greatest among the Chinese, South American, and Dominican women whose mothers worked disproportionately in manufacturing. The women in the three native groups and Russian Jews changed less, but their mothers were better positioned in the first place. Finally, the Chinese, Russian, and South American men showed the greatest change from their fathers, albeit less than their female counterparts. The fact that Dominican, Puerto Rican, West Indian, and native black young men did not move as far suggests that they are having a harder time than minority women in the region's labor market, though the West Indian and native black fathers were better positioned than those of the Dominicans and Puerto Ricans. (The fact that native white men also show little change reflects their fathers' excellent labor market positions.)

The gap between men and women is particularly large among Dominicans. By working in industries similar to those of their fathers, Dominican young men differ sharply from Dominican young women, who have successfully avoided their mothers' industries. Given that Dominican fathers hold low-paying, low-skilled jobs, they provide evidence of second generation stagnation, if not decline, and so extend the story of how Dominican young women outpaced men in education (López 2003, 2004). At first sight, the similarity between parents and their children among

West Indians might also be taken for second generation decline as West Indians become African Americans (Waters 1999). Yet this conclusion is not warranted because the West Indian parents are already well positioned in the labor market. Adopting their parents' pattern may not be a bad idea for young West Indians. This is not a case of clinging to a parent's ethnic economy, however. Speaking English on arrival, the West Indian parents were least likely to work in ethnic niches and most likely to be in the larger service economy.

We also calculated how members of the second generation and their parents compared to the overall distribution of employment of all people their age and sex as measured in the Current Population Survey (see the Methodological Appendix). This produced similar results. The second generation groups have a far less distinct labor market position than did their parents. Immigrant parents are highly concentrated, but the men and women of all second generation groups except West Indians look far more like all young people their age. The Chinese, Dominican, and South American women had the most occupationally segregated mothers, but they were the least segregated. Only West Indians became slightly more

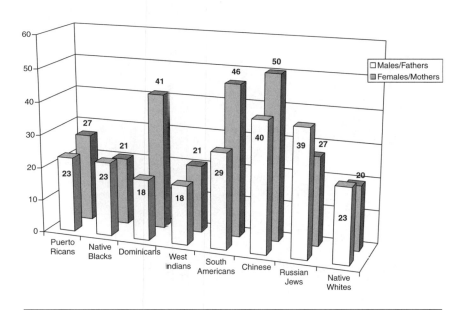

Figure 6.4. Industry Dissimilarity Between Respondents and Their Parents. *Source:* ISGMNY.

different from their generation than were their parents, although the parents were not very segregated to begin with. The West Indian ability to speak English clearly smoothed the parents' incorporation into New York's rapidly growing service sector during the 1970s and 1980s, minimizing their need to rely on co-ethnics for help in finding employment. Their children are taking advantage of these inroads. Western and Pettit (2005) showed that racial discrimination continues to constrain access to entry level jobs, particularly for young men. Our data suggest that discrimination does not lock first or second generation West Indians out of any economic sector in the same way.

Occupations

The main message that comes through from these findings is that the second generation groups are broadly distributed across the labor force and hold jobs quite similar to those of all young people in general. They are not clustered in the ethnic industries and occupations of their parents but have effectively fled them. As Figure 6.5 shows, the most common occupations for second generation and native born groups except native whites are office support workers, service workers, and retail sales. (For

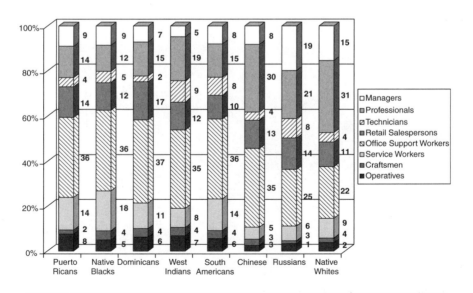

Figure 6.5. Occupational Distribution (%). *Source:* ISGMNY.

native whites, these categories rank behind "professional.") To be sure, some groups show signs of specialization. Many Chinese and Russian Jewish respondents are working in finance- and computer-related occupations. Some Chinese are working in clothing design, the most high status part of the industry in which their mothers work. Many West Indian second generation young women work in health care, though at much lower levels than their mothers. West Indian young people also work as teachers and social workers. West Indians and native blacks both disproportionately work in public and social service jobs. This may help explain why, as we shall see in Chapter 9, these groups are most likely to vote, despite their generation's disdain for the political system. Among the specific occupations most frequently reported by native whites are "media and communications workers," "entertainers and performers," and "food and beverage servers," categories that can overlap.

Still, as with industry, the occupational profiles of the second generation are far less concentrated than for their immigrant parents. Women have avoided blue collar occupations in favor of the service sector, as have men to a lesser extent. The occupational profiles of the groups are roughly similar, though different from their parents. Age and gender seem to play a larger role than ethnicity in determining the type of job one holds, second generation status, or even race. The main intergroup difference is that the best-educated groups—native whites, Russian Jews, and Chinese—are more likely to hold managerial and professional jobs.

Enclaves and Ghettos

The distribution of industries and occupations in which people work must be distinguished from the organization of their places of work. The literature on ethnic economies tends to assume that an ethnic group's concentration in a cell within the larger matrix of industries and occupations must mean that the firms in that industry use ethnic networks to hire their workers, creating ethnic niches at the work site as well as in the larger pattern. Yet as Logan and colleagues (1994) note, this is not necessarily true. To get at this question, we asked our respondents about the racial and ethnic backgrounds of their co-workers and supervisors.

The second generation groups work in settings that vary widely in this regard. No group works in places where their co-ethnics form a majority, as shown in Table 6.2. Native blacks are the most segregated on the job, but only about 40 percent work at places where most of their co-workers are African Americans, though just over 60 percent say they worked in predominantly black (African American, Afro-Caribbean, or African) work sites. Only a quarter reported that their supervisors were African American. Of the second generation groups, the Chinese were most likely to work with fellow Chinese, with a third reporting that their co-workers were mostly Chinese and 27 percent having Chinese supervisors as well as co-workers. (Two-fifths reported their co-workers as mostly Asian, suggesting mixing among Koreans, Vietnamese, and Chinese in some workplaces.) Although the Puerto Ricans, Dominicans, and South Americans were far less likely to work with co-ethnics, they did work with fellow Hispanics, but this reached a majority only among Dominicans. Native whites and Russian Jews worked mainly in predominantly white work sites. Most West Indians and native blacks worked in predominantly black work sites. The Hispanic groups and Chinese were more likely to work in racially mixed workplaces.

Why does the ethnic economy play such a small role for the second generation? Many second generation New Yorkers avoided ethnic economy jobs for the simple reason that they do not pay well. Figure 6.6 compares the weekly earnings of people working where they are surrounded by co-ethnics with those who are not; the latter situation yielded higher pay for every group except native whites. Though the differences were small for most groups, they were large and statistically significant for African Americans and Chinese. African Americans in predominantly African American work sites earn the least of any group, whereas those working in mixed or predominantly white sites earn about the overall median and more than

Table 6.2. Co-ethnic Employment across Second Generation Groups (%)

Group	Supervisor & Co-workers same ethnicity	Co-worker same ethnicity	Supervisor & Co-workers same race	Co-worker same race
Puerto Rican	13.8	28.8	15.9	46.6
Black	23.9	40.3	27.6	60.5
Dominican	6.4	21.0	19.0	52.8
West Indian	6.7	23.4	24.7	56.8
South American	2.1	9.8	13.4	43.1
Chinese	27.4	32.6	29.1	40.0
Russian Jewish	8.7	23.5	72.2	83.6
White	14.3	23.5	74.4	81.7

Source: ISGMNY.

the Hispanic groups or the West Indians. Chinese working in predominantly white work sites earned even more than native whites. Chinese in largely Chinese work sites, on the other hand, earned well below the overall median, about the same as Puerto Ricans. As Zhou (1992) suggests, these low wages could be the effect of restricted workforce participation by women caring for small children. Yet the negative effect of working in co-ethnic work sites remains significant even after controlling for age and gender. The mainstream also yielded better working conditions and higher benefits. Half the Chinese working in mixed settings had health insurance, compared to 28 percent in co-ethnic work sites.

That working in co-ethnic or co-racial work sites has a negative impact for native minorities is not surprising. The finding that it works against members of the second generation is more striking. Many have thought that New York's successful Chinese ethnic enclave (Zhou 1992) and high rates of self-employment among Chinese and Russian parents might yield employment opportunities to the second generation. Yet both groups found large payoffs from leaving the ethnic economy and joining the

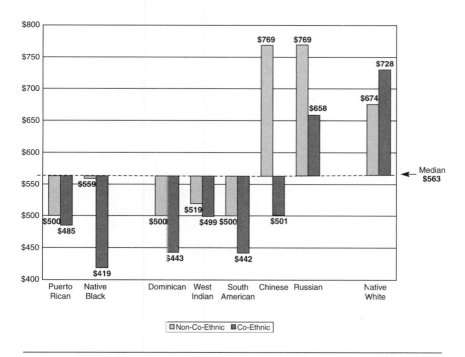

Figure 6.6. Weekly Income by Ethnic Enclave Status ($). *Source:* ISGMNY.

mainstream. In a recent revisiting of the Cuban ethnic enclave in Miami, Portes also found that working there was largely a one-generation phenomenon, with the second generation anxious to find opportunities elsewhere (Portes and Shafer 2007).

Finance was the glamour industry in the late 1990s. Getting a job in this sector meant a lot for the children of immigrants. As one daughter of a Chinatown store owner put it:

> I always knew I wanted to work for J. P. Morgan. I don't know why. I like the name. I thought, J. P. Morgan, yeah, that sounds like an institution that has been around for a long time and it's an old standard of Wall Street, and if I am going to work on Wall Street, I kind of like that name. And I like Goldman Sachs. So I went in, without really researching it. I went to one of those headhunters and told her, I want to apply for a job at J. P. Morgan.

Victoria Malkin's ethnography of retail clerks (2004), conducted for this study, documents the typical second generation work experience in New York. Retail sales provides many young people with their first jobs, including those youth with native born parents. Malkin's participant observation in two branches of a regional housewares chain was revealing. Their twenty-something workforces included Dominicans, South American, Asians, and West Indians as well as native blacks, Puerto Ricans, and the occasional white migrant from another part of the United States. Most employees were high school graduates and many had some college or other post–high school training, although few had four year degrees. The managers were almost exclusively native whites.

By most measures these were bad jobs. The hourly wages were only slightly higher than those in the ethnic economy. Entry level employees got the minimum wage and only slight raises thereafter. The stores were unionized, theoretically entitling full time employees to health insurance and a modest package of other benefits after they worked full time for a set period of time. Yet almost all employees started as part time workers, making them ineligible for union membership or benefits. These "part time" jobs actually required full time availability, as the stores frequently changed workers' hours depending on customer demand. These unpredictable schedules wreaked havoc with the workers' attempts to pursue further education or vocational training, although many were trying to do just that. During slow periods, full time employees struggled to "get enough hours" to maintain full time status—and keep their benefits.

Some could do this only by working a few hours in the morning, then returning at busier times in the late afternoon or evening. Since most workers lived too far from the stores to return home, this meant getting paid for six or eight hours for what was, in effect, a ten or twelve hour day. (For an analogous situation in the fast food industry, see Newman 1999.)

These workers soon realized that they had little chance for advancement. At best they could hope to become supervisors earning a few dollars an hour over minimum wage. Unlike the large department stores of previous decades, this firm rarely promoted workers into the executive office or provided job training that led away from the shop floor. While Malkin's workers dreamed of moving up the ladder of success, few thought they could do so from their current position. This was only one of many jobs they would hold. The company made little commitment to them, and they made little commitment to the company.

Yet most still preferred this job to the ethnic economy jobs held by their parents. They liked working in the middle of the city and having contact with a wide variety of people. Many had grown up in black, Latino, or Asian neighborhoods and attended overwhelmingly black or Latino public schools, so their co-workers were the most diverse social group they had ever been part of. Their friendship and dating networks expanded accordingly. They learned about different ways of doing things and came to share an interest in pan-ethnic, youth-oriented popular music and fashion—a multiethnic mainstream. Unlike ethnic economy workers, the young clerks had to dress neatly in low cost "knock off" versions of high-fashion clothes. While doing this strained their tight budgets, they enjoyed taking full advantage of the sales and changing styles of the stores around them, discount and chic. Few envisioned doing this sort of work for long, but their work was also not in a "ghetto"—and therefore what they did seemed a step up from their parents' parochial lives.

What of the young people who do work in the "ethnic economy"? Some scholars suggest that they did well to do so when their parents had been successful (Zhou and Bankston 1998). Some young people had worked out specifically second generation niches as bridges between the ethnic and mainstream economies. For example, one second generation Dominican man worked as an insurance agent for Dominican immigrant businesses, and several Russian and Chinese second generation respondents were making money as real estate agents, accountants, and attorneys for immigrant clienteles. Some second generation young people even built on the transnational side of contemporary immigrant communities, working in the American branches of corporations based in a parent's home country or for American companies doing business abroad. Since such positions required a knowledge of both the immigrant ethnic economy and mainstream institutions, they seem a natural fit for the second generation. But those respondents who actually did such work were few.

The Chinese were the second generation group most likely to work among co-ethnics. Some Chinese worked in geographically dispersed Chinese small businesses—suburban Chinese restaurants or small stores in native minority neighborhoods—that more closely resembled the "middle man minority" model than a true enclave (Bonacich 1973). Others occupied what Zeltzer-Zubida has called "hidden ethnic niches," where Chinese predominate in a specific work site in a firm or industry that is not particularly Chinese (Zeltzer-Zubida 2004b).

Most Chinese respondents who worked with Chinese co-workers, however, worked in what could reasonably be described as an ethnic enclave. They were geographically concentrated and had Chinese owners and supervisors as well as co-workers, suppliers, and customers. The situation of these young people resembled that of their parents. The Chinese respondents working in their ethnic enclave were more likely to be 1.5 generation as opposed to second generation. They were also younger and more likely to be male. Many found their first job within the enclave and may eventually move out. They were also less educated than other Chinese young people. No more than a handful were professionals serving an immigrant community or capitalizing on their knowledge of both societies.

Often, the ethnic economy provided a safety net for the least well educated members of the Chinese second generation, especially those whose education was interrupted by their migration, as well as for those who faced problems in the mainstream economy. They were much more likely to have been arrested, though that was not common for workers in either kind of setting (14 percent in co-ethnic settings as opposed to 9 percent in ethnically mixed work sites). As bad as their jobs often were, they might have been worse off in the absence of the ethnic economy.

In sum, ethnic enclave jobs were much more like safety nets than springboards. (Kim [2006] reaches a similar conclusion about the Korean second generation in New York.) While ethnic enclaves have clearly been useful for the immigrant first generation, we find little support for the idea that they will be a significant source of upward mobility for the second generation. Even for the children of Chinatown, "moving up" generally means "moving out."

Joining the Mainstream, for Better . . . and for Worse

Members of the second generation have largely assimilated into the mainstream economy. Their labor force participation resembles that of other New Yorkers their own age, and there is little about their jobs to distinguish them as the children of immigrants. Indeed, age, race, and gender remain far more important determinants of second generation status in the labor market. Some groups, of course, tend toward certain occupations and industries over others, but second generation groups are far less clustered than their immigrant parents. Labor market outcomes for members of the second generation do reflect the social capital and labor force position of their parents and the advantages and disadvantages that flow from them. But these influences are largely indirect and often far in the background. Rarely do parents pass jobs or businesses down to their children, and this is most common among the least successful. Even the Chinese ethnic enclave functions more like a safety net than a springboard.

The work lives of the second generation also provide little evidence of second generation decline into an underclass marked by persistent poverty and unemployment. Indeed, the group that most resembles this stereotype, New York's Puerto Rican young adults, raises a concern about possible third generation decline. The most troubled of the second generation groups, Dominicans, though more recently arrived and less well educated, are still more likely to be working or in school and make more money than their Puerto Rican counterparts. Indeed, all of the children of immigrants are more likely than those of native minority respondents to be either in the labor force or in school, and the earnings in most groups are closer to those of the native whites than to those of native minority respondents. The children of immigrants also earn more when they work in the mainstream economy, not in ethnic niches or enclaves. What will happen to these groups as they move fully into their careers is a question we must leave to another generation of social scientists. At this juncture, however, the economic fate of the second generation seems tied more closely to the overall economy than it is either to protective ethnic enclaves or a marginal underclass.

In saying that the second generation is not downwardly mobile, we are not suggesting that they have universally bright economic futures. It is a common mistake to equate assimilation with upward mobility. There are many reasons to be concerned about what the future will hold for the young people we are studying. Household incomes are becoming more unequal, unionized manufacturing and other blue collar jobs with good benefits are dwindling, and labor market insecurity is on the rise. These conditions are particularly challenging for young adults without a college education, which may well characterize the majority of the people in our study even a decade from now. Many of our respondents are working in relatively low wage sectors which are less often unionized and more reliant on young part time workers than was true in times past.

As Katherine Newman (1999) points out, while such jobs may impart more skills and work habits than is generally understood, they may not translate into better-paying positions as the workers get older. Yet these are problems facing all young working and lower middle class New Yorkers, including many local native whites. Further, as Newman's recent followup has shown, over the long term there is considerable mobility from the working poor into the stable working class—particularly among those who do manage to obtain union jobs or to acquire more education (Newman 2006), as many of the second generation are clearly trying to do. The situation is considerably worse for those outside the regularly employed labor force. In general the children of immigrants show less of the weak labor force attachment that we see in a significant minority of native African American and Puerto Rican youth. Yet while distinctive immigrant niches often shaped the lives of immigrant parents, it is the mainstream economy that shapes the lives of the second generation, in no small measure because the children of immigrants *are* the new mainstream.

7

Forming New Families

I feel in the future, soon enough, we're all gonna, you know, get
together and have great and massive sex and we're all going to blend
into one race.

CHINESE MAN, AGED 22

The timing of marriage and childbearing in the United States and the relations between men and women have changed a great deal since the
1960s. Scholars agree that the transition to adulthood has become an increasingly complex and messy affair (Furstenberg et al. 2005). Many
young people spend a period of time living alone or with other young
adults or cohabit for periods before marriage. At the same time, the high
cost of postsecondary education means that many remain dependent on
their families well into their twenties (Schoeni and Ross 2005). While pursuing education leads many people to postpone marriage and children,
many are not marrying or becoming parents at all. At the same time,
single parenthood has become more common, further weakening the relationship between marriage and childbearing. Divorce, separation, and
the formation of second and blended families have all become much more
common (Goldscheider and Waite 1991).

A number of factors contribute to these processes: rising female labor
force participation; declining employment opportunities for men with low
levels of education; changes in public assistance; greater acceptance of
premarital sex, cohabitation, and unmarried parenthood; the availability
of contraception and abortion; and more liberal divorce laws (Ellwood
and Jencks 2001). In a broader sense the women's rights movement led
to greater autonomy for women, opening up opportunities for education
and professional work, and giving women more power in the household.
At the same time, these changes lessened the traditional obligation (and
ability) of men to provide sole support for families and have forced both
women and men to make difficult choices about the balance between
work and family (Gerson 1985, 1993).

Because the second generation is only now reaching young adulthood,
relatively little has been written about their patterns of family formation,

childbearing, and views on gender relations. Many of our respondents were leaving their families of origin and establishing their own households when we interviewed them in their mid-twenties, giving us the opportunity to follow them through these decisions. Just as they grew up in many different kinds of households, our respondents live in a great variety of arrangements as they leave their parents' homes, find their own places, make new bonds with romantic partners, and have children. These decisions have been shaped by structural factors, such as the high cost of housing in the city and the often scant financial resources available to young people and their families. They have also been influenced by cultural norms and values about independent living and the right time for marriage and parenting. Although individuals do not always follow their immigrant parents' expectations, the second and 1.5 generations must contend with their expectations. These differ considerably across the groups and are often different from the expectations of the respondents' American peers.

Norms about the timing of marriage vary considerably across the countries from which our respondents came. The *median* age at marriage in 1984–1994 was only 19 in the Dominican Republic and 21 in Colombia and Peru (Singh and Samara 1996). By contrast, the later-longer-fewer *(wan-xi-shao)* policy in the People's Republic of China promoting late marriage and childbearing means it is rare for Chinese young people to marry before their mid-twenties (Hannum and Liu 2006). Fertility patterns also differ considerably. Although family size in Latin American and Caribbean countries has decreased from around six children in the 1960s to an average of 3.5 in the late 1980s (Wulf and Singh 1991), it is still much higher than in China, where as a consequence of the one-child policy it is only 1.7. Out-of-wedlock fertility is more common and more socially acceptable in the West Indies than in the other home countries in the study, although there, too, family size has fallen in recent decades.

In addition to age at marriage, fertility rates reflect different attitudes toward contraception, which is widely available in China and Russia, and quite common in Colombia, but seems to be less accepted in the Dominican Republic (Fennelly, Cornwell, and Casper 1992). Similarly, abortion is illegal in most South American and Caribbean countries but is widely available and commonly used in China and Russia. In general teenage parenthood is much more common in Latin America and the Caribbean than in Russia and is almost nonexistent in China. In the late 1980s, 19 percent of Dominican women had a child before the age of 18, as did 16 percent of women in Colombia (Wulf and Singh 1991).

Ideas about appropriate roles for men and women in the household and the public sphere also differ considerably. Female labor force participation is higher in the English-speaking Caribbean, for example, than it is in the Dominican Republic or South America. It is also very high in China and Russia. As we will discuss, expectations about fidelity and about men's and women's responsibilities for household tasks also vary considerably across the countries from which our respondents' parents came. Of course, as we have stressed throughout this book, the home-country norms that parents bring with them are not representative of an unchanging national culture. They are often specific to particular migrant flows and to particular times, and they differ by class, religion, rural-urban background, and other factors. For example, Chinese from Taiwan and the People's Republic of China lived under very different state policies that, until recently at least, resulted in the less developed People's Republic having more equitable gender relations than the wealthier but more traditional Taiwan. We must also not forget that migrants sometimes cling to values that have long been eroded in their countries of origin.

In addition to the views of their parents and co-ethnics, children of immigrants are also exposed to the ideas and behaviors of native born Americans they encounter in their neighborhoods, schools, and workplaces and through the media. While the native born seem to share certain ideas about the transition to adulthood—such as a desire to move out of the parental home quite young—there are also significant differences across class and ethnic groups in the timing of family formation. In general, children of more educated, wealthier families tend to postpone marriage and parenting, whereas single parenthood and teenage pregnancy are most common among women from poor families of all racial and ethnic backgrounds, as well as among native blacks and Puerto Ricans in particular (Ellwood and Jencks 2001). Depending on where children of immigrants live and who they mix with, they are exposed to different "immigrant" and "American" approaches to these major life transitions, which sometimes reinforce and sometimes conflict with each other.

We begin by discussing our respondents' views about their parents and their own expectations concerning gender relations. We then focus on the timing of marriage and child-rearing and how our second generation respondents are navigating their ethnicity as they choose partners and raise their children. They must decide how important it is to be with someone from the same background and whether to heed their parents' wishes in this respect. When they become parents and begin to reflect on how much of their ethnic heritage to convey to their children, they also help to frame what ethnic identity will mean to a new generation.

Generation and Gender

Although recent work (Parrado and Flippen 2005) has noted that the effect of migration on gender relations is complex and sometimes contradictory, many scholars of immigration have found that in the first generation, women tend to see the American ideal of equality between men and women as a real plus to migration whereas some men see it as a loss for them (Foner 1999; Levitt 2001). Our study found considerable variation across the groups, but ideas about sex roles, the relative freedom of women, and expectations about appropriate gender behavior that are sometimes starkly different from those in the sending countries (Figure 7.1). Many respondents were shocked by the gender attitudes and behaviors they encountered when visiting their parents' countries. Parents and children often differed on these issues, and we found evidence of a trend toward assimilation to the American context of gender roles. While women were most attuned to these issues, a surprising number of men

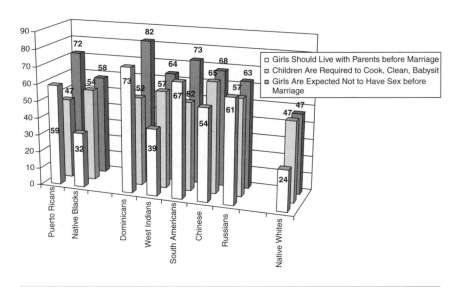

Figure 7.1. Attitudes about Gender Roles (%). *Source:* ISGMNY.

also described gender expectations as a key element of difference between their own more "Americanized" values and beliefs and those of their parents.

We asked three questions in the telephone survey about differential treatment between the genders. We asked whether families expected girls to live in their parents' house until they got married; whether they expected girls not to have sex until they were legally married; and whether the family required the respondents to cook, clean, or do child care while parents worked when the respondents were growing up. Native whites were most egalitarian on all three questions, and native whites and blacks more like each other than similar to the second generation groups. Only 24 percent of native whites and 32 percent of native blacks agreed or somewhat agreed that their families expected girls to live at home until they got married. Puerto Ricans were more like the second generation groups than native whites or blacks, with 59 percent agreeing that their families expected girls to live at home until married. West Indians, who have a long history of high female labor force participation and independent women (Foner 1999), were close to native born blacks, with 39 percent agreeing with the statement. On the other end of the spectrum, Dominicans (73 percent), South Americans (67 percent), and Russians (61 percent) held more traditional views on this question.

The responses to whether girls were expected not to have sex until legally married were quite similar to those for the question about moving out of the parental home. Dominicans, South Americans, and Puerto Ricans were most likely to agree, whereas native blacks and whites were most likely to disagree. The majority of native whites disagreed or somewhat disagreed with this statement, while majorities of the other groups agreed.

In the in-depth interviews Russians and West Indians rarely mentioned their parents' attitudes about gender, although some West Indian women did complain about not being allowed to leave New York for college and about being subject to stricter curfews than their brothers. By contrast, gender relations were a common theme in our conversations with Latino and Chinese respondents. Chinese young people complained that their parents' "traditional" Chinese values held women as less important than men and that their parents worried more about the education and occupation of their sons than of their daughters. Wives, they noted, were expected to be submissive to their husbands and to their mothers-in-law.

This 32-year-old Chinese woman, whose parents were from Hong Kong, describes her parents' traditional views and how they differ from her own:

> *R:* I overheard a conversation [my father] had with his friends when I was in elementary school. We were playing around the house and his friends were bragging about how bright their kids are and stuff like that and my dad said something like, "Well, if one son becomes a doctor and the other becomes a lawyer I will be happy." And his friend was like, "What about your daughter?" "Oh, if she marries well." . . . I couldn't have been that old but it still struck home. And I can't say I have a very close relationship with my father. There was always a distance and I think after hearing comments like that it's even harder to bridge that distance.
>
> *I:* What about your mother? Does she share his views?
>
> *R:* No, she didn't. But as far as decisions around the house and so forth, she left that up to my dad . . . I think her mother-in-law gave her a tough time too. The whole myth about the mother-in-law/daughter-in-law relationship actually in this case did exist. And I think my mom just took it. It's been this way from what I gather for her life. I wouldn't want it. I couldn't live it now, being in the States for twenty-some years. If I was maybe in Hong Kong and kind of kept within the Asian tradition, values and things, being [a] subservient woman, maybe I would have had to but being here and just being exposed to American ideas and so forth, I would never take that.

Chinese men were also keenly aware of their parents' highly gendered expectations:

> In my culture, boys are always more important in the family because the parents are going to be dependent on me when they get old, so I have to take care of them when they are old, so they have to be nicer to me than to my sister. So I'm really more important in the family than my sister.

Dominicans, South Americans, and the Puerto Ricans also brought up gender roles spontaneously in the interview, often in response to the question, "What are the characteristics of your ethnic group that you like the least?" But they differ from the Chinese in that they are more concerned with the "machismo" of Latino culture and with the strict control of girls by parents. While the Chinese are concerned about unequal workloads between men and women within the household and about parents not investing as much in women's as in men's educations and occupations, the concerns of the Latino groups revolve more around sexual relations between men and women. This 30-year-old South American woman chafed at her parents' restrictiveness:

> We could not have boyfriends until we were eighteen. Like I told you, it didn't matter if we were sixteen or seventeen, we had to be home 4:00. If it was a beautiful day and they were generous 6:00. What seventeen year old do you know who has to be home at 6:00? My brother doesn't have that. He can go out. My brother was allowed to have a girlfriend. First of all, what boyfriends would want to date you if you had to be home at 4:00? Whatever boyfriends we had, they had other girlfriends once we went home at 4:00 or 6:00. But if we had them over to the house, like if they really, really liked us and they were being troopers and sticking with us, it was like you're in the living room and that's it. My brother was allowed to have his girlfriend in his room. My parents didn't care because he's a boy. "Double standards" isn't even near to describing it!

Parents often sent strong messages to their children about the behavior they considered appropriate for men and women, and this was often a source of conflict. This Dominican woman objected strongly to her father's expectations that as a woman she should be concerned mostly with housework:

> My father swears I'm never going to get married because I'm assertive and I'm very independent and I don't know how to cook . . . I'm not at all like my mother and I don't plan to be home all day, cooking, cleaning and looking after the kids while he works. I believe it is okay for a man to wash dishes, load the laundry, mop, sweep, whatever. My father feels this is not acceptable and that's woman's work and a man should not have to do that. So he thinks I'm way too liberal and way too independent to ever get married.

Hispanic women often spoke of the importance of "fidelity" in marriage and of the difficulty in finding a Hispanic man who would be faithful. These negative expectations meant an uphill battle for men like this 25-year-old Dominican, who complains:

The stereotype is for Dominican men being womanizers, you know how they say that. Usually when I meet a girl and they're like, "Oh, you're Dominican. Got to watch out for you." I'm like, "No, no, I'm not like that." I have to show them I'm different.

Interestingly, many of these expectations do not translate into behavior. Although whites express more tolerance of premarital sex, few whites had children before marriage. Conversely, while Dominicans and Puerto Ricans said their families disapproved of premarital sex, they were more likely to have children while unmarried. Dominicans, who were the most likely to say their parents expected them to stay at home until marriage, were the least likely of the second generation groups to do so, moving out at a rate much more similar to the native born. Chinese and West Indians, who said it was more acceptable to move out of their parents' homes, actually stayed there longer. While respondents often reported that their families had different expectations about men and women, when we asked about what actually happened when the respondents were growing up, only the South Americans show a gender gap in their treatment by their families, with more girls than boys being asked to cook, clean, or do child care. In all the other groups, parents expected both boys and girls to do roughly similar chores. Although many women had misgivings about the gender attitudes of their male compatriots, in the end most married or partnered with people from the same pan-ethnic group. As we follow our respondents into their adult lives, we can see other ways in which both the expectations of their immigrant parents and the gender norms around them have shaped their decisions.

Leaving the Nest

Leaving the parental home is often an important mark of entering adulthood in American society. Middle class children often leave for college or the armed services at age 18, and when in recent years an increasing number have returned home in their twenties, these "boomerang kids" or "incompletely launched young adults" have been popularly identified as a social problem. Yet the high cost of housing presents a major challenge to young people trying to achieve this mark of adulthood in and around New York. Starting a separate household is quite expensive, and paying rent can eat up funds that could be used to pay for education or saved to buy a home later. For young people in poor or even middle income families, staying at home with parents or other relatives during their young adult years is the easiest way to cut costs.

It is therefore not surprising that young people in New York leave home late compared to those in other parts of the country. Census data for the region in 2000 show that 55.6 percent of those aged 18 to 32 do not live with their parents or other family. By the time they are 30–32, 80 percent are on their own, though a surprising 12 percent are still living with a parent. Table 7.1 shows that our respondents follow a similar pattern, but with some important differences. The children of immigrants are more likely to continue to live with their parents. Over three-quarters live with their parents during the college-age years, compared with only two-thirds of the native born. This gap persists into the early thirties, with more than one in five children of immigrants still living with a parent, compared with only 17 percent of the native born.

The Chinese stay at home longest: nearly half of those aged 28–32 were still living with a parent. Russians, South Americans, and West Indians also tend to stay at home into their mid-twenties, but more have moved out by their early thirties. Dominicans resemble the native born more closely than they do the other children of immigrants. The native born groups are all less likely to live with parents, with native whites being most likely to live independently. Women move out sooner than men. Over a quarter of the older men were still living with their parents, compared with fewer than a fifth of the women. Men from the Hispanic groups were most likely to do this, with West Indians, native whites, Russians, and Chinese less so.

Table 7.1. Percentage of Respondents Living with Parent (only respondents who grew up in metropolitan New York)

Group	Age 18–22	Age 23–27	Age 28–32
Puerto Ricans	69.8	33.6	23.4
Native Blacks	64.7	30.0	15.1
Dominicans	65.3	34.9	19.0
West Indians	72.4	44.0	27.6
South Americans	73.7	51.8	38.3
Chinese	84.7	65.5	49.2
Russians	80.3	39.5	20.5
Native Whites	68.2	33.3	10.8

Source: ISGMNY.

Our in-depth interviews reveal at least three patterns among those still living at home: late launchers, boomerangs, and those engaging in long term multigenerational living. The interviews also suggest that young people from different class and ethnic backgrounds have different ideas about the relationship they should have with their parents and about how leaving their parents' home reflects upon their status as adults.

Late launchers still live with their parents after the age of 22. They are generally attending college or trying to save enough money to rent or buy their own home, which can take many years. Many children of immigrants accept this situation without discomfort and do not think it delays their entry into adulthood. Here is what a 33-year-old West Indian woman who was about to get married said in response to a question about whether she would move out *after* the wedding:

> No. My mother says, "As long as it takes." But I'm giving us two years, at the most . . . To save enough, because she's not charging us rent. I'll be finished paying my car soon, so the money I was using to pay a car note, I can put that into extra savings. So it will help speed up my departure [laugh]. I'm just worried about having enough that if I get sick, or if he gets sick, that the other person can still handle the mortgage without having to worry about "How am I gonna pay this, how am I gonna pay that?"

Our native respondents, regardless of race, generally felt that moving out of the parental home was an important marker of adulthood and that not doing so by their early twenties represented a sort of failure. This is one area in which the second generation groups resembled each other more than they did the native groups. Indeed, while native blacks and Puerto Ricans were slower to move out than the whites, often because of their lower incomes, they were decidedly uncomfortable with this fact and proud to be independent when they could be.

A Puerto Rican woman who grew up on the Upper West Side inherited her parents' apartment when they moved back to Puerto Rico. While acknowledging that she would not have been able to live alone on her salary of $45,000 if the apartment were not rent controlled, she was proud of taking care of herself and felt that her parents now considered her an adult—"not their little girl anymore"—because she could manage alone. She compared herself with a friend who could not afford to move out:

I mean, I have a girlfriend that's my same age, and she can't afford to move out because she doesn't make enough and she doesn't feel that she's an adult, because she's still with mommy and daddy . . . and that's a very big pressure that you have, to prove that "I'm an adult, I can live by myself." You don't feel like an adult if you live with your mom and dad.

This discomfort at living with parents was even more apparent among native *"boomerangs"*: young people who returned to their parents' home after living away proved too expensive, or divorce or unemployment struck. A 27-year-old African American paralegal who plans to go to law school told us that she, her fiancé, and their five children had moved in with her mother and stepfather outside of the metro area in order to save money to buy a house of their own. They had agreed it would be only for a year because "I didn't want to get too comfortable." Despite a good relationship with her mother, she found living with her parents

just aggravating. I mean it's cool, my mom is my best friend but at this point in my life I'm just too old to live at home, 'cause I have my own family and I've lived away from home, so I know that when you come back home it's like 'Oh my God.' I am in somebody else's house, they don't have the same privacies and comfort level and you are kind of shifting . . . I mean I'm ready to go, they are ready for me to go.

By contrast, the children of immigrants seem less reluctant to move back when the need arises. Some do so to save money or to take care of a parent; others do it just for the comfort and company. A Russian Jewish respondent who had returned from a year in Israel happily moved in with her parents and planned to stay for some time. Aware that others might think her "weird," she stressed that staying at home was voluntary and contrasted her relationship with the typical "American" family:

It's free. Nice living conditions and you live with your parents. In our culture, it's like our thing. It's not like you're eighteen and you move out . . . Like American people do it different. So it's not like such a burden. And it's not weird that I'm twenty-four and I'm living at home or anything like that. If I wanted to, I could move out, but it's fine. I have a good relationship with my mother, I like being here with her, knowing her and my brother also. We have our independent lives, but it's nice to come home at night sometimes with them, and I get enough alone time here.

Of course, for all groups, moving in with parents is less than idyllic, and the renegotiation of familial roles is easier for some than for others. A 28-year-old second generation Dominican man moved back in with his parents after dropping out of college. He is separated from the mother of his 5-year-old son, and the boy spends a lot of time at the grandparents' house.

> [It's been] pretty difficult . . . My parents haven't realized the fact that I'm no longer a little kid. I have a kid. And my father really is very old fashioned so it's been mainly a struggle dealing with him in the household. He's a stereotypical old fashioned Hispanic man . . . I guess, the old school fashion of raising your child is like I don't have to have respect for you, you're my child. And it's like hold on a second, I'm a man now. Yes, I am your child but I'm a man.

Most young people in all groups move out when they marry or have children. Yet some choose permanent, or at least open-ended, *multigenerational living* even after they start their own families. A significant percentage of our respondents continued to live with parents even though they were married or cohabiting or had a child. This situation could come about because the parents retire and their children take over the rent payments or mortgage. In other cases, grandparents take on child care, enabling young adult parents to work. Members of some extended families live on different floors of the same building, with unmarried children taking the basement, an arrangement made possible by multiple family or converted homes in the outer boroughs of the city.

Multigenerational living is more common among children of immigrants than among the native born: 17 percent of second generation respondents who were married or cohabiting and 28 percent of those who had a child were living with at least one parent, compared with 7.6 percent and 20 percent of native born respondents. The relatively few Chinese who had married or had a child were most likely to be living in multigenerational families. Dominicans were more likely to form families of their own but less likely to be still living with parents. Only 12.5 percent of those with partners and 23 percent of those with children were doing so, compared with higher numbers of South Americans and West Indians. Less than 10 percent of the native born of any group stayed with their parents after finding a partner, but over 20 percent of native blacks and Puerto Ricans lived with their parents after having a child, probably mostly those who became parents young. In contrast, only 10 percent of whites with children had a parent in the household.

These patterns reflect different ideas about adulthood and family relationships. While the native born generally see moving away from their parents as a necessary step in attaining adulthood, children of immigrants often see living with their parents as being responsible and mature. They sometimes talk in terms of repaying their parents for the care given them when they were children or taking responsibility for the family. A 28-year-old West Indian woman who had been living with her mother, her own daughter, and a sister more or less her daughter's age felt that the girls needed more space, so she started looking for a house for them all two years ago. They were just about to move into a three-family brownstone:

> I think it's part of the West Indian culture, to have an extended family, you know . . . I'm friends with my mother as well, you know, and it's not in my culture to push, to get away from my mother and push her away for my own life and my own family. I think that you can maintain both. To me, it wouldn't be realistic to have had my mother work two jobs and support me with my daughter and do all that she has done for me so that I can attain what she couldn't attain, for me to push her away and to go and form my own life and live high on the hog . . . so I've been placed in an opportunity . . . where I can do these things and also give her the experience of having them through me.

Others are making this arrangement out of preference rather than financial need or family obligation. Some second generation respondents challenged the assumption that it is "normal" to establish a separate household after marriage. A young man with Colombian parents, a degree from a private university, and an accounting job with a big brokerage firm is married and has a son at 33. Although he thinks he may eventually get his own place, he has decided to stay in the upstairs apartment of his parents' house for the foreseeable future:

> I: And why would you say that you keep living with your parents? Do you feel like you're obligated?
> R: No. Not at all. Like I say, I'd move them to Florida because we're

very close-knit. My grandmother, you know, still lives with my mother's sister, my aunt . . . And they both do extremely well. We're just very close.

I: What would you say are the worst things about living with your parents? How does your wife feel?

R: Oh, extremely well. She has her family in Colombia and a lot of South American families live together until whenever you decide to leave—it's not like here in America. In America, when you're eighteen, get out. Get out, you know what I mean? Get out. My wife, her brother is a doctor and he makes money, and he still lives at home with his mother. It's just a close-knit family . . . I'm gonna do the same thing with my son. If you want to go, fine. If you don't want to go, that's fine as well.

Although many of our native born respondents could have benefitted from such a situation, only a few did and they often found it uncomfortable, or at least mildly embarrassing. One 33-year-old white man was renting a two-bedroom apartment with his wife and two children. He took some college courses but did not get a degree and now manages a transportation service. His goal for the next five to ten years is to buy a house, but he feels he cannot afford it, mentioning that homes in suburban New Jersey cost upward of $400,000. Still, living with his parents is not an option.

I: And the last time [we interviewed you] you were living with your wife and your daughter, and your wife was about to have another baby . . . Do you live with anyone else besides them?

R: Just a cat.

I: Any parents?

R: No. I'd have to kill myself.

I: We wouldn't want that [laugh].

These patterns have important implications for mobility and add up to a considerable advantage for the second generation. First, young people who are willing to stay at home are in a better position to attend college without incurring heavy debt. Respondents living at home were much less likely to be working and much more likely to be enrolled in school than those who were not. Our in-depth interviews suggested that this helped many to save to buy a home, either alone or with their families. In an expensive housing market, living with one's parents is highly functional, and it will be interesting to see whether native born people with limited re-sources start to revise their assumption that living apart from parents is a key ingredient of adulthood. For the moment, native born minorities and second generation Dominicans seem to be disadvantaged by their ten-dency to move out early, whereas other groups, particularly low income Chinese, benefit from their willingness to stay at home.

Forming New Families

When they do leave home, some of our respondents are quick to form new households with romantic partners, but most remain single for years. Overall, only 11 percent of our 18- to 22-year-old respondents were mar-ried or living with someone, rising to a third in their mid-twenties and about half in the 28–32 age group. But this varies by group (Table 7.2). It is also clear that people from different backgrounds find partners and have children in different combinations at different ages. In general, those with better-educated parents who stayed in school longer tended to settle down later. The relationship between getting an education and the age at which one chooses a partner or has a child is not straightforward, how-ever. Cultural norms about the "right" age for marriage and childbearing and the expected payoff for postponing a family to complete one's educa-tion also matter.

Native whites often live alone or with roommates for much of their twenties. Only a third are married by the time they reach their thirties, and only then do they begin having children. Yet the equally well-educated

Table 7.2. Share of Respondents with Children and Spouses or Partners by Age and Group (%)

	18–22		23–27		28–32	
	Child	Partner	Child	Partner	Child	Partner
Puerto Ricans	24	17	60	41	63	53
Native Blacks	28	10	62	34	72	47
Dominicans	25	21	54	52	60	68
West Indians	16	11	45	28	52	43
Chinese	1	3	3	16	14	42
Russians	3	11	17	42	42	61
Native Whites	6	11	9	33	27	44

Source: ISGMNY.

Russian Jews tend to live at home until they marry and are usually married by their late twenties. One young Russian man explains:

> R: Russians are more on the marriage thing. You have to get married by age twelve [laughter].
> I: Yesterday.
> E: Yeah. My sister is twenty-nine and she's not married and this is the worst thing for my mother . . . She's an old maid. Listen, twenty-nine is pretty old even by American standards . . . Girls in the Russian community, everybody gets married so early and once she's twenty-five she feels a little pressure.

Meanwhile, although many Chinese American parents have little education, they do not encourage their children to marry young. Most of our Chinese respondents expected to get married when they are about 30 and to put off having children until their early thirties. Getting an education is only one reason they do this, as many Chinese Americans remain single for some years after finishing school. It may also reflect China's state policy that led not only to one-child families but to late marriages even among the poor, with the result that even poor parents put less pressure on their children to marry early than do parents among some other immigrant groups (Greenhalgh and Winkler 2005; Hannum and Liu 2006). In most cases the Chinese have no religious opposition to contraception and abortion. (This would not be true of many of the 20 percent of our Chinese respondents who are Christians.)

More than any other group, the Chinese respondents were concerned about building a solid financial basis *before* getting married and were willing to forgo a period of independent living in order to achieve it. A 27-year-old Chinese man had been dating his girlfriend for a year and a half. They expect to marry, but he is not ready yet. For the time being, he is living at home with his parents and younger brother. His reasons for waiting are partly financial but also stem from a desire to remain single a while longer:

> It's for financial reasons. Plus, you know, I think you can't rush something like marriage. So, you know, I'm a little older and things are different, but financially I'm not ready, and mentally—there's days when I feel I could and days when I feel like I'd rather still be single . . . Not in the sense of go out and play and stuff, but like, you know, I don't feel like I want to come home to a wife.

In contrast, South Americans and Dominicans stress early marriage and both groups settle down relatively young. Dominicans are the most likely to be in a romantic partnership. Over a fifth of those in the earliest age group (18–22) were married or cohabiting, as were 17 percent of the Puerto Ricans and 13 percent of the South Americans, whereas none of the other groups were much over 10 percent (and among the Chinese it was only 3 percent). By their mid-twenties, half the Dominicans are partnered and even more are parents. No other group has moved so strongly into both marriage and parenthood.

Early parenthood is common among West Indians and native blacks but less likely to be associated with getting married. Native black women are particularly skeptical about relationships and marriage and sense that they are unlikely to last. Many respondents stressed that their mothers had raised them not to expect to rely upon a man. Some young women were discouraged by what they had seen in their own families, and others told stories about good relationships that fell apart after the couple married. While arguing that marriage is an unnecessary formality if two people really love each other, the respondents also seemed to feel that marriage gives men unwanted power over women. Said one 34-year-old:

> Marriage, I don't feel like it's really in the cards for me. I mean I really, really, really have to be extremely in love with this person to marry him. Marriage to me is like . . . it's like they own you. [Laugh] I don't want to feel like I'm trapped. I guess it's from the way I was raised. Watching my sister's father, and all these guys. I feel like marriage is just a piece of paper. You know, you love this person, you're with them, you live with them, what's marriage? You're like handcuffed, there's no escape. [Laugh]

Puerto Ricans, native blacks, and West Indians do not expect childbearing to be tied to marriage and often remain single or continue to cohabit after having children. Asked if she had considered marrying the father of her children, this Puerto Rican woman observed:

> This is something we always talk about but we postpone it. We just don't have time, really. But I don't know, maybe one day, but like I said, it would be just something just on a whim. Everyone has already accepted it, you know what I mean, the family. Everyone's accepted that we're just here, you know, but maybe one day we'll

get married, but it isn't a major thing to me, marriage. I mean we've been living together for so long and the only difference is we don't have the license that states that we're married. I don't think about it that much.

The Implications of Early and Delayed Child-Rearing

Our respondents have differing ideas about when to have a child and what circumstances are necessary for parenthood. Overall, just over 5 percent of respondents said they were parents before the age of 18—8.1 percent of women and 2 percent of men—but this was most common among native black women (17 percent), Puerto Rican women (14 percent), and Dominican women (13 percent). West Indian and South American women were next highest (but only at 8 and 7 percent respectively). Fewer than 5 percent of native white women were mothers by 18, and the figure was almost nil among the Chinese and Russians.

Research has shown that positive engagement with school, high educational expectations, and a sense of self-esteem and self-efficacy are important factors in avoiding teenage pregnancy (Plotnick 1992). Middle class families expect their children to attend college and generally have the financial resources and information to make that possible. It is tacitly understood that this means not having children while in high school, and whether by abstinence, contraception, or abortion, most young middle class women avoid becoming teenage parents. This expectation is so ingrained that our middle class respondents said that their parents did not caution them against teenage pregnancy.

The situation is quite different for poor minority women. As a native black woman who had her first child at age 15 remarked, "We had all heard it that you ain't supposed to have children until you get married or whatever." But when many of these young women found themselves in dismal school environments, facing low expectations about their education, and living in neighborhoods where early motherhood was common, many girls ended up becoming young mothers nonetheless (Anderson 1999; Edin and Kefalas 2005).

Teenage parents often talk about pregnancy as "just happening" to them. A closer reading shows, however, that pregnancy tends to happen when other things are not going well in young women's lives (Furstenberg, Brooks-Gunn, and Morgan 1987). The transition to high school, often a larger and more threatening environment than middle school, seemed to lead some girls to withdraw from education and focus more on their boyfriends. A Puerto Rican woman who grew up in the South Bronx, mostly with her mother and grandmother, said that her family encouraged her to finish high school but did not push her hard. Although she was a gifted student, she started cutting class in middle school and had to go to the local zoned high school, which was large and plagued with violence. Feeling that she was learning nothing and the teachers did not respect her, she requested a transfer but was refused and dropped out. It was then that she "came up pregnant."

A 22-year-old South American woman grew up with both her parents, who were Jehovah's Witnesses. They were strict, and her mother insisted that she go to the local high school because it was close to home but did not notice when she started cutting class and hanging out with friends who drank a lot. The young woman always had problems in school and was suspended for yelling at the teachers and other disruptive behavior. She dropped out at 16, "because I was still in ninth grade at sixteen years old and I didn't think I was going to be able to finish high school." She worked for a while at a brokerage firm and became pregnant at 17. She now lives with her parents, brother, and two children and hopes to marry the baby's father in the near future. In the meantime she is on welfare and works only part time.

Although some young mothers thought their parents were too permissive, allowing boyfriends to sleep over when they were only 14 or 15, just as often parents seemed to have overly strict rules but provided no practical guidance about how to avoid pregnancy. In one very sad case, a young woman hid her pregnancy from her deeply religious parents. She tried to tell her mother, but "she didn't want to know and so I realized I had to sort of keep it to myself." Not entirely sure if she was pregnant and having no idea what to do, she wore loose clothes to hide her belly and got no prenatal care. Her son, whom she delivered herself in the bathroom of their home, was born disabled.

The lack of information about sex was fairly common, especially in Catholic or evangelical Protestant families. One Puerto Rican woman who said her mother stressed education and was disappointed when she did not to go to college also said that she got no advice about sex. Although her parents showered her with affection until she was 10 or 11, after that they avoided close physical contact even with each other. As she put it:

They never spoke about the birds and the bees, they never told me how to kiss, they never told me nothing, they were like—I don't remember my parents kissing in front of us. They wouldn't even hold hands in front of us, honestly.

Although parents sometimes send their daughters to Catholic school partly to keep them away from boys, and our data do show that girls who went to Catholic school were less likely to become teenage parents (see Louie and Holdaway 2008), this strategy could also backfire. A Puerto Rican woman who grew up in East Harlem with both her parents went to Catholic school "the whole way through." She became pregnant during her first year in college. Although she felt she was not ready to be a parent, she did not want to have an abortion and had the baby at 20. Family support enabled her to graduate from college, but looking back, she feels she would have been better off knowing more, not less, about sex and birth control:

I think maybe while I was in high school, maybe if I had more access to [knowledge] I mean, we had gym and P.E. and things like that, but I think teens need to be more informed of a lot of things about their sexuality, about birth control. If you're going to a Catholic school, those things are taboo, I mean, you don't talk about those things, you know what I mean.

A Dominican student observed that strict parenting often backfired among her friends, who sometimes left home early and started families to get away from their parents. She said that she herself did all kinds of things her parents disapproved of—"like smoking pot and cutting class and premarital sex and all this other stuff"—without their knowledge and survived. She felt that it was important to let young people make their own decisions even if some of them would go the wrong way, and she points to some of the disadvantages of the second generation experience.

I think that a lot of times with Dominicans when it's like my situation, where my parents were born there and I was born here, I was caught between two cultures . . . A lot of times parents are so strict and so, "no, no, no, no, no." Especially with girls, let's say, they are a lot stricter with girls than with boys. The parents are, "No, no, no, you can't go out with boys." Then a boy is, "It's okay. Come on." Whatever, then the girl does it and then she has trouble and she's,

"But you were too strict." And she leaves. Or you keep pressing that no, no, no, the more the kids are going to want to do it and they are not thinking about the consequences really at that age. So I think just because they are rebellious they will go do something stupid that will affect the rest of their lives.

Many of the young mothers we spoke to do not seem to have considered abortion. This may partly be a religious issue with religious women, who see pregnancy as an act of God. One woman who already had seven children when we interviewed her was working incredibly hard to support them and put them through Catholic school. Asked if she would have more, she replied:

I don't want any; I think I'm comfortable with seven. I think this is about what I can handle, but I shock myself because I always end up doing things, and I adjust pretty quickly, you know, I really do, in any environment. And then, if I do, well, I do. I don't really believe in abortion, because if you make your bed you lay in it, well, you have to pay the consequences and do what you've got to do. So, you know, if I do, I do.

Although rarely immediately forthcoming, parental acceptance was important in enabling young women to deal with motherhood. One woman recalled that when she got pregnant at 17, her mother and grandmother "at first they were like, 'You're too young' and all this other stuff." But in the end, she was not the only one in her family in this situation and in fact compared favorably with some of her cousins. When

they considered, they thought back to everybody else in my family, twelve, thirteen, fourteen with kids, you know, and they said at least I was older, I was maybe eighteen already—I could sign my own baby at the hospital.

Eventually the family rallied round, and by the time of the interview, her mother and grandmother were "crazy about the baby" and helping out with child care.

Indeed, family can sometimes keep early motherhood from derailing a school career. Some very young girls do manage to juggle school and motherhood and sometimes even work. One native black woman was only 14 when she got pregnant, but her mother insisted she finish her education. Working part time in a supermarket, she graduated ahead of schedule and went on to college. By the time we interviewed her at 25, she was working on her bachelor's degree. Support from her mother and her uncles was crucial in helping her manage. In most cases, however, pregnancy makes a difficult situation much harder. One Puerto Rican woman had dropped out of high school and was in a GED program when she became pregnant at the age of 20. Already behind in her education, she feels having her son has slowed her progress further, forcing her to move out of her mother's house and quit the GED program. Now 22, she is looking for work as a nurse's assistant, and her biggest regret is that she didn't finish school.

> *I:* How do you think having a child has changed your life?
> *R:* A lot. I could have been doing a lot of different things now. . . . I could have finished school. I could have done a lot of things different.
> *I:* Before you got pregnant, what were you planning to do in terms of school?
> *R:* Finish.
> *I:* Finish the GED?
> *R:* Yeah. And then go to college.

Becoming a mother in one's late teens or even early twenties can also present difficulties in finishing college. Many native black, West Indian, Puerto Rican, and Dominican women found themselves in this situation. Some were in traditional marriages where the husband was the major breadwinner, and they had decided not to go to university. The parents of one young native white woman who had grown up in Canarsie wanted her to go to college, but she felt it wasn't for her and went to work in a store after graduating from high school. She married at 20 and had her first child two years later. She did not work full time after her two children were born, wanting to raise them herself. Her husband has a secure but not very well-paid job as a custodian at a university, and their traditional family arrangements are possible partly because they live in her childhood home now that her parents have moved away for retirement.

More often, young mothers find themselves juggling work, parenthood, and school, and women who want professional careers are acutely aware of the need to think about timing parenthood. A 20-year-old West Indian woman who hoped to have four children was planning to study to become a lawyer when we interviewed her. She could see no easy time to have children:

> When it comes to when, it's like, I'm between a rock and a hard place, because I know if I have one now, it will slow down my career objectives, but if I don't have one soon, before I start my career, it's gonna be hard to find time then, because you know, I've heard more stories in law firms when a woman becomes pregnant they tend to kick 'em out, you know and I don't want that to happen. If I could have my children before then and they grow with me, then I'll be happy, so it's a toss-up.

Some women are ambivalent about waiting to have children. One Puerto Rican woman, raised in a tough neighborhood by parents without much education, managed to graduate from college and is working on her master's degree while teaching at a public school. By almost any standard her life would seem a success. Yet, at an age when many of her similarly educated white or Chinese peers are just beginning to think about children, she wonders if it is too late for her to start a family, and what she has gained and lost by not having children earlier.

> Oh boy. I think there are two sides of how I feel about that. I am going to be thirty in two months so I see the majority of my friends have had children when they were younger and went through life difficulties. But they made it through and now their kids are a little older and it seems like they are having a second life . . . Now here I am, I've had a good time when I was younger, I've traveled. I've gone out. I've gone to school. I've had different jobs. I've dated different people of all nationalities and I have a boyfriend now and I'm thinking, "Is it too late to have kids?" No, it is not too late biologically, but do I want to have an eighteen- nineteen-, twenty-year-old when I'm fifty-three? Do I want to be a grandparent at sixty or seventy?

At the same time, women were more likely than men to consider not having children at all. Native white and Chinese women were the most likely to express doubts. A Russian Jewish lesbian woman gave the starkest argument for not having children:

> I can't even understand why people begin to want that . . . I see all the negative things and I see zero positive things. You have to take

care of someone, someone's going to be screaming for attention and you will not be able to go to the gym when you want to—life will be completely based around this person for many years and what do I get in return? To me, the answer is absolutely nothing. That's a frightening thought. I'd have to give up everything and get nothing in return. For most people, they get, like you're raising a human being. To me that means absolutely nothing.

Norms and expectations about the timing of marriage and childbearing varied widely across our study groups and resulted in sharp differences in behavior. Native born whites and Chinese wait longest before marrying and having children, while South Americans, Dominicans, and Russians form families much earlier. Parenting outside marriage was most common among native blacks, Puerto Ricans, and West Indians, although West Indian women generally had children at an older age.

Guess Who's Coming to Dinner? Intermarriage and Dating

When people from different backgrounds form families and have children, they are engaging in the most intimate form of ethnic interaction and the only one that might eliminate physical markers of difference. At the same time, immigrant parents who may accept the need to adapt to local norms in the public sphere often feel entitled to exert influence over their children on this more private matter, as indeed may native born parents. Intermarriage is thus a topic on which strong racial and ethnic preferences may be openly expressed. It also raises thorny questions about the value of sustaining cultural differences and the mechanisms for doing so.

We asked our respondents what their parents conveyed to them about whom they should marry, what their own views were, and whom they actually dated and considered marrying. Their answers reveal young people who are struggling to balance values that sometimes conflict. On the one hand, they show an admirable reluctance to judge others on the basis of their race or ethnicity and a desire to be open to relationships with people from different backgrounds. Indeed, a remarkable number in all groups seem to take for granted that having friendships and romantic relationships with people from different backgrounds is a good thing. At the same time, they acknowledge the reality that their parents may not feel the same way and often also wish to sustain their own religious or ethnic culture.

The prospect of raising children from "mixed marriages" raises questions about the compatibility of the parents' religious and cultural traditions; what second language, if any, children should learn; and what connections the children should have with the grandparents. Tracing how interactions in this intimate sphere establish, maintain, or breach ethnic boundaries gives us another way of considering how the children of immigrants are becoming integrated into the larger society. (Recall that a small share of our respondents themselves were the product of intermarriage between different groups.)

While New York is a multiethnic city where people from many different backgrounds rub shoulders in the streets, subways, offices, and shops, many neighborhoods, schools, and workplaces are also quite segregated. Black children can grow up barely knowing a white person of their age, and whites may have little exposure to the lives of blacks and Hispanics. This odd mixture of exposure and segregation plays out in a number of different ways in the lives of our respondents.

For example, if one looks only at the stated preference about whether young people should be open to relationships with people from other cultures, our respondents are overwhelmingly in favor. Fewer than 20 percent of our respondents said it was "important" to marry someone of the same ethnic group. Indeed, among all three Latino groups, the West Indians, and the native whites, the figure was less than 13 percent, whereas slightly more than half the Russian Jews said it was important to marry a fellow Jew, and a quarter of the native blacks and about a fifth of the Chinese felt it "important" to marry someone of the same race. Many respondents told us that they had dated people from many ethnic groups and stressed that it was important not to judge others by their ethnic group but, rather, "look at them as a person."

Nevertheless, one can see distinct boundaries of race, religion, and language among our respondents in terms of the people with whom they are partnering. Figure 7.2 shows that cohabitation is an important part of the picture for our respondents, and it varies by group. In our analysis of intergroup partnering we combine those respondents who are formally married and those who are cohabiting. Though our conclusions about intermarriage can only be tentative, it is striking that most people are partnering with others who share a similar racial or linguistic background (see Figure 7.3). Of those who were married or cohabiting, 84 percent of native whites, 87 percent of native blacks, and 89 percent of West Indians were with someone of the same race. No white or Chinese was married to a native black, though a few whites were with West Indians, and no Russian

Jew was married to a black. While West Indians and native blacks were most likely to be with members of their own groups, they were far more likely to be with each other than with any other group. Finally, while the majority of Russian Jews were with other Russian Jews, they were more likely to be with other whites (often Jewish) than with anyone else.

The Chinese were most likely to be married to or partnered with someone of their own group, followed by the native whites, with native blacks and South Americans least likely to be. Even when people are with partners from other ethnic groups, the range from which they choose is quite limited. Very few Chinese respondents were married at all, making it hard to generalize; but it is clear that those who out-marry do so primarily with whites, with a few marrying other Asians. Only a small handful of Chinese were married to Hispanics, and none were married to blacks. This reflects not only the parents' wishes, as will be discussed, but the kinds of people with whom Chinese Americans live, study, and work.

Among the Hispanics, the South Americans are also the most likely to marry out, usually with other Hispanics. About 20 percent of married or cohabiting South Americans were with Puerto Ricans, and nearly as many

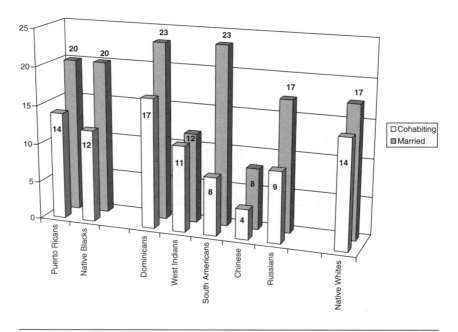

Figure 7.2. Partnering (%). *Source:* ISGMNY.

were with Dominicans and other Hispanics combined. About 10 percent were with non-Hispanic whites, a much higher percentage than for any of the other Spanish-speaking groups in our study. Dominicans and Puerto Ricans primarily intermarried with each other and were also slightly more likely than South Americans to be married to native blacks, although not many were, suggesting that the race boundary is strong even for these "in between" Hispanic groups. South Americans tended to say that the race of their South American partner was white, whereas far more Dominicans and Puerto Ricans described their co-ethnic partners as black. As might be expected, the highest intermarriage rates among native blacks and West Indians are with each other. It is striking that many of the native young blacks are choosing people with family roots outside the United States, another indicator of the dynamic change taking place in the composition of New York's native born black population.

Young people must contend with their parents' opinions about suitable matches, and race looms large in these conversations. Parents in most groups have a clear hierarchy of preferences, and non-black groups almost always put blacks at the bottom. Chinese and Russian Jewish parents most openly expressed anti-black blatant racial prejudice, ranging from the

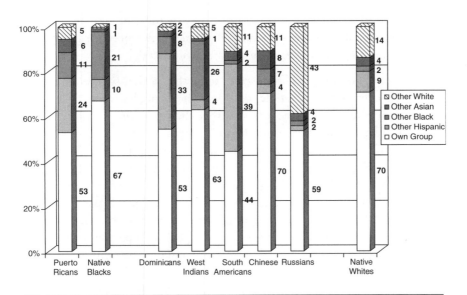

Figure 7.3. Intergroup Partnering of Those Partnered (%). *Source:* ISGMNY.

daughter of two Taiwanese doctors who remarked, "I think they would be slightly appalled if the person I dated was African American," to the blunter

> My mother . . . makes huge cutting generalizations . . . and I think it's on a scale of how brown you are. The browner you get, the more disrespected you are. I think that's how it goes.

Most Hispanic parents preferred a lighter-skinned partner for their children. South American parents did not welcome dark-skinned partners of any race and seem particularly prejudiced against blacks. One parent, according to her daughter, spoke openly about "improving the race"—a common Latin American expression—by marrying white. Dominican parents also sometimes told their children not to date Puerto Ricans, though the advice seems to have had little effect.

Religion was a central issue for Russian Jews. Most parents insisted that their children date only Jews, but the issue was not as simple as that. One woman explained that only a limited range of husbands would be acceptable to her parents, who are Russian Jews from Moscow:

> It's so funny. They are very biased against Hasidic Jews and they think that they are weird and they don't understand very religious Jews, but at the same time I have to marry a Jew so I am extremely limited in the type of Jew that I can marry. It must be a reform or a nondenominational Jew, preferably Russian but not necessarily. Very, very limited scope of who I can marry. [Laughter]

In the end, however, necessity seems to be the mother of tolerance. The longer children remained single, the more their parents relaxed their criteria. Many Russian respondents said that their parents' initial line was, "They can be purple, blue, seven feet tall, anything, but they're Jewish." By the time the children were in their mid-twenties, it was, "They're already like giving up on me, so they'll take anybody at this point." A Chinese respondent said, "At 21 my parents wanted me to marry someone Chinese. I waited till I was 32, and by then they were just happy I married anyone at all!!" Indeed, given the high rate of interracial dating among Chinese women, their very late age of marriage may in part be a conscious or unconscious strategy to "wait out" parental objections to a non-Chinese partner.

While parents sometimes told their children they would disown them if they dated or married out of the group, this never actually happened. In fact, many parents became close to partners they had initially rejected. One of the few situations in which a respondent described discomfort between his father and his wife was because the woman was from mainland China and the father from Taiwan. Both sides had to be careful to avoid the question of Taiwan's independence, which meant nothing to the son but was important to both his wife and his father.

As for the young people, nearly all went out of their way not to be judgmental about other people, and most said that regardless of their own preferences, they would always try to "look at the person, not their skin." Their attitudes markedly departed from those of their parents. Indeed, just as the issue of leaving home often highlighted the differences between "Americans" and members of the second generation, so feelings about intergroup dating sharply differentiated second generation youth from their immigrant parents. That most of the young people had not entered into long term relationships with people of other ethnic groups does not seem to be the result of prejudice, nor did our respondents criticize others who were in interethnic relationships (although this restraint might reflect prejudice and inhibition about owning up to intergroup dating).

When respondents did make a conscious choice to be with someone of the same background, a number of factors seem to be involved. Many respondents mentioned that if they formed a relationship with someone of a different background, their parents would not be able to communicate with their partner, or their children with their grandparents. They also said that they themselves sought a partner who would understand them, and this meant choosing someone who has shared similar experiences.

Older respondents, who may be thinking more seriously about marriage, were more likely to be weighing these considerations and to say that they should marry someone of the same background. Russian Jews, for example, often explained the importance of marrying within the group in terms of raising children, having common values, and avoiding assimilation. As one 24-year-old Russian woman explained:

> The traditional answer is I want to raise my kids Jewish but then that begs the question, Why? Well, I do. You can, he doesn't have to be Jewish but I think it's such a part of my identity that I want somebody who will be able to get upset with me about the same things. Or become excited about the same things that pertain to this identity not merely, "I'm very supportive of you honey and I have no idea what you're talking about."

The sheer fact of who is around within segregated neighborhoods, schools, and work environments also shaped how people find each other. This becomes clear when one hears from the young people who grew up in mixed environments that they were more likely to form relationships outside their race or ethnic group. A Chinese American who grew up in the East Village said that his parents wanted him to marry a Chinese woman. The problem was that all his neighborhood friends were black, white, or Puerto Rican. As a result, he dated "all different kinds of women, actually more out of my own race than Asian or Chinese women, Hispanics, Caucasians, African-Americans." He continued:

> It was weird for me, because my brother and I were the only Asian guys on the block. Kids, you know, so most of my friends, boys, girls, that's where we got used to it. The neighborhood, the school. It's not that I have anything against Asian women, I love all kinds of women, that's just what . . . In America, in New York, I never dated Asian women. When I went to California, that was the first time I dated an Asian woman.

Who wants to date *you* also matters, and it became clear from our interviews that there are powerful gendered stereotypes of desirability. These came across most strongly with the Chinese. Although the young man who grew up on the Lower East Side had no trouble finding dates, several other Chinese men complained that while white men see Asian women as desirable partners, white women do not feel the same way about Asian men. Asked why he always dated Chinese women, one Chinese young man replied:

> It just happened that way. I never had the opportunity to date a white girl or a black girl. They are not interested in Chinese guys. But the other way around when it comes to Chinese girls. A lot of white guys love to date a Chinese girl but white girls would not want to date a Chinese guy. They think Chinese people are geeky and they can't really get nowhere in this country but then when it comes to the females, they think that they will make a good wife. They will stay at home and cook for them and do as they say.

At the same time, the high out-marriage rate among Chinese women seems to reflect their sense that Chinese American men may have more chauvinistic expectations. (They may also be wanting to avoid mothers-in-law with traditional gender ideologies.) One woman recounted her dating woes by explaining that she was not too enthusiastic about the gender norms of traditional Chinese families, especially if the men were not sufficiently "Americanized." Asked what she did not like about being Chinese, she replied:

Where do I start? [Laughter] I definitely don't like this male/female thing. there was one [Chinese] guy I dated where he was the oldest of four kids and sometimes the way he acts and the way he reacts to certain things you can tell that definitely he was first born. He was born here. So there is part of him that's very Americanized but then . . . I felt like he picked and chose whatever was to his favor. He was Americanized on the one hand but I think if he could find the woman who would share the same views, except be willing to accept the fact that she is there to serve him, it would be perfect.

Dominican women voiced similar feelings, expressing concern that even second generation Dominican men had some of the same sexist views as their fathers. One woman explained that there had not been enough generational change for her liking, partly because young men had been taken care of by their mothers and had similar expectations of their wives.

'Cause if he was born and raised there he is like my father and believes all the stuff I said before and now if he is like my brother, let's say, and he was born and raised here and he's Dominican, they like to be with a lot of women. They believe—not all, but the ones I have encountered—to have a wife and then a lot of other girls that they go out with. And that's been my luck. I'm not saying it's true but it's just been my luck. But my brother also, he doesn't believe he has to wash the dishes and clean and stuff like that because I've always done it. My mother's always done it.

Our respondents showed an admirable acceptance of cross-racial and ethnic relationships, and in this are sharply different from their parents. In the end, however, the majority chose a partner of a similar background. In cases where this was a conscious choice, it reflected not rejection of other groups so much as a desire to maintain communication with parents and share language and culture with the partner. At the same time, a great many respondents "in-married" because their pool of possible partners was limited by segregation in schools, workplaces, and neighborhoods or by the stereotypes of others.

Passing the Baton: Child-Rearing and Ethnic Identity

How young people talk about raising their children also tells us how salient ethnic background is in their lives and about the degree to which they are likely to transfer this identity across future generations. Nearly all our second generation respondents said that they would try to teach their children about their grandparents' culture, have the children visit the home country, and help them learn the language. This was partly to retain a connection with their ethnic roots, but also often out of a sense that contact with another culture was valuable in itself. As one Russian Jewish man said:

> *R:* Yeah, of course. I'm gonna try to pass on—I don't want them to be crazy religious children, but, you know, they have to know they're Jewish, they have to know about their religion, a little bit, at least.
> *I:* Do you want them to speak Russian?
> *R:* Yeah, why not. Another language would never hurt.

At the same time, they realize that they will not have the same connection to the home country as their parents do, and that when the parents come from two different backgrounds, it is even harder. This second generation Chinese American woman is married to a Korean. She had originally dated only Chinese men, feeling it would be easier to marry someone of her own culture. She and her husband now face the problem of which language their young son should learn.

> *I:* Do you want Thomas to learn to speak Chinese?
> *R:* My husband and I have a big problem with that right now because my husband's Korean, but he doesn't speak any Korean and so it's hard for him to force a rule onto our son to learn to speak Korean when he himself doesn't speak it. So if we were just to make him learn Chinese, that would be kind of rude to his own heritage too, since he's both. We're having a dilemma right now, whether to not let him learn any one of 'em, [laugh] or learn both or whatever. We're such lazy people right now, we're—yeah, let's just stay with English. But that's just right now. We don't know what we're gonna do in the future.

While many children of immigrants said they wanted to preserve a strong sense of family, most wanted to combine this with a more relaxed and communicative relationship between parents and children than they had experienced. This was a common view among the many Chinese Americans who felt estranged from their parents. One 23-year-old Chinese young man who felt that his mother's strictness led him to drop out of high school and join a gang said he wanted to take a different approach with his own children.

> The biggest problem that Asian parents have with their kids is that they kind of see having an actual relationship with their children and getting their children to do well in school as sort of mutually exclusive things. Asians parents tend not to, in my experience, foster and develop real communicative, caring relationships with their children and that's a problem because things like my joining a gang could have been stopped had I had a better communication with my mother. But there was nothing to stop me . . . It was either her way or no way and once I stepped off track, there was nothing to get me back except my own fear of God or my own fear of dying or whatever . . . The thing I would do differently is to try to foster an actually communicative caring relationship with my children, to take their concerns at whatever age, seriously. And at the same time try to encourage them to appreciate learning and studying hard and things like that. So that's the main difference I guess.

For women, gender often came up as an important topic, and those who had been raised in families with traditional gender roles said that they wanted something different for their children. This young Dominican woman stressed that the especially strict rules for girls were not only unfair but also ineffective:

> I might have some slightly different rules for boys and girls but nothing to the point where like my parents were. 'Cause I know what I did. My parents didn't know what I did so they think that their technique of child-rearing worked wonders and I'm successful and stuff but I know what I did and there were plenty of times where I could have gone that way or this route and really messed up my life.

In mixed-race relationships there was also the question of how to raise children to deal with prejudice. A 30-year-old black lawyer from a middle class family who grew up in white neighborhoods and schools says she will probably marry a white man and dismissed the interviewer's assumptions about the supposed fundamental differences between black and white culture as a question of class. At the same time she is adamant that she would not want her white husband raising their children alone if she were to die:

> If I marry someone who is of a different cultural background, one of the requirements of our relationship will be that if anything happens to me, he will turn my children over to my sisters. I will not have someone who is white raising my children by himself without a lot of black influence because he won't know what the hell he is doing and I'm not going to have that. I don't care how sweet he is, how much I love him, I'm not going to have my children . . . I'm not going to be worried about my children going to my grave. So those are the kinds of realities I deal in, at that level.

As they raise their own children, our respondents have the opportunity to try to learn from what they see as their own parents' successes and failures. For members of the second generation, the process is further complicated by the challenge of seeking to transmit the elements of their parents' culture that they see as valuable while avoiding others—especially excessive strictness and gender biases—that they reject.

Conclusion

Our respondents are still early in the process of choosing partners, having children, and making new homes for themselves, but certain patterns are beginning to emerge. Although there are class differences, the native whites have a model of early adulthood that revolves mainly around proceeding through school and into a career, and postponing marriage and children until their thirties. Of our native minority and second generation respondents, the Chinese are most likely to have followed the native white pattern, marrying and having children late. But they differ in being much more likely to continue to live with their parents well into their twenties and in expecting to retain closer ties with their family of origin.

Native black, Puerto Rican, and Dominican women have high rates of teenage pregnancy, and many also have children during the college-going years, as do a smaller number of West Indian and South American women. Whereas Dominican and South American women often marry young, native black women were more likely to become single parents, a situation also quite common among West Indians and Puerto Ricans. As well as limiting the income available to parents to support their children, single parenthood creates hardship, making it difficult for them to progress through education or to work full time. Single parents' ability to succeed depends greatly on material and practical support from their families. In this respect, West Indians and South Americans, who were more likely to stay at home longer, have better employment options, and purchase a home with family members, were in a much better position than native born minorities and Dominicans, who tended to leave home earlier and had fewer resources to draw upon.

The Russian Jews appear to be replicating a mainstream tradition that is fast disappearing: postponing marriage and childbearing until after college but marrying soon after graduation and having children by their late twenties. The greater levels of education among the parents of the Russians and their tendency to stay together provided some encouragement for following this path. The younger generation also seems to choose, and to have access to, relatively good jobs that pay reasonably well and do not require lengthy credentialing.

The choices our respondents make about forging long term relationships, having children, and becoming independent of their parents' homes reflect both material constraints and the ideas and expectations they are exposed to in their families of origin and the communities in which they grow up. In some situations, these expectations are mutually reinforcing. Chinese parents, for example, come from a country where late marriage and parenting are the norm even among the poor, and because of patterns of settlement and schooling, their children mix largely with middle class whites and other Asians who have similar expectations. At the other end of the spectrum, Dominican parents come from a country where early marriage and teenage and young motherhood are common, and their children grow up in poor neighborhoods in the city where teenage and single parenthood are also common and accepted. Given these differences, it is not surprising that Dominican and Chinese women have very different patterns of family formation.

A more interesting situation arises when second generation young people encounter a creative tension between "immigrant" and "American" practices. Then, if they are able to choose wisely, they have the advantage of being able to pick the path that will serve them best in the circumstances. Confronted with the New York City real estate market, for example, many Chinese, Russian Jews, South Americans, and West Indians choose the "immigrant" option of staying at home and often reap the benefits of doing so. By contrast, the native born, along with the Dominicans, are more likely to move out at younger ages.

The point here is not to generalize about the positive or negative aspects of any particular culture. What works is a matter of context. Staying in the parental home longer is helpful in New York because housing is so expensive and there are many educational opportunities close to home. In a region where young people have to travel farther to attend college, this same trait might become a disadvantage—and as we saw in Chapter 5, the desire to stay close to home curtails the college options of some second generation youth. Cultures are fluid, multifaceted, and evolving, and the different strands of any given culture may be helpful or detrimental in different spheres of life.

An examination of patterns of family formation in early adulthood, however, shows that the process is clearly shaped by cultural factors. This examination argues that researchers should pay more attention to the norms and expectations that young people develop as well as the ways in which those norms and expectations are transmitted across generations and between peers. For researchers who study migrants, this directive includes gaining a better understanding of the cultural repertoires that members of the first generation bring with them and looking at the ways in which those repertoires shape how the second generation thinks about its choices.

8

Culture Matters

Studies of the assimilation of the children and grandchildren of European immigrants in the twentieth century often assumed that upward mobility and Americanization went hand in hand. The more successful members of the ethnic group were the most American not only in terms of their identity, but in terms of the clothes they wore, the foods they ate, and the rapidity with which they abandoned their parents' languages. This strong link between Americanization and socioeconomic mobility is not evident among today's immigrants and their children.

Assimilation works differently in different social spheres. Success in the educational system and successful incorporation into the labor force is one thing. Being comfortable with American ways and sharing American outlooks is another. Indeed, members of the groups that succeed in the educational or economic realm may not be those most at ease with American culture.

Cultural incorporation is hard to measure, in part because "American culture" is a moving target. A nation of immigrants, the United States has a long history of absorbing cultural influences from around the globe and making them our own. The German Christmas tree decorates many American homes, African American jazz, blues, and rap fill our airways, Italian pasta and pizza are an integral part of the American diet, and the remnants of Jewish vaudeville still resonate in our TV shows and movies. Today, salsa and burritos are as ubiquitous as catsup and burgers, presidential candidates use Spanish in their speeches, and Muslim head scarves are appearing next to baseball caps in high school classrooms.

Given all this cultural adaptation and mixing, it can be hard to conceptualize and measure how immigrants and their descendants change culturally, for the "mainstream" they are entering is constantly changing and absorbing new influences (Alba and Nee 2003). Do we see a second

241

generation Chinese American eating a burrito as an example of assimilation but a second generation Mexican American doing the same thing as evidence of cultural retention?

Cultural assimilation can also be a cause or an outcome. We can think of culture as an inventory of behaviors and practices—language use, holiday practices, foods, religion, and transnational activities. We can ask how members of the second generation behave and measure up on these factors compared to their immigrant parents and compared to later-generation native born Americans. But culture—norms and beliefs about how to be in the world—can also influence how people behave and how they make decisions about their lives—as we have just seen in Chapter 7 concerning gender norms and their influences on major life decisions.

This chapter examines how cultural behaviors and practices of the second generation differ across groups and between the second generation and the native born respondents. In the telephone survey we asked questions about formal cultural attributes such as language use, religious practices, use of ethnic media, and transnational ties. While most people claim some attachment to their culture, the content of the culture varies greatly by group. For instance, language is very important to the Russian Jews, the Puerto Ricans, the South Americans, and the Dominicans, but much less so for the Chinese, and obviously not much of an issue for the English-speaking West Indians—although they do think their accent can affect interactions with other Americans. The West Indians talked a lot about their music as a marker of cultural identity. By contrast, most Chinese respondents found the idea of listening to traditional Chinese music laughable, although a few confessed a fondness for Canton pop or Hong Kong movies. They were more likely, however, to mention specific holidays such as Chinese New Year as the key thing they do to celebrate their culture. All the groups mentioned food as an important part of their cultural heritage, but ethnic food matters much more to some groups (Chinese, West Indians) than to others (Russians, South Americans). This variation in what is important to a particular ethnic culture means that we cannot create a scale by equally counting different aspects of culture. That is, we cannot say that one group is more ethnic than others based on a simple count of practices and behaviors. Rather, here we identify three spheres of cultural difference—language, transnationalism, and religion—and discuss how these might influence the lives of the second generation.

Language

Language is one of the most important markers of cultural difference for the second generation. It is also one of the most controversial issues surrounding immigration. The ability of immigrants and their offspring to speak English is a potent political issue. In his critique of Mexican immigration to the United States, political scientist Samuel Huntington (2004) argues that current Latino immigrants and their children form "linguistic enclaves" and do not learn English.

In a 1996 General Social Survey (GSS) question, 63 percent of Americans supported passage of "a law making English the official language of the United States, meaning government business would be conducted in English only." In a 2000 GSS question, 75 percent of Americans agreed with the statement that "speaking English as the common national language is what unites all Americans." Twenty-seven states have responded to this perceived threat by passing official English laws.

The preponderance of social science evidence suggests that this fear is unfounded. The United States has always been efficient at stamping out other languages and getting the children of immigrants to assimilate linguistically. Ample evidence from the Census and other surveys shows that this remains true. Using 1990 Census data, Alba and his colleagues (2002) find that two-thirds of third generation Mexicans and three-quarters of Cubans do not speak any Spanish.

A sharp example of the disconnect between social science findings and public concerns involves the possibility that linguistic assimilation can happen *too quickly*. Portes and Rumbaut (2001) argue that when children abandon a parent's language too quickly, the parents lose authority over the children. This dissonant acculturation leads to a situation where communication between parents and children is impeded—parents cannot understand English well, and children cannot understand the immigrant language well.

Portes and Rumbaut argue that children who maintain fluent bilingualism will do best academically. Other researchers have found a correlation between fluent bilingualism and academic achievement among second generation schoolchildren (Zhou and Bankston 1998; Fernández and Nielsen 1986). In a study of Asian and Latino youth using 1990 Census data, Cynthia Feliciano (2001) found that bilingual students are less likely to drop out than English-only speakers, students in bilingual households are less likely to drop out than those in English-dominant or

English-limited households, and students in immigrant households are less likely to drop out than those in nonimmigrant households.

In the telephone survey, we asked questions about the degree to which the respondent spoke another language growing up; the respondent's ability to understand, speak, and read the parents' language; the language they use most frequently now; and the language they prefer to use. Obviously, one would expect differences in language proficiency between children born in the United States and those who learned to speak in another country and then came to the United States, and we find these differences, but we also find differences by ethnic group.

Figure 8.1 shows the percentage of respondents who grew up speaking either English or the language of their parents' country of origin and whether they prefer to speak that home language now. Figure 8.2 shows the respondents' ability to write, read, speak, and understand their parents' language. (The figures show only the groups whose home country language was not English but who grew up entirely in the United States.) Note that two-thirds of the Russian Jewish respondents grew up speaking English at home, whereas only a third of the other groups benefitted from this. Moreover, the current preference for the home language is highest among Dominicans and lowest among the Russians and Chinese.

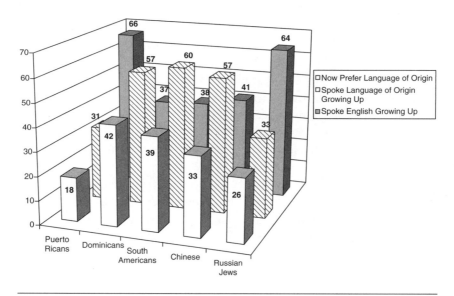

Figure 8.1. Language Practices (%). *Source:* ISGMNY.

Indeed, only a bare majority of the Chinese say they can even speak Chinese well, and far fewer can read it or write it (Figure 8.2). Some of this is clearly related to whether the respondents were born here or spent some of their childhoods in the home country. Among those who were born in China and came after the age of 6, 86 percent say they speak Chinese well. Among the Russian Jews, 91 percent of those who came after age 6 say they speak Russian well, compared to 77 percent of those born here. The Dominicans and South Americans are somewhat more likely to say they can speak Spanish well. Whereas 81 percent of South Americans born in the United States can do so, 98 percent of those who came after age 6 can speak Spanish well; 91 percent of American-born Dominicans can speak Spanish well, as can 99 percent of Dominicans coming after age 6. The same pattern holds for language preference, with a higher reported preference for English among the Chinese and the Russians and a slightly lower preference for English among the South Americans and Dominicans.

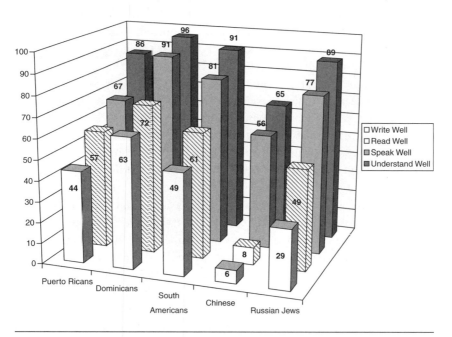

Figure 8.2. Ability in Language of Origin (%). *Source:* ISGMNY.

Overall, Chinese are losing their parents' language most rapidly, followed by the Puerto Ricans and Russians. All the groups clearly prefer English, with Puerto Ricans the most linguistically assimilated—47 percent of them report that they speak mostly English at home, 61 percent prefer English over Spanish, and another 19 percent report speaking only English at home growing up.

A gap is evident between the Spanish-speaking groups (Puerto Ricans, Dominicans, Colombians, Ecuadorans, and Peruvians) and the others from non-English-speaking countries (the Chinese and the Russians). The Puerto Ricans, Dominicans, and South Americans demonstrate rather simple linguistic patterns—they speak either Spanish or English or both. The Russians and the Chinese are from far more linguistically complex sending countries. The group we call Russians includes Jews from a number of different former Soviet Republics and states. This is reflected in their linguistic diversity. For many Russian respondents, Russian was already a second language behind a more local republic-based language spoken primarily in the home.

The Russians in our sample reported speaking thirteen different languages at home growing up: Armenian, Azerbaijani, Estonian, Farsi, Georgian, Hebrew, Hungarian, Kazakh, Lithuanian, Russian, Tadjik, Ukrainian, and Yiddish. The Chinese also reported a variety of linguistic backgrounds—Cantonese, Mandarin, Fukienese, and Taiwanese, as well as a myriad of other dialects including Hainan and Hakka.

Many of the parents of our Russian and Chinese respondents who struggle to learn English have actually mastered several languages or dialects—one young woman who was exasperated about her father's lack of ability in English casually noted that he spoke Mandarin, Cantonese, and Japanese. Some households maintained several languages at once. For example, in one household a grandmother spoke Yiddish, a father spoke Hebrew, and a mother spoke Russian. Another household contained an intermarried couple where the respondent's first language was Spanish, her mother spoke Chinese and Spanish, her father spoke Spanish and English, and her grandmother spoke only Chinese. Many Russian respondents also noted that when they first arrived and went to yeshiva, they struggled not only to learn English but to learn Hebrew at the same time.

Chinese is more difficult to maintain than Spanish for young people born in the United States. Most immigrants speak Cantonese or Fukienese, reflecting the provinces they come from in China. Since written Chinese is not phonetic, even a child who grows up learning to speak to parents and grandparents with relative ease will need a great deal of formal instruction to be literate. Special schools providing after-school and weekend instruction in Chinese are everywhere in New York City, and many parents insisted that their children attend. But many of our respondents report that they hated going, that it was too hard, and that despite their parents' best efforts they quit.

While the thriving network of Chinese schools performs many important functions for Chinese American communities (Zhou and Guoxuan 2002), they are remarkably unsuccessful in teaching second generation young people to read or write Chinese. Even people who attended Chinese school for several years often report that they know only a few characters. In recent years many of these schools have switched their emphasis to preparation for the SAT and other standardized tests, as well as instruction in easier forms of ethnic continuity, such as folk dance.

For some Chinese respondents, loss of the Chinese language was a source of embarrassment

> I live with this family, a grandmother, mother and two daughters, both postcollege age in the same house. And it just reminds me about how uncultured I am, in a sense, because they are a Cantonese-speaking family. My father speaks Toisan. My mother grew up in Hong Kong but she speaks both Cantonese and Toisan. But they never really taught me because for some crazy reason they thought that it would impair my English if they did. And I just get so nervous because my language skills are so lacking. I can't talk to my landlady. When she asked me, "Do you want to join us for dinner today?" I wasn't even sure if she was asking me to dinner. Just to make sure, she told her granddaughter, who told me. I feel very "white" when I'm there.

Many parents make a strategic choice of the language to speak at home in order either to inculcate an ethnic heritage in their American children or to give them a head start in America. Middle class immigrants sometimes know some English before they arrive. Professional immigrants from Russia and Hong Kong, for instance, know some English and choose to speak English at home to their children in order for them to start school without a language deficit. (This was less true for the South Americans and Dominicans, whose much less educated parents generally had no exposure to English prior to immigration.) This omission of the home country language is sometimes seen in retrospect as a shame, since it means the young people are less likely to be fluent in their parents' native language.

Young people who did grow up speaking the native language report that they lost their fluency in it. Once the young people attended school and lived in a mostly English-speaking world, they began speaking to their parents in English. A common pattern is that parents would speak Spanish or Russian or Chinese and the children would respond in English. Young people maintained the ability to understand their parents but became more reticent to speak their parental language. Often, parents who understood English inadvertently hastened the child's path to monolingual English. Many young adults reported that they will speak the immigrant language only to grandparents who cannot understand English. As a result of this rapid switch to English, many respondents reported that they did not know their parents' language anymore, when they recalled knowing more as children. One 30-year-old Chinese woman told us that it was a "watershed moment" when her grandmother died and the family no longer had a reason to speak Chinese. After that, she quickly lost her facility in Chinese.

Since all but a handful of our respondents were completely fluent in English, none reported being embarrassed about their English ability. But in contrast to the numerous stories that the children of earlier European immigrants told about being embarrassed by their parents' poor English skills, our respondents were more troubled by their inability to speak their parents' native language. One young Dominican man told us:

> R: In my house because of my father, we talked English. My father talks a lot of Spanish too but he wanted us to learn English because he wanted us to be successful and when I started school that's when my father was like English, English, English.
> I: Do you feel like you used to speak Spanish better when you were a kid?
> R: My Spanish, oh hell yes. I used to speak much better when I was little. [Little laugh] I don't know what happened. [Now] I have hard time, certain words I get stuck. "How do you say this in Spanish?" [Little laugh]

Embarrassment also prompted this 20-year-old Chinese woman to study Chinese:

> First of all, you go into a Chinese restaurant and you can't even order. That's kind of embarrassing. And another thing was that I remember when I was very young and I was walking in the park and

there was this white guy who spoke perfect Chinese and I couldn't even say my name in Chinese. That was embarrassing too. I'm Chinese, I can't even talk and this guy is white and he can.

It is common for the parents of Chinese respondents not to speak English well, while the respondents themselves do not speak Chinese well. One respondent described the limited amount of communication in his household: "We can hardly understand each other so there is not much talking that goes on." This rapid loss of language means that they lose the ability to teach that language to their own children. If the first generation parents cannot speak English, they are effectively cut off from their grandchildren. Many young people did not want to separate the family by having grandchildren who could not speak with their grandparents or by marrying someone who could not speak to or understand their in-laws.

My sister has a daughter, my niece, and it is absolutely imperative that the kid know Russian. Not because it's such a good language or because we want to promote the culture. Because the bond between a mother and a child and between the grandparents especially cannot exist without language. How can you tell a story? My dad will never learn English to the point where he would be able to communicate. If I were to get married I would want the one I love to speak Russian . . . I want them to have a bond with my parents and that bond would be impossible if he doesn't speak Russian. I would be kind of isolated and I wouldn't want that. I would want to have a house and to invite my family in and have dinner together and to discuss issues at an intelligent level and I can't see how that can happen if it's just in English.

In many families fathers would know more English than mothers; older brothers and sisters could speak the parents' language; but younger siblings, born and raised in the United States, could speak only English. This fluently bilingual South American man chose his language depending on the person being addressed:

I: So when do you speak Spanish, when do you speak English?
R: It just comes natural. I mean, I try not to speak Spanish, especially when I'm uncomfortable with a person, I just like stumble over my words but with my mom, I speak Spanish. She doesn't speak English. But I can't speak Spanish to my brothers, I gotta speak English. It just feels unnatural speaking Spanish.

Because people associate the immigrant language with their parents and grandparents, many feel a warm emotional tie when they do speak it. Other respondents told us that the only words they knew in their parents' language were curses. When this Dominican young man's parents got angry and screamed and yelled at him, they inevitably did so in Spanish:

> We speak Spanish in my house. Like I'll talk to my mom in English, and she'll respond in Spanish or she'll talk to me in English and I'll talk Spanish to her, depending on her mood. If she's mad—she'll definitely talk in Spanish. She'll start screaming real fast in Spanish, but if she wants to like get a point across, or talk to me, she'll talk in English.

Or this Chinese man:

> *I:* When you were growing up, at home, your parents spoke English with you?
> *R:* Yeah. Except when my mom was extremely angry, sometimes it would be the Chinese thing coming out. And I would be in extreme trouble. They would slip into it when they didn't want us to understand what was going on. When one of us was especially in trouble and they wanted to discuss matters they would go off and switch over to another language.

Sometimes respondents refused to speak the home country language in order to make an angry point. One young Chinese American woman told us that she pretends she cannot speak or understand Chinese, although she is fluent in it, whenever someone approaches her expecting her to be able to speak Chinese. In so doing she is making a statement that she should not be treated as a foreigner just because she looks Chinese.

The anti-Semitism faced by Russian Jews before they migrated left them with complex and often contradictory feelings about the Russian language. Often it is the only part of Russian culture they feel warmly toward, since it is the language spoken in their close-knit nuclear families. But one respondent described how his father channeled his anger toward the Soviet Union into his feelings about the language:

> My dad would tell me, "You have to read the English books." He was very upset with me if I was reading Russian books. He would really disapprove and whenever I would raise a concern that I think I'm losing the language, he would just laugh. He really does not have any

value for it. He has an internal dislike of the whole culture that is so deep that if that country were just to go up in flames, he would just say, "Yeah, it's too bad for the people. The end." He really has no value for that. I think I'm more interested and that's weird.

For respondents who came to the United States as young children, it was difficult to start school while not understanding anything people were saying. They described the experience as hard, tearful, and frightening. Said this Russian man:

> The ESL teachers would yell at me because I didn't understand. They would really yell and I couldn't understand. I didn't speak English and I couldn't have my parents come to school because they didn't speak English because their English was worse than mine. I'm not one of the people who are pro-sensitivity. I'm nobody's victim but if the kid comes to the country and does not speak English, and you are the ESL teacher, you don't yell at the kid. How can you yell at the kid?

Or this South American woman:

> I remember when I first went to school, no one really told me that I wouldn't know what everyone was saying. And the school I went to no one spoke Spanish because back then there really wasn't much, you know, bilingual education was not a big thing. There wasn't really integration, anyway, but there was no Spanish teachers, no translators, nothing. I remember my brother and I would cry on the way home on the bus.

Translating for parents was a common experience. A small minority of our respondents reported being embarrassed by it when they were called on to translate at the welfare office or identify bad grades on their report cards or troubles in school. Translation often involved adult business—financial forms or visits to doctors—and the young people felt they were being called on to talk about things they did not understand or use unfamiliar words. At a young age, respondents helped parents with complex medical issues, banking transactions, or insurance forms. One Chinese respondent recalled with disdain how his parents bought a washing machine when he was 10 years old and asked him to translate the manual. "They expected me to be able to install a washing machine at ten years old just because I could speak English."

Most of our respondents reported pride in their ability to translate for their parents. Proud of their language skills and fluency in both languages, many respondents were aware that it was effortless for them to speak English but very difficult for their parents. One young woman told us that when she was a child, translating for her parents made her feel like she was "the smartest person in the world."

Yet translation is not just about literal understanding of words, it is also about knowledge and power. Translators can simply translate the words that are spoken, or they can use their cultural knowledge to better convey the meanings intended in a less literal manner. Indeed, this 23-year-old South American describes how he uses this knowledge to bestow advantages or disadvantages on people:

> R: When I had to go to the welfare office, I had to do translation 'cause sometimes my mother couldn't even receive the benefits and she wanted to know why. My father was working and he couldn't miss the day from work so I was the man to translate. So basically I was the liaison from English to Spanish.
>
> I: How did you feel about translating?
>
> R: At first I wasn't too comfortable because I wasn't sure what I was doing. I knew what everything meant but I wasn't sure how were these people using the information. But now that I know more, I can actually give someone else the upper hand. For example, in the naturalization process, let's say the immigration officer tells me, "Tell this person so and so." Since they don't know Spanish and I know Spanish and probably I know additional information I'll pass it on to the person who doesn't know, who I'm translating to. Giving that person that upper hand and then when they fill out the application or something, everything is legit. Like that. I can give somebody the upper hand or totally blank them out and give them the disadvantage. I have the—not power, but that talent—it makes me feel good about myself because they look up to me to provide good and accurate information to them. I feel wonderful because you're doing that favor for them. When they did you the favor of teaching you Spanish.

Others had a harder time deciding whether to provide their parents' exact words or say what they thought their parents should be saying. This Dominican woman had a combative mother who demanded that her daughter say things that the daughter found inappropriate. She toned down her mother's words in order to make them more palatable:

R: Drama! Drama! "Dile a ese guy lo que yo digo- que se vaya con su maldita . . ." [Tell this guy what I'm saying, that he can get out of here with his damn . . .] My mother said that you could go and do whatever you have to do: "Eso es lo que yo dije, mother fucker." This is what I said. Or if we had to go to an office, any kind of an office. A good example, the Section 8 office. And you know, in these city offices, you have to be a little bit, you know, politically correct, try to do things right. Mami no, "Dile que se mete su maldita . . ." [Tell him to put his damn . . .] And my mother's not the type to use profanity, I'm exaggerating a little bit but she'd want me to curse them out but she wants them to do her a favor! No mom, it doesn't work that way, it doesn't work that way.

Translating often involved a degree of deception. In the case of this Russian man:

I always end up making phone calls for them. When I was eleven I remember distinctly I would call a credit card or a bank and I would just say I was my sister. And the voice is very . . . I was mistaken for a girl on a consistent basis when I was younger so I would do phone calls for her. Lately no. When I do business with my father, he doesn't pick up the phone ever. So I'm always him, without a question or a doubt. I know his Social Security better than he does. I don't mind the translations.

A Chinese respondent recalled going on a trip with his uncles when he was just 11 years old and being forced to lie:

All my uncles could speak English but we were on a trip with one uncle and he backed a Winnebago into another one and he pretended he couldn't speak English. "Mike will translate." Okay. "No, officer, he can't speak English." [Laugh]

Despite the political attention and debate about English-language dominance, the tolerance, acceptance, and even celebration of cultural difference in the United States seems to have made today's immigrants more accepting of a second language than those of a century ago. While members of the second generation are rapidly learning English and losing their parents' language, their openness and pride toward their parents' languages reflect an on-the-ground multiculturalism.

This changed attitude does not mean that bilingualism prevails. Use of

Chinese and Russian declined rapidly among the second generation. For obvious reasons, Spanish was much easier to maintain. Puerto Ricans had the lowest levels of Spanish-language retention. Many Puerto Rican respondents expressed regret about losing their Spanish. Yet the presence of large numbers of immigrants and second generation fluent Spanish-speakers was refreshing the knowledge of Spanish they did have. Many Puerto Ricans said Dominican or South American boyfriends or girlfriends were helping them to relearn some Spanish.

This Puerto Rican saw his ability to speak Spanish as a bonus, something that often came in handy:

R: When I was twelve, when I came back from PR, yeah, I had to translate a lot 'cause I stayed six months in PR and it was nothing but Spanish. When I came back I was speaking nothing but Spanish, and my friends who didn't know Spanish, I used to tell them, "Say this." So they got hooked on it. A couple of my friends are black and they learned Spanish through me. "How you say this to that girl?" Whatever.
I: What about now? Do you speak Spanish?
R: Oh yeah, 'cause right now at the job at Burger King we got a lot of Spanish employees so if they make a mistake I let them know. And the majority of the customers that come into the store are Hispanic so you got to . . . 'cause sometimes their English isn't too good and you let them know you can speak Spanish and they be relieved. "Oh my God, okay." So then you help them out or whatever. I could say in a day the majority I'm speaking Spanish eight-ten hours during the day. Now that my Spanish started to get a whole lot more better now, again. 'Cause I was real rough but I'm getting better.

In contrast, many of the Dominican and South American respondents saw Puerto Ricans as a negative example of what it would mean to lose their language ability. Said this Dominican man:

I: Do you speak Spanish to your children?
R: Oh yeah, definitely. I read books to him, Spanish books to him. I talk to him in Spanish. I try to have my mother speak to him in Spanish.
I: Why do you think it's so important for your child to know both languages?
R: Basically it's another tool for him. It just helps him get along. In the past it was the stereotype, "Oh no, you should only know En-

glish" and that's why honestly, some of my friends who are Puerto Rican don't even know Spanish. We poke fun at them. "Look at you, you don't even know how to speak. Come on."

The Puerto Ricans were most likely to say they spoke "Spanglish." One Puerto Rican man said, "We spoke mainly Spanish in the house. When we were outside we would speak English. It was a mixture. But now I speak Spanglish. People understand me. They know more or less what I'm trying to get across."

New York's large Spanish-speaking community supports a number of radio and television stations. When we asked about listening or watching ethnic TV or radio, the Russians and Chinese reported doing so if their grandmother or parent was watching. Or they described needing to remember which hour the international station broadcast in their language. But the popularity of Latino music and the TV soap operas has transcended generations. Spanish-speaking youth rattled off the names and call letters of a number of radio and TV stations that broadcast all the time in Spanish, as indicated by this South American 27-year-old:

I: How about watching television or listening to the radio in Spanish? Do you do that?

R: Yeah. Six channels on my radio are preset to Spanish. Salsa, merengue.

I: Spanish, not Ecuadorian?

R: There's no Ecuadorian over here.

I: Do you ever read books or magazines? You said you read the newspaper, the Ecuadorian newspaper?

R: Every day.

I: Why do you do that?

R: What's going over there. Right now they have a state of emergency in the place where my mother has the house and so you have to keep good tabs, see how things are there.

About 83 percent of our Dominican respondents, 76 percent of our South American respondents, and 70 percent of Puerto Ricans report watching or listening to Spanish-language programming frequently. Yet only 31 percent of Russians and 41 percent of Chinese watch or listen to ethnic programs. As this South American 23-year-old describes, the bond of Spanish language transcends different sending countries, often through a conscious media strategy to be all-inclusive:

I: Do you listen to Ecuadorian or Spanish radio?

R: Actually, I listen to Spanish radio, La Mega. I don't think there's any Ecuadorian station.

I: Why do you listen to La Mega?

R: Because La Mega is a whole culture put in one. They explain everything from what does this mean in Mexico to what does it mean in Argentina. Also, I like the beat. It just gives a beat that brings out the heart in it. It just makes it move. Every time I hear a good salsa or a good merengue, it just brings out the Spanish person in me and makes me feel proud of what I am. A Spanish-speaking person. Not Ecuadorian. Not Puerto Rican. I'm glad that I can share that with all the people that can speak Spanish. It's something that a South American person can listen to merengue and a Puerto Rican person or Dominican person can come and dance to it over here.

Our respondents saw speaking another language as a positive and welcome aspect of their backgrounds. Said one Russian woman:

It's always good to speak another language and to be able to talk about people and have them not understand. There's a certain richness that comes along with having culture, a different culture to fall back on. And it contributes to your personality and how you can interact with other people, because you have an added perspective. Language, songs that I can sing. People are always intrigued. They ask what does it mean to be Russian and you feel a little special to explain and it adds color to you.

The near-universal use of English among both the true second generation (U.S. born) and the 1.5 generation respondents should reassure anyone worried by the political furor whipped up by debates over English as an endangered language in the United States. The real story among our respondents is about second language retention, and the group differences here are strong—the institutional support of large numbers, media presence, and close proximity and frequent travel to sending countries mean that Spanish is more likely to survive as a second language than is Chinese or Russian. This also has implications for ties to the parents' home country—without a facility in language, members of the second generation will have difficulty maintaining close ties to their parents' country.

Transnationalism

The attachment of our respondents to the home country could not be taken for granted, as in the case of this 18-year-old Colombian:

> *I:* Did your parents ever make a special effort to teach you Colombian history, traditions?
> *R:* They would try to show me the geography of Colombia, "Oh yeah, this province and that province." "Yeah, yeah, yeah, it's all Colombia to me."
> *I:* How did you feel when they were doing that?
> *R:* It's like, "Do we know anybody there? Do we know anyone in the Amazon part of Colombia? No we don't. Do I really need to know that? Not really. All I need to know is where our family is 'cause that's as far as I'm going to go." I'm not going to go to some remote jungle or something.

In light of today's ease of communication and transportation, many people argue that migrants and their children are not really "immigrants" in the traditional sense. Rather they are "transnationals" or "transmigrants"—living in social worlds that cross national borders. This view sometimes theorizes the "transnational option" as being particularly attractive to nonwhite immigrants. Why, after all, would one give up ties to communities and nations where one was part of the ethnic majority in order to become part of a downtrodden minority? Rather than accept racialized minority status, it might seem reasonable to refuse to be incorporated into U.S. society even while functioning within its economy.

Linda Basch, Nina Glick Schiller, and Cristina Szanton Blanc articulated this notion in their influential book *Nations Unbound* (1994). International migrants, they maintain, are increasingly active politically, socially, and economically in two or more societies at the same time, necessitating a major rethinking of categories of nationality and citizenship. This concept has been expanded theoretically by the recent work of sociologist Alejandro Portes (1999, 2001), as well as by the empirical studies of sociologists such as Robert Smith (2006), Peggy Levitt (2001), and José Itzigsohn (2000), among others. While each researcher has his or her own version of transnationalism, they agree that a world of global labor markets and instant communications has made the "either they do or they don't" model of acculturating into U.S. society obsolete.

Transnationalism makes some observers worry that immigration is balkanizing American society. They also fear that maintaining transnational ties will slow the assimilation of the children of immigrants. Samuel Huntington (2004:5) begins his book on immigration's challenge to American identity by warning that "in 2000, the proportion of people in America who were also loyal to and identified with other countries was quite possibly higher than at any time since the American Revolution."

During the nineteenth and the first decades of the twentieth centuries, nativists also frequently invoked the specter of "dual loyalties." Catholic schools, German American bilingualism, and distinctively Jewish dress were all seen as threats to American unity. Others predicted that ties to the home country would fade with time, or at least would mutate into an ethnic culture—different from the mainstream perhaps, but nonetheless a distinctly American creation, with progressively less relationship to the home country.

History largely bore out the latter prediction. To be sure, Irish immigrants and their American-born children remained concerned about Irish independence, and Jews remained active in efforts to create a Zionist homeland in Palestine. Yet these efforts rarely seemed at odds with loyalty to the United States. When immigrant and American identities *did* come into sharp conflict, as happened to German Americans when the United States entered World War I, the ethnic identity almost always disappeared. German American bilingualism, which had flourished for three generations, was dropped almost overnight, as German newspapers shut their doors and thriving German American organizations were suddenly disbanded, or at least renamed. By World War II, few questioned or even noticed the irony of a general named Eisenhower leading the war against Germany.

The possibility of sustained transnational ties is far more viable for today's immigrants. Travel is cheap enough that even working class legal immigrants can return "home" with some frequency—what was once a once-in-a-lifetime trip is now often an annual event. Immigrant neighborhoods are jammed with businesses selling low cost phone calls and instant money transfers to some of the most remote parts of the globe. Video and audio tapes allow immigrants to "participate" in weddings and village festivals in the Andes, Iran, or West Africa. The Internet increasingly makes it possible to do so in "real time."

The governments of sending countries, which until recently tended to ignore their communities abroad, are now encouraging their expatriates to participate economically and politically in the home country; and many countries now grant dual citizenship rights to people in the United States. Indeed, some nation-states now encourage their nationals abroad to become U.S. citizens and lobby their American representatives on behalf of their home country. Paradoxically, as studies by sociologists Douglas Massey, Jorge Durand, and Nolan Malone (2002) have shown, naturalization may actually encourage immigrants to return to their homelands and to invest money there, knowing that if things do not work out, they have the "insurance policy" of an American passport that will always allow them to return to the United States.

Just how transnational will the second generation remain (Levitt and Waters 2002)? Does the strength of transnational ties differ by group? And are transnational ties that do exist into the second generation at odds with integration into American society, as some commentators fear? Our telephone survey asked whether respondents had lived for more than six months in their parents' home country at any time after the initial migration, how often respondents visit that country, how much attention they pay to home country politics, and whether they or their parents send remittances back home. Our in-depth interviews probed whether respondents or their parents had plans to live in the sending country someday, what it was like for them when they visited that country, and how much they felt connected to it.

Figure 8.3 shows that the groups have different patterns of transnational activity. Geographic distance and politics seem to play important roles. Considering the frequency of remittances by respondents, of remittances by parents, and of visits to parents' home country, Dominicans showed the highest combined levels of transnational activity, followed by the South Americans and the West Indians. Chinese and Russian Jewish levels were far lower.

The majority of every group except the Russian Jews had visited their parents' home country at least once. Among the Russians, 82 percent had never been to the former Soviet Union since emigrating (or since birth in the case of the "true" second generation respondents). In a show of transnational activity, however, one-third of this group had visited Israel.

Among the Chinese, 62 percent had visited China (including Taiwan and Hong Kong), a high number given the distance and difficulty of travel, but only about one in ten had visited four or more times (Figure 8.3). By contrast, 48 percent of Dominicans, 39 percent of South Americans, and 35 percent of West Indians had visited this often. Remarkably, one in five Dominicans reported having been to the parents' homeland more than ten times, but only 2 percent of the Chinese and almost no Russians visited that often. The numbers who had spent more than six months in their parents' home country showed the same pattern. Only 9 percent of Chinese and 11 percent of Russians had done so, contrasting with 26 percent of Dominicans, 24 percent of West Indians, and 18 percent of South Americans.

The majority of every group except the Russians reported that their parents sent remittances home, although most of the Chinese reported that their parents did so only about once a year. Many more Dominicans (44 percent), South Americans (44 percent), and West Indians (34 percent) reported that their parents sent money home several times a year or more. Remittance activity among the second generation was much lower than it was among the parents. Of course, given their youth, it is not surprising that most respondents did not regularly send remittances, although a significant minority of Dominicans (20 percent) and South Americans (19 percent) did so. Once the parents retire or die, the second generation may take up some responsibility for caring for relatives back

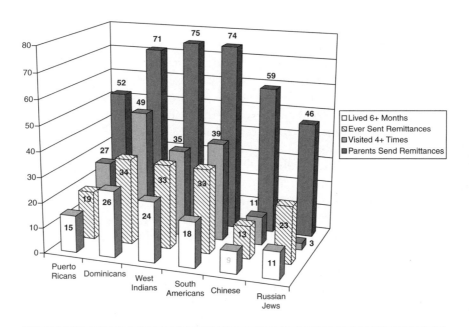

Figure 8.3. Transnational Practices (%). *Source:* ISGMNY.

home. Or they may not, leading to an overall decline in the level of remittances sent abroad.

Respondents with co-ethnic spouses reported higher levels of transnational practices than those who were out-married. More women than men exhibited high levels of transnational practices (Kasinitz et al. 2002). While some studies have found that men have a greater interest in returning home than do women (Grasmuck and Pessar 1991), our finding suggests young women disproportionately bear the burdens of maintaining family ties. Not surprisingly, those who prefer to speak English are slightly less likely to show strong transnational practices, whereas those who prefer the home language are more likely to have strong transnational ties, although multivariate analysis shows that this relationship weakens once other factors are taken into account. Belonging to ethnic organizations is also strongly associated with transnational practices.

Working in a place where most of one's co-workers and one's supervisors are co-ethnics—that is to say, working in an ethnic niche—has surprisingly little impact on transnational practices. Those who work with members of different ethnic groups are actually more likely to show high levels of transnational activity. On the other hand, frequent use of the ethnic broadcast media was closely associated with transnational activity. This relationship is even stronger among the three groups with the highest levels of transnational activity (Dominicans, South Americans, and West Indians).

Some West Indians and Latinos were sent back home to live with relatives at some point during their teen years by parents who were terrified by the dangers of the New York streets. Ironically, these teenagers often found that the education back home stood them in better stead when it came to getting into U.S. colleges or getting U.S. jobs than the education acquired by their cousins in the New York City public schools.

Some young people now use a hiatus in their parents' homeland as a second chance to make it in the United States. One Dominican respondent said that while her grandmother sent her to the Dominican Republic as a "punishment" for disobeying her strict rules prohibiting contact with boys, the effect of spending time in the Dominican Republic was positive:

> She told me that we were going on vacation and in fact, it turned out to be that my vacation lasted three years because she didn't want me to screw up. That's why she sent me there, to save me from myself. I was like eleven to fourteen. Going to the Dominican Republic was

the best thing that ever happened to me. It was. Honest to God, it really really was. I learned the values of being a woman. I learned how to clean a house. I learned how to tend to myself and to others. I learned how to be responsible. I learned what it was to be a woman and it's not just putting on a skirt and shaking your ass. I learned the importance of an education and I'm grateful. When I came back, I had like a whole different set of values.

Yet strong ties to their parents' country are the exception, not the rule. For most of our respondents, the United States was indisputably home. Even those who fondly recalled trips "back home" returned with a profound realization of how they had been shaped by this country (and by New York). Chinese respondents often complained of the strange lifestyle and lack of amenities in China (squat toilets and the lack of air conditioning). One Queens resident dismissed Guangzhou as a dirty and crowded city—"like Chinatown only on a bigger scale." The home country's lack of economic opportunities and amenities was often mentioned by 1.5 generation Dominican and West Indian respondents who could not imagine relocating permanently to the Caribbean. (A striking number of respondents talked with horror about the bugs and lizards they had encountered there.) Therefore few people, even from those groups with high levels of second generation transnationalism, envisioned living in their parents' homeland for any sustained length of time. As one Dominican woman put it:

You go, you visit all these relatives that are there. You kind of see how they live their life. It was fun. It is kind of like country mouse and city mouse, and you get to go to the country and do all sorts of crazy things, like take a bath in a lake. Things that you can't do here. But you are kind of glad that you are going back home to civilization.

Visits to parents' relatives often provided young people a window into their parents' lives and gave them warm feelings about spending carefree summers with their cousins, but these visits ultimately made our respondents feel like New Yorkers and Americans. As one 20-year-old Chinese woman noted:

I: Would you ever consider living in Hong Kong or China?
R: No. Somewhere else, but not there. I'm such a New York City person. I was there for a few days and I was so homesick. Really bad. I'm an American. I don't think I would adapt well because like people

from Hong Kong, their mentality is very traditional. You grow up in America you have this thing where you know, you can do anything you want to. They really don't. They're very family oriented. I'm not. I grew up in America. I'm just like the opposite of them.

Most South Americans and Dominicans who spent time in their parents' countries come home complaining about the corruption and government inefficiency there. Twenty-seven-year-old Eduardo, who was born in Brooklyn, scored very high on our transnationalism scale. He has visited Ecuador more than twenty-two times, he lived there for a year, he regularly sends money to his father-in-law, his family owns land and houses there, and he reads the Ecuadoran newspaper on the Internet very often. Yet his experiences with Ecuador have produced a very strong identification as an American and a New Yorker.

R: My parents ended up wanting to go live in Ecuador. So I went to live in Ecuador when I was seventeen. Lived there a year. A year and three days, to be exact. I hated it. The corruption is ridiculous. Everything, everything is so different. A lot of people get pissed off here if the trains are five minutes late. They don't even have trains over there. They don't got buses over there. The cars there are ridiculous. When I went to live over there, there was a car embargo so no new cars could come in so you saw Toyotas with Ford rebuilt engines.
I: So you were seventeen and your parents decided you were going?
R: They thought it would be a better life for us but that was their time. Not for us. Especially going over there and seeing what we had here, it's just a slap in the face. And the corruption. The corruption is there and if you don't know the right people to grease the right hands, you don't get anything. People always say, "Oh, New York is so bad" and everything. But if you stop and think it's like over there after 7:00 at night you can't go out. There's two kinds of people down there, filthy rich and poor people. No middle class. And you go out there with a new car, they carjack you right in front of your house.

Visits reinforced anti-Communist suspicions for the Chinese. Women who visited sending countries came home horrified at the lack of freedom that women have there compared to the United States. Long term visits provide a civic education program for members of the second generation. Our interviews suggest that the majority of them would return more "American" than they ever were before.

In sum, most groups have low levels of transnationalism, and transnational activities do not always reinforce ties to the homeland. Visiting or hearing about their parents' homeland can actually hasten identification with the United States. Moreover, as we saw in Chapter 5, travel and remittances had a negative association with educational outcomes in the second generation. Sustained transnationalism is therefore unlikely to persist into later generations (Levitt and Waters 2002).

Religion

Scholars of immigrant incorporation have long been interested in religion. Will Herberg's (1960) influential model of immigrant assimilation into a "triple melting pot" of Protestants, Catholics, and Jews shaped a number of studies. Herberg argued that because of the importance of religion in American life and the institutional support that religion provides to identity, immigrants and their descendants would lose a strong association with their ethnic identities as Italians or Poles or Germans but would maintain the sharp boundary between the three major religious groups then present in the United States. Yet the sharp rise in interfaith marriages since the early 1960s and the continuing significance of ethnic boundaries have undermined support for this triple melting pot idea over time.

As immigration from non-European countries developed after the 1960s, American society began to notice that immigrants were bringing to our shores new religious faiths outside the Judeo-Christian tradition. The growth of the Islamic, Hindu, and Buddhist faiths has begun to attract scholarly and popular attention (Eck 2007), refocusing attention on whether strong religious backgrounds lead to better outcomes for immigrants, and most especially for their children. Zhou and Bankston (1998), for instance, argue that the Vietnamese second generation youth who were actively involved in the Catholic Church in New Orleans had better outcomes than those who were less involved.

Overall we find that organized religion plays an important role in the lives of relatively few of our second generation respondents. We asked our respondents if they currently attended a place of worship—a church, synagogue, or temple. Only 46 percent reported that they attended at all. The most actively religious were Dominicans (52 percent attended), West Indians (52 percent), South Americans (50 percent), and native blacks (50 percent). The least active were the Chinese (38 percent) and the

Puerto Ricans (39 percent). Native whites (42 percent) and Russians (41 percent) had similar rates of attending.

Our respondents are, on the whole, less religious than other Americans. Those who are involved in organized religion attend churches and temples where they are likely to come into contact with other ethnic groups. Thus, far from being a cultural reinforcer, religion tends to be an assimilatory force. Given that America is a highly religious country, it is perhaps not surprising that some young people growing up here become more religious than their parents—especially among the Russians and the Chinese, whose parents come from countries where religion was discouraged or even outlawed.

Figure 8.4 shows the religious attachments across our groups compared to a nationwide sample of young adults in the General Social Survey. Nationally, young adults are 46 percent Protestant, 26 percent Catholic, 2 percent Jewish, 6 percent other, and 20 percent no religion. Our respondents are much less Protestant (20 percent), more Catholic (37 percent) and more Jewish (11 percent), and slightly more likely to report no religion (23 percent). But there is wide variation among our groups.

The Chinese are most likely to report that they have no religion (56 percent), although this figure is probably lower than for their parents. A quarter of our West Indian and African American respondents report no religion, as do almost a fifth of native whites. By contrast, only 16 percent each of Dominicans and Puerto Ricans and 17 percent of Russian "Jews" report no religion. In the latter case, however, the religiosity of the group is probably exaggerated by the fact that "Jewish" is both a religious and an ethnic identity and that the sample is selected among people who claim some "Jewish" connection. In fact, only about a third of the Russian "Jews" we surveyed attend a synagogue regularly, and only about a quarter of those attend once a week. The most religious of our groups, South Americans, are also the most homogeneous in terms of their specific religion—80 percent are Catholics. A small number of West Indians and African Americans are Muslim, but the largest non-Judeo-Christian group among our respondents are Buddhists, as 18 percent of our Chinese respondents consider themselves Buddhist and a larger percentage were raised in that tradition.

We asked about the ethnicity of the other people with whom our respondents worshipped. For the most part the second generation does not appear to worship in ethnically specific places. Despite the proliferation of services in a variety of languages throughout New York's immigrant communities (see Carnes and Karpathakis 2001), second generation Catholics and Protestants tend to worship in ethnically mixed congregations, and those Russian Jews who do attend services do so with longtime American Jews, as well as with Jewish immigrants from other parts of the world. Reflecting the broader patterns of segregation in American society and the distinct history of the African American church, native blacks are the group most likely to worship with co-ethnics. Even there, however, the proportion, 42 percent, is lower than one might expect.

Among those who report attending any house of worship, 40 to 60 percent attend nearly every week or more. The minority of Puerto Ricans and Chinese who attend a house of worship are among the most frequent and active attenders. (Fifty-six percent of the Chinese report attending church nearly every week or more, while 55 percent of Puerto Ricans report the same.) Many of these people are also involved in other church activities, such as youth groups or Bible study groups. Indeed, when we examine our respondents' involvement in organized activities, they are more likely to be active in church activities than sports teams or ethnic organizations.

This involvement did not reinforce an ethnic cultural experience, how-

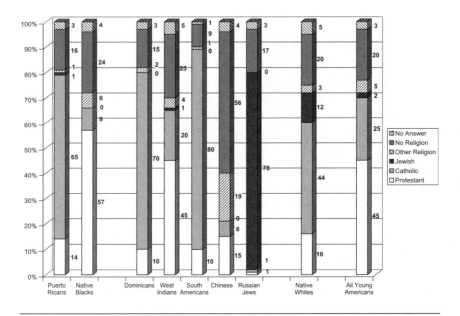

Figure 8.4. Religious Affiliation (%). *Source:* ISGMNY.

ever. Their experiences in churches do not generally emerge from the interviews as sites of interethnic contact. This may be because worship in places like Catholic churches does not lead to sustained interactions among parishioners who come together for mass and then scatter afterward.

Low levels of participation, low levels of religious ethnic segregation, and low levels of interaction while at church all mean that religion does not reinforce cultural differences for the second generation. On the contrary, taking part in organized religion is likely to be a site of integration with people from outside the ethnic group (although often with other first and second generation immigrants and with native minorities more than with native whites).

Even among the self-identified Russians "Jews," a sizable number reflect their secular upbringing by claiming no religion. As mentioned in Chapter 3, while Russian Jews were discriminated against in Russia for being ethnically Jewish, most were secular and far removed from any religious identification. When Russian Jews arrive in the United States, the Jewish settlement agencies that help them very much expect them to begin practicing religion. Many members of the second generation attend Jewish religious schools, yeshivas, where some individuals become very religious and begin to keep kosher homes and attend orthodox synagogues. Others become convinced that though they might be ethnically Jewish, they are completely uninterested in religion and recommit themselves to a secular lifestyle. This 25-year-old Jewish woman describes the clash of American expectations and her own reaction:

> I went to a Jewish Day School that sort of had this project on Russian Jews. They were sort of disappointed with us. They had intended . . . I think . . . this is an Orthodox Day School and they watched all these things on television about Refuseniks and saw these poor Russian Jews wanting so desperately to study Torah and aren't being allowed to! So now they will. But we didn't want to study Torah! [laughter] Amazing. And they were not happy with us.

The Chinese also come from a Communist country where religious expression was discouraged or outlawed; and so many Chinese, like the Russians, were raised in highly secular homes. The majority of Chinese report that they have no religion. Only 18 percent say their current religion is Buddhist, although many of those who now report no religion or who are Catholic or Protestant report that they were raised in Buddhist households. Those who do describe a Buddhist upbringing generally show very little deep knowledge of the religion and do not report that Buddhism made much of an impact on their lives:

> *I:* How important was practicing the Buddhist religion when you were growing up?
>
> *R:* Well, I respect it. Them. So in turn I did everything they wanted me to do. Ceremonial things, like there are certain days of the month . . . I think the first day of the month or the fifteenth day of the month, you do this whole worship thing and there's food and chicken and stuff. They do this whole prayer thing.
>
> *I:* At home or did they go to a temple?
>
> *R:* At home. Yeah, they had the shrine at home. Most people actually go to the temple but they did it at home.
>
> I: So what role would you say religion plays in your life now?
>
> R: I have to honestly say I'm not. I don't know if I would go so far as calling myself an atheist but I'm not a practicing anything.

Even "practicing" Buddhists generally describe a minimal relation to a formal religion. It is more like a philosophy that helps to govern their lives:

> *I:* Would you say Buddhism is an important part of your life?
>
> *R:* Yes. It's not like Christianity where you have to go to church to pretend to be a Christian. It's an irony that some people that believe in Christianity and they could kill a guy and the next day you go to church and pray there, "I did something wrong." And you try to re-lieve your sin, I guess that's what they call it, the next day you're doing the same thing over again. What's the point in that? In Bud-dhism it's different. You do something wrong, you're going to suffer for the consequences. What comes around, goes around. If you did something good, something good will happen to you. Just like that. In Buddhism we also believe in the people who are working hard, will always be luckiest. That's what I believe in.

About a fifth of our Chinese respondents report that they are Christian, 6 percent are Catholic, and 15 percent are Protestant. Although some in-dividuals were raised in these religions, many converted after arrival in the United States, mostly during their college years. These converts tend to be very active Christians and are often members of pan-Asian campus-based, and often evangelical, Christian ministries. While the Chinese have the greatest percentage of people who report no religion, among those

who are religious and attend services, they have the most active partici-
pants, with 59 percent reporting that they attend services nearly every
week or more. Such a high level of religiosity is sometimes a source of tension with the converts' more secular parents (Chai-Kim 2004).

> *R:* I'm a Christian, but I wasn't raised in it, no.
> *I:* You weren't. When did you become a Christian?
> *R:* In college.
> *I:* You're the only Christian in the family.
> *R:* Right.
> *I:* And what role would you say religion plays in your life right now?
> *R:* A big role. It's the source of my creation. I believe in God and He,
> since He is the author of my fate, then, you know, basically the ulti-
> mate purpose of my life is to please my Creator.

Some respondents told us that their parents had converted to Christianity as well, but the most fervent believers tend to be young people
who found religion on their own. In every ethnic group there are a few respondents who were raised in a very strict religious tradition and for
whom religion continues to shape their lives in countless ways. These include Seventh Day Adventists (2 percent of West Indians) and Jehovah's
Witnesses (2 percent of Puerto Ricans and 1 percent of native blacks).
This 20-year-old Chinese man describes how being a Jehovah's Witness
affected his life:

> *I:* And you still go to church about every week?
> *R:* Three times a week.
> *I:* What role would you say religion plays in your life now?
> *R:* Religion is not—I would say it's a way of living. All my decisions
> are dictated by my faith, so if I'm going to choose what music I'm
> going to listen to, religion in some way plays a role. What God
> thinks, how I think God sees my actions, He views my actions. It
> dictates, most of the time. Then again, I'm not perfect, I make mis-
> takes, but most of my decisions are dictated by my religious beliefs.
> *I:* Can you give me an example with music?
> *R:* In junior high school most of my friends, classmates there, were
> African American, hip hop, rap, and reggae. That was the type of
> music that they used to listen to. So it rubbed off on me and it
> became my favorite, but as time has moved on, and I've really
> thought about the message it transmits, I reject that music. I find it

degrading. It glamorizes, in my opinion, it glamorizes the street violence, justifies hustling and dealing as a necessary means to survive.
I reject that completely. I think that is garbage . . . It clashes with
my values.

Since the terrorist attacks of September 11, 2001, the public debate
about religious cultural difference and immigration has focused on the
experience of Muslim immigrants. Given the ways in which Muslim immigrants to Europe have felt marginalized and discriminated against, the
question in the United States is whether immigrants from Muslim countries will face systematic discrimination, thus hardening the boundaries
between Muslims and other groups and preventing assimilation. Few of
our respondents are Muslim, but their experiences do seem markedly
different with respect to intermarriage and intergroup relations. Although only 3 percent of African Americans and 2 percent of West Indians told us they were Muslim, a surprising number of them talked
about issues surrounding Islam. Some African Americans, West Indians,
and Dominicans had either converted themselves (one Dominican man
converted to Islam in prison) or had members of their extended families
convert.

When I was growing up, I was raised to become a Muslim. Not the
black Muslims, but orthodox Muslim, and then as I got older—I
think only like this year—I mean, I still do believe in certain things
that Islam teaches us, however, I'm gearing more toward Christianity. Not because I see anything wrong with Islam, it's just that I
need more focus on it, and—it's a very diligent religion—I need
more time to prepare with that. With Christianity, it's more seen as
acceptable, whereas with Islam, they see it as "Oh, you're fundamen-
talist," or "You're part of the black Muslims, you're following Far-
rakhan," so it gets really difficult.

Intermarriage or dating between Christians and Muslims brought up
more issues and concerns than did Jewish-Christian intermarriage or
dating, as this 29-year-old Dominican woman makes clear:

I: And what about religion? Did they ever talk about that?
R: My boyfriend, the one I was talking about, he was Muslim, so that
really. It brought a lot of conflict because you can't eat pork, you
can't eat this, you can't do that, you can't do this. So that did bring
a lot of conflict in the relationship.

This 21-year-old Catholic Puerto Rican man had trouble with the extended family of a Muslim woman he had married:

I: Everything was always okay. With their parents too?

R: Well, let's see, like my wife right now, when me and her were dating, her parents, since they're Muslim, they couldn't actually appreciate me for myself, 'cause they knew I was Catholic and their house, they didn't believe in the cross symbol, 'cause they have a different symbol and they always used to think wrong about me. They used to try to talk shit about me. But then, after a while they actually got to know me, they didn't have no problems after that.

Although the majority of our respondents in every group were not very involved in organized religion, many described themselves as "spiritual." Like most Americans, they deeply believe that people should choose the religion that is "right for them." "Church shopping" and switching religions is not uncommon. In childhood, church was important both as a place of worship and as an ethnic center to one West Indian man. As he grew older, his attachment lessened and he moved away from organized religion. Still, he retained his spirituality.

R: The church that I grew up in was predominantly West Indian. . . . It probably became important spiritually in me sometime in my teens and I kind of kept going even after the mandatory nature of it had kind of slipped away. And then after that I got disenchanted with it. Disenchanted with that particular denomination and then kind of fell away from that particular church.

I: So what role would you say religion plays in your life right now?

R: Organized religion is not that important. I'm not particularly concerned with going every week. Kind of officially joining a church is not really important to me. Because I think that a lot of what underlies religion is something that I feel regardless of what name you put on it or what building you choose to gather in to observe it. I think there is a force greater than us operating in the world, in the universe and that it is important to pay attention to that force. So that is something that I feel kind of underneath all of that trappings of religion and church and all that.

Some respondents have replaced formal church attendance with meditation or private prayer.

It's like, I don't mind going so Sunday mass but sometimes I feel like I'm better off just being good to myself, because the body, I read somewhere, I was reading that the Guru Book, about the gurus in India—basically it said your body's your temple this and that and it kind of made sense to me.

The spiritual journeys of the second generation have clearly just begun. Many individuals will, no doubt, become more attached to a formal religious tradition and to traditional religious organizations as they get older and particularly as they raise their own children. Some will return to the traditions in which they were raised. Many, we suspect, will not. Yet their religious ideas are fundamentally American. Contrary to the notions of Huntington (2004) and others, who see immigrant religious practices as linking them with the parents' homelands, second generation New Yorkers practice religion in a way that is highly consistent with their American lives.

Even the devout few among the Chinese and Russian Jews are not continuing in their parents' traditions. They have broken with their more secular parents to take up religion anew. Others, in their insistence on finding the religion that is "right for them" and in actively "church shopping," have thoroughly incorporated American individualism and notions of a personal relationship to the divine. In emphasizing the spiritual over the ritualistic and in fully accepting the multiplicity of religious traditions, whether Catholic, Jewish, Buddhist, or Muslim, many members of the second generation have absorbed the secularized Protestant ideas that underlie much of American religious practice.

We should, or course, add an important caveat. There was no predominantly Muslim group in our study. In the post–September 11 context, we must ask how Islam will or will not fit with American attitudes toward religious life. (The few respondents who were Muslim or who had Muslims in their extended families mentioned a number of conflicts and tensions that they felt were present because of religious differences.) That aside, however, religion seems unlikely to be a "bright boundary" separating the largely secular second generation New Yorkers from their fellow Americans (Alba 2005).

Conclusion

Overall, the young adults we spoke with look far more "American" than some debates about immigration would lead one to expect. They almost universally speak English well, they do not sustain strong transnational ties, and they pick and choose their religious identities and attend churches that are diverse. As we saw in Chapter 7, they are far more likely to believe in and practice gender equality than their parents' generation. Two aspects of the cultural assimilation of the second generation stand out. First, it is hard to measure the complexity of the cultural content of ethnicity with a survey question. There is no simple scale for measuring assimilation in the cultural sphere.

Different aspects of culture are more important for some groups than for others—music, for example, is quite important for West Indians and not at all for Chinese. Moreover, different scales yield different insights into the process of cultural assimilation. For instance, the issue of language is both simple, on the one hand, and complex, on the other. Our survey responses confidently tell us that retention of the parental language is no danger among the children of immigrants. When and where to use a language other than English is worked out in the schools and workplaces of New York in complex and subtle ways. Language retention and loss have a clear emotional significance. Religious identity is also far more complex than survey questions can capture. The second generation is undergoing religious conversion, intermarriage, and the borrowing of ideas and beliefs from Eastern and Western traditions to create an individual spirituality.

Second, our young adults easily combine their ethnic backgrounds and their American realities. For the most part, then, ethnicity is not only tolerated, but often celebrated as cultural traditions collide, merge, and coexist. Unlike earlier accounts of the children of European immigrants, these young people rarely feel ashamed of their parents' language and are often proud of their bicultural abilities. Unlike an "uprooted" peasantry who told their American children that they could only imagine what the home country was like, our young adults often visit their parents' countries, watch videos, and communicate with extended families on the Internet and by means of videos and tapes. The advantage of being a second generation immigrant now is that cultural differences at least seem demonstrably easier to both maintain and overcome than they did in the past.

9

Civic and Political Engagement

When I went to Ecuador a few years ago, there was an uprising—
they wanted to get rid of the president—and they *really* united. The
whole town, the indigenous population, everyone gathered in the
streets ready to overthrow the government! You don't see that here.
Here, I protested against the CUNY budget cuts, I was running
around getting signatures from people, and nobody seems to give a
damn. That's what drives me crazy. Yeah, this is the land of opportunity. *Hello?!* You have the right to stand up for yourself! I don't
know, maybe people think they can't make a difference.

ECUADORAN WOMAN, AGED 23

Politics looms large in the literature on how late nineteenth- and early
twentieth-century immigrants became Americans. Scholars of that period
took it for granted that participating in protest movements, joining labor
unions and civic organizations, voting, running candidates, and winning
elections were central to incorporation into American society. Even today
the election of an immigrant or, more often, a child of immigrants to a
significant office, such as mayor of Los Angeles or senator from Illinois, is
usually seen as a watershed moment in an immigrant group's "making it"
in the United States.

Strangely, politics no longer has a prominent role in most contemporary accounts of immigrant assimilation. One reason may be that political
and civic participation play less of a role in the daily lives of all Americans
today. In a nation that "bowls alone," political life may be less important
than in the past, particularly for the young. The 23-year-old student activist quoted at the chapter's opening is struck by how much more politically engaged people seemed to be in her parents' homeland. For her, "assimilation" may mean coming to share the apathy of her American peers.
On the other hand, the lack of emphasis on politics in the contemporary
immigration literature may also be a result of the changing interests of social scientists. Whatever the reason, political and civic participation is an
understudied dimension of the lives of the second and 1.5 generation,

particularly when compared to the voluminous literature on the economic status and educational careers of immigrants and their children.

This is unfortunate. In looking at how the second generation is incorporated in the political sphere, we see a very different pattern than in the labor market or educational attainment. The groups who are the most successful economically are often among the least likely to participate in politics, whereas poorer groups are sometimes among the most politically active. In particular, the African American role in the contemporary public sphere has created opportunities for other groups who share their circumstances. In 2006 a second generation West Indian American woman was elected to Congress from a central Brooklyn district created decades earlier to allow the election of an African American. There are many ironies in this, not the least of which is that the high residential segregation of West Indians helped them gain political representation. Still, that Yvette Clarke, the daughter of immigrants from Jamaica, now sits in the U.S. House of Representatives suggests that politics remains an important facet of incorporation in American society.

Most of our respondents, like many other Americans their age, hold fairly jaundiced views about the value of politics. They question whether politicians care about what they think or whether government is likely to respond to their needs or concerns. Yet many are also aware that government and politics can have a major impact on their lives. In 2000 a quarter of the New York metropolitan area's labor force worked for government or nonprofit social services. About one-eighth of our respondents work for a public agency, and another one-eighth work for a nonprofit organization. Our respondents are also consumers of public services. New York City has a diverse array of public and social services financed by a deep and progressive tax system. From neighborhood sidewalks and parks to the elementary schools, high schools, and public colleges, to the libraries, cultural institutions, sports leagues, and transit system, these services shape the ways in which young people grow up in the city.

Finally, New York is a highly politicized environment. It is populated by a wealth of civic and political organizations and numerous elected or appointed offices, ranging from community boards, precinct councils, and school district parent advisory boards up to the mayoralty (Mollenkopf 1999). The city has a rich heritage of partisan activity. Since the nineteenth century, reformers have periodically squared off against regular party organizations, while political leaders have mobilized voters on the basis of racial and ethnic identities and ideological appeals. Ethnic politics clearly played a central role in integrating the last great wave of immigrants into American life, and its imprint can still be seen today in the prevalence of Irish cops and Jewish teachers.

Political parties clearly play less of a role in the daily lives of New Yorkers today than in the past (Gerstle and Mollenkopf 2001; Jones Correa 2001). Local party organizations are in decline (Adler and Blank 1975; Ware 1985; Wade 1990) and political reforms have reduced, though by no means eliminated, politicians' ability to distribute the patronage jobs, contracts, and other material incentives that made political empowerment so important to earlier working class immigrants (Shefter 1994). Yet this does not mean local politics has ceased to be a factor in the lives of the second generation. Although involvement in parties and campaigns may not have the same payoff it provided in the golden era of the political machines, many young people still find good entry level jobs and suitable careers in the public and nonprofit sectors. Having a political connection with those who make the hiring decisions can still help people get these jobs; these connections, in turn, depend on how the different groups fit within what might be called the "racial and ethnic division of labor" in local politics.

Once again we see that groups matter. Group position can be a resource even when the individual members of the group are unaware of it. Indeed, one paradoxical feature of New York City politics is that members of some economically well-off groups spend little time on politics, whereas members of more disadvantaged groups are often more engaged. Members of less educated and poorer groups may have stronger incentives to be involved in politics. It is an article of faith among political scientists that higher levels of education, income, and occupational status are associated with greater levels of political participation. Among our respondents this is true *within* groups but not at all true when comparing between groups.

The Political Opportunity Structure of New York City

The New York region has a strongly partisan political culture (Mayhew 1986; Shefter 1994). The Democratic Party has dominated New York City and most cities in northeastern New Jersey for a century and a half, while Republican Party machines dominated the outer suburban counties until recently. The white immigrant groups of the nineteenth century and their twentieth-century descendants erected these party establishments, often by successfully challenging a prior group. As a new group gained ascendance, it often sought "ethnic closure" in the particular public sector niches where it came to predominate.

Some rising groups fought their way in by threatening to join other political outsiders to displace the establishment; others spent a long time as subordinates hoping for rewards as loyalists. Jews and Italians, for example, reacted to the Irish-dominated political establishment in New York by voting for Republicans, Socialists, or other third-party candidates between 1920 and 1950. To this day many Italian American officeholders, especially in the suburbs, have come up through the Republican Party. Impatient groups used the threat of defection as a "shotgun behind the door" to compel Democratic county party organizations to absorb and advance their members (Shefter 1994). Sheer numbers sometimes allowed younger candidates from new groups to displace officeholders from earlier groups, leading to a gradual generational succession (Gerson 1990). Once in power, these new coalitions typically sought to expand local spending on functions that were of interest to them and used this expansion to employ members of their electoral base.

Inspired by the civil rights and black power movements, the city's growing African American and Puerto Rican populations began to challenge white ethnic incumbents starting in the 1950s. These efforts culminated in the election of the city's first African American mayor in 1989. Like the Italian and Jewish challenge to Irish political control, the African American and Puerto Rican challenge to the Italians and Jews began by mobilizing newcomers, but it ultimately only became successful when their children—the second generation—could provide the electoral base for a new political majority.

The 2000 Census showed that 28 percent of the ten county study region's African Americans and 20 percent of Puerto Ricans worked in the public sector. The immigrant groups all had lower rates of public employment, although the two groups with greatest proximity to African Americans and Puerto Ricans, the West Indians and Dominicans, had the highest rates (18 and 10 percent respectively). By contrast, South Americans (7 percent), Chinese (8 percent), and Russians (10 percent) all had much lower rates of public sector employment than in the total regional workforce (16 percent).

Our second generation respondents showed a similar pattern. Public employment ranged from a high of 25 percent among African Americans to 16 percent for the Puerto Ricans, 15 percent for the West Indians, 13 percent for the Dominicans, and 12 percent for the South Americans, contrasted with only 10 percent for the native whites, 7 percent for the Chinese, and only 5 percent for the Russian Jews. Thus the second generation groups socially closest to the native minorities, who are often seen as being in danger of downward assimilation and social isolation, are also most likely to work for the public sector. Not coincidentally, they are also the immigrant groups with the largest numbers of local elected officials and the strongest record of political activism.

New Immigrants in the Political Opportunity Structure

The profound impact of immigration on New York and other gateway cities has been felt more slowly among their voting age citizens, but even those populations are changing as first generation immigrants naturalize and second generation immigrants come of age. As a result, New York, Los Angeles, and Miami and the other gateway cities stand on the threshold of a new epoch of racial and ethnic succession in urban politics (Logan and Mollenkopf 2003). The future will be defined less by movements for native minority empowerment like those of the past few decades and more by new immigrant ethnic groups attempting to break into political establishments run not just by white ethnics but by African Americans and Puerto Ricans as well. The huge volume of Caribbean, Latin American, and Asian immigration makes New York a pivotal case for understanding this coming political transformation. In New York City, as in the other gateway cities, native born political incumbents, whether white, black, or Latino, represent districts where their own ethnic electoral base is shrinking and new immigrant voters are growing.

Attempts to analyze the changing nature of the New York City electorate often use the decennial Census to sort people by their racial background and nativity. While this approach reveals the major impact of first generation immigrants on the voting age citizen population—the eligible electorate—it fails to reveal the many native born young adults who are in households headed by immigrants. Because the decennial Census does not ask people where their parents were born, it renders the second generation's members invisible after they have left their parents' homes. (The Current Population Survey [CPS] *does* ask this question on its November voting supplements taken after federal elections. The November 2004 CPS suggests that first generation naturalized citizens accounted for 28 percent of the eligible electorate in New York City and second generation native born individuals another 17 percent.)

In the 2000 Census, New Yorkers living in households headed by native whites constituted only a quarter of the population and a third of the voting age citizens, but today people from such backgrounds serve as mayor, public advocate, three of the five borough presidents, and half the city council seats. Because native whites are older, more likely to speak English, better educated with higher income, and more likely to be property owners, they are more likely to vote than other groups, so their share of actual voters is far larger than their share of the eligible electorate (see also Myers 2007). A less well known but equally important fact is that the declining African American and Puerto Rican populations are also now slightly *over*represented among the city's elected officials. Native African Americans, 14 percent of the city's population and 17 percent of eligible voters, now hold 20 percent of the seats on the city council. The U.S.-born Latinos, mostly Puerto Ricans, are 12 percent of the city population and 13 percent of the voting age citizens, but they hold 18 percent of the council seats. African Americans also hold the third citywide office, comptroller, and one borough presidency, while a Puerto Rican holds the other borough presidency.

By contrast, immigrants of all races are underrepresented. Black immigrants—mostly West Indians—have the most political representation. They make up 10 percent of the city's population but are only 7 percent of the eligible voters, and they hold 6 percent of the city council seats. Latino immigrants are 15 percent of the city's population but only 8 percent of the eligible voters and make up 4 percent of the council. The most underrepresented groups are white immigrants—10 percent of the city's population without a single seat on the council, and Asians. Immigrant and native born Asians combined make up 10 percent of the city's population. Yet there is only one Asian elected official in the city, John Liu, a 1.5 generation Taiwanese American who represents Flushing on the city council.

Candidates from the new immigrant groups won their first public offices after the 1990 redistricting cycle, when two West Indian immigrants and a Dominican took seats on the newly enlarged city council in 1991. (Both of these groups achieved similar "firsts" in state legislative races in the 1992 elections.) The number of first and second generation immigrant officeholders has grown in the intervening decade and a half. After the 2005 elections, the city council included three West Indians, two Dominicans, and the one Chinese-Taiwanese member, for 10 percent of the seats. Although the first and second generation immigrant share of offices falls short of their 30 percent share of the voting age citizen population or their 55 percent share of city residents, gaining these offices nonetheless represents a significant achievement. Their drive to end this underrepresentation creates fertile conditions for new kinds of competition and coalition formation between the new immigrant groups and native born whites, blacks, and Puerto Ricans. Now that native born whites are no longer a majority of the potential electorate, white candidates cannot rely on racial polarization to generate an electoral majority. They must attract crossover support from at least some nonwhite groups.

The different experiences of the parents of our respondents also led to distinctive forms of political socialization for their children. The parents of our young African American respondents lived through the civil rights movement. Formed politically at a time when they could listen to the words of Martin Luther King and Malcolm X, they often taught their children that major sacrifices had been required to gain the franchise. Many ministers of the churches in Harlem and Brooklyn, churches our African American respondents grew up attending, also played important roles in the civil rights movement. The parents of most of our Puerto Rican respondents came of age at a time when the first Puerto Rican elected officials were gaining office, and protests by groups like the Young Lords Party filled the streets (Torres and Velázquez 1998).

African American and Puerto Rican parents are deeply enmeshed in the public sector. Two-fifths of the parents of our African American respondents work for the government, and many others work for social service agencies that receive government funds. African American parents are also more likely than most other groups (except the Russian Jews) to receive government benefits like SSI, welfare, and subsidized housing. They are highly attuned to the importance of politics for the well-being of their communities. Several of our African American respondents reported that their parents had been active in the Black Panthers or other activist groups. Though the parental generation of Puerto Ricans was less likely to work for local government than African Americans, Puerto Ricans are more likely to do so than any other group, with about one in five holding a public sector job. Puerto Rican parents were also highly likely to have received social welfare benefits when our respondents were growing up. Finally, Puerto Rico's high level of political engagement provided members of the parental generation with skills they could apply in New York.

The parents of our second generation immigrant groups had far different political experiences when they were growing up. The West

Indian parents had perhaps the strongest political training, as their islands became independent nations after 1962 and developed robust political competition within British-style parliamentary democracies—although the violence of Jamaican and Guyanese political campaigns deterred some parents from political involvement. The West Indian parents speak English, share a tradition of struggling against racial subordination, and experienced black-led governments. They could relate directly to the African American struggle for political equality (Kasinitz 1992). Indeed, many of New York's African American early political leaders were actually of West Indian origin, though such people began to operate on a distinctly ethnic basis only in recent years. Finally, like African Americans, the West Indian parents have high levels of employment in local government and social services, especially the health-care sector, and also know that politics has a direct bearing on the well-being of their group.

In addition to engaging in formal electoral politics, West Indian respondents and particularly their immigrant parents were far more likely than the other immigrant groups to be involved in community groups, block associations, PTAs, and other local civic groups. Indeed, they were second only to native African Americans in this regard. While many expressed a cynical disdain for "politics" and "politicians," they also took for granted that local issues could and should be addressed through groups and organizations. One 29-year-old West Indian woman described her father, a security guard at a hospital, as very "political," but she went to on clarify that

> when I say "political" I just mean, like, in mind. Not like he's part of any party or nothing like that. But he likes politics and the importance of voting and stuff like that. Even started a block association when we moved here on this block . . . He just thought it would be simpler for everybody to get together and to make sure that certain issues were addressed. like keeping the block clean.

Of course, in New York this sort of activity can also be the first step into more formal political involvement, whether people realize it or not. One African American respondent despised politicians and declared she had never been involved in "politics." She then went on to describe how, when she and her neighbors needed help with a local issue, they sought the assistance of a city councilman who lived around the corner. She did not, however, consider this behavior to be "political."

The political experiences of the Latin American first generation parents were more ambiguous. The Dominican Republic and Colombia, Ecuador, and Peru all experienced periods of authoritarian government, political turmoil, and instability, with stable democratic participation emerging relatively recently. Indeed, the fall of the Trujillo dictatorship and the U.S. invasion were major stimuli to migration to the United States. As Spanish-speakers and residents of countries lacking well-functioning democratic political systems, these parents were less likely to bring political habits and orientations that they could bequeath to their young adult children here. Even when parents had political connections at home, as occasionally happened, this was more often an impetus for migration rather than a basis for political action in the United States.

Dominicans had some experiences that brought them closer to Puerto Ricans in political orientation. They settled in areas nearer to Puerto Ricans than did the South Americans, entered similar economic niches, had relatively high rates of public employment and social welfare benefits, and have become actively connected to Democratic Party politics. Since 1997, Dominican-born people who have become U.S. citizens have had the right to vote in Dominican elections as well. The major Dominican political parties have active branches in New York, and one recent Dominican president lived as a young man in Washington Heights. Thus Dominican politics has more transnational carryover for the émigré community in New York than is true for the South American countries. Since many first generation parents of our Dominican and South American respondents contemplate returning to their homelands for retirement and may own land there, they keep abreast of the political affairs back home. Interest in the home country does not tend to discourage political involvement in the United States. The minority of respondents who followed politics there were generally the same people who had an active interest in politics in New York.

The Soviet and mainland Chinese political situations gave Russian and Chinese first generation immigrants to New York even fewer political skills that might be transferred to the New York setting. The Russian and mainland Chinese parents came from one-party authoritarian systems with little tradition of democratic participation. The Soviet state systematically discriminated against the Russian Jewish parents and often pushed them out of their jobs when they applied to emigrate. Politics thus threatened harm, not opportunity. As refugees, the Russian parents were often highly dependent on public services and were embraced by the politically active Jewish communities of New York City. But the immigrants rarely saw this as a reason to be involved politically. As one male Russian respondent explained:

I don't think they care about it too much. I would say that probably 95 percent of the Russian people don't vote. I think it's just . . . the country they grew up in did not allow them to vote so we never got into it. If you haven't done it for thirty-something years, then you're never going to do it. Voting, they don't care.

The situation was similar for parents from mainland China, many of whom had experienced the shutdown of the Chinese higher education system during the Cultural Revolution. One woman Chinese respondent relates her mother's experience:

R: Yeah, my mom was in the Cultural Revolution. She was in the Red Guard.
I: What did she tell you about that?
R: There was a lot of senseless chanting and class struggle . . . She didn't like that because she didn't get to go to college. Colleges closed down just when she was about to go to college . . .
I: Were they ever penalized or rewarded for their political back-grounds?
R: She had to denounce her father.

Even those respondents whose parents came from Taiwan or Hong Kong had little experience with political engagement as a means of group upward mobility at home. Thus the Russian Jewish and mainland Chinese parents lacked the practices of political engagement that might have prepared them for the American political system.

Youthful Alienation from Political Life

The median age of our respondents was 23 when we interviewed them between 1999 and 2002. The oldest was born in the late 1960s, the youngest in the early 1980s. By the time our respondents entered young adulthood in the latter 1990s, Bill Clinton had been elected president, the country was at peace, and the economy was experiencing its longest sustained expansion, leading to the first marked reduction in urban poverty levels in many decades.

Locally, however, the early childhood of our respondents took place during the worst decade in the city's modern history. Two deep recessions in the first half of the 1970s led to a severe fiscal crisis that reduced opportunities for public employment, diminished public services, and suspended investment in critical parts of the city's infrastructure, including schools. While the economic expansion of the 1980s and the growth of immigration enabled the city's economy and population to gradually recover from these blows, the latter 1980s witnessed the AIDS epidemic, the emergence of crack cocaine, and an alarming increase in violent crime, all of which heavily affected the neighborhoods where many of our respondents passed their adolescent years. Their childhoods also coincided with the administration of Mayor Edward Koch (1977–1989), which faltered on municipal scandal, interracial conflicts, and police corruption.

Although the city elected its first (and only) African American mayor, David Dinkins, in 1989, the 1989–1991 national recession deeply affected New York, undermining his administration. During the Dinkins years the crime rate continued to rise, interracial conflict persisted, and the city experienced painful civil disorder in the Crown Heights riot in August 1991. In a 1993 rematch of the 1989 mayoral election, Republican former federal prosecutor Rudolph W. Giuliani narrowly defeated Mayor Dinkins.

Most of our respondents were adolescents entering adulthood during Giuliani's mayoralty. Giuliani instituted a "zero tolerance" policy to crack down on street crime. Though this helped to reduce violent crime, the Giuliani administration's law enforcement practices sharply increased the number of minority young males who were arrested and "put through the system" (Jacobson 2001). The Giuliani years also saw a number of highly publicized cases in which the police killed or brutalized young black males, often with immigrant backgrounds. This left a deep impression on many respondents.

In part in reaction to the perception that the Giuliani administration was "coming down hard" on minority young people, many of our respondents held negative views of the police—and of city officials. Many respondents pointed to the police killing of Amadiou Diallo, which took place on February 4, 1999, as an example of how the authorities attacked minorities with impunity. (Diallo, a West African immigrant, died when he was hit by nineteen of the forty-one shots fired by members of the Police Department's elite Street Crime Unit who mistook his reaching into his jacket for his wallet to be the drawing of a weapon.)

We were in the field doing our telephone interviews during this event and saw that it clearly influenced our respondents. Interestingly, not only were those African American and West Indian respondents interviewed after the Diallo shooting more likely to express negative feelings toward the police than those interviewed before, they were also significantly more likely to report that they had personally had a bad experience with the police. Many had negative reactions to Mayor Giuliani and his policies: "He's stabbing the poor in the back every day," said one West Indian young man; a South American male said, "I can't stand Giuliani. He's just a big bully." Others admired his firmness in the face of criticism. As one Chinese respondent said, "You know Giuliani is pissing off a lot of people, but he is pointing the city in the right direction." In the main, however, our respondents had very few good things to say about their public officials.

Most of our second generation respondents grew up in immigrant neighborhoods where many adults, including a third of their parents, could not vote. Thus, though our second generation respondents are attending schools that try to socialize them into the norm of civic participation, they live in a youth culture that is skeptical of politicians and in a parental culture that has largely not been incorporated into New York City politics.

What attitudes do these young people hold about the political system? What kind of citizens will the new second generation become? To answer these questions, we focus on the 2,661 respondents who are U.S. citizens, either by birth or naturalization, who live in New York City. This analysis suggests that the ethnic and racial group to which one belongs and that group's position within the larger political opportunity structure of New York City have a considerable impact on the political attitudes and practices of group members, even after controlling for family socioeconomic status.

A Political Profile of Young People in New York City

Political scientists have long established that the political attitudes and practices of young people are strongly shaped by those of their parents, particularly when those parents are politically involved themselves. Parents provide the material resources to help young persons make their way in life and frame their religious and political values and practices; parents also select the communities in which their children grow up (Jennings and Niemi 1974; Gimpel, Lay, and Schuknecht 2003). If parental political leanings and socioeconomic characteristics fully explained the political profile of young New Yorkers, we would expect that those with better-off, better-educated parents would have the most positive evaluations of the political system, hold relatively conservative positions, and be the most likely to participate, whereas those from the poorest families would fall at the opposite end of these spectrums.

Since our native white and Russian respondents have parents with the highest levels of education and income, we might expect them to be the most interested in politics and the most active voters, whereas our Dominican, Puerto Rican, and Chinese respondents would be the least active and interested, since their parents have the lowest education and incomes. Meanwhile, African Americans, West Indians, and South Americans should be between these two poles. Since all the native born groups have been socialized politically completely within an American setting, we might further expect them to be more likely to participate than their second and 1.5 generation counterparts, and perhaps hold more positive evaluations of American political institutions.

In fact, we find a quite different and more complicated pattern when we look at what our respondents think and do about politics and political participation. Two of the native groups, native whites on the high end of socioeconomic status and Puerto Ricans on the low end, do generally conform to the expected model, with whites reporting relatively high participation and Puerto Ricans relatively low. The other groups, however, do not follow the expected pattern. Two relatively disadvantaged groups, native African Americans and second generation West Indians, join whites in being among the most engaged of our respondents—indeed, native blacks are *more* likely to vote than native whites—whereas two groups generally experiencing upward mobility, the Russian Jews and the Chinese, are relatively disinterested in politics and uninvolved in civic life. Moreover, it appears that second generation blacks and Latinos, far from being less interested in politics than their native peers, are equally or more engaged. The political sphere of incorporation thus evidently works differently than the economic one.

We should note that this variation takes place within a generally low level of political involvement and a low opinion of politicians. The second generation shares with their native peers a pervasive cynicism about politics. Overall, a majority of *every* group agrees with the statement that "most elected officials don't care what people like me think." Not surprisingly, Figure 9.1 shows that native whites and Russian second generation respondents are least likely to feel this way, followed by the South Americans, while native blacks and West Indians agree most strongly. This suggests that race, rather than class or immigrant status, influences opinion on this question. Similarly, significant majorities of *all* groups (including whites) agree or somewhat agree that "New York City police generally favor whites over blacks and other minorities." Predictably, outright agreement is particularly strong among native blacks and West Indians, but even three out of ten whites, Russians, and Chinese agree outright with this position.

When we asked our respondents to elaborate on these concerns, respondents told us that they think New York City politicians are hypocrites who tell voters what voters want to hear at election time, then do whatever most furthers their careers, mostly by helping powerful or moneyed interests. One African American woman said:

> They care in the beginning, to get that position. They care because they know they have to get their votes from the middle class and the lower class . . . They make all these promises of what they're gonna do, but as soon as they get elected, they start mixing with the higher-up people that can pull strings, the people who can get you in there no matter what. Then they don't care any more, because the

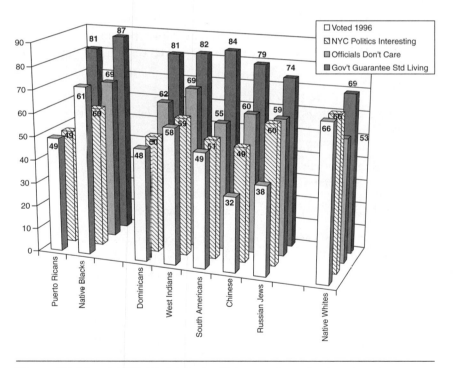

Figure 9.1. Voting and Political Attitudes (% Agree or Somewhat Agree).
Source: ISGMNY.

lower class people are not the ones that are pushing him to where he needs to go. He's there now. Now he's gonna ride the purse strings of the rich and famous to get everything else he wants. So they care until they get to the point they don't need you any more. They'll say anything, that they're gonna help you, help your community, built this, build that. They only care until they get what they're looking out for.

A Puerto Rican woman echoed this sentiment: "The politicians want to make it seem like they care about your issues so they listen to what you have to say around election time. Once they're elected, they really don't come back to your community."

Many of our respondents, even native whites and Russian Jews, the groups most supportive of the police, reacted negatively to the high-profile acts of violence by police against minority young men. One young Russian woman explained, "A lot of injustice is being done to black people. I think it's horrible, especially the police department, the constant murders and beatings and just it's rampant at this point."

Our native black respondents had more direct personal experiences. One older African American male who had served time in the state prison system observed:

The police in there [prison], they were the biggest racists. They are the biggest gang in there. I wasn't in Rikers Island, where mostly black people work [as guards]. I was in facilities upstate where guys have black babies hanging on nooses on their arms and stuff like that. And saying, "Die niggers" or "A happy nigger is a dead nigger" and all that type of crap.

An African American woman has a similar perspective:

I think police officers, the mayor and the commissioner and every-body else that fall in line with politics are in cahoots . . . I think that politics makes the cops feel that they can do anything and get away with it 'cause they make it that way. So they'll go, see somebody.

Even though our respondents are alienated from their elected officials and have a pervasive dislike of politics, they favor an activist government. Figure 9.1 shows that a large portion of each group agrees that "the government in Washington should see to it that every person has a job and a good standard of living." African Americans are most in favor of government help and native whites the least, with the Russian Jews, despite their own substantial involvement with the welfare state, and the Chinese second generation respondents tending toward the white position. Hispanic groups and West Indians are all more positively inclined toward the welfare state, although less so than native blacks.

While our respondents endorse the idea that government should provide a decent standard of living, they show less enthusiasm for New York City politics. Figure 9.1 indicates that most groups are fairly evenly divided over whether they find New York City politics interesting, with native whites and blacks showing the greatest interest and the second generation groups generally showing less interest. Despite their negative feelings about politicians, native blacks express a great deal of interest in local politics, though not as much as native whites. West Indians are only slightly less interested. The Hispanic groups and the Russian Jews are less likely to agree, with the Chinese being the least interested of all. The groups with the most negative views of politicians and politics—African Americans and West Indians—thus somewhat paradoxically have the most interest in New York City politics.

When asked why young people have generally negative opinions about politicians and tend not to be involved in politics, our respondents offered a number of other theories. First, they believe that young people cannot make a difference. One Russian put it bluntly:

> I believe the younger generation knows that whatever the public officials are saying is a bunch of bullshit and it is not really worth their time to go out and vote because nothing is going to change anyway.

A Puerto Rican woman put a slightly different twist on the same thing: "A lot of young people today plain don't care. 'What have I got to vote for? I'm not gonna waste my time.' "

Our respondents also thought that young people are too busy getting established in life or going out and having fun to be involved. They have not yet acquired responsibilities that might motivate them to engage in politics. One Dominican man explained that young people don't vote because

> they got better things to do and it won't affect them directly. Wait 'til they get older and they want to see things change. Then they'll feel it. Young people nowadays just want to have fun and hang out.

Worry about it later when they work and get all these taxes taken out of their paycheck.

How do these attitudes stack up against actual behavior? The rate at which our eligible respondents vote closely tracks their level of interest in New York City politics. Figure 9.1 shows that African Americans and native whites were most likely to vote out of those who were 18 or older and citizens living in New York City in time for the 1996 elections. West Indians were the next most likely, some distance behind the native groups, but markedly ahead of the other second generation groups. The Chinese and Russians, the best educated and most economically successful, participated least in that election. This does not, it should be noted, simply reflect a lack of reliance on state services. The Russians were the most likely to have received public assistance while growing up, and the Chinese rely on public schools for their educations more than any other second generation group. (Since the data on voting are self-reported, the number may be somewhat exaggerated. For our purposes, the differences between the groups are probably more important than the actual numbers.)

Our in-depth interviews gave some indications about why native blacks and West Indians are more apt to vote than their attitudes toward politics suggest. These respondents told us that blacks had to develop electoral clout in a white-dominated world, especially because their parents had made great sacrifices so that they could do so. An African American put it this way:

> If you don't vote, you can't bitch and moan about what the government is doing to you. It is not only a way to get what you want, it is your obligation. Think of all the people who struggled and fought and died just for you to be able to walk into a school and pull down two levers.

A West Indian man elaborated:

> One of the things that is great about this country is that you can raise your voice and one of the ways you raise your voice is by voting. A lot of other countries either came late or still have not gotten to the point where citizens actually have a voice in what goes on in the country and who leads them. It's very American. And as a black person, it is about what it took to give you that. You analogize it to the family context, where people have worked and sacrificed to get you into school and you want to make sure that all that work did not

go for naught. It is very easy to take for granted, but people died. People spilled blood for me to be able to walk into a booth and pull a lever. It's five minutes out of my day. I can do it.

That African Americans hold this attitude is not surprising given the struggles for civil rights and black empowerment. What is striking is that the children of West Indian immigrants have fully absorbed this point of view, assimilating, at least in this context, into black America. Other groups have both less feeling that political representation is important to their success and less connection to the political system. Huckfeldt and Sprague (1995) showed that one's community situation has an impact on one's political behavior (see also Gimpel, Lay, and Schuknecht 2003). This is evident among our respondents. The Chinese respondents, in particular, come from a familial and community milieu that discourages political involvement. One 27-year-old Chinese man noted:

Most of the Jews and the blacks already know English when they get here. The Chinese community, only half. There's a percentage that don't speak English and I think the Chinese families are more passive. They don't have the language and they're less inclined to put themselves in the spotlight.

A 29-year-old Chinese community activist elaborated:

It's a personality trait of Chinese people not to get too involved. And that stems from our parents. Or they kind of look the other way. It's okay, it's no big deal, we'll live, we'll survive, not a big thing.

The problem of low levels of voting, even among those eligible, is compounded, as one Chinese respondent noted, by the absence of efforts to mobilize it.

I don't feel like the politicians support me or Chinese Americans like me because I don't, I never see any platform, you know, that would address me, so to speak. Like, you know, you hear about politicians, they go into Harlem, they talk to black neighborhoods, and they go to Hispanic neighborhoods 'cause they're courting that vote. But I never see like them you know, or hear about politicians like going to, say, Chinese communities to court their vote.

Sometimes this feeling that you are not invited to the political party can be surprisingly direct, as one Chinese woman noted:

I had a bad experience with Giuliani, actually. He was not running at the time but he was helping one of his friends who was running for Senate and he was actually on Main Street when I was waiting for a bus and he was shaking everybody's hand and then when he came up to me, he looked at me and then he turned away. I couldn't tell was it a racial thing or because he thought I was young looking so I'm not a voter.

At the other end of the spectrum were many of our white respondents, who grew up in middle class families and neighborhoods where at least modest levels of civic and political engagement were taken for granted. One native white woman explained:

I guess there are milieus where there's the social expectation that you will vote and milieus where there isn't and I happen to be in one where people vote, so I vote. I'm actually wondering if it runs any deeper than that.

Just as with the encounter with Mayor Giuliani on Main Street in Flushing, the networks connecting white neighborhoods to city politics can be deep and direct. One 32-year-old Italian American man working in a blue collar setting described how his contact with a neighborhood friend produced results:

When we needed the street cleaned, her father has some influence with friends, so I called him. "Hey Joe, can you call somebody? Can they hit our streets when it snows?" Like that. Whether he did anything about it or not, the streets got done. I don't know if it was just him or just timing, but, yeah.

A 31-year-old white woman explained her community activism in the following terms:

I got involved with that through the schools and because my mother and my aunt were involved, again, because of growing up with us so it was just something that was always there.

The ethnographic research conducted for our study sheds light on how community settings and institutions can connect young people to the political system, including Black and Latino Studies programs at City University campuses, unions representing first and second generation social service workers, community organizations in immigrant neighborhoods, and involvement in immigrant churches (Kasinitz, Mollenkopf, and Waters 2004). Participation in these civic organizations often constitutes the foundation of political engagement (Putnam 2000). Religious participation is another important precursor to civic engagement (Verba, Schlozman, and Brady 1995). Such paths can lead people into greater levels of political participation and awareness. Our survey asked our respondents about various forms of membership and civic participation while they were growing up as well as at the current time. In short, we can see the current political practices of our young adult respondents as the product of how they took pathways provided by their parents and their communities.

To ascertain what pathways our respondents took into civic participation as young adults, we asked them about the public and civic facilities—such as parks or libraries—they used while growing up as well as their current involvement with churches, neighborhood associations, PTAs, political clubs, and the like. Even for respondents as children, different patterns of involvement emerged across the groups. As befits a group raised largely in a well-educated, middle class milieu, native whites fit the expectation of "well-rounded involvement." As youngsters, our native white respondents were above average in terms of participating in athletic leagues, but they were also more likely to spend time in libraries and museums and were a bit under the average in terms of attending church.

The other groups, however, fell into several different patterns. All the groups except for the Chinese and Puerto Ricans had relatively high rates of church attendance, with the West Indians, Dominicans, and South Americans all more likely to go to church than the native blacks, who in turn had significantly higher rates than the native whites, Russian Jews, Chinese, or Puerto Ricans. By contrast, the Russian Jews, and to some extent the Chinese, were less likely to be involved in sports activities or playing in the public parks, but they were more likely to use the libraries and museums.

Use of public space, especially the parks, was most prevalent among native blacks, Puerto Ricans, Dominicans, and South Americans. To some degree, this may have compensated for the fact that they were growing up in poorer neighborhoods with less private space. Already, one can see patterns that emerge later in adulthood: native whites fit the "normal model" of civic participation, whereas the other groups do not. The Russians and the Chinese are less likely to use public space and more likely to use facilities for cultural improvement; the native minority groups make substantial use of the civic infrastructure, led by native blacks, but so do their second generation peers.

When we look at current levels of organizational participation, African Americans once more lead the way, with the highest mean score on organizational participation, followed by West Indians. That the group with the lowest opinion of politicians has the highest levels of organizational participation should call our attention to the difference between what people say and what they do. Native whites, on the other hand, has a lower mean score than any other group except the South Americans. Blacks and West Indians are also the most likely to participate regularly in their churches. Closer examination shows that the whites and Russians tend to belong to professional associations, African Americans and West Indians belong to community-oriented organizations like sports leagues, church activities, and PTAs, and the Puerto Ricans and other immigrant groups are involved in ethnic-specific organizations and sports teams.

Fewer than one out of ten of our respondents belongs to a political club, but African Americans, Dominicans, and West Indians are the most likely—or least unlikely—to do so, whereas Russians, whites, and South Americans are the least likely. In every group more than half the respondents belong to some organization, and these memberships connect them to relevant social worlds although usually not directly to the political system. This suggests that the particular kind of social network to which one belongs helps shape political mobilization, along with attitudes, values, and perceptions of group interest.

This pattern of political attitudes and civic participation suggests that members of second generation groups who feel that they can "make it" without the need for much political help to counter discrimination—the Russians and Chinese—participate less in local politics. Groups that do feel this need—specifically African Americans and West Indians—do engage in politics as a way to advance or protect their group interests. This pattern is reinforced by the traditions parents bring with them. West Indian parents came from nations with strong if sometimes troubled democratic traditions, whereas Chinese and Russian parents came from one-party regimes that did not foster political engagement among the first generation parents. The Latino groups, both native and second generation, occupy a somewhat ambiguous position between the more politicized native whites, blacks, and West Indians, on the one hand, and the largely apolitical Russians and Chinese, on the other. The Latino groups' lower socioeconomic status and their lesser ability to speak English work against participation, but this is somewhat countered by their consciousness of discrimination and their connections to African Americans and Puerto Ricans.

The Antecedents and Outcomes of Political Engagement

The scholarly literature on voting in America is largely based on the experience of native whites, who make up the lion's share of the national electorate. Explanatory models based on this population do not always fit the experience of minority and second generation immigrant groups, or even that of those urban native whites who live among them. To determine whether this is so, we undertook a multivariate analysis of the patterns of political attitudes and behavior across our various groups of respondents.

This analysis shows that age, gender, income, and education do not explain much of the overall variation in political attitudes or voting, although each of these standard factors has some bearing. For example, using these four factors to predict whether our citizen respondents living in New York voted explained less than 3 percent of the overall variation in their responses to the four-option question on whether government officials care about people like them. (Only the education variable was statistically significantly associated with less alienation. Controlling for group membership only slightly increased the power of the equation, with blacks and West Indians being statistically significantly more alienated than native whites.) The same independent variables do an equally poor job of explaining how many kinds of organizations respondents have joined, although age, gender, income, and education are all statistically significant. Adding group characteristics shows that blacks are once again the only group statistically *more* likely to have more types of memberships than whites.

To examine the impact of various factors on the likelihood of voting in the 1996 presidential election, we employed a binary logistic regression model using group membership, age, gender, immigrant generation, education, working status, and social capital indicators as predictors among those eligible to do so in 1996. Although the coefficients of the independent variables are in the expected direction (being older, female, better educated, working, born in the United States, and civically engaged all make one more likely to vote) and are statistically significant, the overall power of the model remains modest.

Beginning with group membership (first column in Table 9.1), it is apparent that African Americans seem more likely to vote than native whites (the excluded comparison groups); all the other groups are less likely, with all but the West Indians significantly less likely to vote. As in the previous discussion, the Russian Jews and Chinese are the least likely to vote compared with whites when we just control for group membership. Why does being black, which clearly pushes up the level of alienation, often on the basis of personal experiences with discrimination, produce higher levels of participation? Conversely, why are the most economically successful second generation groups, the Chinese and the Russian Jews, still statistically so much less likely to participate in politics after controlling for these background characteristics?

To answer these questions, we explored a variety of plausible background factors, including having had a child or being married or living with someone, watching ethnic media and using a language other than English at home, working at a unionized job, church participation, parental concern with prejudice against one's group, and respondents' own experiences of prejudice. It is noteworthy that these factors did *not*

Table 9.1. Binary Logistic Model of Likelihood of Voting in the 1996 Presidential Election
(citizens 18 or older by election time, living in New York City)

Constant	.68**	−3.382**	−3.893**
Puerto Rican	−.739**	−.418*	−.461*
Native Black	.266	.555**	.451*
Dominican	−.751**	−.344	−.368
West Indian	−.357	.084	.023
South American	−.740**	−.422**	−.406
Chinese	−1.458**	−1.236**	−1.276**
Russian Jewish	−1.175**	−.942**	−.987**
Age		.098**	.091**
Female		.225*	.182
Education		.327**	.297**
Working		.386**	.362**
1.5 Generation		−.572**	−.593**
Used Libraries & Museums Growing Up			.146**
Organizational Memberships			.268**
Cox & Snell R^2	.067	.137	.158

* Significant at .05 level
** Significant at .01 level

have a statistical impact. Although becoming a teen parent or having been arrested has a palpable impact on many other aspects of the lives of our respondents, neither factor affected the likelihood of voting. Neither did marital status or fertility. Nor, after taking respondents' own education and employment status into account, did parental level of education or respondents' growing up in an intact family. We also looked at what respondents said about such neighborhood problems as crime, youths not respecting authority, neighbors not knowing or being willing to help, and the like. None had a significant or large impact on the likelihood of voting. Finally, even when our respondents' parents told them they "could not trust whites" or needed to worry that "they would face prejudice," this did not make respondents statistically more likely to vote.

We did find that adding controls for age, gender, education, working status, and whether or not a child of immigrants was born in the United States all have important effects, as expected, and double the overall explanatory power of the model (Table 9.1, second column). It is well known that greater age increases the likelihood of voting, although it is interesting to see that effect even within the relatively narrow age range of our respondents. Once more, as with educational attainment, but contrary to the patterns of labor force participation and earnings, being female also has a strong and positive relationship with voting. Finally, incorporation into the larger society, in the form of having a job and more education, also has a strong positive impact, as one might expect. (Interestingly, having been arrested, having a spouse, or having a child has no statistically significant impact compared with these factors.) Those respondents who arrived as small children, rather than being born in the United States, are one of the few instances in our study where 1.5 generation status has a clear and negative impact. It stands to reason that people who are truly "in between" their parents and their native born co-ethnics might take longer to become incorporated into the basic civic process of voting.

The final panel of Table 9.1 reflects the results of this analysis. Many of the additional factors we explored are not significant, but two measures of community involvement are. Even among our youthful sample, the panel shows, civic participation is a midwife to political participation. As evident in Chapter 5, respondents' using libraries and museums while they were growing up has a positive impact on respondents' political engagement. This aspect of growing up represents both a parental commitment that children make use of public facilities designed to produce a well-informed and cultured citizenry and a child's participation in an important municipal service.

Similarly, the literature on the relationship between civic and political engagement (Verba, Schlozman, and Brady 1995; Putnam 2000) makes abundantly clear that the former should promote the latter. Even among our alienated young respondents, this relationship holds. Social context also matters. When we look at all the potentially eligible people in the region, being a New York City resident (as opposed to living the suburbs) has a positive impact on voting, but the statistical significance is only at the .10 level. This outcome may reflect how New York City politics dominates the media in the metropolitan area.

It is worth underscoring that, after controlling for all the background characteristics, native blacks vote at a significantly higher rate than native whites, even though this group is at the bottom end of many other socioeconomic distributions described in this study. Equally noteworthy, West Indians vote at a statistically indistinguishable rate from native whites. The Hispanic groups are all less likely to vote than either the native whites or the two black groups, although the statistical significance is only at the .10 level for Dominicans and South Americans.

Despite their successful incorporation in many other spheres of life in the metropolitan areas, the Chinese and Russians are least likely to participate in politics. This seems counterintuitive, since these groups are experiencing the most upward mobility, are getting good college educations, and are entering professions; but there is clearly something special about Russian and Chinese experiences that works against political participation. This difference is not explained by the groups' holding especially cynical attitudes about politics.

Our respondents have given us some important clues about the sources of these group differences. Compared with other groups, blacks and West Indians are exposed to more racial hostility and discrimination from others, particularly whites, and are more acutely aware of their history of racial subordination. They know that their movement toward political equality—indeed parity, if one considers that blacks hold more city offices than their share of the voting age citizen population or the total population—has been achieved through the civil rights movement and the political struggles that issued from it. Many African Americans work for government agencies or nonprofit organizations funded by government, while many West Indians work in the health-care sector or other social services also heavily dependent on public funding. Their group interests are deeply embedded in local politics. A schematic outline of these different positions in the political dynamics of the city is offered in Figure 9.2.

Other groups regard the Russians as whites who face much less discrimination. Along with the Chinese, they are the most successful second generation group in terms of education and occupational mobility. Thus they may not feel the need for political engagement, nor perhaps do they want to allocate the time for it. Finally, we cannot discount the fact that Russian and Chinese parents of both groups came from authoritarian, if not totalitarian, one-party states where political parties and the state had a bad reputation. Youngsters from both groups heard stories from their parents about how attracting the attention of the authorities could lead to bad outcomes. Unlike Dominicans, South Americans, and West Indians, Russian and Chinese parents had little transnational involvement back in their home countries.

New York's political system is producing new political leadership with greater representation of new immigrant and second generation groups. As such, it is a fascinating laboratory for understanding the emergence of a new phase of urban democracy. Much of that leadership appears likely to come from West Indians and Dominicans rather than from the better-educated, better-off Chinese or Russian Jews. Clearly, the relationship that members of the second generation have to long-standing racial minorities and the institutions they have developed is playing a key role in their incorporation into American political and civic life.

| | | Interest/Participation in Politics | |
		Low	High
Alienation from Politics	Low	Russian Jews, Chinese	Native whites
	High	Puerto Ricans, Dominicans, South Americans	African Americans, West Indians

Figure 9.2. Group Position in Local Politics

10

Race, Prejudice, and Discrimination

Since the resumption of mass immigration in the late 1960s, the United States has incorporated tens of millions of new immigrants, the large majority of whom are non-European. Being neither unambiguously "white," in the way that term had come to be used in late twentieth-century America, nor African American, most of these newcomers did not fit easily into traditional American racial categories. How will this affect their incorporation into the society? Will racial discrimination prevent the full incorporation of new immigrants and their descendants? How are American notions of race being reformulated by the incorporation of so many people who are neither black nor white?

We take for granted that earlier European immigrants were white, or at least potentially "white," and that "racial minorities" were not immigrants. Non-European immigrants make only cameo appearances in the mid-twentieth-century social scientific literature. (The lack of attention paid to the wave of Mexican immigrants at the time of the Mexican revolution by mainstream American social scientists is particularly striking.) Generally, studies of Latino and black immigrants and even most of the studies of Asian immigrants ended up in the "race relations" literature, not the immigration literature. As their experiences were at odds with the dominant, assimilation story, immigration analysts simply defined them out of the picture.

Recent historical works on the incorporation of European immigrants and their descendants have argued that these groups became American by becoming "white." "How the Irish Became White," "Are Italians Whites?" and "How the Jews Become White Folks" argue that the continued sharp exclusion of African Americans has been one reason the United States has been so successful in incorporating immigrants from so many different cultural backgrounds (Ignatiev 1995; Brodkin 1998; Guglielmo 2003; Roediger 2005). As poor, downtrodden, and "different" as European peasants were on arrival in the United States, they immediately had higher social and legal status than African Americans who had been here for generations.

Historians debate whether newly arrived immigrants could indeed be considered "white on arrival" (Guglielmo 2003) or whether the implicit distancing from African Americans was achieved over time (Roediger 2005). Yet whether or not Southern and Eastern European immigrants were initially considered "white," the most important thing seems to be that they clearly were not "black." Recent works on the history of European immigration stress that the price of full inclusion of the European "races" of Jews, Italians, Greeks, Poles, and the like was the acceptance by natives and immigrants alike of a color line separating blacks from whites and the eventual definition of Southern and Eastern Europeans on the "white" side of the line.

The incorporation of the children of the late nineteenth- and early twentieth-century immigrants created a far more broadly inclusive "white society," self-consciously pan-European rather than Anglo-Saxon in its origins. An assumed common Protestant heritage was replaced by newly invented "Judeo-Christian heritage" in religious life, while in the class-rooms the details of English history now had to compete with something called "Western Civ."

Yet this new pluralism hit a distinct limit at the color line, failing to include Asian, Latino, and African Americans. This is not because nonwhite immigrants represented a greater degree of cultural difference from American norms than did their European counterparts, nor because of their colonial origins, as was often argued in the 1970s (Blauner 1972). Shtetl Jews and Sicilian peasants could hardly have been more culturally different from nineteenth-century New Englanders, and Irish famine refugees had certainly known all the horrors of colonialism.

Instead, pluralism stopped at the color line because the United States was still essentially a racial state, in which democracy was fundamentally limited by white supremacy. Color, not ethnic difference, was the key distinction, a fact that is thrown into sharp relief when the United States is contrasted to Western Europe. George Fredrickson (2002: 40) notes that

> a confusion between the need to overcome phenotypic racism, which remains a more basic problem in the United States than for France, and the need for cultural toleration, which is not so difficult a challenge for Americans, has at times muddied the debates over multiculturalism in both countries.

Ethnicity and race have come to stand for two fundamentally different models of incorporation of minority populations in the United States, the former more optimistic than the latter. Some confusion on this point has been caused by the early twentieth-century observers' frequent use of the term "race" to mean what we would now call "nationality" (Banton 1987). The more inclusive vision of a multiethnic *white* America—the vision that begins in the Progressive era and ultimately becomes dominant after World War II—asserts that ongoing ethnic differences among the descendants of Europeans are compatible with "American-ness" and "whiteness" precisely because they are fundamentally different from the "racial" differences imagined to separate Europeans from non-Europeans. Thus, Progressive era celebrations of ethnic diversity usually simply ignored African Americans, despite their large numbers and longstanding presence in the society. James Gavit, in his book *Americans by Choice,* proudly stated that "the American is a product of all races," but he then went on to explain that "all races" meant the "Saxon, Teuton, Kelt, Latin and Slav" (quoted in Glazer 1997:105). In fact, early Mexican American civil rights activists fought school segregation on the grounds that Mexicans were racially *white* and therefore could not legally be segregated as blacks and Asians could. This contrasts sharply with the African American–inspired activism and celebration of *"La Raza"* that began in the 1960s.

Today's immigrants and their children challenge us to examine the nature of our racial definitions, the ways in which race operates in American society, and how nonwhite immigrants and their descendants will be incorporated into the society as members of racial categories and as the descendants of immigrants.

Immigrants and their children are an increasing percentage of all American racial groups. Across the country, the Current Population Survey (CPS) shows that Asians and Hispanics are overwhelmingly first and second generation, but a tenth of blacks and whites are also first and second generation, a number that is much higher in regions like New York. In the United States, it is now impossible to discuss "race relations" separately from immigration.

Here, we examine the extent to which the second generation groups experience racial discrimination and prejudice, how they respond to it, and whether their racial identities impede their full incorporation into American society. The legal scholar David Wilkins (1996:21) asks, "Is the moral significance of racial identity the same for all those groups that are recognized as 'races' in American society?"

This is an especially potent question for the new second generation. Is being nonwhite the same as being a racial minority? Is the African American experience or the European immigrant experience the best model of what will happen to the descendants of the new immigration? Fredrickson (1999:37) has posed the question "Can one model of multiculturalism work both for non-European immigrants who have come recently and voluntarily and also for those who were brought much earlier in chains for forced labor?"

Do members of the second generation see America as a place in which they can be fully accepted, or do they see a color line blocking their full inclusion into society? When the second generation does encounter unequal treatment, do they develop anger and hostility toward mainstream American society or a desire to overcome the barriers they experience? The racial experiences of these second generation nonwhite immigrants raise the question of the shape of the color line in the twenty-first century.

Our examination of the experiences of discrimination and prejudice and the ways our respondents respond to those experiences suggests an answer to Wilkins's question. We argue that our "nonwhite" respondents do not all experience race the same way. African Americans and those who "look like" or could be confused with African Americans, such as West Indians and dark-skinned Latinos, have experiences unlike those of other nonwhite groups. They face more systematic and authoritative racial boundaries than do Asians and light-skinned Latinos. This, we argue, creates more formidable obstacles to full incorporation for them.

Yet, even for those individuals who are defined as black, race is not the monolithic barrier it was in the nineteenth and early twentieth centuries. Although racial prejudice remains alive and well in twenty-first-century New York, it has lost its potent punch in many spheres of life. Most previous work on the second generation argues that it is a distinct disadvantage to be seen as a racial minority. At the same time, at least some members of the second generation have also benefitted from the institutions, political strategies, and notions of rights developed in the aftermath of the civil rights movement precisely because they have been defined as nonwhite. Ironically, affirmative action and other policies designed to redress long-standing American racial inquiries turn out to work better for immigrants and their children than they do for the native minorities for whom they were designed.

Parents' Expectations about Encounters with Race in America

Racial socialization begins at home. Parents' ideas about race and its role in U.S. life shape the childhood experiences of the second generation. We asked our respondents about what their parents might have taught them regarding race, prejudice, and discrimination as well as about their own experiences with discrimination and prejudice. We asked respondents whether their parents or the people who raised them had ever talked with them about prejudice or discrimination against their group; whether their parents had ever told them not to trust white Americans, or not to trust black Americans, or any other particular group; whether parents had ever told them they had to be better than white Americans to get as far as white Americans in life; and whether their parents had ever told them they had to be better than "other people" in general to get as far as "other people" in life.

Figure 10.1 shows that native blacks are much more likely to report that their parents talked to them about discrimination than any other

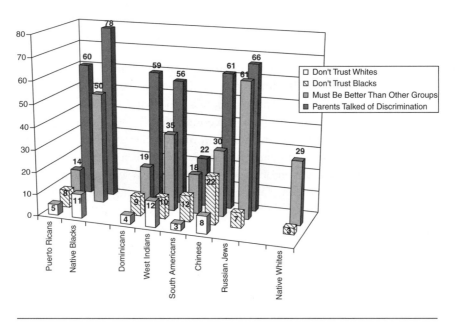

Figure 10.1. Intergroup Attitudes (%). *Source:* ISGMNY.

group, including West Indians (78 percent versus 56 percent). Similar numbers of West Indian and native black parents told their children not to trust white Americans, however, and the respondents in these groups were much more likely to get that message than respondents in other groups. West Indians and African Americans also reported similar levels of discrimination in public places, from the police and from store clerks; native blacks reported higher rates of discrimination while looking for work (35 percent versus 27 percent), which may reflect employers' real preference for black immigrants over African Americans see (Kasinitz and Rosenberg, 1996; Newman 1999; Waters 1999) but it also may reflect differences in the racial attitudes of these two groups.

As Waters (1999) notes, West Indian immigrants who grew up in black majority societies often believe that black and white Americans both tend to "racialize" encounters too much, and that black Americans sometimes focus too much on seeing discrimination where it might not really exist. Therefore, many of Waters's first generation West Indian respondents reported that they specifically did not talk to their children about the likelihood of experiencing racial discrimination, both because they expected it to occur less and because they were wary of "racializing" their children. Yet these first generation West Indians also were clear that they knew that racial discrimination exists in the United States, and so it is not surprising that about a tenth of our second generation West Indian respondents heard from their parents that they should not trust white Americans (see also Vickerman 1999).

We thus see a disconnect between the racial perceptions of West Indians, Dominicans, Chinese, and, perhaps to a lesser extent, South American immigrants parents and their second generation children. Although immigrant parents grew up in societies where they were part of the racial majority, and though they are well aware of racism and discrimination in the United States and attempt to prepare their children to face it, they are wary of imposing a "minority" consciousness on their children. West Indians, in particular, often feel that African Americans—the group they most often compare themselves to—have been hurt by awareness of their stigmatized status as well as by the real fact of pervasive discrimination. They want to protect their children from as much of this negativity and discrimination as they can.

We also asked whether parents had told respondents not to trust black Americans. Native whites were least likely to receive this message from their parents. Interestingly, the Chinese were more than twice as likely to get this message than most of the other groups. Figure 10.1 also shows that Chinese and West Indian parents were far more likely than Latino parents to tell their children that they needed to be better than white Americans to succeed (but approximately one-fifth of the Latino parents said this too). Much of the often celebrated "drive to succeed" among the Chinese and the West Indians is in fact linked to a real fear of discrimination, awareness of minority status, and a belief that they will have to perform better than whites to achieve equal rewards.

Explicit racial socialization was the norm in many households. Some African Americans told us their parents told them to expect racism and not to let it get them down: "They [my parents] said people might try to discourage you from doing what you want to do; it's up to you to make up your mind to do what you want to do."

West Indians described messages from their parents about problems they would encounter because of race, not because of their status as immigrants or ethnics.

> *I:* Do your parents ever say that people might try to limit how far you can go because you're West Indian?
> *R:* Nope, not really. They say they might try to limit me because of my color. They'd say, in this world, a lot of people tend to look at your color before they even give you a chance, so you're prejudged before you even open your mouth. They say don't let that get you down. Just keep going.

Other young people report getting more indirect messages from their parents; not necessarily that racism will affect them directly, but that whites are in control:

> They didn't say it, but they insinuated it. Like they wouldn't say it— maybe they would say stuff like, "white men got the good positions." They would like point out that all the supervisors or bosses were white, so they would say "oh that white guy, this and that." So basically, that stuck.

For some young people it was a burden to hear that they would have to be better than others to get as far:

> [My parents] let me know to watch, just the fact that I was a minority or Dominican, things would be harder for me. So I would have to work harder. People would expect more out of me. They definitely

told me that. Everything was like, "You're going to have to show them." It was almost like I was my parents' representative here. "Okay, you're going to have to do everything to show everybody what we're all about." It made me feel like I was a little burdened. I had too much responsibility but then on the same side it felt like, "Damn, they feel like they have that much trust in me to put me up to that level." It was just too much responsibilities as a kid, I think.

But young people did not just absorb their parents' messages without thinking them through and reflecting on their own experiences. As in so many other facets of life, members of the second generation are well aware that their world is very different from that of their parents. While the second generation West Indians often thought their parents had underestimated the degree of racism they face, many members of other groups actually felt their parents were more fearful of racism than they needed to be, at least in multicultural New York. Some respondents made a point to tell us that their parents' racial views were not their own. One 27-year-old Chinese woman notes:

R: My dad thinks you have to work a lot harder because you have a lot of competition out there. In a way, saying, you really have to prove yourself more than someone else.
I: What do you think?
R: I don't think it has to do with me being Chinese. I think everyone has to prove themselves. I have a particular friend in mind and he works for Solomon [a Wall Street investment bank] and he thinks his peers hold him back because he's Chinese. I don't think so. I just think he's not assertive enough and honestly he just doesn't have what it really takes.

The survey data show that Chinese parents are likely to talk with their children about discrimination and, in most domains (with the exception of school) Chinese are much less likely to experience discrimination than are the other nonwhite groups in our study. These trends are borne out in our interview data, wherein Chinese respondents told us that their parents expected to encounter trouble in the United States, but many of the respondents seemed skeptical that their parents knew what they were talking about.

When I was younger, my parents told me, "Don't start trouble with white people. Or don't start trouble with other groups. Stay away from them. If they push you just avoid them." And I don't like this.

They're trying to teach us to have a passive attitude when there's aggression toward you. When I was a kid, I actually listened to them but now I get older, I just realize how it affected me later on in life. It sounds like they're afraid. They are just passive and they try to make the kids passive too.

Distinguishing between discrimination and unequal treatment may be tricky. Whether one is being treated unfairly because of race or one has just run up against a barrier that confronts everyone may be in question. Given this difficulty, some respondents thought that their parents overprepared them for racial discrimination. This 22-year-old Chinese man was angry with his parents because they did not believe he would be chosen to play baseball for the New York Mets. Although most parents would probably try to diminish their son's hopes of being chosen by the Mets, since the odds are very long, this young man was furious that his parents thought he would not be chosen simply because he was Chinese:

R: When I tried out for the New York Mets, I was much more athletic than I am now, but when I was seventeen I tried out for the Mets at Shea Stadium and they said, "You would never be able to make it, because you're short." They said, "You don't run fast, you don't know how to play ball and you're Chinese." This is coming from people who have never seen me play. Who have never seen my abilities. To even get a try out . . .

I: . . . is a big accomplishment.

R: Yeah. I didn't make it. But I got a tryout. And if another opportunity comes up I won't squander it.

Our one group of "white" immigrants, Russian Jews, also said their parents told them to expect people to discriminate against them because they were Jews. (Indeed, only African Americans were more likely to have discussed discrimination with their parents.) This attitude is understandable given that many of the Russian Jews had fled the former Soviet Union because of anti-Semitism. Yet members of the second generation perceive very little anti-Semitism in the United States and often try to explain to their parents how different the United States is. This 25-year-old woman explains how she changed her middle name back to a Yiddish one, and how much fear doing so caused her mother.

[My parents thought] anti-Semites are everywhere [and] you have to watch out. Especially my father hung on to that idea very strongly.

When I became a citizen I changed my name. I added a middle name. My mother had wanted to name me Brina, after my great-grandmother but in Russia she said, "Well, it's Yiddish, it's gonna give her all these problems and let's not do that. Brina, Ina, Anna. Let's call her Anna. It's close enough." Although it's nothing to do with it. And so when I became a citizen, during that procedure they give you the option to add a name, change a name. So I decided to add Brina as a middle name. I was in college already when I started the citizenship procedure so I was recorded in college without the middle name so I went to tell them to add the name and this made her [my mother] nervous. "Well, this is going to go on your diploma." It's so identifying. So she reacted very instinctively and "You know it's going to go on your diploma. It's going to hang in your office and what if that hurts you professionally?" We had a big argument.

In the former Soviet Union "Jewish" was as much a racial as a cultural or religious identity. Few of our respondents' parents were practicing Jews there, although some became observant in New York. Thus immigration has quite literally meant becoming white for the Russian Jewish second generation. As one young woman noted, "In Russia we were different. We *looked* different," from the majority, but in New York she does not perceive this to be the case. Although she felt a strong cultural connection to being Jewish, for her this ethnic identity was not in conflict with being part of the racial majority (in New York, why should it?). She has thus become "de-racialized" in the New York context—the opposite experience from that of most West Indians and Dominicans.

Unlike African Americans, the Russian Jewish second generation rarely actually experiences discrimination, yet their parents, like those of African Americans, have frequently spoken to their children about discrimination and tried to prepare them to fight for their rights when facing it, all the while worried that it might crush their spirits. The Russian Jewish second generation members have thus entered adult life psychologically and emotionally armored for a battle that, as it turned out, they have almost never actually had to fight.

Experiencing Discrimination and Prejudice

Discrimination and prejudice are experienced by almost everyone in the United States today. Indeed, a national survey of Americans in 1995–1996 found that 33 percent of the total population reported exposure to major lifetime discrimination, and 61 percent reported exposure to day-to-day discrimination (Kessler, Mickelson, and Williams 1999: 208). While the experience was more common among those with disadvantaged social status (women, nonwhites, individuals with low education or low income), a large number of relatively advantaged people still had experienced some type of discrimination.

Whereas 49 percent of blacks reported having experienced at least one lifetime discrimination experience, defined as not being hired for a job, not being given a promotion, denied or refused service, discouraged by a teacher from seeking higher education, being hassled by the police, being prevented from renting or buying a home, being denied a scholarship, being denied medical care, or forced to leave a neighborhood, 31 percent of whites reported experiencing one of these experiences. We live in a world in which any unequal or unfair treatment is often subjectively experienced as an instance of prejudice or discrimination. The widespread use of these terms makes it difficult to identify real differences across subgroups in American society and raises questions about whether the survey questions about prejudice and discrimination mean the same thing to different groups of people.

We asked our respondents about their experiences with discrimination: "Within the past year, did you feel like someone was showing prejudice toward you or discriminating against you?" (For native whites, we added the phrase "because of your ethnicity.") This question is inclusive of experiencing both negative actions (discrimination) and negative attitudes (prejudice). We asked whether the respondent had experienced this prejudice or discrimination at work, when buying something in a store or waiting for a table at a restaurant, by the police, at school, or when looking for work. The pattern of responses is presented in Figure 10.2.

The general pattern is that native born blacks and West Indians report the most prejudice and discrimination, followed by the Hispanic groups, then the Chinese, and then the whites and Russian Jews. (The pattern for experiencing discrimination in schools is different, as will be discussed). As noted earlier, the Hispanic groups differ in their physical appearances, with many Puerto Ricans and Dominicans appearing "black" to most Americans and the South Americans being generally lighter skinned. We do not know from the telephone interview which respondents would be coded as "black" by ordinary Americans, but we do know which ones reported in either our race or ancestry questions that they are some form of black. The results suggest that there are two distinct groups of Puerto Ricans, one dark skinned and the other light skinned, and that they have different experiences. Puerto Ricans with some black ancestry are significantly more likely than Puerto Ricans with no black in their background to report that their parents said they had to be better than white Americans to get just as far as white Americans, and they were more likely to say they had experienced discrimination at a store or a restaurant or at work.

Dominicans do not show the same sharp differences between those reporting black ancestry or race and those who do not, although this may be because Dominicans who do appear black by American standards were less likely to identify themselves as black to us, given the particular history of race relations in the Dominican Republic Among Dominicans the only effect of reporting some black ancestry is to increase the likelihood of having experienced discrimination while looking for work. There were no significant differences between the small group of South Americans who report black ancestry or race and those who do not.

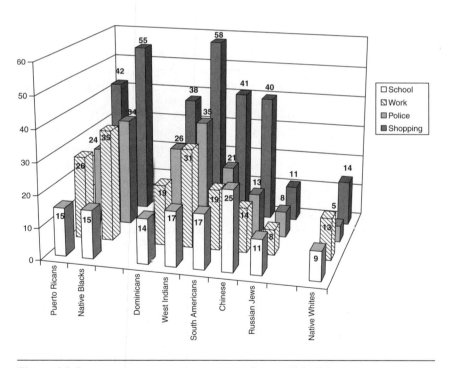

Figure 10.2. Experiences of Discrimination (%). *Source:* ISGMNY.

The qualitative interviews provide further evidence that our respondents fall on different sides of the black/non-black color line. A question we asked about mistaken identity—do other people ever mistake your race or ethnicity?—shows how fluid the color line actually is in New York with respect to some identities and phenotypes and how much color line still exists with respect to others. Light-skinned respondents are often mistaken for other groups, as is this light-skinned Jamaican:

> *I:* Do other people sometimes think you're a different race or ethnicity?
> *R:* Oh yeah. All the time . . . You know that Jewish guy outside? They thought he was the Messiah? [Here the respondent is referring to a poster portraying the late Lubavitcher Rebbe Menachem Schneerson.] I went to his funeral. They thought I was Jewish. They think I'm Spanish. I've been told Mexican. Puerto Rican, Dominican. Every kind of thing. Indian. Everything.
> *I:* How do you feel about that?
> *R:* It's pretty cool actually. I think it is pretty cool. I worked there three summers and this summer they asked me where did I come from. "Jamaica." Just one black guy was, "Oh, wow, we didn't know. Welcome to the group." And I was, "Huh? What are you talking about?" He said, "We didn't know you were black." "What are you talking about?" The whole time they thought I was Spanish because when the Spanish girls talked, I could understand them.

The South Americans often report that they are most often mistaken to be Italian, Greek, and Portuguese. While South Americans and light-skinned Puerto Ricans are "misidentified" onto the white side of the color line, dark-skinned Puerto Ricans and Dominicans are "mis-identified" onto the black side:

> *I:* Do people sometimes think that you're a different race or ethnicity?
> *R:* They think I'm black. I have to speak Spanish in order for people to know. If I don't speak they won't notice. Maybe it's my complexion, maybe it's the way I dress. I don't know.

Even other Hispanics may mis-identify their own members as African American if they do not hear a dark-skinned person speaking Spanish, as this Dominican woman describes in the following incident:

> *I:* Can you recall the last time somebody commented on your racial or ethnic background.

R: Yeah, the guy in Blimpies. He thought that I was black, like, African American, and I had asked him how much was pickle. I asked the girl how much the pickle and she said twenty-five cents, and he said in Spanish, "No, cobra a ella cincuenta." [No, charge her fifty cents.]

I: A Dominican guy?

R: No, he was Cuban. Cóbrala esa cincuenta [Charge this girl fifty cents.] So she was like "No, it's fifty cents." I said it is not fifty cents. He just said to charge me fifty cents. Why? Because I look, and I'm saying in English, is it because I look black? Let me tell you something. I am Dominican. I am proud and I know what you just said." And his face dropped. And I said "Tome tu maldito sándwich coño and mete todo donde puede meter, donde queda mejor. [More or less—take your damn sandwich, you jerk, and shove it where it fits better.] I went off on him!

We also explored gender differences in the reported experiences with prejudice and discrimination. The only significant difference was in experiencing problems with the police. Except among the Chinese, the Russian Jews, and the native whites (few of whom reported problems with the police), males were significantly more likely than females to report problems with the police. This finding aligns with significant differences in arrest rates by gender discussed earlier.

Dominican males are much more likely than South American and Puerto Rican males to report problems with the police. Indeed, the Dominican males are closer to the African American and the West Indian males in this respect. Dominican females, in contrast, are more like the other Hispanic females. West Indian and native black females are much less likely to report prejudice and discrimination from the police than are their male counterparts, but women in these groups are much more likely to report discrimination and prejudice than females of other groups in our study.

It is worth noting that among native white males, the number reporting having experienced "prejudice or discrimination by the police" is actually far *lower* than the number of males who were arrested. We also asked respondents whether they thought that the police favor whites in New York City. Most respondents in every group agreed with that statement, although West Indians and native blacks were most likely to do so. There were no significant gender differences except among the Dominicans, where more males than females thought the police favored whites (79 percent versus 61 percent).

Where respondents encounter discrimination also varies by group, as indicated in Figure 10.2. Every group experienced discrimination when shopping and dining out, ranging from 11 percent of Russian Jews who reported problems in these arenas to 58 percent of West Indians. But among the Chinese, discrimination while shopping is followed by discrimination in school (25 percent). Lower levels of discrimination reportedly happened while Chinese respondents were looking for work or interacted with the police—around 13 percent. For West Indians, being hassled by the police was the next most likely arena (35 percent), followed by work (31 percent), looking for work (27 percent), and being in school (17 percent).

Our in-depth interviews clarified these patterns. It turns out that the different ethnic groups are referring to different phenomena. When the Chinese discuss discrimination at school, they conceive of it differently than do the West Indians and African Americans. The Chinese are mostly discussing discrimination from other nonwhite groups—primarily from black and Hispanic students in their schools who teased or bullied them. The Chinese respondents talked, for example, about kids who tried to copy from their papers in school because as Chinese they were assumed to be very smart, or they mentioned teachers who put them in the hardest math class just because they were Chinese.

Hispanic and black respondents perceived discrimination that was much more likely to come from white teachers or administrators who assumed that they were not smart. These respondents described being put in bilingual education classes when they did not need them or being criticized for not speaking English correctly. They described sometimes blatant racism from white teachers as well as from guidance counselors who steered kids into non–college track courses. One Dominican woman told us that when she was moving into her dorm room as a freshman, her roommate insisted on being present so that she would not steal anything. The Hispanic and black respondents also complained about white professors who had low expectations of their nonwhite students. Teachers who express low expectations or negative racial stereotypes are particularly hurtful to these students.

There was one teacher who I actually admired a lot the way he was, in terms of a teacher, but as a person I was upset by many things he would say to me. Like since I was the only Hispanic in the program, every time he referred to me, he'd say, "the Puerto Rican." I'd say, "I'm not Puerto Rican," and it's like the same shit. I liked him as a person, he was pretty cool, but there were things about him and I knew he was very racist toward another student who was African. He showed it in subtleties that he made into jokes, but I know a joke is not always a joke.

While many respondents were able to deal with teachers whom they knew or suspected were racist, this 18-year-old Dominican woman describes how she was unable to control her anger:

R: I almost got suspended in the seventh grade because this American teacher, she was like, white, Caucasian teacher, she was like "Most of you in the years to come are gonna be on Welfare because all your Spanish mothers do is watch soap operas and sleep with a lot of men." So I got mad, 'cause I take that to the heart, 'cause my mother I appreciate that she's very hard-working so I took a chair and I threw it at the teacher [laugh] and whatever. My mother had to go into school and stuff.

I: What happened to her after you explained what happened.

R: [Sigh] Forget it. A big commotion happened. It was even gonna come out in the news and they were asking my mother's lawyer—we had to get a lawyer because my mother was like she was gonna sue the board of education and whatever, and they apologized and when I dropped out of the school, 'cause I didn't go back, I was like forget it—I'm fed up. They were calling my mother and telling her like no, that they're gonna treat me the way I'm supposed to be treated, to come back.

There was also a disconnect between the way Chinese and native white respondents described their problems with the police and the way blacks, West Indians, and Dominicans did. Young and dark-skinned males are the most likely to describe tense and sometimes violent encounters with the police. So common and expected are such encounters that our dark-skinned male respondents often do not mention them right away in the interviews. For example, this 22-year-old African American male with dreadlocks at first answers a question about race and discrimination by saying he had never experienced anything:

R: I mean, it was nothing obvious. So, I really couldn't say I've been really discriminated against.

I: Any kind of police harassment?

R: All the time! Often, often. Today, since I'm wearing, you know, my regular attire, no, I won't get harassed but if I was just running to the store and I had my fatigue jacket on, automatically I fit every description from every precinct so I have had my problems, yes. They stop me often, harass me, question me, check my pockets, which is against the law, against the law—I want to repeat this again [yells into the tape recorder]—"Against the law." It makes me feel I'm a wanted man. But it makes me feel good because I'm not doing anything, so I mean, it makes me feel like I can laugh in their face, but I don't feel like taking a nightstick to the head so I'll just smile when they leave.

This dark-skinned Colombian man also answers the telephone survey question about discrimination by reporting none, but then he remembers numerous negative experiences with the police:

R: I've always been looked upon as an individual and not necessarily because of my race, you know what I can bring to the table. Hopefully I've never encountered—or if I have encountered it, I don't think I've ever picked up on it.

I: Has there ever been a time when you experienced any problem or difficulty from being Colombian?

R: Oh, your normal harassment by—I don't know why this popped into my head now, 'cause I thought about the question, you know, when you get harassed by cops and stuff like that. You know, "You spics" this and that, you know what I'm saying? Or you get stopped because you're in a nice car, something like that. Because you're Hispanic. Is this car stolen, whatever. So yeah, that happened. It's not that often, but it has happened enough times that it bothers you, everybody. I guess that's why I thought about it now.

Although such experiences with the police do not leap out in response to a general question about discrimination, they commonly emerge among black and Hispanic young men who talk at length about their encounters with the police. People described being stopped if they were "driving while black," or being stopped on the street or on the subway because they "fit the description." Most young men were very angry about their experiences with the police, and most had been advised by parents or teachers or friends to just "take it" and not to talk back because that could lead to far greater trouble. So most of the young men ended up "swallowing" a lot of anger.

R: It was a party in a house and we were partying and someone had done something. I knew nothing about it. I came outside and then all of a sudden they thought it was me and they just took me and just slammed me against the wall, put me in handcuffs. Then they were like, "Oh, okay, sorry," and they let me go.

I: Has anyone ever stopped you walking in the street?

R: Twice they stopped and they just . . . they were, "Can we talk to you for a second?" "Yeah." They are like, "Blah, blah, blah. Where were you?" They start asking me questions and they start getting a little stupid. They start touching and checking me and all that. They're not supposed to do that, you know. So I'm like, "What are you doing? I haven't done anything." "Oh, no, no, whatever." They put me in handcuffs and asked me a whole bunch of questions and all this. Just because somebody around the neighborhood did something and I fit the description.

I: How does that make you feel?

R: Mad. Because it's the system that's made to protect us but at the same time it's not [a] perfect system and I try to live with that. I try to say it's cool until it happens to me and then I understand the anger that some people feel.

This expectation of trouble with the police has led some young people to avoid neighborhoods or situations where their race will stand out:

R: If I go to Bellevue I going to have problems 'cause the cops, they're racist up there. They don't like dark-skinned people. Or Spanish. They don't like them at all. So you try to keep yourself away from that area. Even now, even now you go up there, like I go up there, they're gonna ask me, "Whatchu doin' over here?" Or "whatchu want? I give you five minutes so you could get out of here. You don't belong here." For no reason. I thought it was a free country, you could go anywhere you want as long as you're not messing with nobody, but they all used to kick us out so we just don't go over there.

Although blacks and Hispanics are not the only people to have complaints or run-ins with the police, their complaints are different than those of respondents from other groups. For instance, this 25-year-old Chinese woman answered our telephone survey question by saying she had experienced discrimination from the police, but the problems she describes are very different than the violent incidents described earlier by our dark-skinned male respondents: "It's just sometimes when you have, let's say, the police. If there's a crash, they always think the white guys are right.

They always saying, 'Oh, you're wrong.' Like a witness and then making sure that's a white too and it cannot be Chinese . . . I'm surprised the police are the most prejudiced."

The belief that police favor whites is widespread among our respondents—including whites themselves. A number of whites described incidents of police harassment of blacks that they had witnessed:

> R: I had to remove somebody from a bar I was working in. The guy had thrown a glass at me and then attacked one of my customers, and I removed him from the bar. There were six witnesses in the bar. I didn't strike him. I didn't call him any names. I just had to get him out of the bar. And he was bombed and he fell down outside and busted his head open. I called 911 and I was administering . . . I had a towel on his head . . . When I was putting the towel on his head, there were two young black kids because it was on 9th Avenue and 40th Street, these black teenagers walked by and "Yo, man, this guy is bleeding." They stopped to see what was happening. Two white detectives they jumped out of the car. They were undercover detectives. They got out and walked right up and told them, "Get up against the wall." They were like, "Yo, man, we didn't do anything." And they said, "Shut the fuck up. Get against the wall." I had to tell them, "They didn't do anything. They just stopped. They're just standing here."
>
> I: Was the person that was hurt a white man?
>
> R: Yeah, he was white. But they just assumed, and if I wouldn't have been standing there, they would have arrested them for nothing.

Encounters with the police seem to have a particularly deep and long-lasting effect on young people, particularly young men. Part of this may be because no matter how unfairly one is treated, it is generally imprudent, or actually dangerous, to argue back. This inability to respond leaves one with a bitter sense of frustration. Further, it is hard to dismiss a police officer who treats one badly as simply "ignorant" or a lout, as one could with a peer. The police are armed representatives of the state. Negative treatment by them, in some way, represents negative treatment by the larger society. And if a group, such as African Americans, already has ample reason to feel excluded and stigmatized, repeated negative encounters with the police can reinforce this perception in ways they may not for whites.

Finally, anonymous encounters with shopkeepers, security guards, and particularly the police in public spaces are powerful because such encounters are so purely "racial." Class differences do not count—as the frequent, bitter complaints of middle class African Americans make clear (Feagin 1991). Nor do ethnic differences. Indeed, many of the victims of some of New York's most notorious police brutality cases have been black immigrants. A police officer rarely has a basis for knowing if a young man on a public street is African American or West Indian or middle class or poor. If the police officer discriminates, it is on the basis of race.

Discrimination from the police is an extreme example of the experience of discrimination or prejudice that people experience on the streets. Respondents also reported being referred to with racial slurs such as "nigger," "spick," or "gook" from passersby on the street or on subways. These incidents were described as hurtful but not overly dramatic. Some young men responded to slurs by threatening or actually engaging in physical violence. These incidents, like the ones with the police, are generally unprovoked and unanticipated; they leave little control to the victims other than how to handle their anger and upset.

The most commonly reported type of impersonal encounter occurred during respondents' childhoods, with Russians and Chinese reporting as many incidents as blacks and Hispanics. Russians report having been called "bagels" or "kikes" or "commie" (for Communist) when they were young. The Chinese report having been called "Chinks" or "slant eyes" or "Bruce Lee." These incidents contributed to a sense that other people were identifying them racially and ethnically and that they had to stand up for themselves. But most people remembered the slurs as a regrettable aspect of dealing with other "ignorant kids." In contrast to bad encounters with the police, these incidents did not generally leave lasting scars or deep anger.

By far the most common type of discrimination reported by our respondents happened during shopping or going to a restaurant. Most of the time people reported that shopkeepers follow them to make sure they do not shoplift or actually confront them to ask if they will be buying something. The respondents believe that the shopkeepers think that because of their race or ethnicity, they will not have enough money to buy products for sale in the stores.

> *I:* Have you ever experienced any problems or difficulties from being African American?
>
> *R:* Yeah. I feel I've been discriminated against in my own neighborhood. It was me, my friend . . . He's Haitian, and his sister. And my

sister. All four of us walking together. When we were young we used to walk from here to Kings Plaza Mall and we went into this store and they followed us around saying, "If you don't buy something you'll have to leave." And this is hard to believe but it was a bigger group of whites in there and they weren't doing anything. Neither were we but we got picked on so we just left. And it makes me mad. It kind of hurts and it makes you upset.

Or this Dominican fellow:

R: When I go to stores. When I try to stop a cab downtown. If I try to shop with my credit cards. I face it all the time. Like, one time I was in Macy's and I was shopping and I had to produce more ID than anybody else. You know what I mean? I'm like, "I don't know what you're looking at? I make more money than you." Back then I was really making more money than the vice president. I used to get stopped because I had a big . . . I was young and I had at one time a 928 Porsche . . . If I'm on the Turnpike, I'm dead. I'm definitely going to get pulled over. I get pulled over at least once a week.

People also feel discrimination in restaurants. One Chinese respondent told us that his family always used a "white name" to get a reservation because they thought that by doing so they would get a better table than if they were identifiably Chinese. Other Chinese respondents described waiting for a table and seeing white people who came in after them get seated first, leading the Chinese to conclude that they were being made to wait longer because they were Chinese. Respondents from many different groups were sure that they were given undesirable tables near the kitchen. When they went to fancy restaurants, because of their race.

Discrimination in stores and restaurants was often attributed to racial prejudice, but some people were not so sure. Most respondents said that they dealt with such discrimination by signaling to the store or restaurant employees that they did have money and were not criminals. Sometimes they did this by being sure to dress nicely or by being sure to prominently display their credit cards or the key ring that showed they owned an expensive car.

Respondents were sometimes unsure whether their race assumptions about their class led to bad treatment. One young Dominican woman suspected that her numerous body tattoos and piercing caused people to discriminate against her. Others were quick to point out that bad behavior happened only when they wore sweatpants or cheap clothes. Of course, one must question whether whites who were dressed similarly would also be discriminated against. Yet the employees who discriminate in this way are not all whites—often respondents are perceiving discrimination from clerks or waiters who are themselves members of nonwhite groups. Racism in post–civil rights America is not only real but also quite complicated.

Respondents report having experienced more discrimination when applying for jobs than they did once they were actually on the job. When you are applying for a job, particularly a low wage job, the prospective employer does not know much about you except for your race or ethnicity. Young people applying for such jobs often have little work experience, and their educational credentials are generally not very important. This means employers have little useful information and few rational criteria to help them pick employees, a situation ripe with potential for racial and ethnic discrimination. Often respondents report that when they first speak with interviewers on the phone, the interviewers are encouraging and interested; then when respondents meet the interviewers in person, the interviewers seems uninterested in hiring them because, the respondents surmise, of their race or ethnicity.

> R: I went in there for an interview and I think the person must have thought I was white and they kept on saying, "Rigo?" so they must have thought my last name was Italian or something. So I went to this interview. I'm telling you—at the end of Queens, [the last stop] in Flushing, el último, lo último, three buses, a train, and a plane—put it that way. I get there and they didn't even interview me no more than three minutes.
>
> I: What was the position?
>
> R: A manager for Enterprise Rent-A-Car. And when I walked in, they gave me the look. They all looked at me and then when I walked in, everybody was white in there and I was like, that was the first time I ever felt like that. I was like, you know what? I don't believe this. They came in and said, "Oh, so tell us a little bit about yourself." I said, "Well, I'm a recent college graduate." Whatever, oh, you know, "thank you very much. We'll keep you in our file, we'll just, you know, you'll hear from us."
>
> I: And you're still waiting. [Laugh]
>
> R: No. They sent me a letter! That was the first time I ever felt like I was discriminated against.

One might imagine that nonwhites who report feeling discriminated against themselves in job interviews are talking about whites who refuse to hire them. But this is not always the case. For instance, a 23-year-old second generation Ecuadoran male reported that he felt he was discriminated against by a first generation Ecuadoran supervisor who did not want to hire him because he spoke English without an accent (the supervisor thought the store's customers would assume he was Puerto Rican and therefore would not want to shop there). Our respondent assumes that someone who spoke less English eventually got the job.

Because the workplaces of the second generation are generally diverse places, when different respondents discussed the discrimination they experienced or the or prejudice that they faced on the job, they were describing different phenomena. Some described classic structural racism (Waters 1999) in which they observed a hierarchy in which whites were keeping all the good positions at the top for themselves. West Indians were particularly attuned to this inequality:

> *I:* How do you think Afro-Americans are seen in the U.S.?
> *R:* Not good. We don't get the opportunities. They see us as niggers and if you look [up] the word "nigger," it means wild type of person. That's how they see us.
> *I:* So you say they don't give us opportunities, like employment opportunities?
> *R:* Yeah. Employment opportunities, a lot of stuff. And even in the Army, you can see it in the Army too. They'll give you rank, but you wouldn't see a lot of generals and three stars or four-star generals all that black. They are all white. But you can see it in the Army too. They try to keep you down. They will throw you a bone here or there, but that's it. They won't let you go up any higher.

Yet other respondents described specific actions taken against them that they attributed to racism. In retail, for instance, respondents describe being kept out of direct contact with customers. A Puerto Rican man gave an example: "One job as soon as they saw me as a Puerto Rican, they limited my job. Yeah, they didn't want me helping out the other electronics or some of the other whites because they thought I didn't know, you know, they thought less of me. They thought I didn't know nothing."

Given the variety of people present in these work sites, the reported instances of discrimination may simply be intergroup tensions. The power relations reflected in the incidents recounted by our respondents matter a great deal in the nature and long term consequences of the discrimination. If the discriminator is a member of the white majority in American society (if not the majority in the immediate surroundings), and if the discrimination is by an agent in authority—a teacher, a police officer, or an employer, for instance—the consequences for the target of the discrimination are much more severe than if an equal from another minority group exhibits tensions or resentments. One white respondent, for example, got so upset when his Filipino co-workers spoke in Tagalog that he tried to tape record their conversations and have them translated into English.

A West Indian female describes how different supervisors can make different shifts at her job uncomfortable for different types of people:

> *I:* On your job have you ever experienced unfair treatment from your boss or supervisor?
>
> *R:* Yes [laugh]. We have three shifts, mainly, people work over into other shifts like the morning shift is mostly Latinos. Don't ask how that happened. Actually, I know how that happened, the supervisor is Latino, so mostly new people are hired, he tends to prefer Latinos to come to his shift. If you're a girl, and you look okay, you qualify also. And then the second shift is very mixed, which is the shift I work on. It's black, Asian, and white. And the last shift, which is the night one, is all black people, so according to which shift you work on, you're gonna get treated differently.

Other times casual statements from co-workers bring home to the respondents that their race is something their co-workers are thinking about. A Chinese man said:

> My handwriting isn't that great and one of my co-workers . . . I think she comes from some island in the Mediterranean or something and she said something about, "Yeah, I was working with this Oriental guy before and it took me a while to get used to his handwriting too." To me, it's just because I have bad handwriting doesn't mean that's a racial trait, that we have bad handwriting. She didn't mean to be offensive, it's just one of those things that came up.

Chinese respondents also mentioned that their race was a factor on their jobs, but here once again the consequences of racial awareness differed from what was experienced by blacks and Hispanics. While blacks and Hispanics struggle to overcome negative stereotypes, many Chinese respondents mentioned that non-Chinese people stereotyped Chinese as smart. This positive conception helped the Chinese respondents at work, a Chinese woman suggested.

> *I:* How did your experience getting promoted compare with those of your co-workers?
> *R:* I think that's another thing great about this bank. It's meritocracy.
> *I:* Do you think you've ever been treated differently from your co-workers by your boss or other co-workers?
> *R:* Yeah, like I said, it's a plus and minus being Asian American. They assume you're smart and then again they don't joke with you as much because they tend to see you as more serious.

Many people responded specifically to the idea of workplace discrimination by saying they needed to work harder than others to get as far. Said one 27-year-old native black woman:

> I think as time went on, like in college, I knew that I had to work harder. Have to study harder, study twice as hard if I was going to have the same opportunities to get what other white people might have. I never thought I would be limited though, just that I had to work harder if I was going to.

The cumulative weight of a particular type of discrimination can lead to the kind of anger and reactive ethnicity described by Portes and Rumbaut (2001). This 31-year-old West Indian describes the toll of racism:

> Being a black man—it's the hardest role that you can wear, to me, in this society. I've seen big corporations, you'll see black alongside the Hispanic man in mail rooms. If they want to stay there for the rest of their lives, they probably will . . . From a black man's perspective, every time I walk out the door, I feel I'm pretty much judged every conceivable angle. People from other cultures might say they figure I might want to rob you or shoot you and take whatever. You know, just basically being a damn nigger, and very ignorant, maybe from a white man's point of view—some people might feel—look down on me like I am nothing but pure animal—some of them might actually see somebody that's athletic and talented and actually fear you. So basically from a black man's point of view, when you walk out of the door, you're judged from every conceivable angle. Some of the judgments are very harsh but unfortunately we have a lot of black brothers out there who don't know who the hell they are and they

give power to whatever perceptions there are of them, and it makes it hard for people like me that want to do something about myself. And when I try to do something for me, and shatter this image, it's so much pressure on you to succeed. It's just not easy.

Discrimination clearly occurs in different realms, from different people, with different consequences for the people who experience it. We live in a time of immense racial talk and racial labeling. But this widespread "race talk" means that people use the same terms to describe different phenomena. People who believe they have been treated unfairly and who are not white frequently use the language of race, discrimination, and racism to describe their experiences. But some of them are describing being viewed as stereotypes, some are describing ethnic rivalries, and some are describing workplace disputes among co-workers that take on an ethnic or racial tone.

The white worker who took offense that his co-workers spoke in Tagalog used the language of discrimination, as did the Chinese woman who was upset that people at work assumed she was smart—but these are both different experiences than that of the dark-skinned Dominican woman who got a wonderful reception when she inquired about a job on the phone and yet felt she was denied the job when she was interviewed in person. The former experiences reflect rough-and-tumble ethnic group tension whereas the latter is employment discrimination that can have far-reaching negative consequences for its victims. But the same language is also used to describe much more intense and virulent actions. Blacks and other groups with dark skin experience the same stereotyping, peer tensions, and fights, but they also experience discrimination and unequal treatment from authority figures who have real power over their lives—teachers, police, and employers. Perhaps the worst experiences they have are anonymous encounters in public spaces like subways, parks, and city streets—arenas in which race counts the most and other traits, including ethnicity, count much less.

The model presented in Figure 10.3 captures the differences in the experiences and consequences of different types of discrimination across the groups in our study. Not all "nonwhites" are alike. The "closer" one is perceived to be to African Americans, the more serious the discrimination. Groups differ in the degree and kind of discrimination they experience. So after African Americans, West Indians face the most discrimination, followed by Dominicans and then Puerto Ricans. South Americans experience much less. Chinese experience discrimination even less, and Russians, perceived as whites, even less than that.

A first set of racial incidents (experienced by Dominicans, West Indians, Puerto Ricans, and blacks especially on the streets, in stores and from the police) leaves little control to the nonwhite victim and thus leads to discouragement and to confrontation with whites. These dark-skinned respondents try to avoid racial discrimination by avoiding white neighborhoods so they will not be targeted, or they try to dress nicely so that cabs will stop for them or restaurants will give them good service. They hope to signal their middle class status to differentiate themselves from the "ghetto poor"; or, in the case of Dominicans, West Indians, and Puerto Ricans, they may also signal their ethnic difference from African Americans. But in impersonal encounters on the street or in job applications,

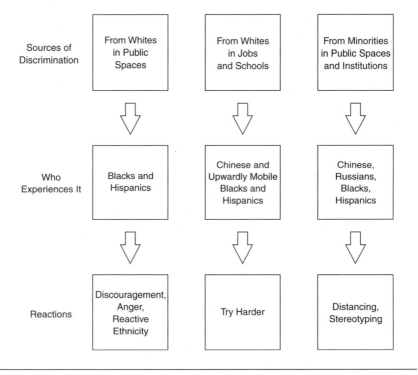

Figure 10.3. Experience and Consequence of Different Types of Discrimination

often the only thing whites know about these dark-skinned applicants is their race, and such techniques cannot always prevent racist treatment.

A second set of racially discriminatory incidents (more common among Chinese, Russians, South Americans, and upwardly mobile blacks, Dominicans, and Puerto Ricans) leads less to discouragement and more to increased efforts to overcome racial stereotypes. When discrimination by whites occurs in an institutional setting where the nonwhite victim perceives some degree of control, such discrimination is experienced as a challenge—a need to try harder to succeed. So workplace discrimination is often interpreted, not as a reason to give up, but as reason to show how good one can be, to show that one is better than all the other workers so that individual characteristics can end up trumping racial stereotypes.

The respondents defined as black also experience such incidents, but in integrated settings—schools, workplaces, churches—where they were exposed to whites' discriminatory practices up close. As a result, poor African Americans, West Indians, and Dominicans don't usually experience this sort of discrimination because, living out much of their lives in segregated neighborhoods, schools, and workplaces, they have so little access to these integrated settings in the first place. These integrated settings are far more likely to be encountered by middle class blacks and Hispanics.

Finally, the third set of racially discriminatory encounters is common—intergroup tensions, fights, and discrimination among nonwhites themselves. The different immigrant and racial groups in New York City fight for resources at work, in schools, and in neighborhoods. The immense diversity in New York City means that there is a great deal of complexity in who is discriminating against whom. Often in-group favoritism—such as black supervisors wanting to hire black workers—is perceived as racism by nonwhite employees vying for the same jobs.

Such rough-and-tumble ethnic rivalry accounts for a great deal of the reported discrimination among all groups and certainly makes young people highly conscious of ethnic differences. Yet the vast number of cross-cutting rivalries also means that although clear ethnic hierarchies may exist among nonwhites, they are less associated with a permanent sense of inferiority or superiority than are the rivalries between whites and nonwhites.

The use of similar racial talk for many different phenomena can also mask social progress. The more integrated one's life, the more likely one is to experience discrimination in a number of spheres. The Chinese, our most successful second generation group, are also the most likely to be in integrated schools, workplaces, and neighborhoods where they are in the minority among other groups. Black and Latino respondents, on the other hand, are more likely, especially during their earliest years of schooling, to be in segregated schools and neighborhoods, where they comprise the majority group. For blacks and Latinos who are upwardly mobile, it is often not until college or getting a full time job that they finally have enough contact with other groups, and particularly with whites, to have much opportunity to be discriminated against. This pattern of differential experiences of discrimination is clearer if we look at class differences within groups.

Respondents' experiences of discrimination at work, show no significant differences related to education, although less educated Dominicans, Puerto Ricans, and Russians report significantly more discrimination in looking for work than do those individuals with more education (see Table 10.1). Discrimination experienced while shopping, however, is variable depending on a respondent's education. For South Americans, Dominicans, Puerto Ricans, West Indians, and native blacks, the more educated people report *more* discrimination. For Chinese it is exactly equal, and for whites and Russians the less educated people report more discrimination. The only two differences that are statistically significant, though,

Table 10.1. Experience of Prejudice and Discrimination (by group and by level of education) (%)

Group	School Education		Looking for Work Education		Work Education		Store/ Restaurant Education		Police Education	
	Low	Hi	Low	Hi	Low	Hi	Low	Hi	Low	Hi
Puerto Rican	14	20	24	14	26	24	39	47	24	15
Native Black	14	19	34	31	35	37	51	70	35	31
Dominican	12	20	24	12	21	14	36	42	27	22
West Indian	15	22	26	25	28	34	54	62	37	31
South American	17	18	19	13	21	18	37	47	24	20
Chinese	33	22	17	11	13	13	41	41	20	11
Russian	10	11	15	7	10	7	15	10	13	6
Native White	12	7	7	5	15	13	20	12	10	3

Low education = Less than a BA. High education = BA or above.

are those among native blacks and native whites (70 percent of blacks with a BA report discrimination while shopping compared with 51 percent of those without one; and 12 percent of whites with a BA report discrimination, whereas 20 percent of those without one do.)

The differences could simply reflect a matter of perception, since better-educated African Americans are more likely to perceive discrimination than are less educated ones (Hochschild 1995). A more likely explanation is that more educated African Americans are more likely to shop in higher-priced stores, patronizing higher-priced restaurants, work in more integrated work settings, and generally have more contact with whites. They thus have greater "opportunities" to be treated badly by whites (Feagin 1991). Ironically, the black poor, who are more likely to experience what we from the outside might see as manifestations of "structural racism"—such as segregation in housing, schools, and jobs—are also actually less likely to have face-to-face encounters with whites other than the police. Thus, in many arenas the black poor may perceive less discrimination or interpersonal racism than do higher class African Americans. In terms of discrimination at school, Dominicans and West Indians are more likely to report discrimination if they are highly educated. Chinese are more likely to report discrimination if they are less educated. For everyone else education makes no significant difference.

The terms "race" and "discrimination" are thus being used to describe all kinds of perceived unfairness. African Americans' experiences, however, are the benchmark against which we compare the experiences of all the groups. African Americans are most likely to report discrimination when looking for work and being at work. They, along with West Indians, report the highest levels of discrimination while shopping and from the police. Further, the discrimination they experience while shopping is very different than what is reported by other groups—it is a consequence not of social class but of race, with better-educated African Americans experiencing the most (the opposite of what occurs among native whites). Indeed, upward mobility in terms of class status may actually expose African Americans to more, rather than less, discrimination in their everyday lives with better-educated African Americans experiencing the most (the opposite of what occurs among native whites).

The interview data again show that different types of discrimination produce different reactions. When demonstrating one's individuality in school or at work was possible, our respondents tended to respond by trying to "outshine" those who doubted them. It is in impersonal instances, such as when a police officer or storekeeper who knows nothing about someone except his or her race and treats that person poorly, that discrimination wreaks its most debilitating and anger-inducing effects. This impersonal prejudice, we argue, is the specific kind of racism that could lead to what Portes and Rumbaut (2001) call "reactive ethnicity." We find such racism most likely to affect blacks, West Indians, and dark-skinned Dominicans and Puerto Ricans. Although Chinese, South Americans, and Russians face a world in which they are sometimes treated unfairly because of their race or ethnicity, their experiences are qualitatively and quantitatively different from the experiences of people with dark skin.

Becoming American after the Civil Rights Movement

The focus on racial discrimination as an integral part of becoming American should not obscure the fact that American mainstream culture has changed drastically in the last half century. As Alba and Nee (2003) argue, the U.S. mainstream has become far more diverse in the last few decades, and the destruction of de jure segregation has led to much more permeable boundaries between racial and ethnic minority groups and the evolving mainstream. Our nonwhite respondents enter a society in which many institutions—especially universities and corporate workplaces—specifically value and try to increase diversity (Bowen, Bok, and Shulman 1998; Massey et al. 2003). Second generation respondents are taking advantage affirmative action programs, which were designed to help native minorities with whom the second generation now shares a broad racial or pan-ethnic identity. Ironically, in many ways the second generation may be better able than the native minorities to qualify for and seek out these programs.

West Indians, to cite the clearest example, have on average more highly educated parents than do the native blacks in our sample. The West Indian parents were socialized in countries where blacks were in the majority and so were likely to believe that race was not an impediment to high leadership, an approach they tried to inculcate in their children (Waters 1999). This means that West Indian youngsters are likely to grow up with parents who have high educational expectations of them, provide support, and know about education.

Yet some of these West Indian second generation students might not qualify for admission to highly selective colleges without the help of affirmative action. After all, they have suffered from growing up in racially segregated neighborhoods and, on average, have attended public schools that are inferior to those attended by whites. Nonetheless, they are generally not as disadvantaged as the native African Americans. Since elite and non-elite colleges are more than willing to count West Indians as "blacks" in order to demonstrate "diversity" in their student admissions, they get in to these institutions and receive the benefits of attending them (Massey et al. 2007). Without the shifts in racial policies that followed the African American–led civil rights movement, such affirmative action opportunities would not have existed The large number of West Indian immigrants who came to New York in the early twentieth century also had higher levels of education than did African Americans (Ried 1939).

Chinese immigrants in earlier times provided levels of human capital as high as that of the many Chinese who arrive today. Yet in a more overtly segregated America, this did not really matter and the life chances of early immigrants were largely circumscribed by race. Today West Indians, Dominicans, South Americans, and the Chinese are all able to take advantage of modern institutions and their desire for diversity. The presence of minorities in top colleges, corporate workforces, and public office is frequently taken as evidence of recent improvements in American race relations and the success of American multiculturalism. The achievements of second generation children of color also is touted as evidence of the country's continuing ability to successfully absorb large numbers of immigrants, especially in contrast to the Western European countries' failure to show the same progress with their own second generation. But the presence of second generation children of color also masks one of the greatest failures of American racial policy—the failure to cope with the heritage of past discrimination, especially with regard to African Americans. The stagnating position of Puerto Ricans and African Americans stands in sharp contrast to the relative successes of our second generation groups. As an immigrant integration policy, affirmative action works exceptionally well. But as a racial justice policy, it has generally been a failure.

Why is this so? One need not subscribe to William Julius Wilson's (1978) view that the significance of race in American is "declining" to share his insight that, for African Americans, racial oppression is multidimensional. It includes overt racist practices, covert racist practices, assumptions within the culture, and residual disadvantage that is the result of *past* racist practices. The civil rights movement greatly reduced, although by no means eliminated, the first of these elements. It was less successful against the second and third. The original, individualistic language of "civil rights" was generally not equipped to address the present-day effects of past discrimination.

Affirmative action, perhaps the most controversial program to be developed after the civil rights movement, is sometimes billed as making up for past injustices against African Americans. It is also often conceived as a program to guarantee "diversity" and minority representation in educational institutions and the workplace. In recent years this diversity rationale has become more common than the redress of past injustice.

For elite colleges, this weaker "diversity" argument has been easy to mesh with past practices. After all, their admissions practices have never been solely meritocractic (Karabel 2005). Such institutions have a long history of adjusting their admissions procedures to ensure a diversity of regional origins, a large presence of children of alumni, and the representation of students with a variety of other characteristics among their student bodies. Extending the logic to include ethnicity was not a significant conceptual stretch. As immigration increased from the 1970s onward, however, it was often not noticed how, in an increasingly diverse America, more and more of the beneficiaries of affirmative action policies were recent immigrants and their children.

Diversity is, of course, a laudable goal. Elite educational institutions and the nation as a whole are better for having pursued it. The emphasis on diversity has, however, also allowed these institutions to sidestep the nation's most vexing racial problem, the persistent poverty and exclusion of so many of the descendants of American slaves.

Thus, whether or not members of the second generation are aware of how much the African American struggles against racism have affected their lives, they are well positioned to take advantage of the results of that struggle. Massey and his colleagues' (2003, 2007) study of higher education reveals that immigrants and their children are by far overrepresented among the nation's black college students, and this is most true at high status institutions. Indeed, in many of America's elite colleges, the majority of the "black" students are immigrants, the children of immigrants, or biracial individuals. Similarly, imprecise definitions have often meant that programs designed for Mexican Americans and Puerto Ricans have been utilized by the children of an ever-broadening category of recent "Latino" immigrants. Institutions have gone along with this because it is, after all, far less wrenching to admit the children of dark-skinned but middle class, often college-educated immigrants than to truly confront the heritage of America's racial past.

That children of immigrants have come to be categorized as members of native minority groups does not mean their experience has been the same as that of the native minorities. The children of immigrants clearly do suffer much of the same prejudice and discrimination, but they do not inherit the scars and handicaps of a long history of racial exclusion and discrimination. Moreover, as the children of positively selected immigrants they have some measurable and no doubt other considerable yet unmeasurable assets and strengths that native minorities do not. The cumulative disadvantages inherited by native minorities mean that they may not be able to succeed in the same ways as the children of recent immigrants can.

This position challenges oversimplified views of what it means to be racialized as a member of a minority group. Too often social scientists have assumed that being racialized as black or Latino can have only negative consequences for the children of immigrants, and this is a view they often share with immigrant parents. Social scientists and immigrant parents often come to see efforts to retain "old country" ways and ethnic traditions as a way to keep at bay the corrosive effects of American racism as well as the frightening realities of the American streets.

Of course, they are partially right. Pervasive racism can indeed be soul crushing, and the nihilism of the American ghetto can lead young people down many a self-destructive path. African American communities have always been more complex than this view implies, however, for they maintain their own institutions and paths of upward mobility (Neckerman, Carter, and Lee 1999). In post–civil rights America, the heritage of the struggle for racial justice has given young people new strategies and resources for upward mobility. Thus, for the second generation today, becoming "black" or "Latino" or "Asian" has positive as well as negative consequences for these three respondents:

I: Have there been any specific times when you feel you've benefitted from being Jamaican?

R: Oh yeah. Actually, yes, because sometimes to get into certain schools, they lower the standards if you are a certain background, ethnicity, so to get into certain colleges, it was pretty okay.

I: Have there ever been times when you felt you benefitted from being Colombian or Hispanic?

R: Just with the financial aid alone. I spoke with some friend outside in financial difficulties. I was telling him, "You've got to look for scholarships." He said, "Where the hell am I going to look for scholarships?" And I said, "Gee, you're white, I really don't know what to tell you." It opens up so many doors, just being a minority. Scholarships I qualified for were outnumbering the ones that other people were [qualifying for]. So definitely a minority title helps in that sense.

I: Have there been any specific times you feel you have benefitted from being Dominican?
R: Yeah, going to law school, I think it will be a big benefit.
I: In what way?
R: I mean, the way that schools are looking for diversity. A lot of law schools is looking for diversity, and the fact that you're Hispanic really helps you out.

Although Asian Americans are doing very well overall and are highly represented in top universities, many of our Chinese respondents told us that the desire for diversity in particular fields or workplaces helped them.

I: Has there been a specific time when you felt you've benefitted from being Chinese American?
R: Yeah. Actually . . . It was really strange . . . all through growing up, being in the sciences and being Asian, you were competing with all the other Asians who are all in the sciences, you know . . . But when I applied to business school, I never applied to Yale, but they sent me an application. They said, "We saw your GMATS, we know you're Asian. Apply and you won't have to pay an application fee because we need Asians." And I went. After so many applications for med school I spent a lot of money on applications and this was like *free*—So I applied. And I guess it kind of came down to, well, in the sciences there are so many friggin' Asians that you don't know what to do with them all, but in business, there are none. So hey, what the hell!

Schools and clubs and curriculums designed to meet the cultural needs of blacks and Hispanics, "Latino" and Asian American Studies programs, and even ethnically based professional groups and associations have also provided avenues for the second generation. For better or worse, the children of nonwhite immigrants have often taken up these models, and this represents a significant change in U.S. society.

Of course, this also means that, often for the first time, African American– and Latino-dominated institutions now face their own ethnic succession struggles. Amy Foerster (2004), for example, writes about the difficulties that the largely older civil rights movement veteran and African

American leadership of a professional trade union has in understanding the concerns of its much younger and largely West Indian and Latino second generation membership. Similarly, Alex Trillo (2004) described a community college currently undergoing ethnic succession in New York. The Puerto Rican Studies course that he took was a product of the civil rights movement. Originally the course was envisioned as a way for Puerto Rican students to learn "about themselves," but Trillo found that though the Puerto Rican Studies class met the requirement for a course on American Studies—the professor was Cuban and all the students were of Dominican, Colombian, Mexican, Ecuadoran, and Peruvian heritage—there was not a single Puerto Rican in the class!

Becoming American on the Color Line

What does racial classification mean in terms of the assimilation of our second generation respondents? Do they feel that racial discrimination will keep them from being American? Do they see the United States as a place that excludes them? Alternatively, do they celebrate the changes, noted earlier, that have created opportunities based on racial identities as nonwhite? A few respondents made the connection between being a racial minority and feeling included or excluded as an American, specifically saying that by being nonwhite they cannot be American. But the majority of our respondents do not think this way. Although they do have a notion of a "white American mainstream," their idea co-exists with a notion of a more multicultural, fluid, and permeable mainstream, perhaps because of the diversity that has developed since the civil rights movement.

In New York City, most respondents encounter this second multicultural mainstream, where even whites are seen as part of a continuum owing to past immigration. When we asked a question about the kinds of people our respondents worked with or lived near, many people never used the word "whites" (and no one used the term "Anglos"); instead, they talked about Italians, Irish, and Jews.

Furthermore, young people had the most contact with each other, not with white native born Americans, who make up only 18 percent of the city's population of people in their age group. Thus they infrequently feel that they must differentiate themselves from their parents to be accepted into mainstream American society. They also feel that their intermarriage and dating patterns and their music and cultural preferences are accepted. When they do think about a larger white American mainstream, they perceive something that they may not have access to. For many of our respondents, "whites" are the people they see on TV or wait on in stores or restaurants. And, as we have seen, for many of our dark-skinned respondents, whites are the people who have directed significant racial prejudice and discrimination against them.

How can we reconcile the easy acceptance and even celebration of difference alongside continued racial discrimination and exclusion? Our respondents really do feel that their cultures are appreciated and even envied by mainstream Americans, and they live in a world where cultural difference is the norm. Yet many simultaneously believe their race will keep them from achieving full equality in the larger American society and may even expose them to hatred and violence. The ethnic and racial world of the second generation is thus best understood in terms of different zones of inclusion and exclusion.

Unlike earlier European immigrant groups, most of our respondents found little stress in reconciling their parents' ethnicity and their own identities as Americans and particularly as New Yorkers. They take for granted the pluralism that earlier white immigrants and later civil rights activists had to struggle for. In terms of their culture, their language, their food, their music, their holidays, and their formal "culture" then, they feel included. Everyone is from somewhere, and the places our respondents and their families came from have given them interesting and appreciated backgrounds. Generally our respondents find that New York not only is tolerant of diversity, with its consequent multiculturalism but also celebrates it.

This 23-year-old West Indian female described how the same person who was prejudiced against her skin color responded well to her ethnic roots:

> There is this [white] guy that works at my job. He's like an ex-pilot and he just loved it that I was Jamaican, he started like whistling a Bob Marley song, while he was passing me. You would be so surprised how those really stuffy white people love Bob Marley and Jamaicans. He may not like black people, but he has a Bob Marley CD in his computer.

Another respondent put it this way:

> There's a Latin craze right now. In the last five years. Spanish people . . . they fall almost into the same category as Italian. They are

not picked on as much as blacks. They don't experience as much prejudice and racism, I think. And right now, at this moment, they are kind of . . . they are running things right now in many ways, as far as the entertainment world and music business and all that. It's something different. It's a different flavor and I think a lot of people like it, whether it be salsa or merengue or tango or the list goes on and on. Antonio Banderas or Jennifer Lopez. They all come from different places.

Most people are well aware that American society has a racial hierarchy that puts darker-skinned people at the bottom and sees them as less smart, less capable, less welcome, than lighter-skinned people. The more a person is likely to be perceived as African American, the quintessentially stigmatized group, the greater his or her reported the difficulty, particularly in public space, where "looks" count for a great deal.

This simultaneous inclusion and exclusion is captured in the dual use of the term "American" by our respondents. On the one hand, they use this term to describe themselves in a zone of societal inclusion when they say they do things the American way in contrast to how their parents do things in more ethnic or less American ways. The Chinese, especially, are likely to make this distinction.

> I'm not that close to my parents because of that and not that close to my family in general because of that, so—because you know, I guess Chinese parents don't really talk to their kids, right? Really. They really don't, you know. They're very strict and they hit you if you're bad and I'm watching television and I'm seeing the white parents talk to their kids and I'm like why don't I get that? Why don't I get encouragement and like, why don't they tell me stuff? When my dad talked to me, it's pretty much he got to yell, so it was always something bad.

But the distinction is also made by many members of other groups, as this South American man illustrates:

> Basically I've had my own values. They would probably be American values. I see values that my father has and my mother has and I see those values and I be like, "No, I saw my parents' values and that's good for them but I told them I'm going to set up my own. So me being American, they had their kind of values when they were growing up, the way their parents taught them. They taught me the same ones but I'm going to take my own type of values. Being in this

country, compared to Ecuador, this is a better country. So my standards are probably going to be a little higher than theirs.

On the other hand, respondents also use "American" as a way to describe the white middle class people they see mostly on TV but hardly ever in real life. In this sense they see themselves as outsiders and view their ethnic or racial identities as markers of their stigmatized and excluded status. Native black respondents, for example, interpreted our question about what it means to be an American in racial terms. They described the alienation they felt from mainstream whites and used the term "American" to describe something they felt excluded from. One African American put this idea in particularly stark racial terms:

I: What do you think it means to be an American?
R: It means that they want you to accept the white mentality and accept the white culture.

Another African American male who had experienced a great deal of discrimination disavowed being an American:

I: Has there ever been a time in your life when being African American was in conflict with being American?
R: Every day. Every day. This society is not made for us to achieve anything. And especially the fact that everything's against us, you know. Now they're trying to take away affirmative action. That proves right there this country's not really for our benefit.

These African American respondents equate anything "American" with this white mainstream and see the connection as incompatible with a racial or minority identity. Whereas none of our Russian respondents have this type of response, a number of West Indians, some of the Puerto Ricans and other Hispanics, and even a few Chinese did. The Chinese respondent who specifically talked about not being able to be American defined "American" in racial as opposed to cultural terms: "I don't have the same exact background as all of the other Americans who have been here for generations. And they have different values and also their look. And their way. Not to be superficial. And they're white. And I look different."

Class, political position, and skin color are all mentioned by those respondents who think of themselves as different from mainstream Americans.

I: What do you think it means to be an American?
R: Probably what it means to be white, maybe have money . . . to have

certain views politically about what type of government is the best type, like their views are the best views. Most of the time they also think that they are the best people in the world. They think that they have the best of everything. Everybody else is always below them.

I: So when you think of an American, who or what do you picture?

R: American could be anybody, but of course we all know the opportunities for black-minority American and white American are not the same.

The paradox is that today's second generation immigrants are located within a very inclusive sphere in terms of certain aspects of popular culture but are also excluded in terms of equality of economic outcomes. Second generation Russians, for example, do not find many people who adopt their parents' food or music or celebrate much about formal Russian culture, yet as whites the second generation Russians quite easily gain access to good schools and good jobs, and they attain invisibility in mainstream institutions. By contrast, the music, dance, and general "coolness" of West Indian culture is celebrated and adopted by any number of other groups, and the whole city seems to become West Indian during the Labor Day West Indian Parade and Carnival. Yet second generation West Indians are stopped by the police, followed in stores, and steered to segregated neighborhoods and schools. Thus they find that race impacts their everyday lives in ways their parents could scarcely have imagined back in the islands. The divergent experiences of these two groups illustrates how multiculturalism and the respect for different cultures that is currently being taught in schools and disseminated in the media ironically co-exists with ongoing exclusion and discrimination.

On balance, however, the majority of our second generation respondents did not perceive either America or being American as something racial. Even those who had experienced a great deal of discrimination tended to see themselves as American and to see America as a place that accepted their culture and their identity. Perhaps this is because they live in New York. Multiculturalism is relatively easy for New Yorkers. The history of the city's incorporation of generations of immigrants, the sheer diversity of its population, and the relative openness of its institutions to a wide variety of groups create a kind of on-the-ground diversity that is perceived as particularly welcoming and inclusive. Most of our respondents did not pick their friends according to race or ethnicity, and they reported that their friends were a diverse lot. When we asked about friendships, the social networks most people described included a veritable United Nations of friends.

> Because of my open-mindedness and I refuse to, most of the time, bow to the barriers of race. I have friends of every conceivable kind. White, black, though I hate those labels, Chinese, Oriental, German, it never matters to me. Just from every part of the world, I know somebody. Australians, Japanese, I feel I'm a pretty universal guy. I have two Italian friends, a white friend, a Guyanese friend. I have a Greek friend. I have a Puerto Rican friend. I have a black friend. It's a lot of different people. A Jewish friend. I go to school with a lot of different types of people.

As a way of circumventing the issue of whether "American" was open to them or not, a number of respondents described themselves proudly as "New Yorkers." This illustrates that they surely perceive New York to be open to them regardless of whether they perceive the rest of the country to be. This second generation Ecuadoran begins by describing the meaning of being American in racial and exclusionary terms, but he then begins thinking about the reality of life in New York and ends with a more hopeful version closer to the idea of a melting pot:

> American is white. White like redneck hick from the middle of nowhere. Raising cattle and drinking beer. That's what I think of as American. There is such a thing as an American. Bland, boring, the American way of dressing, the American way of eating, it's all. But other than that, I don't think there's anything that . . . we're all Americans. America is a big melting pot. People here from every-where. That's what . . . I think that's what makes America, just the fact that there's people from different places living together and learning from one another. That doesn't happen in any other . . . what happened here in America, especially in New York, hasn't hap-pened in any other place in this world. You'd have to say that is America. That is America. All these people and that they're all living under one roof. That's pretty darn difficult, in my opinion. That doesn't happen anywhere else. You go to Argentina, there's not one black person in Argentina. You know how prejudiced they are against black people? They are scared of black people. When I think of that, I think of that as being so ignorant and so ridiculous that . . . I can't believe it.

The extreme diversity experienced in the daily lives of New Yorkers of this age group means that this hopeful cosmopolitan vision, one that is very familiar to most Americans, is becoming something close to a lived reality for our respondents, but that a more pessimistic vision based on continuing prejudice and discrimination is also part of this picture. As of this writing most young people we talked with shared this first optimistic view, but the matter is far from settled. If members of the second generation continues to experience upward mobility on average, and if there is a general perception that the racial prejudice and discrimination they do perceive flaunts the rules of American society, as opposed to being deeply ingrained in the society. then this optimistic view could prevail. If perceived fairness and opportunities for advancement are not forthcoming, a model of exclusion and permanent division is not far out of sight, especially for certain darker-skinned groups.

11

Conclusion:
The Second Generation
Advantage

> I think I have benefitted from being Colombian, from being His-
> panic. It's the best of two worlds. You know that expression? Like
> being able to still keep and appreciate those things in my culture that
> I enjoy and that I think are beautiful and at the same time being able
> to change those things which I think are bad.
>
> 23-YEAR-OLD COLOMBIAN WOMAN

Our research was initially motivated by worries about second generation decline. Like many other social scientists, we were concerned that the children of recent immigrants might be at risk of downward assimilation as they become Americans. We feared that many would earn less than their immigrant parents, get less education, have lower levels of civic participation in their new society, and become more alienated. We also suspected that upwardly mobile children of immigrants might achieve success largely by remaining tied to the ethnic communities and economic niches of their parents. In contemporary America, we speculated, the most successful immigrant families might be the ones who kept large parts of "mainstream" American culture at bay.

Although we found examples of these two scenarios, neither turned out to be common. On the whole, second and 1.5 generation New Yorkers are already doing better than their immigrant parents. The Chinese and Russian Jews have demonstrated particularly rapid upward mobility. This upward trajectory is partly explained by their parents' premigration class backgrounds and "hidden" human capital—but, particularly among the Chinese, even those from working class backgrounds or with poorly educated parents have sometimes achieved stunning upward mobility. Not surprisingly, those second generation respondents who belong to groups that the context of reception has racialized as black or Hispanic have a more mixed record. For these individuals, racial discrimination remains a significant factor in shaping their American lives. Yet even here, most of the chil-

342

dren of immigrants are exceeding their parents' levels of education, if only because the parents' levels were quite low. West Indians, the group in the greatest danger of being negatively racially stereotyped, show real gains over their parents and their native born peers on a number of fronts.

All the second generation groups earn as much or more than the comparable native born group. Controlling for age and gender, Dominicans and South Americans earn more than Puerto Ricans, West Indians earn more than native blacks, and the Russians and Chinese are on par with native whites. In terms of educational attainment, whether or not one controls for age, gender, and parental education, Dominicans and South Americans are doing better than Puerto Ricans, West Indians are doing better than African Americans, Russian Jews are doing better than native whites, and the Chinese are doing better than everyone. While less likely to be working full time than their staggeringly work-oriented immigrant parents, the Chinese and the Russian Jews are either working or going to school full time in slightly higher numbers than native whites (mainly because more are still attending school); the levels of the other second generation groups exceed those of African Americans and Puerto Ricans and, except for the Dominicans, are approaching the rates of native whites. While there are significant differences among the second generation groups in how many get involved in criminal activities, arrest rates are about the same as those of native whites even in those groups whose members are most likely to have had brushes with the law. Moreover, these arrest rates are well below those of native born minority counterparts.

Many respondents of African descent report experiencing racial discrimination, particularly from the police. The experience has clearly left many individuals feeling uncomfortable with their status as "Americans" and alienated them from some aspects of American life. Yet, the second generation group most identified as "black" and most likely to experience such discrimination—West Indians—is also the group most likely to participate in neighborhood and civic affairs and to be interested in New York politics. West Indians vote in numbers comparable to native whites, if somewhat below the very high proportion of native African Americans.

This rapid incorporation into American life does not stem from the second generation's maintaining social or cultural ties with the parents' immigrant communities. The group experiencing the most dramatic upward mobility—the Chinese—is actually the *least* likely to retain the parents' language. Members of every second generation group who work in predominantly ethnic work sites earn less than those who work in mainstream settings. At the same time, today's second generation does not seem overly concerned about shedding those ties or losing ethnic distinctiveness.

Like the 23-year-old Colombian-American young woman quoted earlier, members of the second generation are happy to acculturate "selectively," to use Portes and Rumbaut's (2001) phrase, taking what works the best in their parents' communities and combining it with the best of what they see around them among their native peers. Many respondents cheerfully report that they do not feel fully a part of their parents' immigrant communities nor do they see themselves as fully "American"—a term they use to describe the native whites whom they know primarily through television. Compared to past second generations, the children of immigrants today seem remarkably at ease about living between different worlds. They rarely see their parents' foreignness as posing a serious problem.

This level of second generation incorporation is particularly striking when compared to that of their counterparts in Western Europe. The 2005 riots in France brought worldwide attention to the problems of youth and young adults whose parents are immigrants and who have faced limited socioeconomic mobility. Many of the rioters in Paris live in the suburbs with staggeringly high youth unemployment rates. These unemployed, underemployed, and alienated youth evidently engaged in criminal behavior as a challenge to a racist society that they believe permanently relegates them to an urban underclass. As such, they became symbols of the possible second generation decline throughout Western Europe. For all of the city's problems, New York's relatively open economy, its overtly ethnic and pro-immigrant politics, and the myriad of its educational "second chances" have served the second generation fairly well—far better than they have served our native minority populations.

Despite the city's achievements, how the children of immigrants in and around New York City are incorporated into society remains problematic. Many young people have received substandard educations in the city's worst public schools. Although many of the second generation are working, their jobs often hold limited possibilities for advancement in an economy of stagnant or declining real wages. All too few individuals have found their way through educational routes into the highest-paying professions in the city. On the other hand, these problems are not unique to the children of immigrants but generally face all young working class New York City but face all young working class New Yorkers and are less severe for the children of immigrants than for members of native minority groups.

We should note that the differences among the "centers of gravity" of second generation groups are as large as the overall difference between them and the native born minority groups. The variation within each of the groups is large as well. In the sense that different groups are being incorporated into different parts of American society, their assimilation has indeed been segmented. But this segmentation has not always produced the results predicted by earlier scholarship. Moreover, incorporation turns out to work differently in different spheres of social life. The groups who have done best in the mainstream economy show low levels of civic engagement and political participation, for example. Neither the straight line assimilation model nor the segmented assimilation alternative easily captures the complex ways in which groups have combined economic, political, and cultural incorporation.

Why Are Our Results Different?

Many scholars have speculated that the larger patterns of racial inequality and discrimination in America will force those children of immigrants who are not classified as white into the ranks of persistently poor native minorities. Gans (1992), for example, worried that labeling dark-skinned children of immigrants as black would trump their aspirations for upward mobility. Mary Waters's (1999) ethnography of Afro-Caribbeans in New York City gave support for that position.

The notion that racial and other forms of inequality in host societies will create socioeconomic exclusion for large portions of the second generation has motivated an intense debate in the United States and Europe (Perlmann and Waldinger 1997; Waldinger and Perlmann 1998; Alba and Nee 2003; Smith 2003; Waldinger and Feliciano 2004; Perlmann 2005; Rumbaut 2005a, 2005).

The segmented assimilation hypothesis posits three alternative paths for the second generation: upward assimilation, downward assimilation, and upward assimilation combined with biculturalism. These paths correspond to three types of relationships among the children of immigrants, their parents, and the wider ethnic community. Consonant acculturation occurs when the children and the parents both gradually learn American culture and abandon their home language and culture at about the same pace. As children enter the mainstream, they not only achieve upward mobility, but they do so with the support of their parents. This path is most open to those who are most similar to, or most likely to be accepted by, the white majority.

Dissonant acculturation occurs when children learn English faster and accept American ways more readily than do their parents, who are more likely to cling to immigrant identities. Portes and Rumbaut argue that this process often leads to downward assimilation, as young people face racial discrimination, bifurcated labor markets, and an often nihilistic inner city youth subculture on their own, without strong parental authority and resources and with few community resources and supports. This path is most open to those who are most similar to, or most likely to be classified alongside, native minority groups, especially African Americans.

The third process, selective acculturation, leads to economic upward mobility alongside continued attachment to home country cultures and biculturalism. Selective acculturation (Portes and Rumbaut 2001:52) occurs when "parents and children learn English and American customs at the same rate, where parents and children are inserted into the ethnic community. It is characterized by preservation of parental authority, little or no intergenerational conflict, and fluent bilingualism among children." As such, it forms the "strongest bulwark against effects of external discrimination" (Portes and Rumbaut 2001:54).

Segmented assimilation also takes into account background factors such as parental human capital (including parents' education and income), modes of incorporation (state definitions of immigrant groups, eligibility for welfare, and the degree of social prejudice or discrimination facing immigrant groups in the receiving society), and family structure (single versus married couple families as well as multigenerational versus nuclear family living arrangements). The model points (we believe correctly) to the varying degrees of transnational connection among immigrant groups as an important element of the context of reception.

The most striking innovation in this model lies in two of its predictions. The first is that downward assimilation does *not* occur because the children of immigrants fail to Americanize. It occurs, rather, because they do so too quickly, relative to their parents, or assimilate into the "wrong" segments of American society. The second is that those children whose immigrant parents do not have particularly high educations or incomes can achieve upward mobility through a strategy of selective acculturation—staying at least partially ethnic and embedded in ethnic communities. In making these two predictions, the segmented assimilation model stands the standard assimilation model on its head. For at least some immigrants, the argument goes, coming quickly and easily to share American (or at least lower class American) ways is bad for the second generation. Holding on to immigrant distinctiveness can be an advantage.

This model has proven extraordinarily useful in focusing our attention on how differences in parental human capital, contexts of reception, and ethnic community structure influence second generation outcomes and how the highly segmented nature of American society presents native and immigrant racial and ethnic groups with very different life chances and opportunity structures (Portes, Fernández-Kelly, and Haller 2005:1004):

> If it is true that most descendants of today's immigrants will eventually assimilate to American society, it still makes a great deal of difference whether they do so by ascending into the ranks of a prosperous middle class or join in large numbers the ranks of a racialized, permanently impoverished population at the bottom of society.

Few of our respondents followed either of the two most theoretically innovative predictions of the model. Few experienced downward assimilation resulting from overly rapid Americanization, and few also experienced upward mobility by maintaining their place in an ethnic enclave. Indeed, any sort of second generation downward mobility relative to their immigrant parents is rare. When downward mobility does occur, it is not correlated with rapid differential loss of the parents' ethnic language or culture. (We find no correlation between the ability to understand or speak an ethnic language and educational attainment among our second generation respondents from non-English-speaking backgrounds.) To the contrary, upward mobility is associated with the use of English, employment outside of an ethnic enclave, and learning American ways faster than one's parents. Indeed, joining the mainstream is the most common route to success in this study (Alba and Nee 2003).

Our most successful second generation group, the Chinese, is the least likely to retain the parental language. The Chinese are also among the least likely to participate in ethnic organizations and the most likely to use the public schools. While a minority among the Chinese participates in religious activities, they are generally not connecting to their parents' ethnic ways but often become more religious than their parents in ways that can be a source of tension with them (Chai-Kim 2004). Although the dense social networks of New York's Chinese immigrant community have helped the second generation, this relationship has little to do with maintaining home country traditions or smooth relations with parents. Chinese respondents actually often report difficult, strained, and sometimes unhappy relationships with their parents, despite the fact (or perhaps *because* of the fact) that they tend to live with parents longer than do members of other groups. Finally, whereas first generation Chinese New Yorkers have gone the farthest in establishing a thriving economic ethnic enclave (Zhou 1992), the upwardly mobile majority of the second generation avoids it. Only a downwardly mobile minority of the Chinese second generation has resorted to enclave employment, with its poor wages and working conditions. Enclave employment may well be preferable to unemployment, but it is a safety net, not a springboard.

Why has the experience of New York's second generation not accorded with the predictions of the segmented assimilation model? Our data offer several possible answers. First, members of the second generation have found a way around the "hourglass" model of the U.S. labor market presented by the segmented assimilation model. As Portes, Fernández-Kelly, and Haller (2005:1005) put it:

> The promise of American society, which makes so many foreigners come, lies in the access it provides to well remunerated professional and entrepreneurial careers and the affluent lifestyles associated with them. At the same time, it is obvious that not everyone gains access to those positions and that, at the opposite end of society, there is a very unenviable scenario of youth gangs, drug dictated lifestyles, premature childbearing, imprisonment and early death. Immigrant families navigate between these opposite extremes seeking to steer their youths in the direction of the true mainstream.

Most of the second generation young people with whom we spoke are not affluent professionals, but neither are they perennially unemployed nor part of a "permanently impoverished" underclass. Instead, they are working members of the lower middle class service economy, employed as white collar clerical or service workers in retail or financial services. Their labor market position resembles that of other New Yorkers their age more than it does that of their parents. They rarely drop out of the labor force or become criminals. Most have achieved real, if modest, progress over their parents' generation. They have more education, earn more money, and work in more "mainstream" occupations and sectors.

Second, the studies developing the segmented assimilation model have rarely paid much attention to *native* youth culture beyond documenting the understandable contempt in which immigrant parents hold it. Without including native born comparison groups, however, it is often hard to sort out what aspects of young people's behavior stem from having immigrant parents and what simply reflect being a young person in urban America today. The model posits downward assimilation for those children of immigrants who adopt an "adversarial stance" or "reactive ethnicity" as a result of the experience of prejudice and discrimination. It argues that the emergence of reactive ethnicity reflects the "value contagion" of attending school with members of native minority groups and lacking family and community resources for dealing with ethnic and racial discrimination. Portes and Rumbaut (2001:61) underscore the conflict between parental values of hard work and upward mobility and inner city subcultures:

> Because of their poverty, many immigrants settle in close proximity to urban ghetto areas In this environment, they and their families are often exposed to norms of behavior inimical to upward mobility as well as to an adversarial stance that justifies these behaviors. For second generation youths, the clash of expectations is particularly poignant when the messages that education does not pay and that discrimination prevents people of color from ever succeeding are conveyed by native peers of the same race or ethnic origin.

Without a native comparison group, however, it is easy to confuse the style with the substance of such an "oppositional" identity, as a quick look at the baggy pants and backward baseball caps worn by students on any Ivy League campus will attest. It is worth noting that the features of "ghetto culture" that most alarm these scholars (and immigrant parents!) actually resemble the broader youth culture in America, albeit in a form made more intense by poverty. There is nothing particularly "ghetto" about drug use, materialism, nihilism, and anti-intellectualism. With slight differences in style, these traits are as easy to see in any suburban mall as on inner city street corners.

Drawing on our native white comparison group, we can see that native white males are just as likely to engage in rebellious behaviors as the second generation groups. A comparison of arrest rates among the males in our survey shows that 23 percent of native born white males report having been arrested, compared with 24 percent of West Indian males, 22 percent of Dominican males, and 20 percent of South American males. White males who grew up in New York City get in trouble at even higher rates. Only native born blacks and Puerto Ricans have higher arrest rates than native born whites.

What differs between the native whites and the second generation groups is not the adversarial behaviors but how the larger society reacts to them. Whites who take drugs or get in trouble with the law often have more family resources and face a more lenient criminal justice system (Sullivan 1989). Second generation respondents often face harsher penalties and have fewer resources to deal with the repercussions of the same youthful indiscretions, although a well-networked ethnic group can sometimes provide support for its most troubled young members. Still, second generation youth are less likely to find themselves permanently derailed by youthful missteps than are the Puerto Ricans and native blacks who have fewer economic and family resources and even less societal good will to draw upon when they get into trouble. Indeed, whereas "social capital" helps better-off groups cope with many types of trouble, being heavily "embedded" in networks of reciprocal obligation among the worst off can be a real disadvantage. In such groups, many of the most successful members describe themselves as "loners."

Most standard accounts of second generation incorporation also present a one-dimensional view of how people experience and respond to racial domination. As we argued in Chapter 10, prejudice and discrimination can mean very different phenomena. Discrimination in impersonal sites where the only thing known about a person is his or her race leads to the development of strong feelings of exclusion and reactive ethnicity. This is especially true when the discrimination comes from the police. But this discrimination has implications very different than discrimination that occurs in institutional settings where an individual can signal other nonracial characteristics to would-be discriminators. A young dark-skinned man stopped by the police while walking on the street may reasonably conclude that the officers are responding to his skin color. The same can be said about a dark-skinned young woman who is followed in a store while she looks at clothing. Both individuals get the message that their skin color signals criminal behavior to authority figures. Obviously, they have little individual control in these situations. In this context their race is a "master status," sociologist Robert Merton's (1967) term for a characteristic that trumps all other personal characteristics.

A college student who questions whether his professor has low expectations of him or a young associate in a law firm who wonders if it will treat black or Hispanic associates as well as whites, however, can draw on a wider repertoire of coping skills. Our respondents often told about such situations in which they felt they had indeed experienced racial prejudice and discrimination. Yet instead of just getting angry and discouraged, they learned to develop strategies to overcome such discrimination. The most common strategy was to try to outperform others to disprove negative racial or ethnic stereotypes, something they had within their power to at least try to do. We found that Chinese and light-skinned Hispanics are most likely to report this kind of discrimination. By contrast, people with dark skin who can be coded as black in American racial terms are most likely to experience the more virulent impersonal discrimination from authority figures in anonymous public spaces, an experience that individuals have little real power to overcome (Anderson 1990). Many people experience discrimination, but what it means to them, and how they react to it, depends on social sphere and context.

Finally, previous accounts of second generation incorporation often overlook the possibility that identifying with African Americans or adopting African American–inspired models of racial difference and racial politics can have benefits as well as costs. The claim that the second generation may experience downward assimilation when mainstream American society categorizes them as nonwhite underestimates the extent to which the civil rights movement has changed the meaning of race since the 1960s. However partial its victories or unfulfilled its promise, that movement did delegitimate de jure segregation and overt white supremacy. It also created a repertoire of ideas, institutions, and organizational forms for challenging racial subordination. Affirmative action and other programs designed to promote upward mobility among members of native minority groups are now available to the children of nonwhite immigrants. The emergence of Ethnic Studies programs on American university campuses and the use of blanket categories like "black" or "Hispanic" to enforce the Voting Rights Act and other civil rights era legislation mean that immigrants and their children have access to institutions facilitating social mobility precisely *because* they are considered nonwhite. Assimilating into "black America" or "Latino America" thus does not have universally negative consequences for the contemporary second generation.

Explaining Second Generation Progress

If previous models do not explain the experience of today's second generation New Yorkers, what does? We conclude by answering this question and speculating about what contemporary patterns of second generation integration mean for American public policy and society.

New York City can be tough on any young person, regardless of where his or her parents were born. The children of immigrants face extra difficulties. Only a third of New York City's 3 million households are families with related children under 18. In other words, two-thirds of the households are not currently facing the burdens of rearing children. Among families with children, immigrant parents are much less likely to speak English at home (only 19 percent compared with 60 percent of native parents), and they may not even understand English at all (about a quarter of immigrant parents as compared with only 4 percent of the native parents). Moreover, only half of immigrant parents in New York families are citizens, which gives them far less political influence than native parents.

Most crucially, immigrant parents are less likely to be well educated than native parents: a third lack a high school degree compared with one-fifth of native parents, and only a fifth have college degrees, compared with a quarter of the native parents. As a consequence, they have less income. Immigrant parents had a mean household income of $54,404 in 1999, compared with $73,983 for the native parents. Thus young people growing up in immigrant families have parents with less English facility, less education, less political clout, and less income than those growing up in native families. It would be surprising if these factors did not constitute barriers to progress.

Yet we find that the second generation is generally doing better than natives of comparable racial backgrounds despite these barriers. Why is this so?

The first reason is an obvious factor that is nevertheless consistently overlooked in comparisons between immigrants and natives. Immigrants are a highly selected group. Even when they have relatively modest educations and few financial resources, they have shown that they have the drive, ambition, courage, and strength to move from one nation to another. Their second generation offspring are, therefore, the children of exceptional parents. Although parents may have measurable characteristics that put their children at risk—low education, low incomes, poor language skills, and so on—they have unmeasured characteristics that make them different kinds of parents, mostly in ways that are advantageous for their children.

At first glance a Dominican father who does not speak English and has only a second grade education may appear to have characteristics similar to those of the least well-off New York–born Puerto Rican father, and even fewer resources. Yet as an immigrant parent he has other qualities that separate him from most uneducated Dominican men who stayed at home on the island, qualities that contributed to his success in migrating to New York. His lack of education may not have a negative effect on his ability to instill a desire for education in his son or daughter. So too, a poorly educated Chinese waiter in New York City is quite different from the many comparable men in China who did not make the journey to New York, for he has overcome extraordinary obstacles to change his lot in life. That drive to better his situation is something he is likely to transmit to his children. Thus, when comparing children of natives to the children of immigrants, it is important to remember that while the second generation is not technically a "selected" population, the parents who raised them surely were.

Second, many members of the second generation are well positioned to take advantage of civil rights era institutions and policies for promoting diversity. Indeed, the very presence of many members of the second generation in this country was in large part the result of one important piece of civil rights legislation, the 1965 Hart Celler immigration reforms, which ended national origin quotas in U.S. immigration policy. As the children of parents who come from societies where they typically formed the racial majority, the second generation is far less encumbered by the residue of past discriminatory practices.

Although covert racist practices and assumptions obviously do affect the lives of the second generation today—for example, when the second, third or fourth generation Asian American professional is complimented on his command of English or asked when she is "going home"—we showed in Chapter 10 that such practices and assumptions are less pernicious and less pervasive for many second generation youth than for native minorities whose caste-like subordination has been central to the formation of American identity. Many second generation respondents believed that they had benefitted by being characterized as nonwhite and thus recruited to universities and jobs in order to increase diversity in these institutions. Although nonwhite second generation young adults must cope with racial discrimination, they also profit from a post–civil rights world in which they are able to inherit some of the positive as well as the negative results of America's long, troubled history of race relations.

Finally, the children of immigrants are in a good position to develop their own creative strategies for living their lives. Children of immigrants are often described as being "torn between two worlds" (Child 1943). Social scientists and immigrant parents alike often worry that in navigating between two cultural systems and two languages, their children may never be completely competent in either. It is often feared that growing up in a world where parents who have come of age in a different culture have a hard time guiding their children into adulthood can lead to confusion, alienation, and reversal of authority roles within the family. In the early twentieth century, many children of European immigrants coped with this challenge by rejecting their parents' embarrassing "foreign ways" and trying to become "American." Although our respondents occasionally felt that their parents' cultures were at odds with the American worldview, they rarely saw this as a real problem. Perhaps because of today's ethos of multiculturalism, most of our respondents believe they can choose which aspects of a given cultural model to adopt.

Traditional, straight line assimilation theory implies that the children of immigrants, torn between two worlds, will do best when they assimilate. Doing this may have emotional and psychic costs, but in the end the children of immigrants will come to share the "native advantages" over their immigrant parents (Warner and Srole 1945). Alba and Nee's (2003) contemporary reworking of this notion greatly improved the model by excising its prescriptive aspects, emphasizing that assimilation does not preclude retaining elements of ethnic culture and stressing how assimilation also remakes U.S. culture. Yet they too see the second generation as sharing advantages that come from joining the increasingly multicultural mainstream. By contrast, segmented assimilation theory posits that resisting Americanization can be helpful for the second generation. This theory argues that members of the second generation who assimilate into disadvantaged segments of the native population will suffer, whereas those who partially keep assimilation at bay can continue to share the "immigrant advantages" of relatively better-positioned immigrant communities.

Clearly, today's second generation provides examples of all these paths. However, our study also underscores the importance of a distinct second generation advantage: its location between two different social systems allows for creative and selective combinations of the two that can be highly conducive to success. In developing a strategy for navigating challenges, second generation youngsters do not have to choose whether being foreign or being American is "better." They can draw on both cultures. Members of the groups we have studied clearly have different options depending on their parents' position and their own position in a segmented social structure. Sometimes none of the available choices are particularly conducive to upward mobility. Other things being equal, however, seeing choices where others see constraints is in itself a significant advantage. Further, whereas puritans of various stripes are generally more comfortable with the coherence of traditional cultural systems, New York, more than most places, has historically honored hybridity and rewarded innovation.

In the mid-twentieth century, New York became one of the world's greatest centers of cultural creativity. While American economic ascendancy helped, it is probably not coincidental that the previous second generation came of age in this intensely creative period in American music, art, letters, theater, and criticism. Immigrants and their children played a cultural role far out of proportion to their numbers (Hirschman 2005), and New York, where so much of the second generation was concentrated, became a hothouse for intellectual "scenes" and cultural movements, both mainstream and avant garde. New York gave the children of immigrants the cosmopolitan space in which to make these innovations. And despite the nativists' worries that New York was becoming a place apart, the second generation repaid America with a new, broader, and, we think, better vision of itself. It was Irving Berlin, a 1.5 generation New Yorker, who penned "God Bless America" (a Russian Jew, he also wrote "I'm Dreaming of a White Christmas").

It is too early to say whether New York is experiencing something like this today. The second generation is still young, the world is a different place, and history never quite repeats itself. Yet social scientists may have exaggerated the differences between past experiences of immigrant incorporation and those of the present. The creative mixing of immigrant and native minority cultures already clearly evident in the music, art, dance, and poetry being produced in hyperdiverse cities like New York and Los Angeles is in many ways reminiscent of the best of New York's past. Here we see the second generation advantage most clearly. The greatest spur to creativity in multicultural cities is neither the continuation of immigrant traditions nor the headlong rush to become similar to the host society, but the innovation that occurs when different traditions come together, where no one way of doing things can be taken for granted. For all their problems, the increasingly diverse working class neighborhoods of New York exhibit an undeniable innovative energy.

This creativity is evident in the everyday decisions and behaviors of young people who are growing up with a dual frame of reference. These young people can be, and perhaps must be, creative in their reactions to their environments. For many situations, second generation members cannot blindly repeat the received wisdom of their parents, which is best suited to a different society. More than most of us, members of the second generation know that their parents' ways cannot always be their ways. Nor can they unreflectively take up an American culture they are only beginning to understand. Instead, they must choose among the ways of their parents, of broader American society, and of their native minority peers or, perhaps, create something altogether new and different.

We often attribute drive and creativity to the self-selection of immigrants or to ethnicity itself, but the real second generation advantage comes from being located between two cultures. The creativity inherent in occupying a position at the crossroads of two groups has been widely recognized in a variety of situations, but we believe it has been insufficiently recognized with respect to the second generation. Sociologist Ron Burt describes the situation of being between two social networks as being in a "structural hole." He notes that

> opinion and behavior are more homogeneous within than between groups, so people connected across groups are more familiar with alternative ways of thinking and behaving which give them more options to select from and synthesize. New ideas emerge from selection and synthesis across the structural holes between groups. (Burt 2004:349–350)

This insight is not new. At the beginning of the last century Georg Simmel (1922) recorded it in his classic discussion of conflicting group affiliations and the role of the stranger. Burt (2004:350) goes back even further, quoting John Stuart Mill:

> It is hardly possible to overrate the value . . . of placing human beings in contact with persons dissimilar to themselves, and with modes of thought and action unlike those with which they are familiar . . . Such communication has always been, and is particularly in the present age, one of the primary sources of progress.

Yet, if anything, this has become more true for today's second genera-tion than it was for the children of immigrants in the past. The ethos of multiculturalism and the reality of globalization and the unprecedented diversity that characterizes cities like New York multiply the second gener-ation advantage. The contemporary second generation does not feel undue pressure to reject the languages, beliefs, and behaviors of its immi-grant forebears. Nor do its members feel the need to cling to them to keep the dangers of assimilation at bay. They are individuals who grew up in a world in which being different can be "cool," and they insist that they are free to assert certain aspects of their parents' ways and to reject others—thus allowing this cultural creativity to flower.

Consider an example of how this can work. When we asked about the age at which young people were expected to leave home, there was wide-spread agreement among native white, native black, and Puerto Rican re-spondents that living with your parents after age 21 was difficult at best, and definitely not conducive to "being an adult." By contrast, most of our second generation respondents in every group grew up with a different norm transmitted to them by their parents and their ethnic group—that living with parents and other extended family members until marriage and maybe even after was normal and did not have to be fraught with conflict and angst. In many cases living in the parental home was a sign of respon-sibility and maturity and thus completely compatible with being an adult. As one 24-year-old Russian Jewish woman notes:

> In our culture. It's like, it's not like our thing. It's not like you're eighteen and you move out. American people do it different. So it's not like such a burden. And it's not weird that I'm twenty-four and I'm living at home or anything like that. If I wanted to, I could move out, but it's fine. I have a good relationship with my mother, I like being here with her, knowing her and my brother also. We have our independent lives, but it's nice to come home at night sometimes with them, and I get enough alone time here.

On the other hand, our native born respondents also grew up with an expectation that men and women would receive the same amount of edu-cation and that there was no reason that women should not expect to get as much education as men. Many of our Hispanic and Chinese respon-dents received messages from their parents that girls did not need as much education as boys.

These two sets of ideas, the first about the timing of establishing one's own household and the second about the length of education, interact with the structure of the New York City housing market, one of the most expensive in the world. While many native white families had the financial resources to help their children attain independent living or owned homes that they could give to their offspring when they retired, the black and Puerto Rican families had far less ability to support their children in their desire to live independently. Regardless of race, however, most of our native respondents expected that they should strike out on their own and have their own apartments, if not by age 18, then certainly by their early twenties. They struggled to do so and often felt like failures when they could not. The second generation respondents, by contrast, often continued to live with their parents until they felt able to afford to live on their own. This allowed many second generation women to continue their schooling, even if they had children, because their parents could help with child care or because they did not have to work full time to support high rents.

Thus a second generation young woman is able to combine the norm of education and career ambitions that pushes her toward college and the norm of multigenerational living that allows her to live at home while she attains that goal. Most CUNY schools and other low cost New York colleges have no dormitories; those that do charge far more for them than the cost of living "at home." (Once again, this is not so different than in times past. In the "glory days" of the City College in the 1930s, its mostly second generation student body lived at home with immigrant parents. A generation later, how many of their thoroughly Americanized children would have done the same?)

A young second generation woman may not be aware that she is choosing to maintain one norm and shed another. These are simply norms that fit with the realities of a labor market that rewards education, a primary education system that has equal expectations of men and women, and a housing market that makes it hard for a young single woman attending college to find an apartment. Her ability to combine an American norm about education with an immigrant norm about living with parents nevertheless means that she is better off than her native minority neighbor who cannot conceive of living with her parents at age 25, even though she would like to finish college. It also makes her better off than her first generation counterpart who has just arrived at age 18 believing that her brother should finish college but that she can be successful if she can just get a high school degree and a job. The creativity of this second generation comes from its members' ability to meet structural environment needs with a wider repertoire of options about beliefs and behaviors than is available to people who have grown up in the same society as their parents and who consequently have only a single frame of reference.

Being located between two or more cultural systems can, of course, sometimes have negative consequences. The Dominican American student attending Fordham whom we quoted in Chapter 7 about the inadequacy of the guidance Dominican parents gave their children in sexual matters and the problems this had caused her peers presents a good example. Of course, the extent of the advantage derived from combining two sets of norms does depend on which immigrant norms the second generation person draws upon and which segment of U.S. society the person is being incorporated into. We are not suggesting that the positive side of being between cultural systems always outweighs the limitations and constraints faced by the most disadvantaged of the second generation. This second generation advantage is but one factor among many shaping young people's lives today. Most of the time, however, we suspect it is on the positive side of the balance sheet, and that too often previous observers have ignored its impact or have been too quick to see combining two sets of norms as negative.

The creativity that comes from being between cultural systems was clearly evident among earlier generations of European immigrants as well. Yet even while they remade America on their own "ethnic" terms, they often did so in the face of very real pressures to assimilate that left them profoundly aware of their outsider status and embarrassed, or at least ambivalent, about their parents' "foreign" ways (see Hansen 1938; Gordon 1964). In part because of their successful integration into U.S. society, and in part because of changes in American attitudes about difference in the wake of the civil rights movement, today's second generation members live in an America in which the pressures for cultural conformity have lessened substantially. Far from being embarrassed, many of our informants felt proud of the ways in which they bridged two worlds in what Monica Boyd and Elizabeth Grieco have called their "triumphant transitions" (1998). We saw this in the pride with which young people described using their ability to translate to help their parents or other people with limited English, in the easy ways in which young people described their multiethnic friendship networks, and in the extensive use of ethnic music and media, especially among the Spanish speakers. Indeed, our respondents were more likely to be embarrassed that they had too rapidly assimilated into American society—a number described how bad they felt about losing their parents' language. This reflects the stronger appreciation of diversity in America in general as well as the particularly cosmopolitan ethos of New York.

In New York City the second generation inherits an environment where the second generation advantages work to particularly good effect. While these young people feel the sting of disadvantage and discrimination, they move in a world where being from somewhere else has long been the norm. For them being a New Yorker means being both ethnic and American, being different both from native whites and from their immigrant parents. In this feeling they are reaping the benefits of New York's long history of absorbing new immigrants. As Glazer and Moynihan put it in *Beyond the Melting Pot* (1963/1970:xiii):

> New York is not Chicago, Detroit or Los Angeles. It is a city in which the dominant racial group has been marked by ethnic variety and all ethnic groups have experienced ethnic diversity. Any one ethnic group can count on seeing its position and power wax and wane and none has become accustomed to long term domination, though each may be influential in a given area or domain. None can find challenges from new groups unexpected or outrageous . . . The evolving system of inter-group relations permits accommodation, change and the rise of new groups.

This situation has persisted despite the nonwhite origins of most new immigrant groups. No doubt New York City still has an entrenched white establishment that can trace its roots in the United States back many generations. But the new second generation rarely encounters such people on the job, in the unions, or around the neighborhoods, schools, and subways of New York. Instead, the children of immigrants see a continuum of "whites" who trace their origins to Italy, Ireland, Germany, Russia, Poland, Greece, or Israel. If Italians are yesterday's newcomers and today's establishment, then perhaps Colombians are the new Italians and, potentially, tomorrow's establishment. New Yorkers, old and new, are happy to tell themselves this story. It may not be completely true. But the fact they tell it, and believe it, is significant and may serve to help make it come true.

Why Do Some Groups Do Better Than Others?

Why do some of our groups do so much better than others? Members of the second generation, as we outlined, are creative partly because of the variety of strategies they have available for how to be in the world. A logical extension of this is that different groups have different strategies or concepts that they have brought with them, and as we have tried to make clear throughout the book, these groups face different structural realities once they get to the Unites States.

As argued earlier, the groups differ in terms of parental human capital, reasons for migration, and the contexts of reception they encounter. Thus, the relative success of the Russian Jewish second generation respondents is not unexpected—their parents had high levels of education, they came as refugees, and while they were getting established and retrained in the United States, a large percentage of the families took advantage of welfare, food stamps, and other government programs. Indeed, in contrast to native minority groups, it is striking how little stigma was attached to the Russians' use of widespread public assistance, either within the group or from other New Yorkers. As Jews, the Russian immigrants were also given special attention and aid from established Jewish organizations that helped them with everything from housing to job referrals and English-language lessons. As whites the Russians found housing in better neighborhoods with less crime, better schools, and better stores and services. It is no surprise, then, that their children have done well.

Obvious factors do less to explain the success of our Chinese respondents. Twenty-two percent of our Chinese respondents are from families with highly educated parents, and one would expect these respondents to do well. But 67 percent of our Chinese parents have very low levels of education. Unlike the Russians, few entered the country as refugees, and thus they did not initially qualify for welfare or other government programs. In addition, the Chinese sometimes faced racial and ethnic discrimination in schools and the labor market. But the Chinese in our study are doing exceptionally well, better, by most measures, than groups in which parental education is, on average, considerably higher.

Explaining the relative success of the Chinese suggests that what we might call "family strategies for the accumulation and intergenerational transfer of capital" may be more important than race or parents' nativity. The most successful children come from groups that are more likely to have two parents and even other adult wage earners and caretakers in the household supporting relatively few children. The Chinese have a high ratio of working adults to children in the household. While it is true that Chinese parents relentlessly expect their children to perform well in schools, they also provide the means for them to do so in the form of higher *household* incomes (even when individual incomes are modest), living in neighborhoods with better schools, keeping their children out of the labor force while they pursue higher education, and navigating the bureaucratic pathways toward the best schools in the New York City public school system. It is worth noting that unlike native whites or better-off African Americans, the Chinese rarely turn to private schools as an alternative, although they do spend money on supplemental educational and exam preparation, often in weekend "Chinese schools."

The Chinese are able to provide the means for their children to do well because of several other important factors. First, while the group has low median parental education and income, the first generation is marked by a great diversity of class origins. Despite this class diversity, the group is very much a cohesive group, with a high degree of social connection between its better- and worse-off members. Perhaps because of language barriers, perhaps because of race, many Chinese professionals continue to inhabit the same social world as their poorer compatriots; whereas South American professionals—particularly if they are light skinned—often leave the community and become functionally white.

Social networks link middle and working class Chinese immigrants, and all the Chinese share ethnic newspapers, ethnic churches, and ethnic broadcast media. Guides to the New York City public school system published in the Chinese-language newspapers pass on information provided by the middle class immigrants who have used their own education and class-based cultural capital to figure out how the system works and how to navigate it. This knowledge is shared with working class immigrants. In this way the Chinese respondent who told us that her barely literate mother who worked in a garment factory but who "somehow" knew her daughter should go to Stuyvesant (the premier public high school in the city, accessible only by test) is a beneficiary of both the class heterogeneity and ethnic solidarity of the Chinese ethnic group.

As Burt (2004:351) defines it, "Social capital exists where people have an advantage because of their location in a social structure." Working class Chinese second generation youth acquire social capital because they are embedded in a social structure—the networks encompassing their immigrant parents—with educational and class diversity. This social capital is not available to Dominican youth, whose parents' community is homogeneously poor, nor to South American youth, whose group exhibits less ethnic solidarity.

At the same time, the context of reception by the wider society also shapes group experience. One reason the Chinese are able to take advantage of the islands of excellence in New York's public school system is that, despite their racial distinctiveness, they face little discrimination in the housing market. Chinese immigrants can move into white neighborhoods without causing rapid white out-migration. By contrast, West Indians or Dominicans, regardless of income, face much higher levels of discrimination in housing. They are less able to move into white neighborhoods in search of better schools or safer streets. When they do, "white flight" often leads to declines in school quality and public safety, much as it would if the newcomers were native African Americans or Puerto Ricans. Added to these advantages is the stereotype of the Chinese as successful students. One of the strongest findings in educational research is that high expectations from teachers have a positive effect on student outcomes (Rosenthal and Jacobsen 1968). Unlike Hispanic and black students, who often have to overcome low expectations, the Chinese enter schools that expect them to do well.

Finally, cultural factors are at play in the success of the Chinese. The pattern of obligations that keeps working class mothers and fathers from divorcing even when they are miserable together and that keeps young adults living at home and supporting their parents even when they do not communicate with them promotes socioeconomic mobility for the Chinese second generation. Second generation Chinese put off marriage and childbearing until they have finished school and established themselves in their careers. This does not necessarily make them happier than others their age—we interviewed a lot of lonely and bitter Chinese young adults. But it does facilitate academic and career success. While they may not always be having a good time, they are experiencing very high rates of upward social mobility.

The other groups we studied have different mixes of behaviors and beliefs and face different structures of barriers and opportunities. The Dominicans probably present the clearest cause for concern. With a comparatively high level of African ancestry, Dominicans face high levels of discrimination, both in public space and in the housing market. Unlike the parents of West Indians, few of their parents spoke English on arrival. They arrived in the United States with very low levels of education and continue to have low incomes. Their nearest "proximal host" population, Puerto Ricans, are also quite poor, and the neighborhoods they share have some of New York's worst schools.

It is not clear whether Dominicans, caught between remaining in one of the poorest immigrant communities and assimilating into the poorest of the native communities, enjoy much second generation advantage. Many have formed single-parent households, and the ratio of children to working adults in the household is low. By New York standards, many of the Dominican first generation arrived in the United States undocumented, and their high level of remittances to and investments in the Dominican Republic drains capital out of the community.

Nevertheless, despite these disadvantages, members of the Dominican second generation are in many respects doing at least marginally better than their Puerto Rican counterparts and even native born African Americans. They are much better educated than their parents, although less well educated than most other New Yorkers their age. Finally, those Dominicans who do achieve high levels of education show little evidence of disadvantage relative to native whites, something that is not true for the native minorities.

Immigration, Race, and Public Policy: Looking into the Future

While our story is cautiously optimistic, we must underscore several caveats. First, our study began at an auspicious time—from 1999 to early 2001. The labor market was tight, unemployment was low, and the financial services industry in New York was pumping money into the local economy. After decades of rising income inequality and stagnant median wages, the local and national economy experienced some good years at the end of the 1990s. Our young respondents reaped the benefits of that particular time and place, even though they generally held entry-level jobs without much security. Most of our respondents could find work, and most were optimistic about their own futures.

The collapse of the dot-com boom and the economic shock of the terrorist attack on the World Trade Center in September 2001 shook that confidence. When we reinterviewed many of our in-depth respondents in 2002 and 2003, some had lost their jobs and had not been able to replace them. Given that most of our respondents were working and lower middle class people with some college education and relatively low-paying jobs, severe economic downturns like the one in 2001–2003 could change stories of modest upward mobility and rosy outlooks into stories of stagnation, pessimism, and worry about the future.

We can also ask whether the social mobility and general optimism we found will carry over to the third and fourth generation or whether the grandchildren and great-grandchildren of the immigrants will experience a reversal of fortune, as seems to be true of the Puerto Ricans. Academics and policymakers have not paid nearly enough attention to Puerto Ricans in recent decades. Dwarfed by the arrival of new immigrant groups, Puerto Ricans have often disappeared statistically into the broader Hispanic category. Neither immigrants nor natives, they have a special political status that also allowed them to fall through the cracks. Even the rediscovery of urban poverty in the United States in the 1980s and 1990s has focused almost exclusively on African Americans, and the new immigration literature has left Puerto Ricans out of the picture entirely.

While "off stage," in New York, at least, the Puerto Ricans' situation has deteriorated. The poorest group in our sample, the Puerto Ricans show distressing evidence of persistent poverty and intergenerational socioeconomic decline. Perhaps this is because the special selectivity of immigrants does not apply to the third generation families our respondents grew up in. It is also possible that there is a reverse selectivity effect, with the more successful Puerto Ricans moving to other parts of the country or even out-marrying and losing their identity as Puerto Rican. Nonetheless, the New York–based sample we spoke with is doing poorly. Racial discrimination, poor urban schools, language issues, and dysfunctional families all play a part.

Another clear pattern in our findings is deeply troubling. Race and racial discrimination continue to shape the life chances of second generation respondents with dark skin, who can be confused or associated with, or who see themselves as becoming, African Americans. Although we find little evidence of second generation decline, the continuing disadvantages faced by native African Americans, the status of the New York–born Puerto Ricans, the poverty and incarceration of many second generation Dominicans, and the high levels of discrimination reported by even the relatively well-off West Indians clearly point to the possibility of third generation decline. Because race encapsulates a complex dynamic of scarce family resources, high obstacles to success, and a risky environment, it still counts very much in New York City. That many children of immigrant minority parents manage to avoid racism's worst impacts does not lessen the sting for those who cannot. There is a distinct possibility that some portion of Dominicans and West Indians experience marked downward mobility as they become less distinguishable from African Americans over time and as residual immigrant and second generation advantages fade into the third or fourth generation. West Indians, despite relatively high incomes and levels of education, are the most likely of our second generation groups to report experiencing discrimination from the police and in public places, where their interactions with whites seem little different from those of African Americans.

Several public policies can make a difference in continuing second generation integration and preventing third generation decline. The shameful inequality in the educational system has to be lessened. The New York City public schools vary so much in quality that it is difficult to imagine they are part of the same system. The variation begins at the very earliest grades, and the effects of attending a substandard school are compounded and reinforced year after year until it is too late to undo the damage by the time students enter high school. At the other end of the spectrum are students who enter some of the best elementary schools and can navigate the system. They end up in one of the magnet schools and achieve an education as good as any obtainable in private school. This inequality maps onto racial and income disparities and is inexcusable. In order to ensure continued positive integration of generations of immigrants, we must make good on America's promise of equality of opportunity.

Affirmative action in higher education, while intended primarily to address the long-standing grievances of native minority groups, especially African Americans, is in fact a policy that has worked well for the children of immigrants and should be supported. Hampered by racial discrimination, some substandard schools, and a lack of knowledge about the American educational system, yet ambitious and coming from families who invest a great deal in the success of the next generation, the children of nonwhite immigrants are perhaps best suited to a program designed to locate and help qualified but disadvantaged youth. Affirmative action and other programs that seek to facilitate the upward mobility of minority youth have, in fact, served us well in integrating the children of nonwhite immigrants. That this was not their original intention should not obscure this important success.

In addition, the government should continue to monitor and fight both overt and subtle racial discrimination in housing, jobs, and schools and by the police. Discrimination is a fact of life for dark-skinned young people, but how that discrimination feels is very different if they know that the law will protect them and that their society does not countenance such behavior.

We began this study worried about downward mobility of some of the children of immigrants. We now feel that it is, in some ways, the opposite problem that is actually a greater cause for concern. It has become clear that the relative success of the children of immigrants is now obscuring the depth of continuing poverty and discrimination, limited opportunities, staggering rates of incarceration, and the general social exclusion of large segments of the native minority youth population. When elite colleges point with pride to their increasing "diversity" and to the growing numbers of "blacks" and "Latinos" among their students and faculty, it is easy to overlook how much of that diversity is provided by the growing numbers of immigrants and their children, and how little by the descendants of American slaves or by long-present Puerto Ricans or Mexican Americans. When institutions like the CUNY colleges or New York's selective public magnet schools express concern over their declining "black" and "Latino" enrollments, it is easy to miss how much more dramatic those declines would be if it were not for the children of West Indian, Dominican, and South American immigrants.

Let us be clear. The increasing diversity of American institutions and of American society is a good thing. The reduction of racial barriers, initiated by the civil rights movement, however partial, has created a fairer and thus better society. In fact, the use of affirmative action and the active pursuit of diversity have facilitated the incorporation of the children of immigrants. However unintentionally, such policies and practices have helped members of the second generation find their place in American society. They are part of the reason the situation in New York and other American cities looks so different than that in Europe. Good for the immigrants and their children, this unintended incorporation policy has also been good for the United States. In an era of globalization, it has brought new and different skills, fresh talent, and extraordinary drive to an America that needs them now as much as ever. At the same time, such policies and practices have been less successful in addressing the problems of the very populations they were originally designed for, and whose struggles for justice brought them about in the first place. This is a fact that must be faced squarely. When, out of ignorance or misguided notions of solidarity, politicians and social scientists lump native and immigrant minorities together under rubrics such as "Hispanic," or worse, "people of color," they make such issues more difficult to talk about, much less address.

Further, for the children of non-black, nonwhite immigrants it is important to remember that race is mutable and that the color line may be moving. The central cleavage in American life was once clearly between whites and nonwhites. Today there is mounting evidence that it is between blacks and non-blacks. This has tremendous salience for much of the second generation. The changing position of Asian Americans—once as racially excluded as anyone—on most indicators of acculturation and assimilation in the last two decades should remind us that there is nothing permanent about what we call race. Perhaps the ties of language will, in the next century, make of the children of Colombians, Ecuadorans, Cubans, and Mexicans (along with the grandchildren of Puerto Ricans and the great-grandchildren and great-great-grandchildren of southwestern "Hispanos") a single "Latino" race. But this is hardly the only possible outcome, or even the most likely one, given the consistent finding that many of the second generation children of Latino immigrants prefer to use English anyway.

Finally, we must remember that incorporation is a two-way street. The second generation has been successful partly because New York, compared to many other places, has put few barriers in their way. In this regard it is important to remember that the number of undocumented immigrants among our 1.5 generation respondents was relatively low. Indeed, most of our respondents' parents entered the country legally; and of those who did not enter legally, most eventually managed to regularize their status. Few of our respondents reported that their own legal status or that of their parents had posed a major problem as they were growing up in the 1980s and 1990s. This finding presents a sharp contrast to cities in which more of the immigrant population is undocumented. It is also a contrast to the situation of the children of today's newest immigrants, since even in New York the proportion of undocumented immigrants has risen and legalization has become more difficult. While efforts to "get tough" on undocumented immigrants and plug the various loopholes used to legalize an immigrant's status have been singularly unsuccessful in keeping undocumented immigrants out of the country, they do keep immigrants undocumented longer. As a result many immigrants are now permanently locked out of meaningful participation in American civic life. Whatever one thinks of the situation that created today's large undocumented population, one can easily see how much the presence of such a large, permanent population who are part of our nation economically, socially, and culturally, but not politically, ill serves a democratic society. The situation is bad for the immigrants, bad for America, and particularly bad for the immigrants' American children. This, far more than downward assimilation, is where we feel the true danger of creating an underclass lies. If we are truly concerned about the integration of the children of immigrants into American society, policies that keep their parents undocumented can only be judged highly counterproductive.

The elements of the civic culture of New York and America that welcome and celebrate immigration and ethnic diversity should be maintained and reinforced. The history of America's treatment of immigrants has many shameful aspects—forced assimilation, forced repatriation, imprisonment in concentration camps, blatant prejudice, discrimination, violence, and exclusion. Through it all, however, America has also maintained an ideology of equality and openness to immigrants and a bedrock rule that anyone born in the United States is a citizen. We can see this ideology as a hypocritical story we have told ourselves, and sometimes it is. But it has also been a resource for the immigrants, for their children, and for members of native minority groups fighting for inclusion and fair treatment.

One need only look at the continued exclusion of the second and third generation of post–World War II immigrants in Western Europe to see how much worse the situation could have been. Every year for the last few decades some misguided lawmaker proposes to deny birthright citizenship to the children of undocumented migrants or even to the children of immigrants more generally. This would be a terrible mistake. Not only would it create a permanently excluded but permanently present class of noncitizens in our midst, it would send a terrible message to our newcomers.

America can be proud of its ideology of inclusion, and New York, on its best days, can be proud of the reality of inclusion it offers to the second generation. The hold that members of the second generation have on that promise of a better life may be precarious, but, combined with their youthful optimism, it leaves us hopeful about their future and about the future of the city that they inherit.

Methodological Appendix

Overall Approach

A pilot study to test the feasibility of surveying the second generation in New York began in July 1996 with funding from the Russell Sage Foundation. Any such survey faces the immediate challenge of deciding whether to sample a cross section of the whole second generation, which would include members of many groups for which we could not economically gather a statistically reliable subsample, or to sample specific groups in order to explore how group membership might or might not influence individual differences, even though the result would not be a true cross section. Since new immigrants to the New York area come from world regions that differ strongly in terms of racial, ethnic, economic, and cultural traits, and since they enter a resident population that is also sharply differentiated on these dimensions, we opted to stratify our sample in terms of race and ethnicity as well as region of origin. In other words, we sought to sample the most important groups, not develop a random cross section.

The pilot study sought to determine the feasibility of completing in-person interviews with members of important immigrant groups in each major racial-ethnic category: Chinese and Koreans among the Asians; Dominicans and Colombian, Ecuadoran, and Peruvian Hispanics; and West Indian and Haitian blacks; as well as the native control groups—whites, blacks, and Puerto Ricans.

This experience taught us that the Korean and Haitian second generation populations were too small and too dispersed to be found in a cost-effective manner. Moreover, it became clear that trying to reach people in person would yield far worse response rates than would be obtained through telephone interviews, in part because people were often reluctant to open their doors or were not at home. This convinced us to switch to screening and interviewing respondents by telephone. As a result, our interview instrument would have to be much shorter than if we were attempting in-person interviews. Since we felt, however, that we could only capture many complexities of the respondents' racial and ethnic identifications and personal experiences through in-depth interviews, we decided to ask a subsample of the telephone respondents to complete an in-person interview to probe these issues.

To evaluate and refine our draft questionnaire, we commenced a pilot telephone survey of respondents in fall 1997. That experience and some preliminary in-depth interviews yielded a revised telephone questionnaire that we used with a supplemental sample gathered in distant suburbs beginning in fall 1998. For this supplemental sample, we called households with Chinese and Hispanic last names with listed telephone numbers and dialed randomly into known suburban concentrations of black residents. This pilot phase yielded 657 suburban respondents. Since these data were not gathered by the same method as the main sample, we do not analyze them in this study.

The Telephone Survey

With the validity of the questionnaire confirmed, we initiated the random digit dialing (RDD) of the main telephone survey in late 1998, completing a total of 3,415 additional interviews by early 2000. We used an innovative two-stage sampling methodology. A screening telephone call enumerated members of the household, identified its racial and ethnic background, and determined if an eligible 18 –32-year-old child of immigrants from one of our groups lived in the household. Because our interviewers were often speaking with immigrant parents and household members, we used multilingual interviewers who could conduct the screening interview in English, Spanish, Cantonese, Mandarin, and Russian. (Once the main interview began, we also offered the second generation respondents the opportunity to continue in another language, but only three chose to do the interview in Spanish.) Once the screening call identified an eligible person, the main interview begin or was scheduled.

The screening for the telephone survey covered the four boroughs of New York City (excluding Staten Island), two inner city counties in northeastern New Jersey (Hudson and Passaic), and four inner suburban New Jersey and New York counties (Essex, Hudson, Nassau, and Westchester), where the 1990 Census Public Use Microdata Sample showed that our target respondents were present in at least 3 percent of the microdata area's households. This sampling frame eliminated two-fifths of the total population of the New York metropolitan area but retained four-fifths of the target second generation groups and two-thirds of the blacks and Puerto Ricans. (The sampling area had a total population of 11.9 million in 2000, and our target groups made up 75 percent of the total.)

In the first wave of RDD screening, our survey firm, SRBI, Inc., made calls to 91,331 randomly selected telephone numbers and identified 32,401 households as eligible for screening (see Table A.1). Of these, we successfully screened 22,504 and identified 4,405 households containing at least one respondent who fit one of our target categories. Completed in

Table A.1. Screened and Eligible Households and Interviews Completed

Total Phase 1 Screening Calls	91,331
Not Residential/No Answer/No Response after Callbacks	54,789
Household Did Not Speak English, Spanish, Chinese, or Russian	4,141
Eligible to Be Screened	32,401
Refused to Be Screened	4,862
Began Phase 1 Screening	27,089
Failed to Complete Screening	4,585
Completed Screening	22,504
% Eligible Successfully Screened	69.5
Found Eligible in Phase 1 Screening	*4,405*
Total Phase 2 Screening Calls	196,063
Not Residential/No Answer/No Response after Callbacks	109,283
Household Did Not Speak English, Spanish, Chinese, or Russian	6,330
Eligible to Be Screened	80,450
Refused to Be Screened	10,066
Started Screening	70,384
Completed Screening	64,290
% Eligible Successfully Screened	79.9
Found Eligible in Phase 2 Screening	*2,399*
Total Eligible in Phase 1 and Phase 2	6,804
Total over Quota	363
Total Final Respondents	*3,415*
Yield Rate (R/E)	*53.2%*

March 1999, this first wave of screening enabled us to complete 2,015 interviews, filling our quotas for native whites, native blacks, and Puerto Ricans and providing substantial numbers of Dominican, West Indian, South American, and Chinese respondents as well as a good beginning on the Russian Jewish respondents.

In May 1999, we commenced a second wave of screening of 196,063 calls only to households in telephone exchanges that produced at least one qualified respondent in the first wave. This wave of screening identified 80,450 households eligible for screening, successfully screened 64,290 households, and identified 2,399 households containing a member of the remaining target groups, with 1,417 interviews being completed by February 2000. By May 2000, the resulting data were compiled, checked for errors, and corrected through callbacks. Tables A.1 and A.2 indicate the number of screening calls, the number of households identified with one or more eligible respondents, the number of interviews commenced, and the number of interviews completed for each group by screening phase.

In essence, this study collected independent random samples of eligible members of the eight target groups. The two-stage sampling enhanced our efficiency in reaching eligible second generation individuals while staying within a random dialing sampling methodology. The second stage was equivalent to using the first stage as a separate Waksberg-style RDD sample for each group. Since the first stage yielded 119 or more eligible households for every group, it provided at least that many starting points for the second stage samples. This second stage sample was thus far more diverse than most sample-point-based in-person samples or even many Waksberg samples. (Since almost all the interviews that would have been completed by screening in the entire sampling area would have come from these exchanges anyway, seeking cases outside these telephone exchanges would have doubled the number and cost of screening calls without significantly enhancing the sample.) We found only small age, gender, and second or 1.5 generation status differences and developed separate weights for the second stage cases to bring them in line with the first stage.

Only a few screening calls produced an immediate refusal to speak with us, but about 10 percent of the households that began screening terminated before completion. Once a household was determined to have at least one eligible 18- to 32-year-old member, another 13 percent refused to undertake the main survey; but the great majority of those respondents who began the main interview, 87 percent, completed it. We calculated

Table A.2. Detailed Disposition of Eligible Households by Group and Screening Phase

	Puerto Rican	Native Black	Dominican	West Indian	South American	Chinese	Russian Jewish	Native White
Phase 1 Eligible	952	1020	306	613	236	143	119	1,016
Refused	371	398	119	238	101	63	52	447
Over Quota	40	151	0	0	0	0	0	67
Began Interview	541	468	187	375	135	80	67	*472*
Completed Interviews	*429*	*421*	163	343	122	80	47	*410*
% of Phase 1 Eligible Quota	47.0	48.6	53.3	56.0	51.7	55.9	39.5	43.2
Phase 2 Eligible			446	120	481	870	482	
Over Quota			0	0	0	102	0	
Refused			155	42	167	200	167	
Began Interview			291	78	314	568	315	
Completed Interviews			*264*	*64*	288	537	264	
% of Phase 2 Eligible Quota			59.2	53.3	59.9	69.9	54.8	
Total Completed	429	421	427	407	410	617	311	410
Edits	+4	0	−1	0	−8	−10	−2	−2
Final	433	421	428	407	402	607	309	40
Yield CI/E	47.5	48.6	56.9	55.5	56.1	66.6	51.4	43.0

Note: Italicized completed interview totals indicate group quota was met in Phase 1.

response rates for each group by dividing the number of completed interviews by the total number of eligible respondents identified in the screener.

We gathered data on 400 or more respondents from each group, except that we sampled about 600 Chinese respondents to capture their great variation in class and origin and had to limit our sample of Russian Jews to about 300 because of financial constraints. We asked respondents who qualified for more than one group—for example, who had a Puerto Rican father and a Dominican mother—which group they felt closest to and assigned them to that group for analysis. The yield of completed interviews among those determined to be eligible is 53.3 percent, ranging from a low of 41.3 among native blacks to a high of 66.6 percent among the Chinese (see the final row of Table A-2). These rates compare well for survey research in the New York area.

Our 18 to 32-year-old respondents seem generally representative of the larger universe of young people as identified in the 2000 Census Public Use Microdata Sample, as shown in Table A.3. (Since the decennial Census does not ask parents' place of birth, comparisons cannot be exact. The Current Population Survey, which does ask this question, does not contain enough cases for this age group in the sampling area to permit statistical comparison.) Note that although our survey sample seems slightly younger and more likely to be female than these populations as defined in the 2000 Census microdata, the differences are small and the patterns across groups are quite similar. Only among the Chinese and the Russians

Table A.3. Comparison of Survey Respondents and 2000 Public Use Microdata Sample

	Puerto Rican	Native Black	Dominican	West Indian	South American	Chinese	Russian	Native White
Median Age in Survey	24.2	25.5	23.7	23.4	24.0	22.0	22.0	25.8
Median Age in Census	25.0	25.2	24.7	24.8	25.4	25.6	25.2	26.2
Female Share in Survey	59.2	61.4	59.3	52.8	48.9	46.0	49.7	54.9
Female Share in Census	52.5	57.1	52.8	55.2	45.4	50.4	47.9	51.5

are the age differences more than a year and a half, and this is partly a reflection of our effort to secure true second generation respondents, who are less present in the overall population and likely to be younger. The gender balances in our survey respondents, which reflect the difficulty in securing responses from young minority men, especially those in poor neighborhoods, tend to be more female than in the population at large as reflected in the 2000 Census microdata but follow cross-group patterns that are quite similar to those in the larger population. We feel confident, therefore, that our data are highly reflective of the actual population at the time of our survey.

Once the quantitative data were collected, we coded the open-ended items concerning the high schools and colleges attended and the industries and occupations of employment for respondents and their parents. We also geocoded the respondents' current place of residence using the addresses to which incentive checks were mailed, responses to the question about where people lived, or the geocenter of the telephone exchange when that information was missing. This enabled us to identify the 1990 and 2000 Census Tracts associated with the current place of residence as well as the Zip codes of current residence and neighborhood in which the respondent grew up. In addition, we identified the political precinct of the New York City residents. This allowed us to associate each respondent with a variety of indicators of neighborhood context drawn from the Census or the election results.

Where our analysis compares groups, we have weighted the data to take account of age and gender differences between the first and second waves of interviews. When we undertake multivariate analysis of the entire sample, we have weighted the individuals to represent their incidence in the entire population eligible for study. In other words, this analysis is not biased by the fact that we set similar quota sizes for each group even though their incidence in the larger population varies tremendously. On publication of this study, we are making a public use version of the data available at www.urbanresearch.org.

The In-Depth Interviews

As the telephone survey got under way, we trained sixteen advanced graduate students to complete 333 in-depth interviews with a subset of the telephone respondents, chosen where possible to represent cases of upward and downward mobility. (Table A.4 shows that the gender, age, and parental education levels of the in-depth respondents are generally comparable to those of the overall telephone survey sample.) These interviews took several hours, and each produced 80 to 100 pages when transcribed. Interviewing commenced in January 1999 and was completed at the end of 2000. The research directors provided rigorous training of the interviewers and met with them in a weekly seminar to discuss field issues and substantive findings. In 2001–2002, with funding from the MacArthur Foundation Research Network on the Transition to Adulthood, we re-interviewed 123 of these respondents to cover their experiences in the wake of the September 11th attack on the city and the associated economic downturn.

As the transcripts of the in-depth interviews became available, we used the qualitative data analysis program Atlas Ti to code them for themes and topics. We also appended an abstract of the telephone survey results to each case. In total, the transcripts yielded about 17,000 pages of data. Our respondents told us vivid, rich, insightful, and even painful stories. The first round of coding identified basic subjects like work, education, family, and political participation. The attached data from the telephone survey allowed us to control for group, gender, or any other characteristic when searching text. A second round of coding introduced analytical subcodes on success, job characteristics, identity, citizenship, high school choice, English as a Second Language, partner choice, child-rearing,

Table A.4. Comparison of Survey Respondents and In-Depth Interviewees

Group	Survey Respondents			In-Depth Interviewees		
	Female Percent	Average Age	A Parent Has BA	Female Percent	Average Age	A Parent Has BA
PR	60	24.1	14.8	53	24.6	16.7
NB	61	25.5	27.6	63	25.7	40.7
DR	59	23.7	15.2	44	23.4	18.6
WI	52	23.4	30.0	55	24.3	26.3
SA	49	24.0	23.6	54	24.6	15.4
CH	46	22.5	22.7	50	24.6	28.9
RJ	48	22.4	70.2	45	23.0	65.8
NW	56	25.7	55.6	50	27.2	58.3
Total Sample	54	23.9	30.6	51	24.6	32.7

PR = Puerto Rican; NB = Native Black; DR = Dominican; WI = West Indian; SA = South American; CH = Chinese; RJ = Russian Jewish; NW = Native White.

neighborhoods (highlighting themes like ethnic succession), college choice, career path, transnational ties, religion, experiences with CUNY, and community colleges.

These codes allowed us to relate quantitative findings (such as the impact of high school quality on educational attainment) to the qualitative data (such as what respondents say about their high school experiences). From late 2003 through 2005, we analyzed the results of the qualitative interviews, cleaned the quantitative data set, coded a series of open-ended questions in that data set, geocoded the locations where respondents lived and had grown up during their childhood, and added contextual information from the 1990 and 2000 Censuses.

One unanticipated by-product of the in-depth interviewing was it helped us improve the data quality of the telephone survey. As we followed up with respondents, we could monitor the quality of telephone survey data collection and respond promptly to problems. As a result, we believe the telephone survey data to be of high quality. In-depth respondents did, however, occasionally gave our interviewers information that differed from that collected by the telephone survey. These were not "errors" so much as nuances in the way the different methods collect information.

The Ethnographies

Finally, we recruited six ethnographers to investigate key sites where second generation individuals were interacting with each other and native born groups between September 1999 to August 2000, while a seventh predoctoral fellow replicated our survey and in-depth interview with 200 Korean second generation individuals located through a distinctive surname approach with additional support from the National Science Foundation (Kim 2001). The ethnographic sites include a public community college with many Latin American second generation students; the Black Studies courses and student activities in a four year college with many African American and West Indian students; a retail workplace with second generation and native minority workers and native white customers; a social service union led by African Americans whose membership is largely West Indian and Latino; three protestant congregations with different mixes of first and second generation Chinese, Korean, and white members; and community organizations in a heavily Dominican neighborhood compared with those in a more mixed Latino neighborhood.

Because we wanted to capture a diversity of experiences, we undertook parallel ethnographies in different sites, not a "team ethnography" in one site. We retained the meta-ethnographic benefits of a team approach, however, by meeting weekly to discuss field research findings, organize our work around common themes, and bring out comparisons across research settings. The survey data informed the ethnographic work, including site selection. For example, the ethnographers studying the union and the retail site used the survey data to determine the occupational and industry distribution of second generation respondents and whether their jobs were unionized. The ethnographies are reported in a companion volume (Kasinitz, Mollenkopf, and Waters 2004).

Sample Characteristics

We defined the eligible age range for our respondents as 18–32 because we were interested in the transition to adulthood among the offspring of the post-1965 immigration to the United States. Age 32 was the oldest a person could be in 1997 if born to parents who immigrated in 1965. Because only a few children could have been born at this time, it is no surprise that the age distribution of our second generation and 1.5 generation respondents is weighted toward the younger end of our age range even though we took steps to increase the number of older respondents. (All subsequent tables report only unweighted distributions from the main sample. In the tables in the book we use weights to adjust group sizes back to their original distribution in the population sampled.)

Table A.5. Age by Group (in percent)

Group	18–20	21–23	24–26	27–29	30–32	Total
Puerto Rican	26.1	22.4	17.7	18.6	15.2	429
Native Black	17.8	16.9	19.7	23.0	22.6	421
Dominican	23.7	33.3	15.5	16.4	11.2	427
West Indian	31.4	23.8	19.4	13.8	11.5	407
South American	23.4	29.3	19.8	15.4	12.2	410
Chinese	41.4	21.8	18.7	10.3	7.7	609
Russian Jewish	40.2	25.4	18.3	9.6	6.4	311
Native White	13.4	20.5	20.0	23.2	22.9	410
Total Sample	27.6	24.0	18.6	16.2	13.6	3415

Table A.5 gives the age distribution among the different groups. The native black, white, and Puerto Rican respondents are spread relatively evenly, though Puerto Ricans are somewhat younger than whites and blacks. On average, the second generation respondents are younger, markedly so for the Chinese and Russian Jews. We believe that this reflects the recency of the immigration of these latter groups to New York City and the actual distribution of the total population and is not an artifact of sampling procedures.

Table A.6 shows similar pattern in the distribution of these groups across the immigrant generations. West Indians, Colombians, Ecuadorans, and Peruvians, and Dominicans are mostly second generation, but the majority of Russian Jews and Chinese are 1.5 generation (born abroad but arrived in the United States as children below age 12). (To find a suitable sample of Russians, we had to relax the 1.5 generation age constraint to 18, so these are termed "1.25 generation.") Owing to their parents' recent migration, only 42 percent of the Chinese and 12 percent of the Russian Jewish respondents in our sample are true second generation. We had some concern that our greater reliance on targeted screening to secure Chinese respondents had contributed to their relative youth and predominance of 1.5 generation respondents. As discussed earlier, this targeted screening was necessary because the Chinese second generation is a smaller and less concentrated group than the others. However, a comparison of the two waves indicated no difference in age distribution or household type among the Chinese. We concluded that our approach had yielded the true age distribution of the Chinese second and 1.5 generation. This is true of the Russians as well.

Table A.6. Immigration Cohort by Group (in percent)

Group	U.S./2nd Gen	1.5 Gen	1.25 Gen
Puerto Rican	100.0		
Native Black	100.0		
Dominican	61.9	37.9	
West Indian	54.1	45.5	
South American	59.3	40.5	
Chinese	42.4	57.5	
Russian	12.2	60.8	26.7
Native White	100.0		
Total Sample	66.7	30.7	2.4

As is often the case with surveys of young adults, our sampling resulted in more female than male respondents, particularly among native born blacks and Puerto Ricans and the Dominicans, and to a lesser degree among native whites and West Indians, as shown in Table A.4. Male representation was at parity or greater among the South Americans, Russians, and Chinese, however. As Table A.3 has shown, this outcome reflects actual difference in the gender distributions of the various populations, at least insofar as the Census captures the "actual." It also reflects the differentially greater difficulty of finding and securing information from young minority males, as well as some cultural differences across groups in the willingness of females to divulge information.

The Issue of Selectivity

Conclusions drawn from a survey of just one city and its surrounding suburbs obviously raise questions of selection bias. Are we truly looking at characteristics that can be generalized to larger populations, or are we only looking at the consequences of who ends up living (or not living) in the sampling area? For groups that are earning relatively low incomes, is it because they are really generally poor, or is it only that more of the poor members have remained in the New York metropolitan area while some of the better-off ones have moved somewhere else? We worried about this question especially with respect to the Puerto Ricans, whose outcomes are lower than other groups on such measures as income and education. While we cannot examine all the potential dimensions of selectivity across our groups, we did use the 2000 Census microdata sample to cross-classify in-movers, out-movers, and stayers across three broad income brackets by group to see whether they showed differential out-migration by income.

Table A.7 presents the results. In general, lower-income households were more likely to leave the New York metropolitan area than higher-income households, and members of the native born groups were more likely to leave than the immigrant groups. In particular, the Puerto Rican population does not show a differentially larger out-migration of its higher income members. On this basis, we believe that selective out-migration of higher income households does not explain the poor outcomes among Puerto Ricans in our sample. If anything, the relatively larger departure of poor and middle income Puerto Ricans would slightly understate how poorly the group is doing.

Table A.7. Movement Out of New York Consolidated Metropolitan Area between 1995 and 2000 by Group and Income (percent who moved)

Group	Household Income <$30K	Household Income $30–60K	Household Income Above
Puerto Ricans	7.9	8.1	5.5
Native Blacks	9.8	9.3	6.1
Dominicans	6.7	5.7	4.2
West Indians	10.0	7.8	4.2
South Americans	8.5	6.5	5.1
Chinese	7.8	6.8	6.6
Russians	3.7	5.9	4.1
Native Whites	15.0	9.8	6.2
Other	10.3	8.8	7.0
Total Sample	11.1	8.9	6.1

Source: U.S. Census, 2000, 5% Public Use Microdata Sample.

Variable Construction

Beyond the cleaning and reconstruction of responses to the questions in our survey, we constructed a number of additional variables used in the analysis of this book. Here, we further explain the school quality index, the college quality measures, the household variables, the comparison of employment patterns with the overall values in the March 2000 Current Population Survey, and the transnationalism index.

High School Quality Index

Our survey instrument asked each respondent for the name of the high school he or she last attended as well as the highest level of education he or she completed. For all those who attended a public high school in New York City, we first developed a high school quality index based on performance data collected by the Division of Assessment and Accountability of the New York City Board of Education (now the Department of Education) for the 1995. That was the earliest year for which comprehensive public school data were available. It would have been preferable to have data either from the exact years in which our respondents were attending high school or a somewhat earlier year, but this was not possible. (The median year in which our respondents were 17, the senior year for those who are at the age-appropriate grade, is 1992). Nonetheless, we believe that the relative distribution of high school performance levels was fairly stable through the late 1980s and early 1990s, so 1995 is a reasonable proxy year for such data.

We undertook a correlation analysis of the 1995 public high school data to understand the relationships among the variables the data contain. This led us to exclude many variables that had no relationship to the most positive educational outcome (graduation rates). Next, we converted the remaining variables to z-scores to ensure comparison and conducted a second correlation analysis, eliminating further variables that had no significant relationship with graduation rates. This led to the final creation of a high school quality scale. We ranked all the high schools into five quintiles and assigned the high school quality quintile score to each respondent. (A few of our respondents attended high schools that had been closed or substantially restructured by the time the 1995 data were published, and these were assigned to the lowest quality quintile.)

The College Quality Index

We relied on the 1998 *U.S. News and World Report* (*USNWR*, published September 1, 1997) ranking of colleges and universities in the United States to develop this index. We picked this year because it reflected a year in which many of our respondents might have attended college, because the ranking methodology had stabilized at that point, and because we had access to an online version of the ranking. The *USNWR* rankings are based on surveys of educational elites about institutional quality and on data provided by the institutions themselves (on such things as retention rates, SAT scores, institutional resources, and alumni giving). While the *USNWR*'s methodology has been subject to criticism, changes over time, and its underlying data and weighting system are not transparent, the ranking is probably the most influential one in public opinion. In the 1998 ranking, the system distinguished colleges and universities as national or regional in scope and sorted them into four tiers. In Figure 5.4, we group colleges in Tier I as "top," Tiers II and III as "middle," and Tier IV as "lowest."

The Household Variables

One weakness of our telephone survey is that neither the screener nor the main questionnaire specifically conducted a full inventory of the household and the respondent's relationship to each member of that household. The screening process did identify how many adults over 50, between 33 and 50, and 18 to 32 lived in the household and whether one or more eligible individuals lived in the household. The main questionnaire also asked detailed questions about the form of the respondent's household during the years he or she was between the ages of 6 and 18, including whether the respondent lived with both biological parents, and if not, who, if anyone, served as the respondent's father and mother figures and which other adults in the household might have helped raise the respondent. We also asked whether the respondents still lived where they were born, where they lived longest between 6 and 18, and how many times they moved in those years. We also asked how long they have lived at their current address; whether they lived with their parents, owned, or rented; and whether they had a spouse, partner, or children living with them. Using the screening information and these questions, we constructed the likely current form of the household as well as the form of the family when the respondent was growing up.

We assume that respondents living with an adult over 50 in their household are living with a parent or older relative. Where there is only one person over 32 in the household and the respondent is living with a spouse or partner, we assume the respondent is not living with parents. When respondents volunteered that they were living with their parents in answer to whether they owned or rented their home we classified them as living with their parents. When the years living at the current address subtracted from the respondent's age was under 17 and the respondent was living with an adult over 32 who was not a partner, we also classified them as living with a parent or older relative. This approach allowed us to assign most people to a likely current household form, with 2.4 percent having missing data and 9 percent being unclassifiable by this approach.

Employment Comparison

In order to measure the similarity and differences of the occupational distribution of our respondents with that of the general population, we constructed a file from the March 2000 Current Population Survey (CPS) that contained both the cases of the first generation parents (age 40 to 60) and our second generation and native born young people (age 18 to 32) to see what industries and occupations were held by those who were working. This enabled us to generate measures of dissimilarity both between parents and their children and between the respondents and the entire 18 to 32-year-old cohort in the sampling area. The CPS is the main source of labor market experience in the United States, and it contains detailed information on industry and occupation of employment, as well as weeks and hours worked and wages received.

Measures of Transnationalism

Our survey asked numerous questions about relationships with the home country, including number of visits, whether the respondent had ever lived there for six months or longer (and why), and whether they or their parents sent remittances home. In addition, we determined the extent to which respondents used the parents' language and whether they watched mass media in that language. With the answers to the items on parents sending cash to the home country, respondents sending cash to the home country, and respondents visiting their parents' home countries, we constructed an additive scale of transnational activities ranging from 0 to 9 (average inter-item correlation = .35, alpha = .53, N = 1810).

References

Adler, Norman, and Blanche Davis Blank. 1975. *Political Clubs in New York*. New York: Praeger.

Alba, Richard D. 1990. *Ethnic Identity: The Transformation of White America*. New Haven, Conn.: Yale University Press.

———. 2005. "Bright vs. Blurred Boundaries: Second-Generation Assimilation and Exclusion in France, Germany, and the United States." *Ethnic and Racial Studies* 28:20–49.

Alba, Richard D., Johann Handl, and Walter Müller. 1994. "Ethnische Ungleichheit im Deutachen Bildungasystem." *Kölner Zeitschrift für Soziologie und Sozialpsychologie* 46:209–237.

Alba, Richard D., John R. Logan, Amy Lutz, and Brian J. Stults. 2002. "Only English by the Third Generation? Loss and Preservation of the Mother Tongue among the Grandchildren of Contemporary Immigrants." *Demography* 39:467–484.

Alba, Richard D., and Victor Nee. 2003. *Remaking the American Mainstream: Assimilation and Contemporary Immigration*. Cambridge, Mass.: Harvard University Press.

Anbinder, Tyler. 2001. *Five Points: The 19th Century New York City Neighborhood That Invented Tap Dance, Stole Elections, and Became the World's Most Notorious Slum*. New York: Free Press.

Anderson, Elijah. 1990. *Streetwise: Race, Class, and Change in an Urban Community*. Chicago: University of Chicago Press.

———. 1999. *Code of the Street: Decency, Violence, and the Moral Life of the Inner City*. New York: W. W. Norton.

———. 2004. "The Cosmopolitan Canopy." *Annals of the American Academy of Political and Social Science* 595:14–31.

Appelbaum, Eileen, Arnette Bernhardt, and Richard J. Murnane (eds.). 2003. *Low-Wage America. How Employers Are Reshaping Opportunity in the Workplace*. New York: Russell Sage Foundation.

Attewell, Paul, and David E. Lavin. 2007. *Passing the Torch: Does Higher Education Pay Off across the Generations?* New York: Russell Sage Foundation.

387

Baker, Susan S. 2002. *Understanding Mainland Puerto Rican Poverty.* Philadelphia: Temple University Press.

Balfanz, Robert, and Nottre Letgers. 2004. "Locating the Dupont Crisis," Baltimore, Md.: Center for the Social Organization of Schools, Johns Hopkins University, Report 70.

Banton, Michael P. 1987. *Racial Theories.* New York: Cambridge University Press.

Barth, Fredrik. 1996. "Ethnic Groups and Boundaries." Pp. 294–324 in *Theories of Ethnicity: A Classical Reader,* edited by Werner Sollors. New York: Macmillan.

Basch, Linda G., Nina G. Schiller, and Cristina Szanton Blanc. 1994. *Nations Unbound: Transnational Projects, Postcolonial Predicaments, and Deterritorialized Nation-States.* Langhorne, Pa.: Gordon and Breach.

Bean, Frank, and Marta Tienda. 1987. *The Hispanic Population of the United States.* New York: Russell Sage Foundation.

Bengtson, Vern L., Timothy J. Biblarz, and Robert E. L. Roberts. 2002. *How Families Still Matter: A Longitudinal Study of Youth in Two Generations.* New York: Cambridge University Press.

Binder, Frederick M., and David M. Reimers. 1995. *All the Nations under Heaven: An Ethnic and Racial History of New York City.* New York: Columbia University Press.

Blauner, Bob. 1972. *Racial Oppression in America.* New York: Harper and Row.

Bonacich, Edna. 1973. "A Theory of Middleman Minorities." *American Sociological Review* 38:583–594.

Borjas, George J. 1999. *Heaven's Door: Immigration Policy and the American Economy.* Princeton, N.J.: Princeton University Press.

Bowen, William G., Derek C. Bok, and James S. Shulman. 1998. *The Shape of the River: Long-Term Consequences of Considering Race in College and University Admissions.* Princeton, N.J.: Princeton University Press.

Boyd, Monica, and Elizabeth M. Grieco. 1998. "Triumphant Transitions: Socioeconomic Achievements of the Second Generation in Canada." *International Migration Review* 32:853–876.

Brint, Steven, and Jerome Karabel. 1989. *The Diverted Dream: Community Colleges and the Promise of Educational Opportunity in America, 1900–1985.* New York: Oxford University Press.

Brodkin, Karen. 1998. *How Jews Became White Folks and What That Says about Race in America.* New Brunswick, N.J.: Rutgers University Press.

Browning, Rufus P., Dale Rogers Marshall, and David H. Tabb (eds.). 1984. *Protest Is Not Enough: The Struggle of Blacks and Hispanics for Equality in Urban Politics.* Berkeley: University of California Press.

———. 2003. *Racial Politics in American Cities* (3rd edition). New York: Longman Publishers.

Brubaker, Rogers. 2004. *Ethnicity without Groups.* Cambridge, Mass.: Harvard University Press.

Bryce-Laporte, Roy Simon. 1972. "Black Immigrants: The Experience of Invisibility and Inequality." *Journal of Black Studies* 3:29–56.

Burrows, Edwin G., and Mike Wallace. 1999. *Gotham: A History of New York City to 1898.* New York: Oxford University Press.

Burt, Ronald S. 2004. "Structural Holes and Good Ideas." *American Journal of Sociology* 110:349–399.

Butterfield, Sherri-Ann. 2004. " 'We're Just Black': The Racial and Ethnic Identities of Second-Generation West Indians in New York." Pp. 288–312 in *Becoming New Yorkers: Ethnographies of the New Second Generation,* edited by Philip Kasinitz, John H. Mollenkopf, and Mary C. Waters. New York: Russell Sage Foundation.

Capps, Randolph, Michael E. Fix, Julie Murray, Jason Ost, Jeffrey S. Passel, and Shinta Herwantoro Hernández. 2005. "The New Demography of America's Schools: Immigration and the No Child Left Behind Act." Washington, D.C.: Urban Institute, September 30.

Carlson, Barbara C., and Rebecca L. Scharf. 2004. *Lost in the Maze: Reforming New York City's Fragmented Child Care Subsidy System.* New York: Welfare Law Center.

Carnes, Tony, and Anna Karpathakis (eds.). 2001. *New York Glory: Religions in the City.* New York: New York University Press.

Carter, Susan B., and Richard Sutch. 1999. "Historical Perspectives on the Economic Consequences of Immigration into the United States." Pp. 319–341 in *The Handbook of International Migration: The American Experience,* edited by Charles Hirschman, Philip Kasinitz, and Josh DeWind. New York: Russell Sage Foundation.

Chai-Kim, Karen. 2004. "Chinatown or Uptown? Second Generation Chinese American Protestants in New York City." Pp. 257–279 in *Becoming New Yorkers: Ethnographies of the New Second Generation,* edited by Philip Kasinitz, John H. Mollenkopf, and Mary C. Waters. New York: Russell Sage Foundation.

Chan, Sewell. 2006. "Mayor Attacks 2 Main Ideas on Immigrants." *New York Times* (March 31), p. B6.

Chen, Hsiang-shui. 1992. *Chinatown No More: Taiwan Immigrants in Contemporary New York.* Ithaca, N.Y.: Cornell University Press.

Child, Irwin. 1943. *Italian or American? The Second Generation in Conflict.* New York: Russell and Russell.

Chin, Margaret M. 2005. *Sewing Women: Immigrants and the New York City Garment Industry.* New York: Columbia University Press.

Citizens Budget Commission. 2003. "Five Problems That Hurt New York and What Can Be Done about Them." New York: Document prepared for Citizens Budget Commission Conference, November 13–14.

Cohen, Abner. 1974. "The Lesson of Ethnicity." Pp. ix–xxii, Introduction in *Urban Ethnicity,* edited by Abner Cohen. London: Tavistock Publications.

Cohen, Cathy J., and Michael C. Dawson. 1993. "Neighborhood Poverty and African American Politics." *American Political Science Review* 87:286–302.

Collier, Michael W., and Eduardo A. Gamarra. 2001. "The Colombian Diaspora in South Florida: A Report of the Colombian Studies Institute's Colombian

Diaspora Project." Miami: Latin American and Caribbean Center, Florida International University, Working Paper Series WPS no. 1, May 2001. http://lacc.fiu.edu/publications_resources/publications_frm.htm.

Conley, Dalton. 1999. *Being Black, Living in the Red: Race, Wealth, and Social Policy in America*. Berkeley: University of California Press.

———. 2001. "A Room with a View or a Room of One's Own? Housing and Social Stratification." *Sociological Forum* 16:263–280.

Contreras, Randol. Forthcoming. "Damn, Yo, Who's That Girl? An Ethnographic Analysis of Masculinity in Drug Robberies." *Journal of Contemporary Ethnography*.

Crul, Maurice, and J. Doomernik. 2003. "The Turkish and Moroccan Second Generation in the Netherlands: Divergent Trends between Polarization within the Two Groups." *International Migration Review* 37(4):1039–1064.

Danziger, Sheldon, and Peter Gottschalk. 1995. *America Unequal*. New York: Russell Sage Foundation.

Denton, Nancy A., and Douglas S. Massey. 1989. "Racial Identity among Caribbean Hispanics: The Effect of Double Minority Status on Residential Segregation." *American Sociological Review* 54:790–808.

Division of Adolescent and School Health (DASH), Center for Chronic Disease Prevention and Health Promotion. 1993. "New York City Youth Violence Survey." Atlanta, Ga.: Centers for Disease Control and Prevention.

Dougherty, Kevin. 1992. "Community Colleges and Baccalaureate Attainment" *Journal of Higher Education* 63(2):188–214.

Dreier, Peter, John H. Mollenkopf, and Todd Swanstrom. 2001. *Place Matters: Metropolitics for the Twenty-first Century*. Lawrence: University Press of Kansas.

Duany, Jorge. 2002. *The Puerto Rican Nation on the Move: Identities on the Island and in the United States*. Chapel Hill: University of North Carolina Press.

Duncan, Otis Dudley, and Beverly Duncan. 1955. "A Methodological Analysis of Segregation Indexes." *American Sociological Review* 20:210–217.

Eck, Diana. 2007. "Religious and Cultural Institutions." Pp. 214–227 in *The New Americans: A Guide to Immigration since 1965*, edited by Mary C. Waters and Reed Ueda, with Helen Marrow. Cambridge, Mass.: Harvard University Press.

Edin, Kathryn, and Maria Kefalas. 2005. *Promises I Can Keep: Why Poor Women Put Motherhood before Marriage*. Berkeley: University of California Press.

Eisinger, Peter. 1973. "The Conditions of Protest Behavior in American Cities." *American Political Science Review* 67:11–28.

Ellen, Ingrid Gould, Katherine O'Regan, Amy Ellen Schwartz, and Leanna Stiefel. 2002. "Immigrant Children and Urban Schools: Lessons from New York on Segregation, Resources and School Attendance Patterns." Washington, D.C.: Brookings-Wharton Papers on Urban Affairs. http://www.brookings.edu/press/books/bwpapersonurbanaffairs2002.htm.

Ellwood, David T., and Christopher Jencks. 2001. "The Growing Differences in Family Structure: What Do We Know? Where Do We Look for Answers?"

Working Paper on the Social Dimensions of Inequality, Russell Sage Foundation, New York, NY.

Fagan, Jeffrey, and Garth Davies. 2004. "The Natural History of Neighborhood Violence." *Journal of Contemporary Criminal Justice* 20(2): 127–147.

Fagan, Jeffrey, Valerie West, and Jan Holland. 2003. "Reciprocal Effects of Crime and Incarceration in New York City Neighborhoods." *Fordham Urban Law Journal* 30:1551–1602.

Farley, Reynolds, and Richard Alba. 2002. "The New Second Generation in the United States." *International Migration Review* 36:669–701.

Feagin, Joe R. 1991. "The Continuing Significance of Race: Antiblack Discrimination in Public Places." *American Sociological Review* 56:101–116.

Feliciano, Cynthia. 2001. "The Benefits of Biculturalism: Exposure to Immigrant Culture and Dropping Out of School among Asian and Latino Youths." *Social Science Quarterly* 82:865–879.

Feliciano, Cynthia, and Rubén G. Rumbaut. 2005. "Gendered Paths: Educational and Occupational Expectations and Outcomes among Adult Children of Immigrants." *Ethnic and Racial Studies* 28:1087–1118.

Fennelly, Katherine, Gretchen Cornwell, and Lynn Casper. 1992. "A Comparison of the Fertility of Dominican, Puerto Rican and Mainland Puerto Rican Adolescents." *Family Planning Perspectives* 24:107–110, 134.

Fernández, Roberto M., and François Nielsen. 1986. "Bilingualism and Hispanic Scholastic Achievement: Some Baseline Results." *Social Science Research* 15(1):43–70.

Fernández, Roberto M., and Celina Su. 2004. "Space in the Study of Labor Markets." *Annual Review of Sociology* 30(1):545–569.

Fernández-Kelly, Patricia, and Richard Schauffler. 1996. "Divided Fates: Immigrant Children in a Restructured U.S. Economy." Pp. 30–53 in *The New Second Generation,* edited by Alejandro Portes. New York: Russell Sage Foundation.

Fitzgerald, Joan. 2006. *Moving Up in the New Economy: Career Paths for U.S. Workers.* Ithaca, N.Y.: ILR Press.

Flores, Juan. 2000. *From Bomba to Hip-Hop: Puerto Rican Culture and Latino Identity.* New York: Columbia University Press.

Foerster, Amy. 2004. "Isn't Anyone Here from Alabama? Solidarity and Struggle in a Mighty, Mighty Union." Pp. 197–226 in *Becoming New Yorkers: Ethnographies of the New Second Generation,* edited by Philip Kasinitz, John H. Mollenkopf, and Mary C. Waters. New York: Russell Sage Foundation.

Foner, Nancy. 1987. "The Jamaicans: Race and Ethnicity among Migrants in New York City." Pp. 195–218 in *New Immigrants in New York,* edited by Nancy Foner. New York: Columbia University Press.

———. 1994. *The Caregiving Dilemma: Work in an American Nursing Home.* Berkeley: University of California Press.

———. 1999. "The Immigrant Family: Cultural Legacies and Cultural Changes." Pp. 257–274 in *Handbook of International Migration: The American Experi-*

ence, edited by Charles Hirschman, Philip Kasinitz, and Josh DeWind. New York: Russell Sage Foundation.

————. 2000. *From Ellis Island to JFK: New York's Two Great Waves of Immigration.* New Haven, Conn.: Yale University Press.

———— (ed.). 2001. *Islands in the City: West Indian Migration to New York.* Berkeley: University of California Press.

————. 2005. *In a New Land: A Comparative View of Immigration.* New York: New York University Press.

Foner, Nancy, and Philip Kasinitz. 2007. "The Second Generation." Pp. 270–282 in *The New Americans: A Guide to Immigration since 1965,* edited by Mary C. Waters and Reed Ueda, with Helen Marrow. Cambridge, Mass.: Harvard University Press.

Foote, Thelma W. 2003. *Black and White Manhattan: The History of Racial Formation in Colonial New York City.* New York: Oxford University Press.

Fredrickson, George M. 1999. "Mosaics and Melting Pots." *Dissent* 46(3):36–42.

————. 2002. *Racism: A Short History.* Princeton, N.J.: Princeton University Press.

Friedberg, Rachel M., and Jennifer Hunt. 1999. "Immigration and the Receiving Economy." Pp. 342–359 in *The Handbook of International Migration: The American Experience,* edited by Charles Hirschman, Philip Kasinitz, and Josh DeWind. New York: Russell Sage Foundation.

Friedman, Robert I. 2000. *Red Mafiya: How the Russian Mob Has Invaded America.* Boston, Mass.: Little, Brown.

Fuligni, Andrew J. 1997. "The Academic Achievement of Adolescents from Immigrant Families: The Roles of Family Background, Attitudes and Behavior." *Child Development* 68:351–363.

————. 1998. "The Adjustment of Children from Immigrant Families." *Current Directions in Psychological Science* 7:99–103.

————. 2006. "Family Obligation among Children in Immigrant Families." In *Migration Information Source.* Washington, D.C.: Migration Policy Institute.

Furstenberg, Frank F., Jeanne Brooks-Gunn, and S. P. Morgan. 1987. *Adolescent Mothers in Later Life.* New York: Cambridge University Press.

Furstenberg, Frank F. Jr., Thomas D. Cook, Jaquelynne Eccles, Glen Elder, Jr., and Arnold Sameroff. 1999. *Managing to Make It: Urban Families and Adolescent Success.* Chicago: University of Chicago Press.

Furstenberg, Frank F. Jr., Rubén G. Rumbaut, and Richard A. Settersten. 2005. "On the Frontier of Adulthood: Emerging Themes and New Directions." Pp. 3–25 in *On the Frontier of Adulthood: Theory, Research, and Public Policy,* edited by Richard A. Settersten, Frank F. Furstenberg, Jr., and Rubén G. Rumbaut. Chicago: University of Chicago Press.

Gans, Herbert J. 1979. "Symbolic Ethnicity: Future of Ethnic Groups and Cultures in America." *Ethnic and Racial Studies* 2:1–20.

————. 1992. "Second Generation Decline: Scenarios for the Economic and Ethnic Futures of the Post-1965 American Immigrants." *Ethnic and Racial Studies* 15:173–192.

————. 1999. "The Possibility of a New Racial Hierarchy in the Twenty-first

Century United States." Pp. 371–389 in *The Cultural Territories of Race: Black and White Boundaries,* edited by Michèle Lamont. Chicago: University of Chicago Press.

Gerson, Jeffrey. 1990. "Building the Brooklyn Machine: Irish, Jewish, and Black Political Succession in Central Brooklyn, 1919–1964." PhD dissertation, City University of New York Graduate School and University Center.

Gerson, Kathleen. 1985. *Hard Choices: How Women Decide about Work, Career and Motherhood.* Berkeley: University of California Press.

———. 1993. *No Man's Land: Men's Changing Commitments to Family and Work.* New York: Basic Books.

———. 2002. "Moral Dilemmas, Moral Strategies, and the Transformation of Gender: Lessons from Two Generations of Work and Family Change." *Gender and Society* 16:8–28.

Gerstle, Gary. 1999. "Liberty, Coercion, and the Making of Americans." Pp. 275–293 in *The Handbook of International Migration: The American Experience,* edited by Charles Hirschman, Philip Kasinitz, and Josh DeWind. New York: Russell Sage Foundation.

Gerstle, Gary, and John H. Mollenkopf (eds.). 2001. *E Pluribus Unum? Contemporary and Historical Perspectives on Immigrant Political Incorporation.* New York: Russell Sage Foundation.

Gibson, Margaret A. 1988. *Accommodation without Assimilation: Sikh Immigrants in an American High School.* Ithaca, N.Y.: Cornell University Press.

Gibson, Margaret A., Patricia C. Gándara, and Jill Peterson Koyama (eds.). 2004. *School Connections: U S. Mexican Youth, Peers, and School Achievement.* New York: Teachers College Press.

Gimpel, James G., J. Celeste Lay, and Jason E. Schuknecht. 2003. *Cultivating Democracy: Civic Environments and Political Socialization in America.* Washington, D.C.: Brookings Institution Press.

Glazer, Elizabeth. 1999. "How Federal Prosecutors Can Reduce Crime." *Public Interest* 99:85–99.

Glazer, Nathan. 1997. *We Are All Multiculturalists Now.* Cambridge, Mass.: Harvard University Press.

Glazer, Nathan, and Daniel P. Moynihan. 1963. *Beyond the Melting Pot: The Negroes, Puerto Ricans, Jews, Italians, and Irish of New York City.* Cambridge, Mass.: MIT Press and Harvard University Press.

Goldscheider, Frances K., and Calvin Goldscheider. 1993. *Leaving Home before Marriage: Ethnicity, Familism, and Generational Relationships.* Madison: University of Wisconsin Press.

Goldscheider, Frances K., and Linda J. Waite. 1991. *New Families, No Families? The Transformation of the American Home.* Berkeley: University of California Press.

Goldsmith, Victor, Philip McGuire, John H. Mollenkopf, and Timothy Ross (eds.). 2000. *Analyzing Crime Patterns: Frontiers of Practice.* Thousand Oaks, Calif.: Sage Publications.

Gordon, Milton M. 1964. *Assimilation in American Life: The Role of Race, Religion, and National Origins.* New York: Oxford University Press.

Granovetter, Mark S. 1973. "The Strength of Weak Ties." *American Journal of Sociology* 78:1360–1380.

Grasmuck, Sherri, and Patricia R. Pessar. 1991. *Between Two Islands: Dominican International Migration.* Berkeley: University of California Press.

Greeley, Andrew. 1976. "The Ethnic Miracle." *The Public Interest* 45:20–36.

Greenhalgh, Susan, and Edwin A. Winkler. 2005. *Governing china's Population: From Jerimist to Neo-Jelseral Biopolitics.* Stanford, Calif.: Stanford University Press.

Grosfoguel, Ramon. 1999. "Puerto Ricans in the USA: A Comparative Approach." *Journal of Ethnic and Migration Studies* 25:233–249.

Guarnizo, Luis, and Marilyn Espitia. 2007. "Colombia." Pp. 371–385 in *The New Americans: A Guide to Immigration since 1965,* edited by Mary C. Waters and Reed Ueda, with Helen Marrow. Cambridge, Mass.: Harvard University Press.

Guglielmo, Jennifer, and Salvatore Salerno. 2003. *Are Italians White? How Race Is Made in America.* New York: Routledge.

Guglielmo, Thomas A. 2003. *White on Arrival: Italians, Race, Color, and Power in Chicago, 1890–1945.* Oxford: Oxford University Press.

Hannum, Emily, and Jihong Liu. 2006. "Adolescent Transitions to Adulthood in Reform-Era China." Pp. 270–319 in *Changing Transitions to Adulthood in Developing Countries: Selected Studies,* edited by Cynthia B. Lloyd, Jere R. Behrman, Nelly P. Stromquist, and Barney Cohen. Washington, D.C.: National Academies Press.

Hansen, Marcus Lee. 1938/1990. "The Problem of the Third Generation Immigrant." Pp. 191–216 in *American Immigrants and Their Generations: Studies and Commentaries on the Hansen Thesis after Fifty Years,* edited by Peter Kivisto and Dag Blanck. Urbana: University of Illinois Press. (Originally published in Augustana Historical Society Publications.)

Hao, Lingxin, and Melissa Bonstead-Bruns. 1998. "Parent-Child Differences in Educational Expectations and the Academic Achievement of Immigrant and Native Students." *Sociology of Education* 71:175–198.

Harris, Kathleen Mullan, Frank F. Furstenberg, Jr., and Jeremy K. Marmer. 1998. "Paternal Involvement with Adolescents in Intact Families: The Influence of Fathers over the Life Course." *Demography* 35:201–216.

Hauser, Robert M., William H. Sewell, John A. Logan, Taissa Hauser, Carol Ryff, and Maurice M. MacDonald. 1992. "The Wisconsin Longitudinal Study: Adults as Parents and Children at Age 50." *IASSIST Quarterly* 16(1/2):23–38.

Herberg, Will. 1960. *Protestant, Catholic, Jew: An Essay in American Religious Sociology.* New York: Anchor Books.

Hernández, Ramona, and Francisco Rivera-Batiz. 1997. "Dominican New Yorkers: A Socioeconomic Profile." New York: CUNY Dominican Studies Center.

Hernández, Ramona, and Silvio Torres-Saillant. 1996. "Dominicans in New York: Men, Women and Prospects." Pp. 30–56 in *Latinos in New York: Communities in Transition,* edited by Gabriel Haslip-Viera and Sherrie L. Baver. Notre Dame, Ill.: University of Notre Dame Press.

Hirschman, Charles. 1983. "The Melting Pot Reconsidered." *Annual Review of Sociology* 9:397–423.

———. 1996. "Problems and Prospects of Studying Immigrant Adaptation from the 1990 Population Census: From Generational Comparisons to the Process of 'Becoming American.'" Pp. 54–81 in *The New Second Generation*, edited by Alejandro Portes. New York: Russell Sage Foundation.

———. 2001. "The Educational Enrollment of Immigrant Youth: A Test of the Segmented-Assimilation Hypothesis." *Demography* 38:317–336.

———. 2005. "Immigration and the American Century." *Demography* 42: 595–620.

Hochschild, Jennifer L. 1995. *Facing Up to the American Dream: Race, Class, and the Soul of the Nation*. Princeton, N.J.: Princeton University Press.

Holdaway, Jennifer. 2005. "Slaves of New York: Real Estate, Kinship Relations, and Intergenerational Social Mobility in New York City." Paper presented at the Annual Meeting of the Population Association of America, Philadelphia, April.

———. 2007. "China: Outside the People's Republic of China." Pp. 355–370 in *The New Americans: A Guide to Immigration since 1965*, edited by Mary C. Waters and Reed Ueda, with Helen Marrow. Cambridge, Mass.: Harvard University Press.

Hollinger, David A. 1995. *Postethnic America: Beyond Multiculturalism*. New York: Basic Books.

Horowitz, Carl F. 2001. *An Examination of U.S. Immigration Policy and Serious Crime*. Washington, D.C.: Center for Immigration Studies.

Huckfeldt, R. Robert, and John D. Sprague. 1995. *Citizens, Politics, and Social Communication: Information and Influence in an Election Campaign*. Cambridge: Cambridge University Press.

Huntington, Samuel P. 2004. *Who Are We? The Challenges to American National Identity*. New York: Simon and Schuster.

Ignatiev, Noel. 1995. *How the Irish Became White*. New York: Routledge.

Iorizzo, Luciano J., and Salvatore Mondello. 1980. *The Italian Americans*. Boston: G. K. Hall.

Itzigsohn, José. 2000. "Immigration and the Boundaries of Citizenship: The Institutions of Immigrants' Political Transnationalism." *International Migration Review* 34:1126–1154.

Itzigsohn, José, and Carlos Dore-Cabral. 2000. "Competing Identities? Race, Ethnicity, and Panethnicity among Dominicans in the United States." *Sociological Forum* 15:225–247.

Itzigsohn, José, Silvia Giorguli, and Obed Vazquez. 2005. "Immigrant Incorporation and Racial Identity: Racial Self-Identification among Dominican Immigrants." *Ethnic and Racial Studies* 28:50–78.

Jackall, Robert. 1997. *Wild Cowboys: Urban Marauders and the Forces of Order*. Cambridge, Mass.: Harvard University Press.

Jacobs, Jane. 1961. *The Death and Life of Great American Cities*. New York: Random House.

Jacobs, Jerry A. 1996. "Gender Inequality and Higher Education." *Annual Review of Sociology* 22:153–185.

Jacobson, Matthew Frye. 1998. *Whiteness of a Different Color: European Immigrants and the Alchemy of Race.* Cambridge, Mass.: Harvard University Press.

Jacobson, Michael. 2001. "From the 'Back' to the 'Front': The Changing Character of Punishment in New York City." In *Rethinking the Urban Agenda: Reinvigorating the Liberal Tradition in New York City and Urban America,* edited by John H. Mollenkopf and Ken Emerson. New York: Twentieth Century Foundation Press.

Jacobson, Michael, and Philip Kasinitz. 1986. "Arson and the Burning of the Bronx." *The Nation,* November 15.

Jargowsky, Paul A. 1997. *Poverty and Place: Ghettos, Barrios, and the American City.* New York: Russell Sage Foundation.

Jennings, M. K., and Richard G. Niemi. 1974. *The Political Character of Adolescence: The Influence of Families and Schools.* Princeton, N.J.: Princeton University Press.

Jensen, Leif, and Yoshimi Chitose. 1994. "Today's Second Generation: Evidence from the 1990 U.S. Census." *International Migration Review* 28:714–735.

Jones-Correa, Michael. 1998. *Between Two Nations: The Political Predicament of Latinos in New York City.* Ithaca, N.Y.: Cornell University Press.

——— (ed.). 2001. *Governing American Cities: Interethnic Coalitions, Competition, and Conflict.* New York: Russell Sage Foundation.

———. 2003. "Term-Limits and Openings for New Political Actors in Urban Settings: The Case of New York City." Paper presented at the Western Political Science Association Meeting, Denver, Colo., March 27–29.

Kahn, Bonnie M. 1987. *Cosmopolitan Culture: The Gilt-Edged Dream of a Tolerant City.* New York: Atheneum.

Kao, Grace. 2004. "Parental Influences on the Educational Outcomes of Immigrant Youth." *International Migration Review* 38:427–449.

Kao, Grace, and Jennifer S. Thompson. 2003. "Racial and Ethnic Stratification in Educational Achievement and Attainment." *Annual Review of Sociology* 29:417–442.

Kao, Grace, and Marta Tienda. 1995. "Optimism and Achievement: The Educational Performance of Immigrant Youth." *Social Science Quarterly* 76:1–19.

Karabel, Jerome. 2005. *The Chosen: The Hidden History of Admission and Exclusion at Harvard, Yale, and Princeton.* Boston: Houghton Mifflin.

Karmen, Andrew. 2000. *New York Murder Mystery: The True Story behind the Crime Crash of the 1990s.* New York: New York University Press.

Kasinitz, Philip. 1992. *Caribbean New York: Black Immigrants and the Politics of Race.* Ithaca, N.Y.: Cornell University Press.

———. 2000. "Red Hook: The Paradoxes of Poverty and Place in Brooklyn." *Research in Urban Sociology* 5:253–274.

———. 2001. "Children of America: The Second Generation Comes of Age." *Common Quest* 4:32–41.

———. 2004. "Race, Assimilation and Second Generations: Past and Present." Pp. 278–298 in *Not Just Black and White: Historical and Contemporary Perspectives on Immigration, Race, and Ethnicity in the United States,* edited by Nancy Foner and George M. Fredrickson. New York: Russell Sage Foundation.

Kasinitz, Philip, Juan Battle, and Ines Miyares. 2001. "Fade to Black? The Children of West Indian Immigrants in South Florida." Pp. 267–300 in *Ethnicities: Coming of Age in Immigrant America,* edited by Rubén G. Rumbaut and Alejandro Portes. New York: Russell Sage Foundation.

Kasinitz, Philip, Mohamad Bazzi, and Randal Doane. 1998. "Creating and Maintaining Sustainable Diversity: The Case of Jackson Heights." *Cityscape* 4:161–178.

Kasinitz, Philip, John H. Mollenkopf, and Mary C. Waters. 2002. "Becoming Americans / Becoming New Yorkers: Immigrant Incorporation in a Majority Minority City." *International Migration Review* 36:1020–1036.

———. (eds.). 2004. *Becoming New Yorkers: Ethnographies of the New Second Generation.* New York: Russell Sage Foundation.

Kasinitz, Philip, and Jan Rosenberg. 1996. "Missing the Connection: Social Isolation and Employment on the Brooklyn Waterfront." *Social Problems* 43:180–196.

Kasinitz, Philip, and Milton Vickerman. 2001. "Ethnic Niches and Racial Traps: Jamaicans in the New York Regional Economy." Pp. 191–211 in *Migration, Transnationalization and Race in a Changing New York,* edited by Héctor Cordero-Guzmán, Robert C. Smith, and Ramón Grosfoguel. Philadelphia: Temple University Press.

Kasinitz, Philip, Mary C. Waters, John H. Mollenkopf, and Merih Anil. 2002. "Transnationalism and the Children of Immigrants in Contemporary New York." Pp. 96–122 in *The Changing Face of Home: The Transnational Lives of the Second Generation,* edited by Mary C. Waters and Peggy Levitt. New York: Russell Sage Foundation.

Kasinitz, Philip, Aviva Zeltzer-Zubida, and Zoya Simakhodskaya. 2001. "The Next Generation: Russian Jewish Young Adults in Contemporary New York." New York: Russell Sage Foundation Working Paper Number 178.

Kelly, Jennell. 2005. *Child Care in New York City: A Neighborhood Analysis of Supply and Demand.* New York: New York Office of Child Care and Family Services.

Kelly, Robbin D. G. 1997. *Yo' Mama's Disfunktional: Fighting the Culture Wars in Urban America.* Boston: Beacon Press.

Kessler, Ronald C., Kristin D. Mickelson, and David R. Williams. 1999. "The Prevalence, Distribution and Mental Health Correlates of Perceived Discrimination in the United States." *Journal of Health and Social Behavior* 40 (3): 208–230.

Kim, Dae Young. 2001. "Entrepreneurship and Intergenerational Mobility among Second-Generation Korean Americans in New York." PhD dissertation, City University of New York.

————. 2004. "Leaving the Ethnic Economy: The Rapid Integration of Second-Generation Korean Americans in New York." Pp. 154–188 in *Becoming New Yorkers: Ethnographies of the New Second Generation,* edited by Philip Kasinitz, John H. Mollenkopf, and Mary C. Waters. New York: Russell Sage Foundation.

————. 2006. "Stepping-Stone to Intergenerational Mobility? The Springboard, Safety Net, or Mobility Trap Functions of Korean Immigrant Entrepreneurship for the Second Generation." *International Migration Review* 40:927–962.

Kwong, Peter. 1996. *The New Chinatown* (Revised edition). New York: Hill and Wang.

Kyle, David. 2000. *Transnational Peasants: Migrations, Networks and Ethnicity in Andean Ecuador.* Baltimore, Md.: Johns Hopkins University Press.

Lahiri, Jhumpa. 1999. *Interpreter of Maladies: Stories.* Boston: Houghton Mifflin.

Lamont, Michèle (ed.). 1999. *The Cultural Territories of Race: Black and White Boundaries.* Chicago: University of Chicago Press.

Landale, Nancy S., and R. S. Oropesa. 2002. "White, Black, or Puerto Rican? Radical Self-Identification among Mainland and Island Puerto Ricans." *Social Forces* 81:231–254.

Landesman, Alter F. 1969. *Brownsville: The Birth, Development and Passing of a Jewish Community in New York.* New York: Bloch Pub. Co.

Lareau, Annette. 2003. *Unequal Childhoods: Class, Race, and Family Life.* Berkeley: University of California Press.

Lee, Sara S. 2004. "Class Matters: Racial and Ethnic Identities of Working and Middle-Class Second-Generation Korean Americans in New York City." Pp. 313–338 in *Becoming New Yorkers: Ethnographies of the New Second Generation,* edited by Philip Kasinitz, John H. Mollenkopf, and Mary C. Waters. New York: Russell Sage Foundation.

Levitt, Peggy. 2001. *The Transnational Villagers.* Berkeley: University of California Press.

————. 2007. *God Needs No Passport: Immigrants and the Changing American Religious Landscape.* New York: New Press.

Levitt, Peggy, and Mary C. Waters (eds.). 2002. *The Changing Face of Home: The Transnational Lives of the Second Generation.* New York: Russell Sage Foundation.

Lewis, Oscar. 1966. *La Vida: A Puerto Rican Family in the Culture of Poverty—San Juan and New York.* New York: Random House.

Lieberson, Stanley, and Mary C. Waters. 1988. *From Many Strands: Ethnic and Racial Groups in Contemporary America.* New York: Russell Sage Foundation.

Liebow, Elliot. 1967. *Tally's Corner: A Study of Negro Streetcorner Men.* Boston: Little, Brown.

Light, Ivan H., and Steven J. Gold. 2000. *Ethnic Economies.* San Diego: Academic Press.

Lin, Jan. 1998. *Reconstructing Chinatown: Ethnic Enclave, Global Change.* Minneapolis: University of Minnesota Press.

Logan, John R., Richard D. Alba, and Thomas L. McNulty. 1994. "Ethnic Economies in Metropolitan Regions: Miami and Beyond." *Social Forces* 72:691–724.

Logan, John R., and John H. Mollenkopf. 2003. "People and Politics in Urban America." Report to the Drum Major Institute, New York City.

Logan, John R., and Glenna D. Spitze. 1996. *Family Ties: Enduring Relations between Parents and Their Grown Children*. Philadelphia: Temple University Press.

Logan, John R., Brian J. Stults, and Reynolds Farley. 2004. "Segregation of Minorities in the Metropolis: Two Decades of Change." *Demography* 41:1–22.

López, Nancy. 2003. *Hopeful Girls, Troubled Boys: Race and Gender Disparity in Urban Education*. New York: Routledge.

———. 2004. "Unraveling the Race-Gender Gap in Education: Second Generation Dominican Men's High School Experiences." Pp. 28–56 in *Becoming New Yorkers: Ethnographies of the New Second Generation*, edited by Philip Kasinitz, John H. Mollenkopf, and Mary C. Waters. New York: Russell Sage Foundation.

Louie, Vivian S. 2004. *Compelled to Excel: Immigration, Education, and Opportunity among Chinese Americans*. Stanford, Calif.: Stanford University Press.

Louie, Vivian, and Jennifer Holdaway. 2008. "Immigrants and Catholic Schools: A New Generation." *In Immigrant Communities and American Schools. Special Issue of Teachers College Record*, edited by R. Alba and J. Holdaway.

Lowi, Theodore J. 1964. *At the Pleasure of the Mayor: Patronage and Power in New York City, 1898–1958*. New York: Free Press.

Malkin, Victoria. 2004. "Who's behind the Counter? Retail Workers in New York City." Pp. 115–153 in *Becoming New Yorkers: Ethnographies of the New Second Generation*, edited by Philip Kasinitz, John H. Mollenkopf, and Mary C. Waters. New York: Russell Sage Foundation.

Maly, Michael T. 2005. *Beyond Segregation: Multiracial And Multiethnic Neighborhoods in the United States*. Philadelphia: Temple University Press.

Marrow, Helen. 2007. "South America: Ecuador, Peru, Brazil, Argentina, Venezuela." Pp. 593–611 in *The New Americans: A Guide to Immigration since 1965*, edited by Mary C. Waters and Reed Ueda, with Helen Marrow. Cambridge, Mass.: Harvard University Press.

Martinez, Ramiro, Jr., and Abel Valenzuela, Jr. (eds.). 2006. *Immigration and Crime: Race, Ethnicity, and Violence*. New York: New York University Press.

Marwell, Nicole P. 2004. "Ethnic and Postethnic Politics in New York City: The Dominican Second Generation." Pp. 227–256 in *Becoming New Yorkers: Ethnographies of the New Second Generation*, edited by Philip Kasinitz, John H. Mollenkopf, and Mary C. Waters. New York: Russell Sage Foundation.

Massey, Douglas S., and Brooks Bitterman. 1985. "Explaining the Paradox of Puerto Rican Segregation." *Social Forces* 64:306–331.

Massey, Douglas S., Camille Z. Charles, Garvey F. Lundy, and Mary J. Fischer. 2003. *The Source of the River: The Social Origins of Freshmen at America's Selective Colleges and Universities*. Princeton, N.J.: Princeton University Press.

Massey, Douglas S., and Nancy A. Denton. 1989. "Residential Segregation of Mexicans, Puerto Ricans and Cubans in selected Metropolitan Arcade." *Sociology and Social Research* 73: 73–83.

———. 1993. *American Apartheid: Segregation and the Making of the American Underclass*. Cambridge, Mass.: Harvard University Press.

Massey, Douglas S., Jorge Durand, and Nolan J. Malone. 2002. *Beyond Smoke and Mirrors: Mexican Immigration in an Era of Economic Integration*. New York: Russell Sage Foundation.

Massey, Douglas, Margarita Mooney, Camille Charles, and Kimberly Torres. 2007. "Black Immigrants and Black Natives Attending Selective Colleges and Universities in the United States." *American Journal of Education* 113(2): 243–271.

Matza, David. 1964. *Delinquency and Drift. From the Research Program of the Center for the Study of Law and Society, University of California, Berkeley*. New York: Wiley.

Mayhew, David R. 1986. *Placing Parties in American Politics: Organization, Electoral Settings, and Government Activity in the Twentieth Century*. Princeton, N.J.: Princeton University Press.

McLanahan, Sarah S. 1999. "Father Absence and the Welfare of Children." Pp. 117–145 in *Coping with Divorce, Single Parenting, and Remarriage: A Risk and Resiliency Perspective*, edited by E. Mavis Hetherington. Mahwah, N.J.: Lawrence Erlbaum Associates.

———. 2001. "Life without Father: What Happens to the Children?" Princeton, N.J.: Princeton University Center for Research on Child Wellbeing.

Mei, Lori, Jennifer Bell-Ellwanger, and Ron Miller. 2002. "An Examination of Four-Year Cohort Graduation and Dropout Rates for the New York City Schools' Class of 2001 and Final School Completion Outcomes for the Class of 1990." Paper presented at the Annual Meeting of the American Education Research Association, New Orleans, La, April 1–5.

Merton, Robert K. 1967. *Social Theory and Social Structure*. New York: Free Press.

Min, Pyong Gap. 1998. *Changes and Conflicts: Korean Immigrant Families in New York*. Boston: Allyn and Bacon.

——— (ed.). 2002. *The Second Generation: Ethnic Identity among Asian Americans*. Walnut Creek, Calif.: AltaMira Press.

Mittelberg, David, and Mary C. Waters. 1992. "The Process of Ethnogenesis among Haitian and Israeli Immigrants in the United States." *Ethnic and Racial Studies* 15:412–435.

Model, Suzanne. 1993. "The Ethnic Niche and the Structure of Opportunity: Immigrants and Minorities in New York City." Pp. 161–193 in *The Underclass Debate: Views from History*, edited by Michael B. Katz. Princeton, N.J.: Princeton University Press.

Mollenkopf, John H. 1994. *A Phoenix in the Ashes: The Rise and Fall of the Koch Coalition in New York City Politics*. Princeton, N.J.: Princeton University Press.

———. 1999. "Urban Political Conflicts and Alliances: New York and Los Angeles Compared." Pp. 412–422 in *The Handbook of International Migration: The American Experience*, edited by Charles Hirschman, Philip Kasinitz, and Josh DeWind. New York: Russell Sage Foundation.

———. 2005a. "9/11 Reshapes the Political Environment." In *Contentious City: The Politics of Recovery in New York City*, edited by John H. Mollenkopf. New York: Russell Sage Foundation.

———. 2005b. "A Changing City." In *New York Comes Back: The Mayoralty of Edward I. Koch*, edited by Michael Goodwin. New York: Power House Books in association with the Museum of the City of New York.

Mollenkopf, John H., and Lorraine Minnite. 2001. "Between White and Black: Asian and Latino Political Participation in the 2000 Presidential Election in New York City." Paper presented at the Annual Meeting of the American Political Science Association, San Francisco, August 30–September 2.

Mollenkopf, John H., David Olson, and Timothy Ross. 2001. "Immigrant Political Participation in New York and Los Angeles." Pp. 17–70 in *Governing American Cities: Interethnic Coalitions, Competition, and Conflict*, edited by Michael Jones-Correa. New York: Russell Sage.

Moore, Deborah Dash. 1994. *To the Golden Cities: Pursuing the American Jewish Dream in Miami and L.A.* New York: Free Press.

Morawksa, Ewa. 2007. "Transnationalism." Pp. 149–163 in *The New Americans: A Guide to Immigration since 1965*, edited by Mary C. Waters and Reed Ueda, with Helen Marrow. Cambridge, Mass.: Harvard University Press.

Mouw, Ted. 2003. "Social Capital and Finding a Job: Do Contacts Matter?" *American Sociological Review* 68:868–898.

Myers, Dowell. 2007. *Immigrants and Boomers: Forging a New Social Contract for the Future of America*. New York: Russell Sage Foundation.

Nardulli, Peter F., Jon K. Dalager, and Donald E. Greco. 1996. "Voter Turnout in U.S. Presidential Elections: An Historical View and Some Speculation." *PS: Political Science and Politics* 29:480–490.

Neckerman, Kathryn. 2007. *Schools Betrayed: Roots of Failure in Inner-City Education*. Chicago: University of Chicago Press.

Neckerman, Kathryn M., Prudence Carter, and Jennifer Lee. 1999. "Segmented Assimilation and Minority Cultures of Mobility." *Ethnic and Racial Studies* 22:945–965.

Nee, Victor, Jimy Sanders, and Scott Sernau. 1994. "Job Transitions in an Immigrant Metropolis." *American Sociological Review* 59:849–871.

Nee, Victor, and Jimy M. Sanders. 2001. "Trust in Ethnic Ties: Social Capital and Immigrants." Pp 374–392 in *Trust and Society*, edited by Karen Cook. New York: Russell Sage Foundation.

New York City Department of Education. 2002. "The Class of 2001 Four-Year Graduation and Dropout Report and 2000–2001 Event Dropout Rates." New York: Division of Assessment and Accountability.

Neidert, Lisa J., and Reynolds Farley. 1985. "Assimilation in the United States:

An Analysis of Ethnic and Generation Differences in Status and Achievement." *American Sociological Review* 50(6): 840–850.

Newman, Katherine S. 1999. *No Shame in My Game: The Working Poor in the Inner City.* New York: Knopf.

———. 2006. *Chutes and Ladders: Navigating the Low Wage Labor Market.* New York: Russell Sage Foundation.

Novak, Michael. 1974. "The Seventies: The Decade of the Ethnics." Pp. 137–147 in *Race and Ethnicity in Modern America,* edited by Richard J. Meister. Lexington, Ky.: Heath.

Nyden, Philip, John Lukehart, Michael T. Maly, and William Peterman. 1998. "Neighborhood Racial and Ethnic Diversity in the U.S. Cities." *Cityscape* 4:1–18.

Oliver, Melvin L., and Thomas M. Shapiro. 1995. *Black Wealth, White Wealth: A New Perspective on Racial Inequality.* New York: Routledge.

Ong, Paul, Edna Bonacich, and Lucie Cheng. 1994. *The New Asian Immigration in Los Angeles and Global Restructuring.* Philadelphia: Temple University Press.

Osofsky, Gilbert. 1966. *Harlem: The Making of a Ghetto: Negro New York, 1980–1930,* New York: Harper and Row.

Pager, Devah. 2005. "Double Jeopardy: Race, Crime, and Getting a Job." *Wisconsin Law Review* 2005:617–660.

Park, Robert. 1950. *Race and Culture.* Glencoe, Ill.: Free Press.

Parrado, Emilio A., and Chenoa A. Flippen. 2005. "Migration and Gender among Mexican Women." *American Sociological Review* 70:606–632.

Passel, Jeffrey S. 2005. "Estimates of the Size and Characteristics of the Undocumented Population." Washington, D.C.: Pew Hispanic Center Report, March 21.

Patterson, Orlando. 2000. "Taking Culture Seriously: A Framework and an Afro-American Illustration." Pp. 202–222 in *Culture Matters: How Values Shape Human Progress,* edited by Lawrence E. Harrison and Samuel P. Huntington. New York: Basic Books.

———. 2004. "Culture and Continuity: Causal Structures in Socio-Cultural Persistence." In *Matters of Culture: Cultural Sociology in Practice,* edited by Roger Friedland and John W. Mohr. New York: Cambridge University Press.

Paulino, Edward. 2006. "Dominican Apartheid: Dominico-Haitianos and Their 21st Century Struggle for Citizenship and Dignity." Paper presented at the 2006 Annual Meeting of the Latin American Studies Association, San Juan, Puerto Rico, March 15–18.

Perlmann, Joel. 2005. *Italians Then, Mexicans Now: Immigrant Origins and Second-Generation Progress, 1890 to 2000.* New York: Russell Sage Foundation.

Perlmann, Joel, and Roger Waldinger. 1997. "Second Generation Decline? Children of Immigrants, Past and Present: A Reconsideration." *International Migration Review* 31:893–922.

———. 1999. "Immigrants, Past and Present: A Reconsideration." Pp. 223–238 in *The Handbook of International Immigration: The American Experience,* edited by Charles Hirschman, Philip Kasinitz, and Josh DeWind. New York: Russell Sage Foundation.

Perlmann, Joel, and Mary C. Waters. 2002. *The New Race Question: How the Census Counts Multiracial Individuals.* New York: Russell Sage Foundation.

———. 2004. "Intermarriage Then and Now: Race, Generation and the Changing Meaning of Marriage." Pp. 262–277 in *Not Just Black and White: Historical and Contemporary Perspectives on Immigration, Race, and Ethnicity in the United States,* edited by Nancy Foner and George M. Fredrickson. New York: Russell Sage Foundation.

Pessar, Patricia R. 1995. *A Visa for a Dream: Dominicans in the United States.* Boston: Allyn and Bacon.

Pessar, Patricia, Pamela M. Graham. 2001. "The Dominicans: Transnational Identities and Local Politics." Pp. 251–274 in *New Immigrants in New York,* edited by Nancy Foner. New York: Columbia University Press.

Peterson, Ruth D., Lauren J. Krivo, and John Hagan. 2006. *The Many Colors of Crime: Inequalities of Race, Ethnicity, and Crime in America.* New York: New York University Press.

Pleck, Joseph H., and Brian P. Masciadrelli. 2004. "Paternal Involvement by U.S. Residential Fathers." Pp. 222–271 in *The Role of the Father in Child Development* (4th edition), edited by M. E. Lamb. New York: Wiley.

Plotnick, Robert D. 1992. "The Effects of Attitudes on Teenage Premarital Pregnancy and Its Resolution." *American Sociological Review* 57:800–811.

Pong, Suet-ling, Lingxin Hao, and Erica Gardner. 2005. "The Roles of Parenting Styles and Social Capital in the School Performance of Immigrant Asian and Hispanic Adolescents." *Social Science Quarterly* 86:928–950.

Portes, Alejandro. (ed.). 1996. *The New Second Generation.* New York: Russell Sage Foundation.

———. 1999. "Conclusion: Towards a New World—The Origins and Effects of Transnational Activities." *Ethnic and Racial Studies* 22:463–477.

———. 2001. "Introduction: The Debates and Significance of Immigrant Transnationalism." *Global Networks* 1:181–194.

Portes, Alejandro, and Robert L. Bach. 1985. *Latin Journey: Cuban and Mexican Immigrants in the United States.* Berkeley: University of California Press.

Portes, Alejandro, Patricia Fernández-Kelly, and William Haller. 2005. "Segmented Assimilation on the Ground: The New Second Generation in Early Adulthood." *Ethnic and Racial Studies* 28:1000–1040.

Portes, Alejandro, and Lingxin Hao. 2004. "The Schooling of Children of Immigrants: Contextual Effects on the Educational Attainment of the Second Generation." *Proceedings of the National Academy of Sciences of the United States of America* 101:11920–11927.

Portes, Alejandro, and Leif Jensen. 1989. "The Enclave and the Entrants: Patterns of Ethnic Enterprise in Miami before and after Mariel." *American Sociological Review* 54: 929–949.

Portes, Alejandro, and Rubén G. Rumbaut. 2001. *Legacies: The Story of the Immigrant Second Generation.* Berkeley: University of California Press.

———. 2005. "Introduction: The Second Generation and the Children of Immigrants Longitudinal Study." *Ethnic and Racial Studies* 28:983–999.

Portes, Alejandro, and Richard Schauffler. 1996. "Language and the Second Generation: Bilingualism Yesterday and Today." Pp. 8–29 in *The New Second Generation,* edited by Alejandro Portes. New York: Russell Sage Foundation.

Portes, Alejandro, and Steven Shafer. 2007. "Revisiting the Enclave Hypothesis: Miami Twenty Five Years Later. The Sociology of Entrepreneurship." *Research in the Sociology of Organizations* 25:175–190.

Portes, Alejandro, and Min Zhou. 1992. "Gaining the Upper Hand: Economic Mobility among Immigrant and Domestic Minorities." *Ethnic and Racial Studies* 15:491–521.

———. 1993. "The New Second Generation: Segmented Assimilation and Its Variants among Post-1965 Immigrant Youth." *Annals of the American Academy of Political and Social Science* 530:74–96.

Powell, Roslyn. 2000. *Nowhere to Turn: New York City's Failure to Inform Parents on Public Assistance about Their Child Care Rights.* New York: NOW Legal Defense and Education Fund.

Prell, Riv-Ellen. 1999. *Fighting to Become Americans: Jews, Gender, and the Anxiety of Assimilation.* Boston: Beacon Press.

Putnam, Robert D. 2000. *Bowling Alone: The Collapse and Revival of American Community.* New York: Simon and Schuster.

Qin, Desiree Baolian. 2006. "Our Child Doesn't Talk to Us Anymore: Alienation in Immigrant Chinese Families." *Anthropology and Education Quarterly* 37:162–179.

Ramos, Fernando A. 1992. "Out-migration and Return Migration of Puerto Ricans." Pp. 49–66 in *Immigration and the Work Force: Economic Consequences for the United States and Source Areas,* edited by George J. Borjas and Richard B. Freeman. Chicago: University of Chicago Press.

Richardson, Bonham C. 1992. *The Caribbean in the Wider World, 1492–1992: A Regional Geography.* Cambridge: Cambridge University Press.

Ried, Ira de A. 1939. *The Negro Immigrant: His Background, Characteristics, and Social Adjustment, 1899–1937.* New York: AMS Press.

Rivera, Raquel. 2003. *New York Ricans from the Hip Hop Zone.* Basingstoke, UK: Palgrave Macmillan.

Rivera-Batiz, Francisco L., and Carlos E. Santiago. 1996. *Island Paradox: Puerto Rico in the 1990s.* New York: Russell Sage Foundation.

Rodríguez, Clara E. 1989. *Puerto Rican: Born in the USA.* Boston: Unwin Hyman.

———. 2000. *Changing Race: Latinos, the Census, and the History of Ethnicity in the United States.* New York: New York University Press.

Roediger, David R. 1999. *The Wages of Whiteness: Race and the Making of the American Working Class* (Revised edition). London: Verso.

———. 2005. *Working toward Whiteness: How America's Immigrants Became White: The Strange Journey from Ellis Island to the Suburbs.* New York: Basic Books.

Rosenbaum, Emily. 1994. "The Constraints on Minority Housing Choices, New York City 1978–1987." *Social Forces* 72 (3): 725–747.

Rosenthal, Robert, and Lenore Jacobsen. 1968. *Pygmalion in the Classroom: Teacher Expectation and Pupils' Intellectual Development.* New York: Holt, Rinehart and Winston.

Rosenwaike, Ira. 1972. *Population History of New York City.* Syracuse, N.Y.: Syracuse University Press.

Roth, Wendy. 2006. "Caribbean Race and American Dreams: How Migration Shapes Dominicans' and Puerto Ricans' Racial Identities and Its Impact on Socioeconomic Mobility." PhD dissertation, Harvard University.

Rouse, Cecilia E. 1995. "Democratization or Diversion? The Effect of Community Colleges on Educational Attainment." *Journal of Business and Economics Statistics* 13(2):217–224.

Rumbaut, Rubén G. 1995. "The New Californians: Comparative Research Findings on the Educational Progress of Immigrant Children." Pp. 17–69 in *California's Immigrant Children: Theory, Research, and Implications for Educational Policy,* edited by Rubén G. Rumbaut and Wayne A. Cornelius. La Jolla, Calif.: Center for U.S.-Mexican Studies, University of California San Diego.

———. 1996a. "The Crucible Within: Ethnicity Identity, Self-Esteem, and Segmented Assimilation among Children of Immigrants." Pp. 119–170 in *The New Second Generation,* edited by Alejandro Portes. New York: Russell Sage Foundation.

———. 1996b. "Origins and Destinies: Immigration, Race, and Ethnicity in Contemporary America." Pp. 21–42 in *Origins and Destinies: Immigration, Race, and Ethnicity in America,* edited by Silvia Pedraza and Rubén G. Rumbaut. Belmont, Calif.: Wadsworth.

———. 1997. "Ties That Bind: Immigration and Immigrant Families in the U.S." Pp. 3–45 in *Immigration and the Family: Research and Policy on U.S. Immigrants,* edited by Alan Booth, Ann C. Crouter, and Nancy Landale. Mahwah, N.J.: Lawrence Erlbaum Associates.

———. 1999. "Assimilation and Its Discontents: Ironies and Paradoxes." Pp. 172–195 in *The Handbook of International Immigration: The American Experience,* edited by Charles Hirschmann, Philip Kasinitz, and Josh DeWind. New York: Russell Sage Foundation.

———. 2004. "Ages, Life Stages and Generational Cohorts: Decomposing the Immigrant First and Second Generations in the United States." *International Migration Review* 38:1160–1205.

———. 2005a. "The Melting and the Pot: Assimilation and Variety in American Life." Pp. 154–173 in *Incorporating Diversity: Rethinking Assimilation in a Multicultural Era,* edited by Peter Kivisto. Boulder, Colo.: Paradigm Publishers.

———. 2005b. "Turning Points in the Transition to Adulthood: Determinants of Educational Attainment, Incarceration, and Early Childbearing among Children of Immigrants." *Ethnic and Racial Studies* 28:1041–1086.

Rumbaut, Rubén G., and Alejandro Portes (eds.). 2001. *Ethnicities: Children of Immigrants in America.* Berkeley: University of California Press.

Sabogal, Elena. 2005. "*Viviendo en la sombra:* The Immigration of Peruvian Professionals to South Florida." *Latino Studies* 3:113–131.

Saegert, Susan, J. Phillip Thompson, and Mark R. Warren (eds.). 2005. *Social Capital and Poor Communities.* New York: Russell Sage Foundation.

Salamon, Lester M. 1995. *Partners in Public Service: Government-Nonprofit Relations in the Modern Welfare State.* Baltimore, Md.: Johns Hopkins University Press.

Sampson, Robert J., and John Laub. 2003. *Shared Beginnings, Divergent Lives: Delinquent Boys to Age 70.* Cambridge, Mass.: Harvard University Press.

Sampson, Robert J., Jeffrey D. Morenoff, and Thomas Gannon-Rowley. 2002. "Assessing 'Neighborhood Effects': Social Processes and New Directions in Research." *Annual Review of Sociology* 28:443–478.

Sampson, Robert J., Jeffrey D. Morenoff, and Stephen Raudenbush. 2005. "Social Anatomy of Racial and Ethnic Disparities in Violence." *American Journal of Public Health* 95:224–231.

Sampson, Robert J., Stephen W. Raudenbush, and Felton Earls. 1997. "Neighborhoods and Violent Crime: A Multilevel Study of Collective Efficacy." *Science* 277:918–924.

Sanjek, Roger. 1998. *The Future of Us All: Race and Neighborhood Politics in New York City.* Ithaca, N.Y.: Cornell University Press.

Sauerzopf, Richard, and Todd Swanstrom. 1999. "The Urban Electorate in Presidential Elections, 1920–1996." *Urban Affairs Review* 35:72–91.

Schoeni, Robert F., and Karen E. Ross. 2005. "Material Assistance from Families during the Transition to Adulthood." In *On the Fronteir of Adulthood: Theory, Research, and Public Policy,* edited by Richard A. Settersten, Frank F. Furstenberg, Jr., and Rubén E., Rumbaut. Chicago: University of Chicago Press.

Sennett, Richard. 1974. *Families against the City: Middle Class Homes of Industrial Chicago, 1872–1890.* Cambridge, Mass.: Harvard University Press.

Shefter, Martin. 1992. *Political Crisis / Fiscal Crisis: The Collapse and Revival of New York City* (2nd edition). New York: Columbia University Press.

———. 1994. *Political Parties and the State: The American Historical Experience.* Princeton, N.J.: Princeton University Press.

Shibutani, Tomatsu, and Kian Kwan. 1965. *Ethnic Stratification: A Comparative Approach.* New York: Macmillan.

Simmel, Georg. (1922) 1955. *Conflict and the Web of Group Affiliations.* New York: Free Press.

Singer, Audrey, and Greta Gilbertson. 2000. "Naturalization in the Wake of Anti-immigrant Legislation: Dominicans in New York City." Washington, D.C.: Carnegie Endowment. Working Paper 10.

Singh, Susheela, and Renee Samara. 1996. "Early Marriage among Women in Developing Countries." *International Family Planning Perspectives* 22:148–157, 175.

Skeldon, Ronald. 1994. *Reluctant Exiles? Migration from Hong Kong and the New Overseas Chinese.* Armonk, N.Y.: M. E. Sharpe.

Skogan, G. Wesley. 2006. *Police and Community in Chicago: A Tale of Three Cities.* New York: Oxford University Press.

Small, Mario. 2007. "Racial Differences in Networks: Do Neighborhood Conditions Matter?" *Social Science Quarterly* 88(2):320–343.

Small, Mario Luis, and Monica McDermott. 2006. "The Presence of Organizational Resources in Poor Urban Neighborhoods: An Analysis of Average and Contextual Effects." *Social Forces* 84:1697–1724.

Small, Mario Luis, and Katherine Newman. 2001. "Urban Poverty after the Truly Disadvantaged: The Rediscovery of the Family, the Neighborhood, and Culture." *Annual Review of Sociology* 27:23–45.

Smith, James P. 2003. "Assimilation across the Latino Generations." *American Economic Review* 93:315–319.

Smith, James P., and Barry Edmonston. 1997. *The New Americans: Economic, Demographic, and Fiscal Effects of Immigration.* Washington, D.C.: National Academy Press.

Smith, Robert C. 2006. *Mexican New York: Transnational Lives of New Immigrants.* Berkeley: University of California Press.

Smith, Sandra. 2005. " 'Don't put my name on it': (Dis) Trust and Job-Finding Assistance among the Black Urban Poor." *American Journal of Sociology* 111(1):1–57.

Stack, Carol B. 1974. *All Our Kin: Strategies for Survival in a Black Community.* New York: Harper and Row.

Steinberg, Stephen. 2007. *Race Relations: A Critique.* Stanford, Calif.: Stanford University Press.

Suárez-Orozco, Carola, and Marcelo M. Suárez-Orozco. 2001. *Children of Immigration.* Cambridge, Mass.: Harvard University Press.

Suárez-Orozco, Carola, Marcelo E. Suárez-Orozco, and Irina Todorova. 2007. *Learning in a New Land: Immigrant Students in American Society.* Cambridge, Mass.: Harvard University Press.

Suárez-Orozco, Carola, Irina L. G. Todorova, and Josephine Louie. 2002. "Making Up for Lost Time: The Experience of Separation and Reunification among Immigrant Families." *Family Process* 41:625–643.

Suárez-Orozco, Marcelo M., and Carola E. Suárez-Orozco. 1995. "The Cultural Patterning of Achievement Motivation: A Comparison of Mexican, Mexican Immigrant, Mexican American, and Non-Latino White American Students." Pp. 161–190 in *California's Immigrant Children: Theory, Research, and Implications for Educational Policy,* edited by Rubén G. Rumbaut and Wayne A. Cornelius. San Diego: Center for U.S.-Mexican Studies, University of California San Diego.

Sullivan, Mercer L. 1989. *"Getting Paid": Youth, Crime and Work in the Inner City.* Ithaca, N.Y.: Cornell University Press.

Thomas, William Isaac, and Florian Znaniecki. 1927. *The Polish Peasant in Europe and America*. New York: Knopf.

Thompson, E. P. 1966. *The Making of the English Working Class*. New York: Vintage Books.

Tienda, Marta. 1989. "Puerto Ricans and the Underclass Debate." *Annals of the American Academy of Political and Social Science* 501:105–119.

Torres, Andrés, and José E. Velaquez, (eds.). 1998. *The Pureto Rican Movement: Voices from the Diaspora*. Philadelphia: Temple University Press.

Torres-Saillant, Silvio. 1998. "The Tribulations of Blackness: Stages in Dominican Racial Identity." *Latin American Perspectives* 25:126–146.

Torres-Saillant, Silvio, and Ramona Hernández. 1998. *The Dominican Americans*. Westport, Conn.: Greenwood Press.

Trillo, Alex. 2004. "Somewhere between Wall Street and El Barrio: Community College as a Second Chance for Second-Generation Latino Students." Pp. 57–78 in *Becoming New Yorkers: Ethnographies of the New Second Generation*, edited by Philip Kasinitz, John H. Mollenkopf, and Mary C. Waters. New York: Russell Sage Foundation.

Tuan, Mia. 1998. *Forever Foreigners or Honorary Whites? The Asian Ethnic Experience Today*. New Brunswick, N.J.: Rutgers University Press.

———. 2002. "Second Generation Asian American Identity: Clues from the Second Generation Experience." Pp. 209–238 in *The Second Generation: Ethnic Identity among Asian Americans*, edited by Pyong Gap Min. Walnut Creek, Calif.: AltaMira Press.

Verba, Sidney, Kay Lehman Schlozman, and Henry E. Brady. 1995. *Voice and Equality: Civic Voluntarism in American Politics*. Cambridge, Mass.: Harvard University Press.

Vickerman, Milton. 1999. Crosscurrents: West Indian Immigrants and Race. New York: Oxford University Press.

Wade, Richard C. 1990. "The Withering Away of the Party System." Pp. 271–295 in *Urban Politics, New York Style*, edited by Jewel Bellush and Dick Netzer. Armonk, N.Y.: M. E. Sharpe.

Waldinger, Roger. 1986. *Through the Eye of the Needle: Immigrants and Enterprise in New York's Garment Trades*. New York: New York University Press.

———. 1996. Still the Promised City? African-Americans and New Immigrants in Postindustrial New York. Cambridge, Mass.: Harvard University Press.

———. 2000. "The Sociology of Immigration: Second Thoughts and Reconsiderations." Paper presented at Conference on Migration and Development, Princeton University, April 28.

Waldinger, Roger, and Cynthia Feliciano. 2004. "Will the Second Generation Experience 'Downward Assimilation'? Segmented Assimilation Re-assessed." *Ethnic and Racial Studies* 27:376–402.

Waldinger, Roger, and Michael I. Lichter. 2003. *How the Other Half Works: Immigration and the Social Organization of Labor*. Berkeley: University of California Press.

Waldinger, Roger, and Joel Perlmann. 1998. "Second Generation: Past, Present and Future." *Journal of Ethnic and Migration Studies* 24:5–24.

Ware, Alan. 1985. *The Breakdown of Democratic Party Organization, 1940–1980.* Oxford: Clarendon Press.

Warikoo, Natasha. 2004. "Cosmopolitan Ethnicity: Second Generation Indo-Caribbean Identities." Pp. 361–391 in *Becoming New Yorkers: Ethnographies of the New Second Generation,* edited by Philip Kasinitz, John H. Mollenkopf, and Mary C. Waters. New York: Russell Sage Foundation.

Warner, William Lloyd, and Leo Srole. 1945. *The Social Systems of American Ethnic Groups.* New Haven, Conn.: Yale University Press.

Waters, Mary C. 1990. *Ethnic Options: Choosing Identities in America.* Berkeley: University of California Press.

———. 1999. *Black Identities: West Indian Immigrant Dreams and American Realities.* Cambridge, Mass.: Harvard University Press.

Waters, Mary C., and Tomás Jiménez. 2005. "Assessing Immigrant Assimilation: New Empirical and Theoretical Challenges." *Annual Review of Sociology* 31:105–125.

West, Cornel. 1994. *Race Matters.* New York: Vintage Books.

Western, Bruce, and Becky Pettit. 2005. "Black-White Wage Inequality, Employment Rates, and Incarceration." *American Journal of Sociology* 111:553–578.

Whyte, William H. 1988. *City: Rediscovering the Center.* New York: Doubleday.

Wilkins, David B. 1996. "Introduction: The Context of Race." In *Color Conscious: The Political Morality of Race,* edited by A. Appiah and A. Gutmann. Princeton, N.J.: Princeton University Press.

Williams, Terry M. 1992. *Crackhouse: Notes from the End of the Line.* Reading, Mass.: Addison-Wesley.

Williams, Terry M., and William Kornblum. 1985. *Growing Up Poor.* Lexington, Mass.: Lexington Books.

Wilson, Kenneth L., and Alejandro Portes. 1980. "Immigrant Enclaves: An Analysis of the Labor Market Experiences of Cubans in Miami." *American Journal of Sociology* 86:295–319.

Wilson, William Julius. 1978. *The Declining Significance of Race: Blacks and Changing American Institutions.* Chicago: University of Chicago Press.

———. 1987. *The Truly Disadvantaged: The Inner City, the Underclass, and Public Policy.* Chicago: University of Chicago Press.

———. 1996. *When Work Disappears: The World of the New Urban Poor.* New York: Knopf.

Winnick, Louis. 1990. *New People in Old Neighborhoods: The Role of New Immigrants in Rejuvenating New York's Communities.* New York: Russell Sage Foundation.

Wong, Siu-lun. 1999. "Deciding to Stay, Deciding to Move, Deciding Not to Decide." In *Cosmopolitan Capitalists: Hong Kong and the Chinese Diaspora at the End of the Twentieth Century,* edited by G. Hamilton. Seattle: University of Washington Press.

Wulf, Deirdre, and Susheela Singh. 1991. "Sexual Activity, Union and Childbearing among Adolescent Women in the Americas." *International Family Planning Perspectives* 17:137–144.

Yin, Xiao-huang. 2007. "China: People's Republic of China." Pp. 340–354 in *The New Americans: A Guide to Immigration since 1965,* edited by Mary C. Waters and Reed Ueda, with Helen Marrow. Cambridge, Mass.: Harvard University Press.

Yinger, John. 1997. "Cash in Your Face: The Cost of Racial and Ethnic Discrimination in Housing." *Journal of Urban Economics* 42:339–365.

———. 1998. "Housing Discrimination Is Still Worth Worrying About." *Housing Policy Debate* 9:893–927.

Zeltzer-Zubida, Aviva. 2004a. "Affinities and Affiliations: The Many Ways of Being a Russian Jewish American." Pp. 339–360 in *Becoming New Yorkers: Ethnographies of the New Second Generation,* edited by Philip Kasinitz, John H. Mollenkopf, and Mary C. Waters. New York: Russell Sage Foundation.

Zeltzer-Zubida, Aviva. 2004b. "The Multiple Logics of Economic Incorporation: Second Generation Immigrants in the Metropolitan New York Labor Market." City University of New York.

Zeltzer-Zubida, Aviva, and Philip Kasinitz. 2005. "The Next Generation: Russian Jewish Young Adults in Contemporary New York." *Contemporary Jewry* 25:193–225.

Zephir, Flore. 2001. *Trends in Ethnic Identification among Second-Generation Haitian Immigrants in New York City.* Westport, Conn.: Bergin and Garvey.

Zhou, Min. 1992. *Chinatown: The Socioeconomic Potential of an Urban Enclave.* Philadelphia: Temple University Press.

———. 1997a. "Growing Up American: The Challenge Confronting Immigrant Children and Children of Immigrants." *Annual Review of Sociology* 23:69–95.

———. 1997b. "Segmented Assimilation: Issues, Controversies, and Recent Research on the New Second Generation." *International Migration Review* 31:975–1008.

———. 2000. "Contemporary Immigration and the Dynamics of Race and Ethnicity." Pp. 200–242 in *America Becoming: Racial Trends and Their Consequences,* edited by Neil J. Smelser, William J. Wilson, and Faith Mitchell. Washington, D.C.: National Academy Press.

———. 2001. "Progress, Decline, Stagnation? The New Second Generation Comes of Age." Pp. 272–307 in *Strangers at the Gates: New Immigrants in Urban America,* edited by Roger Waldinger. Berkeley: University of California Press.

Zhou, Min, and Carl L. Bankston III. 1996. "Social Capital and the Adaptation of the Second Generation: The Case of Vietnamese Youth in New Orleans." Pp. 197–220 in *The New Second Generation,* edited by Alejandro Portes. New York: Russell Sage Foundation.

———. 1998. *Growing Up American: How Vietnamese Children Adapt to Life in the United States.* New York: Russell Sage Foundation.

Zhou, Min, and Cai Guoxuan. 2002. "Chinese Language Media in the United States: Immigration and Assimilation in American Life." *Qualitative Sociology* 25:419–441.

Zhou, Min, and Mingang Lin. 2005. "Community Transformation and the Formation of Ethnic Capital: The Case of Immigrant Chinese Communities in the United States." *Journal on Chinese Overseas* 1(2): 260–284.

Zhou, Min, and John R. Logan. 1991. "In and out of Chinatown: Residential Mobility and Segregation of New York City's Chinese." *Social Forces* 70:387–407.

Zhou, Min, and Yang Sao Xiong. 2005. "The Multifaceted American Experiences of the Children of Asian Immigrants: Lessons for Segmented Assimilation." *Ethnic and Racial Studies* 28:1119–1152.

Zolberg, Aristide R. 2006. A Nation by Design: *Immigration Policy in the Fashioning of America*. New York: Russell Sage Foundation.

Zolberg, Aristide R., and Long Litt Woon. 1999. "Why Islam Is Like Spanish: Cultural Incorporation in Europe and the United States." *Politics and Society* 27:5.

Index